Inside the IBM RISC System/6000

Marcus Bennett

Inside the IBM RISC
System/6000

McGRAW-HILL BOOK COMPANY

London · New York · St Louis · San Francisco ·Auckland
Bogotá · Caracas · Lisbon · Madrid · Mexico
Milan · Montreal · New Delhi · Panama · Paris · San Juan
São Paulo · Singapore · Sydney · Tokyo · Toronto

Published by
McGRAW-HILL Book Company Europe
Shoppenhangers Road, Maidenhead, Berkshire, SL6 2QL, England
Tel 0628 23432; Fax 0628 770224

British Library Cataloguing in Publication Data

Bennett, Marcus
  Inside the IBM RISC System/6000
  I. Title
  004.2

ISBN 0–07–707688–5

Library of Congress Cataloging-in-Publication Data
Bennett, Marcus
    Inside the IBM RISC System/6000 / Marcus Bennett.
        p.   cm.
    Includes bibliographical references and index.
    ISBN 0–07–707688–5
    1. IBM RISC System/6000 computers. I. Title.
    QA76.8.I25975B45   1993
    004.165—dc20   93–13494
                                                              CIP

1234 CUP 9654

Typeset by Datix International Limited, Bungay, Suffolk
and printed and bound in Great Britain at the University Press, Cambridge

Contents

Acknowledgements

I am grateful to the following people without whose patience, help and contributions this book would not have been possible: **Raymond Wordsworth Bennett**, for taking the trouble to proofread this work continually; **Angela Christi**, for help with the proofreading and semantics; **Johnny Lauridsen**, IBM Denmark, for NCS programs and APPC sections; **Liz Lewis**, IBM UK, for accounting, auditing and superusers sections; **Tim Hayashi**, IBM Japan, for advice and guidance regarding NLS; **Nelson Strother**, IBM Hawthorne, NY, USA, for technically sharpening this work; **Valerie Sangwine**, IBM UK Press and Publicity for colour slides; and **Jim McArdle**, IBM Test Equipment Engineering, USA, for his continued proofreading.

The following figures require acknowledgement: Figs. 2.1, 2.2, 8.6, 8.7 and A1.1—Valerie Sangwine, IBM Press and Publicity; Fig. 8.1—IBM Press and Publicity; Fig. 12.7—Johnny Lauridsen and Marcus Bennett; Fig. 12.8, 12.9, 13.6 and 13.7—Johnny Lauridsen; Fig. 13.2—Ian Stimpson; Fig. 14.4—Liz Lewis. All other figures provided by Marcus Bennett.

Acknowledgements

Preface

Development of UNIX-based systems has come a long way in the last 10 years. UNIX systems today are designed to be of use in ordinary offices in the world of commerce and industry generally. IBM is committed to producing high-quality UNIX computer systems such as the IBM RISC System/6000 to meet today's needs.

In 1978 (about five years before IBM launched its first UNIX computer) I remember putting the finishing touches to my very first personal UNIX computer system. It was the result of a great amount of hard work. Although this system still works today, it bears little similarity to the nineties generation of UNIX workstation and is considerably removed from the IBM RISC System/6000 which is the subject of this text.

This book is intended to cover a wide audience. If you feel at one with any of the categories listed below then I am confident that you will find it worthwhile reading.

If you are part of a corporate computing department you will probably have had experience of IBM's mainframe computing systems. This book will show how and why IBM is embracing the open systems marketplace with the IBM RISC System/6000. You will see how IBM has tried to ensure that the RISC system integrates well into both traditional IBM and UNIX environments. To this end we will discuss the range of IBM systems network architecture (SNA) and UNIX TCP/IP communications options available for the IBM RISC System/6000.

If you work within a computer vendor you may often be frustrated by the inaccuracy of information sometimes reported by the media. What has been the true picture of IBM's RISC system development to date? This publication discusses the history behind IBM's involvement with UNIX to enable you to understand the changing times at IBM that have culminated in the IBM RISC System/6000.

Many users of today's computer systems are personal computer users. IBM and Microsoft DOS have their place on over 40 million desktops worldwide. DOS is, and will continue to be, a powerful force in the PC and workstation market of the future. This book will show how IBM provides DOS integration across its entire range of UNIX platforms and how close the RISC system comes to providing users with 'a better DOS than DOS'. For the established DOS user we will also cover tools that enable DOS to link to the RISC system.

If you are an established UNIX developer or architect you will be interested in the many in-depth technical sections in this book. What is MicroChannel, how good is it technically, is it IBM's future direction? Why does IBM refer to the RISC system as second-generation RISC? How does the RISC system address the challenges of the nineties generation of UNIX systems in terms of security or usability? Does the RISC system provide the latest facilities such as optical storage, reliable filesystems and networking? These topics are covered in depth.

For the consultant this book includes numerous references that provide an insight into the design of the RISC system project and its future direction. How should the RISC system be positioned in the open systems marketplace? Does it conform to accepted UNIX or internationally agreed standards? What can be expected of future RISC systems? These points are covered.

If you are an existing IBM RISC System/6000 or UNIX user note that this book is not a hands-on guide or a technical reference manual. These topics are worthy of publications in themselves and IBM already publishes a vast array of such material. To this end we will be explaining how to obtain these texts in an optimal manner, including demonstrations of the IBM electronic customer support system. We will also be discussing the facilities that stand out in IBM's implementation of UNIX such as systems administration, hypertext help and error recovery.

How this book is organized

Chapter 1 is the introduction. Chapter 2 outlines the current range of IBM RISC systems and peripherals. For readers new to UNIX or AIX it should be read in conjunction with Appendix 1, 'The history of UNIX and IBM's involvement', on page 296 which discusses the origins of the UNIX operating system and IBM's long involvement with this technology.

AIX provides a significant number of enhancements to traditional UNIX. Chapter 3 details the fundamental extensions made to UNIX System V that form the basis of AIX. This includes a discussion of the pre-emptible and real-time kernel, improved international language support for traditional IBM codepages and ISO codesets and details of the object data manager, object-oriented database.

IBM makes reference to reduced instruction set computing (RISC) as a technology pioneered and patented by IBM. What are the origins of RISC technology; why is the RISC system known as second-generation RISC technology? Chapter 4 also discusses the XL series of compilers which are tailored specifically to exploit the underlying hardware.

UNIX has always provided a strong programming environment. AIX has extended the traditional UNIX environment to include support for advanced computer and software engineering tools. Chapter 5 discusses these tools. It also discusses the changes made to the AIX kernel to support dynamic binding.

Graphical end user interfaces are an expected part of a modern UNIX system. AIX is a strong performer in this area. Chapter 6 examines programming in traditional character-based applications and describes the new challenges that graphical user interface development brings. Also discussed is the range of offerings that form the AIXwindows product, including the support for PHIGS, PEX and Silicon Graphics GL.

UNIX systems have traditionally been provided with the *man* page help. AIX version 3, however, provides a comprehensive hypertext help system called InfoExplorer. We will examine InfoExplorer and take a closer look at IBM's information strategy in general, including the move to the IBM electronic customer support system in Chapter 7.

In order to provide a well-balanced and reliable environment AIX's enhanced UNIX operating system needs to be matched with an enhanced hardware environment. Chapter 8 focuses on some key hardware architectural advances. This includes diskless workstations, X-stations, the MicroChannel peripherals bus and high-performance graphics.

IBM provides a comprehensive and easy-to-use systems management interface tool (SMIT). Chapter 9 explains the operation of this tool and also considers the installation of AIX in large network environments.

Chapter 10 looks at storage. One of the highlights of AIX on the IBM RISC System/6000 is the advanced journalled filesystem. What is it, and why did IBM rework the traditional UNIX filesystem? What are the benefits to the business user?

AIX includes the ability to work with DOS data files and executable programs for users who have already made investments in DOS technology. We look at what users can and cannot do with the DOS simulator and learn how to connect existing personal computer networks into AIX in Chapter 11.

Chapter 12 considers the standard UNIX networking components of AIX. We look at the elementary basic network utilities component of AIX as well as the implementation of transmission control protocol/internet protocol (TCP/IP). We also consider Sun's Network File System (NFS) and Apollo's Network Computing System (NCS) and their integration into AIX.

Chapter 13 examines ways of communicating from existing IBM personal computers, minicomputers and mainframe computers to the IBM RISC System/6000, using traditional IBM vendor communications protocols. This includes a discussion of the advanced program-to-program communication protocol called APPC.

We define and explain the *de facto* 'Orange Book' security standards in Chapter 14. We then look at how the IBM RISC System/6000 enforces physical and software security policies.

IBM has traditionally been very strong in the area of diagnostics. AIX provides a complete range of standalone and online diagnostics. We examine these facilities and also describe how the IBM hardware and software support system operates in Chapter 15.

The UNIX world is driven by standards. But whose standards, and what do they really mean? Chapter 16 takes a conciliatory look at various standards bodies. It includes a discussion of both vendor, open systems and performance standards and looks at how well the IBM RISC System/6000 meets them.

IBM is trying very hard to encourage customers and other computer vendors to invest in IBM RISC System/6000 technology. In so doing IBM hopes to make the RISC system a leading if not the leading architecture in the UNIX marketplace in the nineties. Chapter 17 examines this strategy and implementation more closely.

Trademarks

AIX/6000, AIX, AIX CASE, AIX Interface Composer, AIXwindows, AIXwindows Desktop, Application System /400, BookMaster, ES/9000, GDDM, graPHIGS, High Availability Cluster Multi-Processing/6000, IBM, InfoCrafter, InfoExplorer, InfoTrainer, LoadLeveler MVS, MicroChannel, MVS/ESA, NetView, OS/2, Operating System/2, PS/2, Personal System/2, Power PC, POWERserver, POWERstation, Presentation Manager, RISC System/6000, SAA, Scalable POWERparallel, SCLM, S/390, 9076 SP1, VM, Xstation Manager are trademarks or pending trademarks of International Business Machines Corporation.

1-2-3 is a trademark of Lotus Development Corporation.

AFS is a trademark of TransArc Corporation.

AlphaWindows is a trademark of the Display Industry Association.

Apple Laserwriter is a trademark of Apple Inc.

C + + is a trademark of AT&T.

DECnet is a trademark of Dec.

Display PostScript is a trademark of Adobe Corporation.

Ethernet is a trademark of Xerox Corporation.

FORGE 90 is a trademark of Applied Parallel Research Inc.

HP, NetWork Node Manager and **SoftBench** are trademarks of Hewlett-Packard Inc.

Informix is a registered trademark of Informix Software, Inc.

Ingres and **Sybase** are trademarks of Sybase.

Intel 386 and **Intel 486** are registered trademarks of the Intel Corporation.

Interleaf and **Interleaf Desktop Publisher** are registered trademarks of Interleaf, Inc.

IXI is a trademark of IXI Inc.

Legato Networker and **Networker Jukebox** are trademarks of Legato Inc.

MIPS is a registered trademark of MIPS Computer Systems, Inc.

NCS is a trademark of Apollo Microsystems, Inc.

Netware, Netwire and **Novell** are registered trademarks of Novell, Inc.

NeWS, NFS, Sunsoft's Tooltalk, are registered trademarks of Sun Microsystems, Inc.

Oracle is a trademark of Oracle Inc.

OSF, OSF/1, OSF/Motif Window Manager and **Motif** are trademarks of the Open Software Foundation.

PC/IX, INed are trademarks of Interactive Systems.

PEX, X11.4, X11.5, Andrew filesystem and **X Window system** are trademarks of the Massachusetts Institute of Technology.

POSIX is a trademark of the Institute of Electrical and Electronics Engineers.

PostScript is a trademark of Adobe Systems, Inc.

PVCS is a trademark of Intersolv.

Silicon Graphics GL is a trademark of Silicon Graphics Inc.

SPEC, SPECint92, SPECfp92 are trademarks of Standard Performance Evaluation Corporation.

Sun, SPARC and **SPARCstation 2** are trademarks of Sun Microsystems, Inc.

Tektronix 4014 is a trademark of Tektronix.

UIM/X is a trademark of Visual Edge.

Ultrix and **VAX** are trademarks of Digital Equipment Corporation.

Uniplex is a trademark of Uniplex Inc.

UniTree is a trademark of General Atomics / DISCOS

UNIX is a registered trademark of UNIX System Laboratories, Inc.

Windows is a trademark of Microsoft Corporation.

WizDOM is a trademark of Tivoli Inc.

X/Open is a registered trademark of X/Open Ltd.

XPG3 is a trademark of X/Open Ltd.

Conventions

Considerable effort has been expended in using a consistent set of typefaces and styles to make this book logical and easy to understand. The rules are:

- System programs or commands: in italics   *make*, *ls*,
- Programming functions: in bold   **XtInitialize()**
- Program code and command output: in monospace   `a = b + c`
- Pathnames, files: in monospace   `/usr/lpp/X11/Xamples`
- Emphasis: in italic   *This is important*

Throughout this publication, numerous examples and opinions are put forward. These opinions are the result of my personal experience and therefore I will express them in the first person. Also note that unless otherwise specified:

- Generic UNIX facilities implemented in AIX are described as UNIX facilities.
- The term AIX when used should be taken to mean features of AIX version 3 as implemented on the IBM RISC System/6000. The current level of AIX at the time of writing is 3.2.4 (announced in June 1993).
- The term RISC system should be taken to mean the IBM RISC System/6000.

A full list of acronyms used in this publication is given in Appendix 4.

1
Introduction

I remember a radio report well from the spring of 1989: 'We advise all residents to take particular care and not to drive unless absolutely necessary.' The local radio station was advising me and other inhabitants in Austin Texas that owing to the extraordinary weather conditions (namely strong hailstorms) driving was to be avoided. However, this was not the only unusual event that was taking place right in the heart of Texas.

I had been sent to IBM Austin to co-write a programming guide for IBM on the X Window System, the graphical user interface for AIX (AIX is the name for IBM's implementation of UNIX), but one morning I and a number of colleagues got a break from our gruelling schedule. We were ushered into a large windowless room to speak to the developers of a new IBM UNIX computer system. The machine we saw that day was of course a prepreproduction model. It had a transparent plexiglass case so that curious systems engineers such as myself could cluster round and marvel at the new technology. Even at that time the IBM RISC System/6000 was fast. This model sat beside a model 135 RT personal computer, at that time IBM's fastest workstation UNIX system. Running on each machine was a looping compile and run benchmark, already showing the RISC System/6000 at twice the speed of its parent. This was my first glimpse of the IBM RISC System/6000, a computer that has redefined even IBM's competitors' view of IBM's presence in and commitment to the UNIX and open systems marketplace

1.1   Open systems

Open systems is one of the latest terms to enter the information technology (IT) industry. Ignorance of open systems in today's marketplace is tantamount to professional negligence. So exactly what is an open system? It is a computing system whose components are not owned or controlled by any single vendor. It is built upon a comprehensive and consistent set of information technology standards and functional standards' profiles.

UNIX is an example, perhaps the principal example, of an open system, but it

1

is by no means the only one. Many vendors' operating systems and architectures are open in the sense that their architectures and specifications are clearly defined. IBM's Systems Network Architecture (SNA) is open in this respect but the standard is controlled by a single vendor—IBM. Perhaps a better way to look at open systems is to look at the requirements of today's customer and how those requirements are fulfilled by open systems.

1.1.1   Customer requirements and open systems solutions

Multivendor connectivity

The basis for interoperability is connectivity. Users need to make use of their information on an enterprise-wide basis.

Transparent data access

Information needs to be accessible in a transparent and nondisruptive way. Applications (usually) and users (certainly) should not be concerned about the physical location of their data resources. Applications need to be able to move through vendor and protocol barriers, a process made easier if open systems fundamental protocols are the same.

Remote application access

Users must be able to access applications throughout the network. The physical terminal screen to which the user is connected should be the gateway to and not the jailer of the user's computing network.

Multivendor systems management

Tools and procedures must be defined to allow systems resources to be managed effectively. A vendor's proprietary environment allows tighter control since specifications are under the control of a single manufacturer allowing in principle for more complete systems management. Open systems are controlled by many vendors so the specification and adherence to systems management standards by a multiplicity of vendors is crucially important in order to avoid systems management chaos.

Transaction processing

Users now expect distributed computer applications that use cooperative processing to solve customers' data processing needs. An effective open system needs to support communication protocol standards and optionally support that vendor's previous protocol standards to enable integration and migration from existing customer systems.

Multivendor security

As the user gains interoperability and interconnectivity between network-connected systems, the user must ensure that security is not compromised. As many vendors and large corporate computing departments begin to make electronic links to other customers and clients over public telephone networks, open systems must employ security standards to protect information from accidental and intentional misuse or destruction.

Consistent look and feel

Users now expect a consistent user interface while operating in a multivendor open systems environment. A common interface maximizes user productivity because the behaviour of the application interface is consistent with a user's expectations. A user has a correspondingly reduced learning time and makes fewer mistakes.

Heterogeneous display and printing

Users expect to be able to access their applications from network-connected workstations or terminals placed throughout the organization and to direct hard copy output to their local printers.

Consistent programming look and feel

Application developers prefer a common set of programming interfaces, development environments and tools to enable them to deliver the user's expectations discussed above.

1.1.2   The benefits of open systems

The move to open systems is driven by the perceived benefits of this form of IT. It is interesting to note that the lowest cost provider is no longer the fundamental driving force; it is usually customer independence. What are the benefits?

Interoperability

Interoperability means being able to interconnect systems from many different manufacturers and have them integrated to solve a business need. Interoperability is more than just network interconnection, it includes the ability for integrated messaging and mail, the sharing of data (preferably transparently to the user) and also shared resources (for example printing).

Investment protection

By far the greatest cost to a user in a total IT environment is the investment made in the applications to run that user's business. By using open systems the user is free to choose from a wide variety of computer systems from different vendors and select the one which meets current and future total business needs.

Portability and scalability

Portability enables a customer to relocate system resources, for example to relocate data and applications to platforms that best suit requirements. Portability should also be applied to the professional staff whose skills should be useful across varying systems. For example, professionals skilled with UNIX computer systems can easily adapt to the minor differences in any one vendor's implementation of UNIX. This is true at the operational level and, even more importantly, true at the more involved programming and application design level.

Price/performance

For customers purchasing open systems many hardware and software elements of a computer system are designed to be interchangeable. Thus, the freedom to choose between vendors for these items tends to lead to increased competition and commodity pricing, so reducing the price.

Time to market

Time to market (TTM) and break-even after release (BEAR) are two critical measurements that vendors use to measure the success of their products and services. Open systems, which are based around portable and recognized software standards, enable hardware and applications vendors to improve TTM and BEAR.

1.1.3   Open systems driving factors

A recent study of over 80 leading companies, conducted by the Open Systems and Workstations Consultancy (OSWC), concluded that:

- Seventy per cent believe that there is a general trend towards open systems in their business environment.

- Eighty-five per cent believe they will be moving to open systems within five years.

Perhaps for all the reasons outlined above, IT and business professionals are now insisting on open systems, and because of this paradigm shift it is likely to be a self-fulfilling prophecy. In summary, open systems are not a threat; they are a certainty.

2
The IBM RISC System/6000 family

The IBM RISC System/6000 was announced by IBM at 10.00 a.m., American Eastern Standard time, on Thursday, 15 February 1990. Right from the day of announcement, the IBM RISC System/6000 has represented a considerable advance in technology over its forerunner the IBM RT PC system.

2.1   RISC system family outline

A variety of models exist, from the entry-level diskless workstation models M20 and 220 (discussed in more detail in Sec. 8.3), right up to the high-performance, rack-mounted model 980B. All IBM RISC System/6000 computers are binary compatible with one another and run the same Advanced Interactive eXecutive (AIX) Operating System, IBM's name for its enhanced UNIX operating system. Binary compatibility allows an applications developer to develop a product that runs on all RISC systems, and correspondingly allows a user to move these applications from the model M20 up to the model 980B, without recompilation, as their needs develop.

Broadly speaking, the models divide into five power bands and three physical sizes, as Table 2.1 shows. Figure 2.1 shows the family, including some members of entry level, desktop and deskside RISC systems. Harris (1993) is an excellent guide to all models, peripherals and software available in the IBM RISC System/6000 family. The guide includes more comprehensive specifications than covered here.

2.1.1   Entry-level RISC systems

The basic entry-level IBM RISC System/6000 is the model 220 diskless workstation. This small form factor desktop workstation may also be configured with a single floppy disk and hard disk drive, turning it into a basic level workstation, with two I/O bus slots for future expansion.

An even lower cost RISC system entry workstation is the model M20. This system can be regarded as a model 220 packaged inside a 17 inch colour screen.

Table 2.1. RISC system classification

Speed	Desktop	Deskside	Rack
25 MHz	320H	520H	930
33 MHz	M20 220	530H	
41 MHz	340H 350 355	550	950
50 MHz	360 365	560 570	970B
62.5 MHz	370 375	580	980

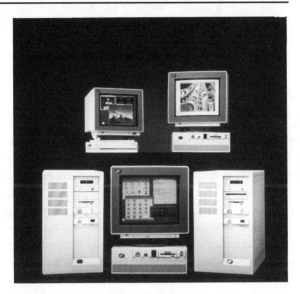

Figure 2.1. The IBM System/6000 family. From left to right and top to bottom the models are: 220, 350, 520H, 340H and 560.

Its typical application is as a nonexpandable diskless workstation, though it is possible to use a locally attached SCSI port to attach external peripherals such as disks and tapes.

2.1.2 Desktop RISC systems

The desktop RISC system family is the 300 series. The models are 320H, 340H, 350, 355, 360, 365, 370 and 375. Fully configured these desktop machines can house at least 128 Mb of system memory, 2000 Mb of internal disk (entry-level desktop model 32H is restricted to 800 Mb), an internal 3.5 inch diskette drive and external tape and CD-ROM drives. Large amounts of external disk may also be attached using the IBM 9333 serial link disk subsystem (see Sec. 8.1; a single MicroChannel card can attach 16 Gb of disk storage). Processor speeds of the 300 series are listed in Table 2.1. The model 320H has three free bus slots; models 340H, 350, 360 and 370 have four because their planar electronics include Ethernet networking adapters and integrated hard disk (actually an integrated small computer systems interface (SCSI)-1 interface, which can interface hard disk and other peripherals; see Appendix 2).

For customers who require the power of the 300 series at a lower cost, but who are willing to accept a slightly less expandable series of machines, consider models 355, 365 and 375. These have the power of their model 350, 360 and 370 counterparts but have two bus slots (instead of four) and one memory slot (instead of two). This limits a configuration to 128 Mb of internal memory, 2 Gb of internal hard disk and one free bus slot (assuming a graphics adapter is installed).

2.1.3   Deskside RISC systems

The IBM RISC System/6000 500 models are the most popular RISC system models and are packaged as deskside units with processors in five different speeds. Models 520H, 530H, 550L, 560, 570 and 580 have the processor speeds 25, 33, 41, 50 and 62.5 MHz respectively. These deskside systems have seven free MicroChannel bus slots (four for model 550L and eight for models 570 and 580) for greater expandability. As with the model 300 series, external tape, CD-ROM or serial link hard disk drives may be attached. However, most customer requirements can usually be satisfied by using a fully internally configured model 500 machine. For example, a 500 series has eight system memory slots, seven free MicroChannel bus slots, three full-height 5.25 inch hard disk bays, three half-height 5.25 inch peripheral bays and a floppy diskette drive. So a fully configured model 570 could have 1024 Mb of system memory, six 2 Gb hard disks (12 Gb), a CD-ROM drive, an 8 mm digital tape drive, a 1.44 Mb diskette drive, a graphics, SCSI disk and LAN adapters and still have five free MicroChannel card slots.

The input and output bus used on the IBM RISC System/6000 is the IBM MicroChannel for which a great variety of high-performance cards are available. The list includes:

* Console graphics terminal adapters
* The Ethernet high-performance LAN adapter
* The Token Ring high-performance LAN adapter
* The 128-port asynchronous controller adapter
* The four-port multiprotocol communications controller
* The X.25 interface coprocessor
* The 3270 connection adapter
* The block multiplexor channel adapter
* The enterprise systems connection (ESCON) adapter
* The FDDI network adapter

Each model 500 series machine also has a special optical channel converter slot which can form the basis of an extremely high speed (220 Mbit per second) optical network. The optical channel converter is discussed in detail in Sec. 8.6.

2.1.4 Rack RISC systems

For greater expansion still, select the 900 series of systems. These comprise rack-mounted systems in a range of processor speeds from 25 to 62.5 MHz. These models, 930 and 950, have no more slots than their 500 series counterparts; their principal advantage is rack mounting. As with models 570 and 580, the 970 and 980 have eight free MicroChannel slots because the native disk interfaces are integrated onto the planar (i.e. already included in the non-removable circuit cards of the systems). Further, Models 970 and 980 can attach a MicroChannel expansion cage for a total of 16 free MicroChannel adapter card slots. The racks are the same as those used on IBM's AS/400 minicomputer and even on entry-level IBM mainframe computers. They allow customers with large disk or peripheral requirements to order a complete system in one unit. For example, a fully configured model 980B is capable of attaching over 400 Gb of disk storage.

Lastly, note that all RISC system systems contain integrated planar support for basic devices including:

- A parallel port
- One or two serial ports
- One tablet port
- Keyboard and mouse ports

2.1.5 Peripherals

To complete this overview of the IBM RISC System/6000 family we will introduce some of the peripheral devices that can be ordered with the IBM RISC System/6000. First, consider internal hard disk drives. Model 220 has space for a single 3.25 inch hard disk, Model 300 has two 3.25 inch hard disk drives. The 500 series of models has space for three 5.25 inch full-height (or six 3.5 inch) hard disk drives. A customer has the choice of adding in the following drives:

- 160, 212, 320, 400, 1004, 2000 Mb 3.5 inch form factor hard disks
- 355, 670, 800, 857, 1370 or 2467 Mb 5.25 inch form factor hard disks

The portable disk option is shown in Fig. 2.2.

Removable disks are connected via the small computer systems interface (SCSI). The portable disk unit consists of a power unit into which a single removable disk of 355 Mb, 670 Mb or 1 Gb can be plugged. Also available is the securable disk, comprising a smaller self-contained, removable disk with power supply. It provides 320 Mb or 1 Gb of external disk storage.

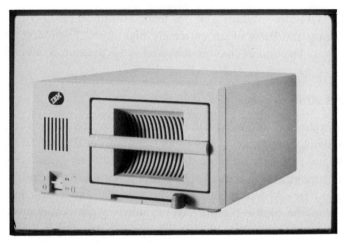

Figure 2.2.   The RISC system portable disk drive.

Other removable media options are shown in Table 2.2. The $\frac{1}{4}$ inch streaming tape drive is available in three models with formatted tape capacities of 150 or 525 Mb or 1.2 Gb. The 4 mm tape drive uses the audio industry standard 4 mm digital audio tape (DAT) to store 2 Gb of data. The 8 mm high-capacity tape drive has a capacity of 2.3 or 5.0 Gb (depending on the model) and is more fully described in Sec. 8.4. The $\frac{1}{2}$ inch tape drive accommodates standard 2450 feet 'mainframe' reel tapes and enables data interchange via these tapes with IBM mainframes. The capacities are as for standard mainframe tapes, that is to say, 160 Mb when recorded at a density of 6250 bits per inch and 44 Mb at a recording density of 1600 bits per inch.

Table 2.3 on page 13 summarizes machine specifications across the IBM RISC System/6000 family.

2.2   Ordering a complete system

Ordering a system should start first by analysing the business needs for a RISC system. Whatever the environment, business, applications development or research, one should clearly work from these requirements. These typically include the following interrelated issues:

- Software solution   Does a readily available software package exist that satisfies user needs? Or is it the intention to use RISC systems for bespoke software development?
- User considerations   How many users will need to use the system? Will they require use of single or multiple applications? Are these applications to be used from character-based ASCII screens or from graphics screens. For graphics, will this be provided using local area network (LAN) connected

Table 2.2. Removable media options

Removable media	Internal	External
¼ inch streaming tape	N	Y
4 mm DAT tape	N	Y
8 mm high capacity tape	Y	Y
8 mm tape library	N	Y
½ inch 9-track tape	N	Y
CD-ROM	Y	Y
Rewritable optical disk drive	N	Y
5.25 inch 1.2 Mb diskette	N	Y

personal computers, or via an X-station? Or will each user have their own IBM RISC System/6000?

- Timing and financing   What allowance is to be made for upgrading of the system? What are the expected growth rates in terms of expected users and applications? In the long term it may be sensible to choose a RISC system hardware platform that allows the current system to be upgraded rather than be replaced by a newer IBM RISC System/6000 platform.

- Operational considerations   How often will the business application be run: 24 hours a day, 7 days a week, or only during normal office hours? What priorities do these applications have? Are there any corresponding requirements for high-availability components?

- Other considerations   Are the applications and the resulting systems to be standalone or do they need integrating into an existing IT network, perhaps to allow users to run applications locally on the chosen RISC system and connect into existing systems, for example an IBM mainframe. Perhaps applications will be migrated from an existing computing platform, and in a transition period a user will be expected to run their new local application and 'passthru' to their existing applications.

All these considerations and more need to be taken into account when choosing a RISC system to meet the needs of the customer. Customers should be clear what they need. When this has been established, a customer can normally contact their IBM marketing office or IBM value added reseller who will be able to size the system and select the software packages that meet all their requirements. Base system needs such as required memory and hard disk will be governed by the choice of application solution or development requirement needs. (As a guide any RISC system should be equipped with at least 16 Mb of memory and 400 Mb of hard disk.) A basic solution may comprise one or more desktop, deskside or rack-mounted RISC systems. Every system unit includes two serial and parallel ports, a console, a mouse and a keyboard port. A tape drive should be ordered to load the AIX operating system and probably the IBM or third-party software solution. This tape drive is also necessary for systems backup. For systems which do not require graphics, a low-cost solution may comprise a RISC system with only ASCII-attached terminals. (IBM markets two principal ranges of terminals, the 3151 and 3152 series.) In this case multiport asynchronous terminal adapters will need to be ordered. For a 'workstation' configuration, it would be more usual to include a graphics adapter, a graphics screen, a console mouse and console keyboard. Further, 'graphics' users can be attached via an LAN using IBM X-station 150s or suitably configured PCs. Other communications requirements will dictate the selection of cards such as the 3270 connection or the X.25 network adapters. Usually the number of adapter cards and the size of hard disk will make the choice of a desktop, deskside or rack-mounted RISC system clear.

The breadth of configurations that comprise the RISC system family is large, with systems to cater from one to over a hundred users. To put this into perspective, a single RISC system could cost from as little as £4000 to over £300 000.

2.2.1   POWERstations and POWERservers

IBM provides two families of popular configurations for the IBM RISC System/ 6000:

- An IBM RISC System/6000 POWERstation consists of a RISC system with a single native high-resolution graphics display attached via a graphics adapter. This workstation also has a console keyboard and mouse. This configuration is usually used as a single-user workstation by an applications developer, a UNIX professional or engineering/scientific user. Normally such a user would maintain a LAN connection to a POWERserver to access shared data.
- An IBM RISC System/6000 POWERserver is usually the basis for a multiuser commercial RISC system solution or as a disk server for POWERstation users. 'Multiuser commercial' is taken to mean that users are connected by ASCII displays to the serial ports on the system console or on multiport asynchronous port adapter cards.

In fact, to use IBM terminology the IBM RISC System/6000 is an example of a 'build to order' computer system (as compared to a 'build to plan' system like the IBM PS/2 computer). This means that each computer system is built exactly to a customer's requirements. So any customer can choose exactly the system that meets their needs. This would normally be done by the IBM value added reseller, IBM marketing personnel, or by the customers themselves should they have IBM electronic customer support (described in detail in Sec. 7.6).

Table 2.3. The IBM RISC System/6000 family specification summary

Model	M20	220	230	320H	340H	350	355	360	365	370	375	520H	530H	550L	560	570	580	950	970B	980B
Configuration	DT	DT	DT	DT	DT	DT	DT	DT	DT	DT	DT	DS	DS	DS	DS	DS	DS	Rack	Rack	Rack
Clock speed	33	33	45	25	41	41	41	50	50	62.5	62.5	25	33	41	50	50	62.5	41	50	62.5
Std memory (Mb)	16	16	16	16	16	32	16	16	16	32	32	16	32	64	64	32	64	64	128	128
Max memory (Mb)	64	64	64	128	256	256	128	256	128	256	128	512	512	1024	1024	1024	1024	512	1024	1024
Std int. disk (Mb)	0	0	0	400	540	540	540	540	540	540	540	400	800	2000	800	2000	2000	1714	4096	4096
Max int. disk (Gb)	0.0	2.0	2.0	0.8	4.0	4.0	4.0	4.0	4.0	4.0	4.0	12.0	7.2	12.0	12.0	12.0	12.0	19.2	47.0	47.0
Max disk (Gb)	7.0	20.4	20.4	8.8	237.2	237.2	100.0	237.2	100.0	237.2	100.0	140	140	396	396	460	460	70.5	840	840
Memory slots	8[1]	8[1]	8[1]	2	2	2	1	2	1	2	1	8	8	8	8	8	8	8	8	8
MCA slots[2]	1	1	1	2	3	3	1	3	1	3	1	7	7	4	7	7	7	7	15	15

[1] Up to eight, 8 Mb, single inline memory modules (SIMMs).
[2] Slots free after providing for a SCSI hard disk controller and graphics adapter. An additional slot would be available (not M20) for ASCII terminal attach configurations.

3
AIX facilities

In one of its most forward looking decisions, IBM merged the two leading UNIX technologies—UNIX System Laboratories (USL) UNIX System V and Berkeley Software Distribution (BSD) UNIX version 4 to create AIX on the RISC system. Entire publications exist on both of those operating systems and this chapter does not attempt to review either. Instead it concentrates on some of the most interesting changes made to produce AIX for the IBM RISC System/6000.

3.1   How does the IBM RISC System/6000 boot?

Starting AIX on the RISC system is an automatic process, but it differs dramatically from the startup of many other UNIX systems. The RISC system boot process is designed to be reliable, fast and flexible. Reliable, because the initial machine startup does not depend on the RISC system processor at all but on a hardcoded on-card sequencer (OCS). Flexible, because boot parameters are stored in nonvolatile RAM (NVRAM) and the user therefore has a choice from which device to boot. Fast, because the boot code is stored in a compressed format in a reserved area of the hard disk. Also, the startup code is run from a RAM disk. Let us look at this in more detail.

The overall boot process is shown in Fig. 3.1. Each on-planar processor designed by IBM contains a small amount of test circuitry (about three per cent of gates per chip) known as the common on-chip processor (COP). A serial bus links COP areas to the OCS which is an Intel 8051 CPU with an internal 4 kb ROM and 128 byte RAM. This also has access to 64 kb ROM and at least 16 kb of NVRAM for startup. On system startup the OCS gets control of the system and performs the following built-in self-tests (BISTs):

- Embedded memory checking
- DC logic
- AC logic

It then resets the hardware registers in the processors to a known state and marks

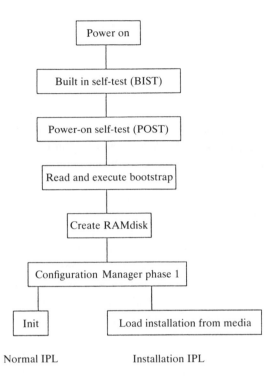

Figure 3.1.   The AIX boot process.

all software caches as invalid. The OCS program is an on-board version of the engineering support processor (ESP) used in the design of the IBM RISC System/6000. In fact every IBM RISC System/6000 still has an ESP connector on the CPU planar which could, in principle, be used for extended diagnostics.

Should the OCS detect an error it displays it on the three-digit LED front panel and waits for human intervention. (See Chapter 15 for more details on maintaining the IBM RISC System/6000.)

Once the processors have been error-checked they are started and they then begin to execute instructions from the initial program load (IPL) ROM to perform further power-on self-tests (POSTs). This includes checking all adapter cards on the MicroChannel I/O bus and a full memory check.

After completing the POSTs the normal device list is read from NVRAM. NVRAM contains an ordered list of devices, from which the RISC system should boot with the keyswitch set to the 'normal' position, and a service list of devices that are used when the keyswitch is in 'service' position. If the NVRAM is invalid a default boot device is selected from the IPL ROM. (The NVRAM is unpopulated for the first-ever RISC system boot. From experience though, if the NVRAM battery is disconnected the contents are also lost, from which I can only conclude that IBM's definition of NVRAM really means battery backed-up

RAM!) The IPL file is now read from that device. This is a simple three-part file containing:

- A bootstrap header
- The AIX kernel
- The boot filesystem image

The header contains a description of the IPL media in use, for example, the number of sectors per track of the device, the position of the start of executable boot code and where to place this code when running the kernel. The boot filesystem is a special prototype filesystem containing programs, adapter description files and scripts needed to initialize the system.

Control is now passed to a ROM program that expands this IPL file, relocates the kernel to real address 0 and then copies the header into the kernel for later use. A C language environment is now set-up by creating a stack, and control is passed to the IPL file at entry point **main()**. Main initializes the virtual memory hardware and data structures. It also defines a boot filesystem created in RAM. At this stage in the boot process no real physical filesystems are available but a filesystem environment is required to execute the initialization programs. The RAMdisk is built for this purpose.

The RAMdisk stores essential information including the installation shell scripts that will be executed, as well as the kernel, that is to say /unix itself. This means that the /unix kernel file stored in the real physical filesystem is not used for systems boot. It is there for compatibility reasons. If subsequently relinked or altered it will automatically be copied into the boot file.

Next, the kernel debugger (if present) is initialized and process entries for the processes **swapper()**, **init()** and **wait()** defined. Next, extended device-checking self-test routines are run: for example, extended testing on the floating-point processor.

When all this is done **init()** gets control and all the kernel initialization routines are run, for example, machine device driver, trace dump, filesystem, to name but a few. **init()** then starts the swapper and frees up all that memory used up to this point but no longer required. (The swapper is a program that allows the RISC system to run concurrently more applications than will fit into the real memory contained in a system. It places inactive or unused parts of an application from real memory into a reserved disk area, called a swapspace, until required.)

3.1.1 Running /etc/init and /etc/inittab

The RAMdisk binary file /etc/init is now executed. First this runs the phase 1 configuration manager to make available all base devices such as disk and diskette drives, etc. The real root filesystem is then mounted onto /mnt of the RAMdisk and configuration information thus far discovered is transferred to the physical object data manager database on the real root filesystem. Phase 1

```
@(#)inittab   1.22 com/cfg/etc,3.1,9021 4/6/90 17:18:07
#Identifier:  Runlevel :action   :command
init:     2:  initdefault:
brc:      :   sysinit:/etc/brc >/dev/console 2>&1   # Phase 2 of system boot
rc:       2:  wait:    /etc/rc >/dev/console 2>&1   # Multi-User checks
srcmstr:  2:  respawn:/etc/srcmstr                  # System Resource Controller
rctcpip:  2:  wait:    /etc/rc.tcpip >/dev/console 2>&1  # Start TCP/IP daemons
rcnfs:    2:  wait:    /etc/rc.nfs >/dev/console 2>&1 # Start NFS Daemons
cons:     012 34 56789:  respawn:/etc/getty/dev/console
piobe:    2:  once:    /bin/rm -f/usr/lpd/pio/flags/*  # Clean up printer flags files
cron:     2:  respawn:/etc/cron
qdaemon:  2:  once:    /bin/startsrc -sqdaemon
writesrv: 2:  once:    /bin/startsrc -swritesrv
tty1:     2:  off:     /etc/getty /dev/tty1
rcncs:    2:  wait:    sh /etc/rc.ncs
hcon:     2:  once:    /bin/startsrc -s hcon
```

Figure 3.2. A sample /etc/inittab startup file.

configuration is now complete and the root filesystem is overmounted onto root.

Now that the real physical root filesystem is available the contents of the /etc/inittab file are processed. A typical file is shown in Fig. 3.2. Running the inittab file is part of the standard AT&T System V initialization procedure; a BSD UNIX system finishes booting by running *init* and then enabling terminals in /etc/ttys. By executing inittab, **inetd**, **nfs**, **getty**, **piobe**, **cron**, **qdaemon** and other traditional UNIX processes are started. The system is now in operation and users can log on.

To give an idea of the boot process time, using an IBM RISC System/6000 model 560 with about 2 Gb of disk and 48 Mb of memory the boot process was timed at about 80 seconds. The RISC system can boot this quickly primarily because the journalled filesystem (described in Sec. 10.1) overcomes the need to run the *fsck* program at startup.

3.1.2   *The systems resource controller*

Entries in inittab include references to the *startsrc* program, that is the systems resource controller (SRC). This is a facility carried over from AIX version 2 used in the IBM RT PC system. A subsystem is defined as a set of related programs that are started and stopped as a unit. The complex interaction of modern UNIX tasks such as TCP/IP networking needs more than a set of raw startup lines in a startup file like inittab. The SRC first requires a subsystem to be defined by name. A subsystem contains a list or programs (called methods or actions) that need to be executed when a subsystem is started, restarted or stopped. Also included is a list of actions that need to be taken if part of the subsystem fails. All this information is stored in an object oriented database supplied with AIX called the object data manager (ODM) and accessed through standard ODM subroutine calls.

AIX provides a set of subroutines (in general **src...()**) to enable a systems programmer to add user-defined subsystems into AIX. Examples of subsystems that already use the SRC are AIX spooling, TCP/IP networking, error logging and SNA communications.

It is interesting to compare the AIX SRC with the System V release 4 service access facility (SAF). The SAF is a new feature of System V release 4 that provides a way to manage the connection of terminals (direct connect or network) to a system. The SAF controls a number of monitors, each one being responsible for the connection of terminals to a port type. Therefore in SAF terms the **ttymon** process replaces the traditional UNIX **getty** program, in that it scans unused, directly attached TTY ports waiting for a connection. The SAF talks via a named pipe to the *sacadm* dedicated administrative command. The SAF typically stores required information in flat files in /etc/saf. It therefore provides a consistent way to add both directly attached and networked terminals to a system.

The AIX SRC by contrast is a more general-purpose facility that can be concerned with terminal management but is not limited to it. Additionally, the SRC stores its configuration information in the AIX object database ODM, not in a flat ASCII file format.

3.2   The object data manager

The ODM is an object-oriented database supplied with AIX. The ODM however is not intended to store vast applications databases but is optimized to store system information. Within AIX itself the ODM is already used to store:

- Detailed technical characteristics of each adapter card or hardware subsystem. For example, the name of the device to be placed in the /dev directory, the unique programmable option select ID (POS-ID) identifying the MicroChannel card adapter and the LED number to be displayed on the front panel as this system is configured at AIX boot.
- The hardware and software configuration actually selected. For example, for an available tape drive, that the name is rmt0, that the parent disk controller is scsi0 and that the absolute physical location is 00-08-00-50 (drawer 0, slot 8, connector 0, port 50).
- Vital product data (VPD) for installation and update procedures. For example, that the SCSI controller card has firmware dated 13 Nov 1991 and is at level 2.01.5.
- Communications configuration information. For example, the SNA peer and host information required to communicate successfully using the SNA services component of AIX.
- Systems management information. For example, the menu structures and

```
class AIXers
  {
  char   szName      [20];
  char   szBirthday  [10];
  short  nAge;
  char   szFirstMeet [60];
  char   location    [90];
  method connection;
  };

AIXers:                              AIXers:
  szName      = "Johnny"               szName      = "Susan"
  szBirthday  = "29 Aug"               szBirthday  = "09 Feb"
  nAge        = 28                     nAge        = 24
  szFirstMeet = "IBM Austin"           szFirstMeet = "IBM Southbank"
  location    = "Denmark"              location    = "England"
  connection  = /usr/bin/connect       connection  = /usr/bin/hcon
```

Figure 3.3.   A sample ODM class and entries.

dialog panels used by the systems management interface tool (SMIT). Hence dynamic modifications to the ODM are naturally reflected by the SMIT. For example, after installing the network management product NetView/6000 users will find new menus added to the SMIT.

3.2.1   ODM objects and classes

ODM stores data by class and instance of that class, that is to say, a definition of a datastructure and an example use of that datastructure. A user can add, change, get, show, delete and drop objects and classes in three ways. Either using command line ODM commands, and using the ODM API, or via the full-screen ODM editor *odme*.

Figure 3.3 is an example of a fictional database class called AIXers that was created with the *odmcreate* command and added to using the *odmadd* command. It shows the database definition of the class AIXers and two database entries for the individuals named Johnny and Susan. Notice from the database definition that most of the entries are just C language style numbers or character arrays. But there is also the definition of connection variable, an example of a method. This is analogous to the ability to imbed functions within structures in the object oriented language C + +. In this example the method is the name of the program executed on my AIX system to send these colleagues electronic mail.

3.2.2   ODM and dynamically configurable device drivers

ODM plays an important role in providing AIX's ability to support dynamically configurable device drivers. (In traditional UNIX systems device drivers cannot be dynamically configured. For more information see Sec. 5.4.). There are nine main ODM database classes interrelated as shown in Fig. 3.4. The definitions of these classes are:

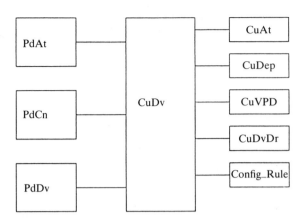

Figure 3.4   ODM class relationships.

PdDv   Predefined devices: lists the physical devices that could be supported
            in the system, for example, tape drives, adapter cards. PdDv includes
            pseudo-physical devices such as disk logical volumes.

PdCn   Predefined connections: lists the devices that can be connected to
            intermediate devices, for example, the devices that can be connected
            to a 64-port asynchronous card.

PdAt   Predefined attributes: a listing of attribute values for entries in the
            PdDv class, for example, that an 8 mm tape drive has an attribute
            called block size, which has a default value of 1024.

CuDv   Customized devices: an entry for each device defined or installed in
            the system.

CuAt   Customized attributes: device-specific information for a defined or
            installed device.

CuDep   Customized dependencies: a list of the dependence links between
            logical devices or from logical to physical devices, for example, that
            the 'inet0' device is dependent on the token ring device 'tr0'.

CuDvDr   Customized device drivers: Information about critical resources
            needed to ensure correct device serialization.

CuVPD   Customized vital product data: a listing of the hardware, software
            and microcode revision levels defined or installed in the system.

Config_   Configuration rules: a list of programs which need to be run as the
Rules   system starts. The configuration rules class is ordered by phase and
            sequence. Phase 1 describes the IPL and is followed by phase 2 (for
            the keyswitch in normal position) or phase 3 (for the keyswitch in
            service position). The sequence number, for example 1, 5 or 6,
            would indicate what order to run that program in the particular
            phase.

```
PdDv:                                     CuDv:
    type        = "8mm"                       name        = "rmt0"
    class       = "tape"                      status      = 1
    subclass    = "scsi"                      ddins       = "tape"
    prefix      = "rmt"                       loc         = 00-08-00-50
    devid       = ""                          parent      = scsi0
    detachable  = 1                           PdDvLn      = tape/scsi/8mm
    led         = 2418
    DvDr        = "tape"                   PdAt:
    Define      = /etc/methods/define         uniquetype  = "tape/scsi/8mm"
    Configure   = /etc/methods/cfgsctape      attribute   = "block_size"
    Unconfigure = /etc/methods/ucfgdevice     deflt       = 1024
                                              values      = 0-245760,1
```

Figure 3.5. A sample ODM device.

Figure 3.5 is a simple example of some of these classes in action. Here the predefined database is that of an 8 mm tape drive. From this the customized device /dev/rmt0 is derived. The *PdAt* predefined attributes indicate that the default tape block size is set to 1024 bytes but may have a range of values up to 245 760 bytes.

3.2.3 The vital product database

Another good example of the use of the ODM is to store vital product data (VPD) in what AIX refers to as the vital product database. The database comprises a set of ODM object classes and a function library API libvpd. a to access the information. Software installation and update programs such as *installp* store information in this database. For example, looking in the header swvpd. h reveals that information like:

LPP_ NAME	The name of the licensed program product installed
INSTALL	The level of the program being installed
VER	The program version number
REL	The release level of the program
MOD	The modification level of the program
CHECKSUM	The checksum of all files for this package

is stored in the ODM for each installed software product. This is an important advance over many other implementations of UNIX that simply install a program without any checks, and have no method of tracking program versions or fix

levels once installed. It also allows postinstallation security checks via the
checksums in the inventory files to detect altered files.

3.3   Printing

AIX has a printer spooling subsystem which is derived in its most basic form
from the port of UNIX to IBM platforms by interactive systems. There have of
course been some major changes.

Let us first review the basics of printing via the standard device driver then
build on this knowledge to understand the AIX extensions.

3.3.1   *Printing via the device driver*

At the most fundamental level a real physical printer can be seen by a user as an
entry in the AIX filesystem. For example, consider a workstation with an Apple
Laserwriter PostScript printer configured as the device /dev/lp0. Without
using any print spooling facilities at all, the printer may be accessed directly. For
example, the following command:

```
cat /etc/passwd > /dev/lp0
```

sends a listing of the password file to the printer connected to /dev/lp0. The
file is sent via the device driver to the real physical printer. By passing through
the device driver the file undergoes some conversion according to the printer
driver characteristics. For example, an end-of-line character (ASCII line-feed) is
translated into two characters, an ASCII carriage-return character, followed by
an ASCII line-feed character.

The printer device driver's characteristics are modified using the standard
ioctl() function call. An applications developer may use this knowledge to
advantage. For example, assume that the /dev/lp0 port was really connected
to the IBM graphics printer (this is actually a circa 1980 Epson graphics printer).
In order to print graphics an applications developer needs to send the printer the
correct device-specific Escape codes. That is to say:

1   Tell /dev/lp0 printer device driver to pass all subsequent characters to the
    printer unaltered, and not to perform any page formatting, for example,
    page numbering, headers or footers. Use **ioctl()** function.
2   Send data to the printer. For example:
    a   Send form feed character to position to top of new page.
    b   Send Escape, followed by character 'L' to begin 960-bit image graphics
        mode.
    c   Send correct number of data bits. Printer now automatically out of
        graphics mode.
    d   Send Escape followed by character 'J' followed by number of 0.1176 mm
        increments to feed paper forward.

    e Send carriage-return character to reset print head to character position 0.

    f Repeat the above 5 steps a–e until the full graphic is drawn.

3   Call **ioctl()** again to restore printer driver state.

As you can observe, this is a fairly involved process and works only because the exact characteristics of the printer are known. If the connected printer was not an IBM graphics or compatible then the Escape sequences sent would be meaningless.

3.3.2   *Print spooling*

Usually output is not sent directly to the printer with the `cat` command. It is much easier to use the printer spooling subsystem. Why? First, by printing directly to the device driver the file being printed is inaccessible until after the physical printer has finished printing it. Second, the results of many different users, each sending their output to the printer, may result in a mix-up of everyone's information. It is much more sensible to send files to a print spooler which takes a copy of the file and then prints it in an orderly manner.

Under AIX, files are sent to a named queue, which is actually part of a three-part hierarchy as shown in Fig. 3.6. A print queue has a name: laser or lineprt in our example. Each print queue has a one-to-many mapping with one or more virtual printers. For example, printout sent to the queue named lineprt can be sent to one of two virtual printers. Virtual printers map many-to-one real physical printers.

A queue is a named virtual device to which output is sent. A print queue can have only a single datastream type. A virtual printer represents a particular datastream and printer setting on a particular printer. Virtual printers are required because modern printers can usually understand more than a single datastream. For example, a Lexmark 4029 laser printer can understand ASCII, Hewlett-Packard PCL4, and PostScript datastreams and so can be defined as three different virtual printers.

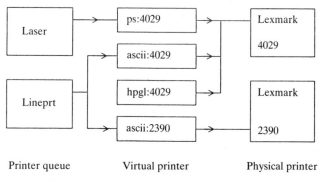

Figure 3.6.   Queues, virtual printers and real printers.

```
ascii:
      discipline=fcfs          # first come first served
      device = lpd             # matches stanza to come
      acctfile = /var/adm/qacct

lpd:
      backend=/usr/lpd/piobe   # backend program
      file=/dev/lp0            # real printer device
      header=always            # printer a header
      trailer=never            # but never a trailer
```

Figure 3.7. Sample qconfig entries.

From our logical view of the printing process here is a view of how AIX interprets user requests. First, note that configuring the real and virtual printers and queues is done via the SMIT (see Sec. 9.1). Theoretically, it is possible to use the numerous native AIX commands to create these entities. Unfortunately, I have found that the time spent configuring them manually is a complex and error-prone process—I recommend you use SMIT!

When a print request is submitted, the printer command copies the file and places it in a queue of files to be processed. A program called *qdaemon* (an example of an endless background process known as a 'daemon' process) takes files from this queue and consults the *qconfig* file to determine to what real printer to send the output. The printfile is sent to the real printer after passing through a program declared in the *qconfig* file called a backend. The backend creates a datastream including any necessary printer initialization codes to set-up the printer as the required virtual printer, then prints the file. For example, an ASCII printer such as an IBM 4201 Proprinter may be capable of printing in multiple fonts, e.g. Courier and Roman. Sending the output to the ASCII queue means sending it via a particular virtual printer which will have a predetermined font.

How does *qdaemon* know what to do? The answer is that the /etc/qconfig file contains a list of parameters. Figure 3.7 shows the entries mapping the queue named *ascii* to the physical /dev/lp0. To speed up the lookup, /etc/ qconfig is translated into a binary file /usr/lpd/qconfig.bin by a program known as a digester.

3.3.3 *Remote printing*

Though local printing is sound, remote printing has a number of advantages:

- Someone else has the responsibility for software configuration and physical maintenance of the printers.
- It is quieter.
- Your personal workstation processor is not loaded.
- It enables printer sharing among a group of workstations.

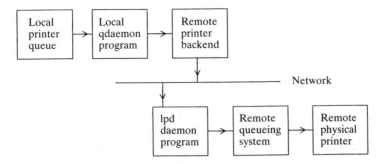

Figure 3.8.   Remote printing.

Under AIX, remote printing is achieved by feeding the output from the *qdaemon* to a special printer backend. This process is shown in Fig. 3.8, which shows the special backend program *rembak* that sends the print file across the network to the destination machine's *lpd* daemon program. From there it is sent to that remote system's *qdaemon* program and then to the remote physical printer.

3.3.4   Printing limitations

Although AIX has done much to make the printing process both flexible and reliable it has not until recently addressed the major shortcoming of device dependence that still plagues UNIX printing. In plain terms, different printers print text and graphics using different command sequences. UNIX does not solve this problem. Here is an example.

A user creates some charts using AP/6000 (essentially an office automation package for AIX based on UNIPLEX). The charts display graphically under X-Windows. Using the standard X-Windows program *xwd* a user can dump the screen image of the chart and send this to an IBM 3812 or PostScript printer. But what if the user does not have one of these printers? Even a simple window display cannot easily be printed!

Let us now consider an X-Windows applications developer, for example Interleaf Corporation, and their product Interleaf Desktop Publisher. Interleaf needs to be able to perform more than a program-initiated window print. Users of this high-function desktop publishing package will clearly expect to be able to print the document they have composed to any graphics capable printer attached to their IBM RISC System/6000. However UNIX does not provide a device-independent way to print. It is still the responsibility of the application developer's program to generate the correct printer datastream and send it to the printer driver directly (by suitable calls to **ioctl()** as outlined before).

This implies that an application program needs to be able to generate PostScript and a variety of other printer formats. How does the applications developer map a colour screen output to greyscale printer? How do they compensate for the different aspect ratios of screen and printer? How do they test their resultant printer drivers?

This is an important area since many other personal operating systems provide these facilities with ease. For example, Microsoft Windows and IBM OS/2 Presentation Manager both allow the programmer to print to any operating system supported printer. The application just says print. The operating system transforms anything displayed on the graphics screen into a datastream suitable for a printer (or spooler). AIX has also introduced some facilities to overcome this problem (see Sec. 6.7). There are some other non-vendor-specific mechanisms to enable device independent printing. Bristol Technologies market a product that allows an X-windows program to write device independently to either the screen or a Hewlett-Packard PCL (printer control language) or PostScript printer. But there is no standard to date.

AIX does however provide the transcript utilities which enable output to be manipulated to PostScript printers. For example:

enscript   Converts text files to PostScript format

psc   Converts troff format to PostScript format

psrev   Reorders and selects pages in a PostScript file

psplot   Converts files in plot format to PostScript format

ps4014   Converts a Tektronix 4014 file to PostScript format.

3.4   Real-time computing

A real-time application is different from a regular program in that it must perform or respond to certain program actions within a strict timeframe.

3.4.1   Real-time UNIX systems

The initial design point for UNIX was as a multiuser, multitasking operating system. However, real-time systems need facilities not provided by that traditional environment. Let us look at some of the requirements.

Short interrupt latency

Interrupt latency is the maximum time a requesting interrupt may have to wait before being serviced. Why need it wait at all? Well, a UNIX device driver may need to disable interrupts during certain critical sections of code. For example, consider a high-speed optical network link between two IBM RISC System/6000 computer systems. A packet is received by one system and is being processed when another arrives. Unless interrupts are disabled while the packet is removed from the input queue the queue may be left in an indeterminate state destroying its integrity.

Fast context switching

Context switching means stopping the currently executing task, saving its registers (context), loading another task's context, then setting it running. Under UNIX a program runs in user mode until it needs to execute a system call, at which time the processor will begin executing code in the kernel mode. Unfortunately the standard UNIX kernel is not pre-emptible, so while executing a system call on behalf of a user, UNIX cannot task switch. Some system calls like **fork()**, **exec()** are notorious for requiring a substantial time to execute, thus preventing a UNIX system from responding in real time.

Pinning memory

This is the process of locking a program's code and/or data into real memory. Why do this? If a user's UNIX system is loaded or has little real memory, then their application program may be paged out to disk. When a real-time interrupt arrives, the program needs to be paged back in and resumed; this will take time which might be unacceptable for real-time applications.

Scheduling

In UNIX scheduling is via a policy that favours interactive programs over batch programs: the smaller the priority number the more important is the process. The priority number of a process is increased by UNIX if the process remains inactive for a long time, and decreased if it uses large amounts of processor time. Many real-time programs remain inactive for long periods but when awoken require immediate attention. Using this scheduling policy real-time programs would not fare well.

Timer services

In UNIX these are provided by the **sleep()** and **select()** calls. **sleep()** allows only a one-second resolution (useless for real time). **select()** allows for microsecond resolution in principle, however this is dependent upon the hardware implementation. There is also a limit of one interval timer per process, again useless for real-time applications.

3.4.2 *The AIX approach to real-time UNIX*

Many vendors produce special versions of their UNIX operating system specializing in real time. AIX took a fundamentally different approach in that a policy decision was made to implement real-time facilities from the start. Developers welcome this approach because regular AIX applications can include real-time components as and when required. Also, specialized real-time applications can use AIX instead of developing and executing on a specialized real-time (and usually cut down) UNIX.

AIX kernel pre-emption

The fundamental traditional UNIX limitation is that processes running in kernel mode may not be pre-empted at any time. That is to say, if a more favoured priority process were blocked waiting for an event, it cannot be unblocked even if that event arrives, and another process is executing a call in kernel mode. The reason that UNIX was not initially designed to be pre-emptible was that all kernel data structures were made globally accessible to any process executing in kernel mode. This was for simplicity; to prevent contention (and deadlock) between processes for the same kernel data structure system calls were made atomic. That means, each system call must run to completion, or voluntarily give up the processor, before another can be scheduled.

In UNIX System V Release 4, USL has tried to improve the real-time characteristics by the introduction of *pre-emption* points into the kernel. A pre-emption point is a section of code within a system call where the process does not care if it is interrupted. If these pre-emption points are scattered extensively throughout the kernel, then the worst case context switch is the duration of the longest running section of code without pre-emption points.

Under AIX, however, all kernel code that accesses data has been modified (this was not a trivial task). A process executing in kernel mode must protect any shared data structure by locking. With this scheme the kernel is pre-emptible by default and not by exception. Consequently, context switching time is now reduced; real-time applications may now be executed as regular user (as opposed to kernel) programs. AIX therefore provides numerous user facilities for real-time programming and these are integrated into the base AIX operating system.

AIX also allows the real-time performance of an application to be improved by coding critical parts of the application as a kernel extension. Since AIX has a dynamically expandable kernel this may be done on the fly without recompiling or relinking existing kernel code.

Now let us list a few of the real-time facilities that AIX provides.

Memory pinning

Some applications may not be able to afford page-in delays, but may benefit from having their code, data and stack always resident in memory. In such cases it is advisable to use the **plock()** system call to pin user memory. Since AIX allocates a 32 Mb stack for each process, it is advisable to use the **setrlimit()** call to reduce this to a sensible value. Developers writing (kernel) interrupt handlers use separate kernel routines, including the **pin()**, **unpin()** and **pincode()**, **unpincode()** functions.

Timer services

The recommended timer services for real-time programs are based on those specified by POSIX 1003.4. The functions enable per process interrupt timers with a 10 millisecond resolution. The cost of each interrupt is about 300 microseconds. The main routines are:

gettimerid()	Allocates the interval timer
incinterval()	Changes the time to the next interval interrupt, or changes the default interrupt interval after the next interrupt
absinterval()	Sets the timer to an absolute value immediately
getinterval()	Finds the time left before the next interrupt

Also available is a set of fine granularity kernel timer services which can be used for sub 10 millisecond resolution timers. Of course these are executable in kernel mode only, which means that a kernel extension needs to be written.

Real-time priorities

All processes in AIX have a priority between 0 and 127. A real-time process should allocate a fixed priority value (by allocating between 0 and 40) using the **setpri()** call. Such a process will run until it voluntarily gives up the processor by sleeping, or until an interrupt occurs. Since the system timer interrupt is 10 milliseconds this will be every 10 milliseconds or less.

User processes run at variable priorities in the range 40 to 127. User processes are scheduled using the traditional UNIX algorithm where priority increases with more processor usage. The original priority of a process is inherited from its parent. If however, **nice()** or **setpriority()** is called, AIX takes your priority (in the range 0 to 40) and maps it into the range 40 to 127 based on your value *and a number of other factors.*

Enhanced context switching

As described earlier, the traditional UNIX kernel is not pre-emptible, so the worst case context switch is the time through the longest running system call. Since AIX has a fully pre-emptible kernel any user or kernel process may be interrupted at any time. If the process is not pre-empted it will run for a fixed amount of time (usually 10 milliseconds). When it expires the scheduler will recalculate the priority and the dispatcher will choose the runnable process with the most favoured priority to be executed in the next time slice. Interrupt handlers are not time sliced and therefore run to completion except in the case where they become interrupted by a higher priority handler. AIX also made changes to the kernel dispatcher data structures (a common modification for USL UNIX System V.3 onward also). The original structures were a simple but long queue. These have been replaced by 128 process scheduling *run queues* as described in Fig. 3.9.

Each run queue corresponds to the fixed (real-time) and variable (user) priorities supported by the dispatcher. Each run queue is a circularly linked list of runnable processes. When choosing the process to be run next, a bit array is scanned to see if the run queue contains any process, and if it contains one or more processes (bit set) it indexes into the the list and dispatches the process at the head of the list. If this process completes its time slice and is still runnable, it is placed at the tail of the queue. Finally, note that the time to **fork()** a process in AIX is further reduced since when forking, that is, copying the parent process, kernel data is global to the virtual memory manager, so need not be copied.

3.5   International language support

Writing this book in the United Kingdom meant remembering that national language support (NLS) involves more than translating dollar symbols to pounds while reading American documentation. IBM has traditionally been very strong in the area of NLS both for European and Asian languages, and the RISC system is particularly capable when it comes to NLS. However, since NLS is a very confusing area, we will start with a few definitions that explain some of the challenges which face an applications developer who wishes to provide internationalized applications.

3.5.1   Single and multi-byte character sets

When using all eight bits of a byte there are 256 possible values for characters. This is fine for alphabetic languages, that is, the ones in which phonetic symbols are combined to form words, but inadequate for ideographic languages like Japanese and Chinese. In these Asian languages each word is a unique ideographic symbol (or rarely two or more symbols). Such languages require two or more bytes per character to encode the language, and a graphics terminal to display the several thousand different ideographs. IBM uses the acronym SBCS (single byte character set) for character sets that require only a single byte; for characters that need to be stored in two or more bytes IBM uses the acronym MBCS (multibyte character set)—this is a replacement for the now obsolete IBM term DBCS (double byte character set).

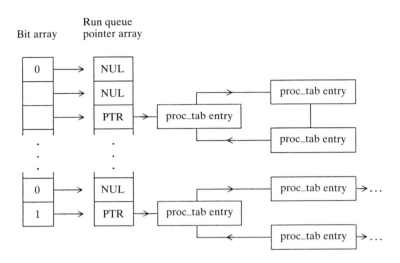

Figure 3.9.   AIX run queues.

3.5.2   *Collation*

English sorting rules are very simple, each letter sorts to one and only one place. However in other languages this is not so. In French, for example, the letters e, è, é, sort in that order even though they may not be arranged in this sequence in the character set.

In German there may be a one-to-many character mapping, for example the German 'ß' (scharfes S) is collated as if it were 'ss'.

Some languages, for example Spanish, treat a sequence of characters as a single sorting character. For example the 'ch' and 'll' sequences have their own collating positions.

Classification and formatting

Many Asian languages have only one case so C programming functions like **islower()** and **isupper()** become meaningless. Many countries have different date, time and numeric formats. For example, date formats for Friday, 13 December 1991 are shown in Table 3.1 on page 33.

3.5.3   *Program messages*

A truly international program requires its program panels, help text and error messages all to be translated into the local language. It is common to separate all these messages, called machine-readable information (MRI), and put them into a separate file, then when the language is changed only the messages file need be changed.

Mixing it all together

In today's environment one may naturally expect to work on computer systems in the language of one's choice. For example, an English-speaking user can use the native system in Belgium (where a Belgian–French keyboard is different to a regular French keyboard). This user can use a set of keystrokes to get uniquely English characters at the Belgian–French keyboard, and have them displayed on the screen.

3.5.4   NLS support in AIX

IBM's strategy on NLS is to support existing industry standards as well as IBM's international codepage standard. At the time of writing, AIX includes support for the following SBCS and MBCS languages: Danish, Finnish, French, German, Icelandic, Italian, Japanese, Korean, Norwegian, Spanish, Swiss, Swedish, Traditional Chinese, Turkish, UK English and US English.

Of course, even though every copy of AIX that is shipped contains support for all these languages, the user will often not be able to enter all of a country's national language characters unless they have the correct keyboard. For example, it is possible to display Japanese kanji on the screen of a US-based AIX system but not enter Japanese characters.

3.5.5   Codepages and ISO character sets

IBM has standardized on *codepage* technology across its entire range of traditional non-UNIX computer systems be they microcomputer, minicomputer or mainframe based. For example, the codepages 437 and 850 are used by the DOS operating system for US English and Western European character sets respectively.

The UNIX world, however, uses ISO standard character sets. In Europe, for example, ISO 8859/1 is known as *Latin-1*. ISO 8859 and codepage 850 are not identical, but their intentions are the same, namely that a single codepage provides all the necessary characters for Western European languages such as French, German, Italian and Spanish. The traditional ASCII characters are arranged in positions hexadecimal 0x00–0x7F and the 'extra' characters for the Western languages are in positions 0xA0–0xFF.

While for ASCII the letters are arranged in alphabetical order, this is not true for Latin-1 or codepage 850. This means that AIX has to build a collation table independent of its encoded hex value. In fact AIX also has to know what country is being collated. For example, in codepage 850 both Germany and Sweden have the 'ä' character, but in Germany this sorts like an 'a' character, and in Swedish it sorts after lowercase z!

The other common ISO codesets are shown in Table 3.2 (on page 34).

Table 3.1. International date formats

Country	Date	Format
USA	12/13/91	month/day/year
UK	13/12/91	day/month/year
(ISO)	91/12/13	year/month/day
Japan	03/12/13	91-emp[1]/month/day

[1] The Japanese year is calculated as years since the last emperor came to power.

One extremely important change made from past releases of AIX is the support of ISO standard codesets for a user. Before AIX version 3.2, the AIX operating system was shipped in two different object forms, one using the IBM codepage 850 for Western Europe and the other using IBM codepage 932 for Japan. Since most UNIX users use codeset standards, AIX 3.2 and later allows the user the flexibility to use ISO codesets as their primary mode of international operation. Correspondingly, AIX is now shipped worldwide in a single package. In Western Europe the ISO 8859/1 codeset should be used and in Japan the EUC-JP codeset (described later).

3.5.6 Setting up NLS

In order to use NLS a user simply needs to set a system *locale*. This is done by setting the LANG variable at the shell prompt to the current country in the form:

```
Language_territory.codeset-modifier
e.g export LANG=fr_CH.8859-1
```

AIX now supports ISO 8859 codesets 1, 7 and 9.

3.5.7 Multibyte character set support

The Asian-style languages currently supported are Traditional Chinese and Japanese. The only requirement necessary to support these is that the customer has a suitable keyboard. For example, for Japanese a keyboard includes a multipart space bar and Japanese keytop engravings. The rest of this discussion relates to Japanese support. Japanese kanji characters are stored in extended UNIX codes Japanese (EUC JP, often named UJIS). Prior to AIX 3.2, Japanese characters were stored in SJIS (shift JIS) format which, like its PC codepage 850 SBCS counterpart, was the standard for Japanese PCs. However, other Japanese UNIX systems use EUC JP, so AIX now supports UJIS and SJIS.

Table 3.2. ISO codeset standards

Language	Formal ISO	Informal ISO
Western European	ISO 8859/1	Latin-1
Eastern European	ISO 8859/2	Latin-2
Southeastern European	ISO 8859/3	Latin-3
Northern European	ISO 8859/4	Latin-4
English and Cyrillic	ISO 8859/5	Latin-5
English and Arabic	ISO 8859/6	Latin-6
English and Greek	ISO 8859/7	Latin-7
English and Hebrew	ISO 8859/8	Latin-8
Western European and Turkish	ISO 8859/9	Latin-9

The format of UJIS characters under AIX is as follows:

```
#1   0 xxxxxxx
#2   1xxxxxxx    1xxxxxxx
#2   ss2         1xxxxxxx
#3   ss3         1xxxxxxx    1xxxxxxx
```

Each character is stored in one of four formats. First, all characters in the form hex 0x00 to 0x7F are straight ASCII. The second type of character classification is a two-byte character pair, each byte having the most significant bit set. The third classification begins with a byte called ss2 for single shift 2, actually the hex character 0x8e. It is a two-byte pair whose second byte has the most significant bit set. The fourth classification is a three-byte sequence, beginning with the byte called ss3, called single shift 3, actually the hex character 0x8F, followed by a two-byte pair, whose bytes are in the range 0x80 to 0xFF. A quick calculation, therefore, will show that this character encoding scheme can currently accommodate over 30 000 different multibyte characters.

While we have discussed how Japanese characters are stored (as multibyte characters), how does one enter a Japanese kanji character? First, we need to understand that in addition to ideographic kanji characters, there are also two phonetic language systems katakana and hiragana. Generally, katakana is used for non-Japanese words and hiragana for native Japanese words. Together the two systems are known as kana and constitute about 100 characters (only!).

So, to enter a kanji character, either kana or English characters are entered using a special Japanese keyboard. This has a special five-part spacebar as well as kana and English keytop engravings. By using a special compose key, AIX is instructed to convert the entered characters to kanji. However, several kanji characters may have the same phonetic representation, and in that case a menu of choices is presented at the bottom of the screen. If the translation is unambiguous then no selection is necessary. Kana to kanji translation is now performed by the AIX operating system, so regular character or OSF/Motif applications do not include special code to do this, though they must of course include code to cope with these multibyte wide characters.

3.5.8 NLS setup and programming considerations

Actual NLS support may be coded in different ways. AIX 3.2 and later programming guides recommend the Single Source Single Object (SSSO) approach. This means that a single object supports both single and multibyte language support. Alternatively the application may be packaged as Single Source Dual Object (SSDO) meaning that although a single set of source code exists, conditional compilation flags inside the code enable two different versions of the program to be built. Less than ideally, AIX 3.2 is packaged as SSDO, although this does have the advantage of providing two objects, one optimized for single byte character set operation, while the second has generalized support for both multi- and single byte character sets.

IBM advises that application writers should ideally strive towards delivering SSSO applications. A checklist of producing such an application might read:

1   Assume the user has setup the LANG environment variable.
2   All machine readable information, that is to say, messages, should be stored in message catalogues (explained below).
3   Use the **setlocale()** function as the first statement in an application's **main()** function to inform the program of user's LANG preferences.
4   Convert all data read in from user or disk input from its storage form of file code characters to a useful internal form of wide characters using supplied AIX functions.
5   Manipulate the wide character information using **wc.....()** functions.

NLS support in X-Windows

The standard X-Windows fonts use the ISO 8859 codeset standard. IBM also supplies another set of fonts that provide support for the IBM codepage 850. This is primarily of use in connecting from an AIX system to other systems using IBM codepage standards. For example, under X-Windows, using the windowed *aixterm* terminal emulator a user can use the *telnet* command to connect to a remote IBM OS/2 system running TCP/IP. The OS/2 system will be running codepage 850 (in Western Europe) and the user can display the OS/2 session on their X-Windows screen by using codepage 850 in the aixterm window.

Message catalogues

AIX uses the X/Open XPG3 message cataloguing system. This system has been adopted by many other UNIX vendors, notably the Open Software Foundation.

The idea behind a message catalogue is to remove all message text from the body of an application and place it in a message catalogue. According to the run-time environment variable LANG, the program should retrieve the correct country message from the catalogue and display it in a suitable form, for example in a popup message dialog within an OSF/Motif program.

Here is a sample message cataloguing program:

```
/* this is the message file example.msg */
/* process with the command runcmd example example.msg */
/* set MS_SET1 */
MSG1 "Hello World \n"

/* this is the file example.c */
#include <locale.h>
#include <nl_types.h>
#include "example.h" /* machine generated with runcat */
nl_catd catd;

main()

    (void) setlocale (LC_ALL, ""); /* check LANG environment */

    catd = catopen (MF_EXAMPLE, 0);

    printf ( catgets (catd, MS_SET1, MSG1, "Default msg \n" ));

    catclose (catd);
}
```

4
RISC technology

The concept of RISC was due, at least in part, to the pioneering work done by the IBM TJ Watson research centre, and in particular John Cocke, on the 801 reduced instruction set computer (RISC) project. The fundamental idea was to produce a processor whose minimal or 'reduced' instruction set was optimized to satisfy the needs of the vast majority of any program code. More complex and infrequently used instructions were to be simulated using the basic set.

Recall that the trend in microprocessors in the late seventies and early eighties was to produce processors with complex instruction sets, hence the term CISC (complex instruction set computer). Unfortunately, compiler design could not and still can not easily produce code to take advantage of these increases in complexity.

RISC can therefore be seen as a reaction to that trend, with the goal of providing a smaller (in transistor circuits per processor) and more effective processor. A processor with a smaller and simpler instruction set is easier to design and debug. Hardware designers can therefore concentrate on deciding what is the very best minimal instruction set and then focus on decreasing the number of processor cycles required to load, decode and execute those instructions. One instruction per cycle was seen as the ultimate goal. The IBM RT PC system (see Appendix 1) was IBM's first attempt at a commercial RISC-based UNIX workstation and followed this goal.

In 1985, most of the original IBM 801 design team embarked on a new effort, the 'America project', to reconsider the issues of machine architecture. The team performed studies on floating-point organization and performance, understanding what hardware design features could really be used by state-of-the-art compilers, and, most importantly, whether instruction-level parallelism techniques could be employed to achieve an architecture called 'superscalar' that would achieve what had been previously thought impossible, less than one machine cycle per instruction executed. By 1986, the team had designed a second-generation RISC architecture which embodied these principles, but now RISC became the acronym for reduced instruction set cycles. By reading more than one instruction from memory at a time and designing an architecture comprised of a number of

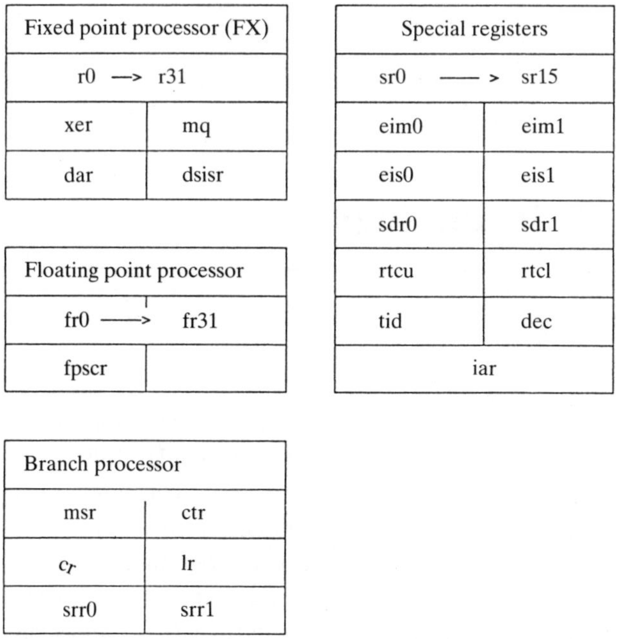

Fixed point processor (FX)	
r0 —→ r31	
xer	mq
dar	dsisr

Special registers	
sr0 —— > sr15	
eim0	eim1
eis0	eis1
sdr0	sdr1
rtcu	rtcl
tid	dec
iar	

Floating point processor	
fr0 ——→ fr31	
fpscr	

Branch processor	
msr	ctr
cr	lr
srr0	srr1

Figure 4.1.   The IBM RISC System/6000 register programming model.

processor execution units, more than one instruction could be executed concurrently. In 1986, a group at IBM's Austin Texas laboratory accepted these ideas. The result is the IBM RISC System/6000.

The overall architecture of the RISC system has been termed POWER—performance optimization with enhanced RISC. The IBM POWER architecture therefore describes a family of binary compatible processors used by IBM for the AIX operating system. The goal of this chapter is first to explain the POWER architecture in terms of the low-level programming and associated memory management, and then to show how this is integrated with the XL family of RISC system compilers.

4.1   Register model

Figure 4.1 shows the logical view of the IBM RISC System/6000 central processing unit (CPU). From an assembler programming perspective, a programmer is made explicitly aware that the CPU is divided into three areas (the branch, fixed and floating-point units). This mirrors the physical design of the original hardware chipset which was packaged into three physically separate units.[1] Any program that uses data references to create instructions, for example, a program loader or

[1] Later RISC Systems, models 220 and 230, use a single chip implementation of the POWER architecture and are discussed in Sec. 8.3.

debugger, must explicitly force instructions from the data cache into the instruction cache (see Sec. 4.3). Of the 184 processor instructions, 18 are used in the branch processor, 116 in the fixed-point processor and 42 in the floating-point processor. The remaining 8 are used for cache manipulation.

Referring to Fig. 4.1:

Fixed point-processor registers

r0–r31   General-purpose registers: main 32-bit register set used by the system.

xer   Fixed-point exception register: this 32-bit register indicates the state of the fixed-point operation, for example, that an overflow or carry has occurred.

mq   Multiply quotient register: this provides a 32-bit register extension to store the results of a multiply or divide operation.

dar   Data address register: contains the 32-bit address that caused a data storage or alignment exception.

dsisr   Data storage interrupt status register: defines the cause of the interrupt whose address was placed in the dar.

Branch processor registers

msr   Machine state register: defines the state of the processor, for example, whether external interrupts are disabled, whether the floating-point processor is available or whether an incorrectly aligned address was selected.

cr   Condition register: a 32-bit register that reflects the result of certain operations and provides a mechanism for testing and branching.

lr   Link register: a 32-bit register that contains the destination address of conditional branch instructions or the return address for subroutine instructions.

ctr   Count register: a 32-bit register that is automatically decremented with branch and count instructions. It can also represent an address for the branch to count register instruction. The count register is also used as a fast save area for the msr register when a supervisor call occurs.

srr0   Status save/restore register 0: this 32-bit register saves the machine state on interrupt and restores the machine state on a return from interrupt instruction. srr0 contains the address that caused the interrupt.

srr1   Status save/restore register 1: as srr0, but srr1 contains specific information on the interrupt cause as well as part of the msr register when the interrupt occurs.

Floating-point processor registers

fr0–fr31   Floating-point registers: thirty-two, 64-bit floating-point registers.

fpscr   Floating-point status and control register: controls the handling of floating-point exceptions and results.

Special-purpose registers

dec   Decrementer register: a counter that provides a mechanism for causing an external interrupt. This is achieved by loading the register with a number that is decremented at regular intervals until the register reaches zero when an interrupt is made.

eim0,   External interrupt mask low and high, 32 bits.
eim1

eis0, eis1 External interrupt summary low and high, 32 bits.

iar   Instruction address register (program counter).

rtcu   Real-time clock upper register: the 32-bit time in seconds.

rtcl   Real time clock lower register: the lower 32 bits of the time in nanoseconds.

sr0–   Segment registers: sixteen, 32-bit registers used for virtual-to-real address
sr15   translation.

sdr0   Storage description register 0: a pointer to the higher order bits of the real address of the page frame table (PFT).

sdr1   Storage description register 1: contains the high-order bits of the real address of the hash anchor table (HAT) and a HAT mask used by virtual-to-real address translation hardware to index into the PFT pointed to by sdr0.

tid   Transaction ID register: the 32-bit transaction ID of the executing process.

4.2   Virtual memory addressing

Figure 4.2 shows the translation from an effective address that programmers use to a physical address used to access actual memory. The programming register model is that of a 32-bit processor. Addresses are 32 bits in size allowing for a per process address space of 4 Gb (but, by using and swapping shared segments and mapped files, an applications developer can considerably expand the total amount of data accessible should this be necessary). To generate a physical address the effective address is divided into three parts: a 4-bit segment index, a 16-bit virtual page index, and a 12-bit offset as follows:

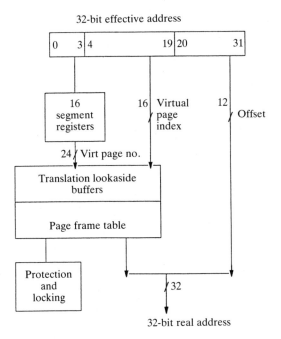

Figure 4.2.   Virtual address translation.

Stage 1　　The index selects one of the segment registers from sr0 to sr15. Each
segment register is 32 bits in size. If the most significant bit is 1 then
the lowest 24 bits read and write from memory addresses on the
MicroChannel I/O bus. If the bit is 0, these 24 bits form the upper 24
bits of the virtual address which will lead to an address in system
memory.

Stage 2　　The 24-bit segment ID is concatenated to the 16-bit virtual page
index to form a 40-bit virtual page number. The virtual page number
provides an index into the PFT to produce a 20-bit real page
number.

Stage 3　　The real page number from the PFT lookup is combined with the 12
bits of the original effective address to form a physical 32-bit
address.

Stage 4　　The physical 32-bit address is used to address real system memory.

By convention, certain segment registers are used for the same purposes systemwide.
This is shown in Fig. 4.3.

　　How exactly does a 40-bit virtual page number become translated into a 20-bit
physical address? This is explained in Fig. 4.4. The sdr1 register points to a table
in real memory called a hash anchor table (HAT). The virtual page number
(VPN) indexes into the HAT and the HAT points to a linked list of entries in a

Registers	Segments	
0	Primary kernel segment	Global
1	User text segment	Shared
2	Process private segment	Private
3		
4		
5	Attached	Private
6	data segments	or
7	and	shared
8	mapped files	
9		
10		
11	Reserved	
12	Reserved	
13	Shared library text segment	Shared
14	Secondary kernel segment	Global
15	Shared data segment	Shared

Figure 4.3.   Virtual memory segments.

PFT. The PFT is addressed using the sdr0 register. The linked list is traversed (indexed) for a matching VPN. If a matching VPN is found, then the real 20-bit address is determined in hardware by applying a simple equation based on the HAT address and the number of traversals required to find the VPN. If, however, there is no match (pointer to next PFT is zero), then the virtual memory address is not in real memory. A page fault then occurs, requiring that page of memory to be read from the hard disk into real memory. Note also from Fig. 4.4 that the PFT entry stores the access rights for the page of memory.

4.3   Understanding caches

If any RISC system processor had to translate every effective address to a physical address using the two large index tables (the HAT and the PFT) this would be the performance-limiting part of the processor. Similarly, a processor's operation would also be slow if it had always to access system memory for program data and instructions. Instead, frequently used effective address to physical

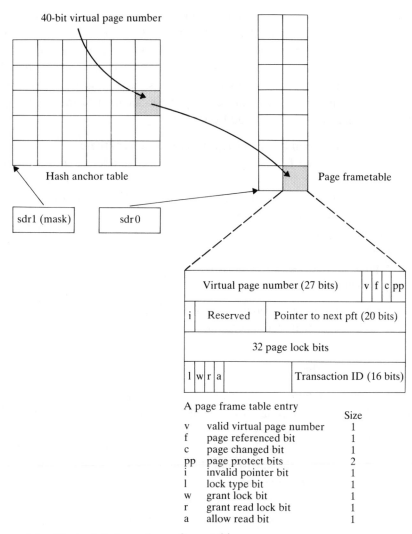

Figure 4.4. The hash index and page frame tables.

address translations are stored in a memory cache called a translation lookaside buffer (TLB). The memory cache architecture provides a cache to system memory throughput of up to 480 Mb per second depending on RISC system model.

Starting with the TLB, this contains two 64-entry tables that maintain the effective address to physical address translations for 128 pages, that is to say, 512 kb of real memory. An additional two caches are also provided, a data cache and an instruction cache. A 64 kb data cache stores the most recently accessed data. The cache is organized as four, 16 kb set associative areas, that is to say, each of the four areas is searched in parallel for a matching data address. The search is made for an effective address and if any of the 128 addresses match, then the 128 byte data line is accessed instead of system memory. The instruction cache unit is a 32 kb cache that fetches instructions, executes branch and condition register logic and dispatches up to two instructions per cycle to the fixed- and floating-point units. It is organized as a two-way set associative cache, each set has 64 entries of 16 four-byte instructions. Lastly, an eight-instruction buffer is used for normal instruction fetching. So to summarize the hierarchy of the RISC system memory effective address access:

- If the information is in the data cache it is selected from there.
- The TLB is searched for a way to map the effective address into a physical address.
- If the TLB does not contain the mapping, the HAT and PFT must be searched for the physical address.
- Usually the physical address found is in system memory and read into the processors.
- If the physical address is not present it is page faulted from hard disk into physical memory.

The addition of numerous models into the RISC system family has meant a variety of cache sizes are now utilized as shown in Table 4.1.

4.4   CPU walkthru

The reader can understand the operation of the RISC system processing units by starting with the branch processor as follows. The branch processor fetches instructions from cache memory (or from system memory for a cache miss) at four bytes per cycle, executing all branch instructions it finds and dispatching the remaining instructions to the fixed-point (FX) and floating-point (FP) processors. This continues until either the queue of instructions waiting at the FX and FP processors is full, or a conditional branch is encountered which depends upon the result of a computation which has already been dispatched, but which has not yet completed execution.

The condition register (cr) is a 32-bit register divided into eight condition fields. The FP and FX processors each drive an individual field in the cr to indicate the result of their operations. This design prevents conflicts of sharing a common condition code in separate processors. (For example, comparing a fixed-point register to 0 and simultaneously comparing a floating-point register value with 0 might try and set the zero bit twice in a conventional architecture.) To increase parallelism further, the results of an instruction only set condition codes in the cr register if the record bit part of the instruction opcode is set.

Overall, branch processor instructions are defined so that all information and resources needed to execute reside in the branch processor itself. For example, information required for logical operations, conditional or absolute addressing is contained in the branch processor.

Table 4.1. Data and instruction cache sizes

Model	Data cache (kb)	Instruction cache (kb)
M20 220	8	Combined
340 520H	32	8
355 360 365 370 375 560 570	32	32
530H 540 550 930 950	64	8
580 970 980	64	32

For large sequences of real code, branch processor instructions are completely overlapped giving rise to the term zero cycle branching. That is to say, the time delays in branching from one part of a program to another in the branch processor are totally hidden by the underlying concurrency of the other processing units.

4.4.1   The fixed-point processor

The fixed-point (FX) processor handles all integer and string operations as well as data address calculations for itself and the floating-point (FP) processor. It also handles actual movement of data from the data cache to itself and the FP processor.

Instructions support byte (8 bit), half-word (16 bit) and word (32 bit) data types. The FX processor supports logical, shift and arithmetic instructions and also a number of string manipulation instructions, and is thus particularly suitable for C programs.

4.4.2   The floating-point processor

The FP processor was designed to perform ANSI/IEEE 754-1985 standard arithmetic. It includes the usual facilities, for example, sign, absolute, multiply and divide instructions. Importantly this processor also supports multiply and add instructions of the form a = b * c + d. Research has indicated that many real-life programs make use of this combination. Also, this single instruction reduces the overall rounding error as compared to executing the two separate multiply then add instructions.

A register renaming facility enables optimizations on the fly, by using the internal 38 registers instead of the declared 32. For example, in the pseudo-code segment:

```
Load Reg10 with Reg9 + Reg8
Save Reg10
Load Reg10 with new value
```

For the purposes of the second *Load* instruction another unused register is used instead of register 10. This enables *Load* to proceed without waiting for the preceding store to complete. This is particularly effective for example, if this code sequence is performed within a loop, effectively overlapping the register *Save* with other instructions in the loop.

4.5   Virtual memory management

AIX virtual memory management is more complex than for traditional UNIX systems because it is tightly integrated with the filesystem. When a file is opened, the kernel maps the whole file into virtual memory. This means that the file is now represented by an address range in the virtual memory space of the system. System calls that read from and write to the file are translated into memory addresses and a memory read or write is attempted at that virtual memory address. If that memory address is not resident in real memory then a page fault occurs, and the virtual memory management paging subsystem brings that page into real memory for read/write. That is to say, under AIX, file I/O is done through the virtual memory management paging subsystem, not via the traditional UNIX buffer cache. This rationalization results in improved filesystem performance, but complicates the process for the virtual memory management algorithms. Why? Because UNIX (and in this case AIX) manages processes and memory pages independently, so when running a process, AIX cannot tell what memory pages belong to that process. Consider the case when users perform a large amount of manipulation on files in the filesystem. When the requirements for virtual memory pages exceed the physical memory available, AIX needs to page out infrequently used or *stale* pages. However, AIX could (if not checked) page out programs (even part of the process that was being executed) and page in large parts of files users were working on. The real memory of the RISC system would then be filled with mostly data, causing heavy page faulting to read in executable program code, resulting in poor performance.

For sensible memory management AIX provides a memory load control algorithm. The algorithm corrects a well-known UNIX problem by trying to ensure that no matter how many new processes are started, AIX *will not thrash.* (Thrashing occurs when the memory requirement of all processes wanting to run greatly exceeds the amount of real physical memory available. In these circumstances most UNIX systems perform no useful work but spend all their time moving memory pages between real memory and disk.)

AIX monitors the ratio between the number of memory pages written out to paging spaces in the last second compared to the number of pages stolen from other processes by the running process. If this ratio is close to 1.0 then thrashing is guaranteed. The smaller the ratio the less chance of thrashing. AIX considers the system to be thrashing if this ratio is 0.17 or greater. When this memory overcommitment condition is detected any new processes are placed onto a 'suspend' queue, that is to say, a list of programs that will not be run. Additionally, some existing processes are removed from the run queue and placed on a suspend queue. How does AIX know which processes to suspend? By measuring for each process its repaging rate. A repage represents the movement of a page from disk into real memory of a page that was recently paged from memory to disk. If the repaging rate is too high the process becomes eligible for suspension. Once suspended a process may not be reactivated (that is to say placed back on the run queue) for at least one second. The pages of the suspended process quickly become stale, and the virtual memory management page replacement algorithm pages them out to disk thus releasing enough real memory to stop thrashing. To guarantee a recently reactivated process processor time, once reactivated a process may not be suspended for two seconds. All the numbers quoted here are defaults used in the scheduling algorithm. An experienced systems administrator can alter these settings using the *schedtune* command.

4.6 Compiler design

The reverse side of developing a RISC instead of a CISC processor is that the compiler designer has a much higher overall responsibility for the net performance of the RISC-based computer system.

IBM is no stranger to advanced compiler development. IBM research division had already produced the *advanced optimizing C compiler* for the first IBM RISC computing platform—the IBM RT PC system. For the IBM RISC System/ 6000, IBM Toronto and IBM Yorktown Research, established centres of excellence in compiler design, were faced with a really challenging task. They had to extract every last ounce of performance from the new hardware architecture. Since superscalar architecture (see page 37) was new to the RISC system, the design team was moving into uncharted waters. They did have some tough objectives to meet, as follows:

- The compiler should include two modes of operation. A fast, non-optimizing compilation mode for program development, and a reliable, optimizing mode for code production.
- It should be designed in such a way as to support multiple languages, including C, C + +, Fortran and Pascal.
- The C compiler needed to support the four programming standards:
  —ANSI standard X3J11
  —IBM systems application architecture C, level 2
  —The IBM RT PC system C compiler
  —The IBM RT PC system advanced optimizing C compiler

The result is the IBM XL series of compilers that support C, C + +, Fortran and Pascal. The Fortran XL compiler accepts Fortran based on the Fortran 77 standard as well as Fortran written for IBM mainframe VS Fortran. It also accepts selected features of the Fortran 90 standard.

Additionally, IBM has available other languages:

- APL2/6000—an APL interpreter compatible with IBM's mainframe and personal computer language APL2.
- COBOL—a COBOL compiler written by MicroFocus accepting ANSI, FIPS and SAA COBOL programming dialects.
- Ada/6000—an Ada Validation Organization validated Ada compiler.

The remainder of this chapter discusses the XL series of compilers.

4.6.1   What is a compiler?

A compiler takes a programmer's input source code that (one would hope) the programmer understands and translates it into machine code that a computer can understand. Essentially a compiler is a two-step process.

The compiler first analyses the program to determine its net effect. The results of this analysis are passed to a translator which generates the object code for the target hardware. Unfortunately:

1 Programmers occasionally include errors in their programs. These errors must be detected and reported to the programmer and compilation continued by trying to find a point after the error from which analysis can continue.
2 Programmers expect to be able to compile parts of their program separately, perhaps in separate languages, and use a linker to put the component parts together.
3 At link time AIX allows for dynamic linking; as such the linker may not be able to resolve all program references at link time and has to construct special tables of 'to be resolved' addresses. At program load, special 'stub' code is first executed to resolve these references before proceeding (see Sec. 5.5).

For all these reasons the internal design of the XL series of compilers is more complicated and is shown in Fig. 4.5.

Each of the C, Fortran or Pascal compilers has a compiler-specific component (the first four phases of the figure). From intermediate code optimization downward, each compiler uses common routines to translate the intermediate code into actual optimized object code for the RISC system branch, fixed- and floating-point processing units, scheduling instructions to achieve maximum concurrency and thus minimum execution time. For those who are less familiar with the terms outlined, here is an explanation of the various stages used in the compiler before we turn our attention to the optimization techniques used in the XL compliers.

The *read phase* simply reads characters from the source program to be compiled. It can be a simple subroutine called from the lexical analyser phase. For the C compiler it needs to implement the C macro preprocessor.

The *lexical analyser* receives characters from the read process and assembles

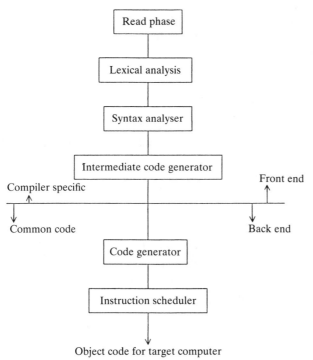

Figure 4.5.   The structure of the XL family compilers.

them into legal tokens. For example, the tokens **if, else** and the floating-point number 5.678. The results are stored in a symbol table accessible to later phases of the compiler.

The *syntax analyser* performs pattern matching on the list of tokens generated by the lexical analyser. It builds a hierarchical tree structure describing the net effect of a program. For example, in the assignment a = b + c, a subtree may be generated to indicate that the addition of variables b, c are of type integer, and are of type *automatic* since they were declared on a stack frame, are to be added together, and the result placed into static variable a whose visibility is only in the environment of the file test.c.

The *intermediate code generator* generates an idealized extended intermediate language which is assembler-like in character. The language assumes an infinite register machine and is designed to retain enough structural information to be amenable to optimization techniques. The intermediate code forms a stable and documented interface between the front and back ends. So, for example, there is no reason in principle why a future back end version of this compiler could not be designed to produce code for AIX on IBM PS/2 platforms.

The *intermediate code optimizer and scheduler* optimizes the code that is presented to them so that it executes more efficiently on the IBM RISC System/ 6000 processors. This is described in some detail in the following section.

The *code generator* translates the intermediate code into IBM RISC System/

6000 machine-specific code. It also has to make the translation from an unlimited register machine to one of finite proportions, a process achieved using a technique known as *graph colouring*.

4.6.2 *XL compiler optimization*

We will now consider the optimization techniques used by the XL compilers. For simplicity, these will be explained as though they were performed upon the program source, though the reader should note that optimizations are actually carried out on an internal representation of a user's program.

Elementary optimizations

Like most 'industry' optimizing compilers, the XL compilers use a range of well-known techniques. *Constant expression evaluation* evaluates as much of an expression as is possible based on known values. *Expression reordering* rearranges the sequence of evaluation while maintaining the overall net effect of the compilation block. For example:

```
a=3;
if (a<b)                              if (3<b)
     { x=a; y=a-1; }                       y=2;
else { x=a; y=x+1; }                  else y=3;
a=0;                                  a=x=0;
x=0;
```

Initial Code   Optimized

Redundant code elimination identifies code that can never be executed and does not compile it. *Strength reduction* replaces more difficult to execute operators with easier ones.   For example, multiplication of integer numbers by 2, 4, 8 etc. ... can be performed using a bit shift of the binary number. Raising any number to the power of 2 (squaring it) can be replaced by multiplication by itself. *Straightening* tries to analyse typically Fortran *spaghetti* code containing **gotos** and rearranges it for efficiency. For example:

```
10    if (mean.eq.10)  goto 20    10    if (mean.eq.10)  goto 60
15    if (life.eq.42)  goto 30    15    if (life.eq.42)  goto 60
      a=999.0                           a=999.0
20    continue
30    goto 60
60    do 100 i=1,100                60    do 100 i=1,100
```

Initially   Straightened

Common subexpression elimination analyses code for sequences which are used more than once in a basic block and can be assigned to a temporary register variable without side effects. For example:

```
int a, b, c;                int a, b, c;
int block (int d)           int block (int d)
{                           {
                            register int _tmp;
a = b + c;                    a = _tmp = b + c;
f = b + c - d                 f = _tmp - d


}                           }
```

Initially   Eliminated

Code motion moves statements from inner to outer loops wherever possible. For example:

```
{                           {
int  i, perfect;            int   i, perfect;
long bench;                 long bench;
bench = time();             bench = time();

for (i = 0; i<10000; i++)   perfect=496;
   perfect=496;               for  (i=0; i<10000; i++);

printf( "took %d \n",       printf ( "took %d \n",
   time()-bench);              time()-bench);
}                           }
```

Initially   Rearranged

Rearranging the assignment of the perfect variable before the loop therefore makes a nonsense of this program's attempt to measure the time taken to perform 10 000 assignments.

Restructuring

Restructuring uses a number of simple techniques that add object code into a program to increase execution speed.

Inlining identifies calls to short, nonrecursive subroutines. Instead of executing a subroutine call to that subroutine the code for that function is placed in line. The XL compilers do this for functions which expand to less than 100 instructions when the − Q flag is selected.

Unrolling involves copying the body of a loop's code one or more times and performing the loop a correspondingly fewer number of times. Since it is unusual for the number of iterations to be able to be reduced exactly, it is also usually necessary to keep an additional copy of the loop body to be executed to make up the remaining total. For example, consider the statement a = a + (a/7) to be executed in a loop 99 times. Placing two of these statements in a loop, and executing this 49 times means the compiler still needs to execute this statement once more (99 − (49 * 2) = 1) at the termination of the unrolled loop.

Recurrence recognition

A recurrence is an expression whose value depends upon the value of the same expression in an earlier iteration. For example, in the code fragment:

```
void induction ( int size, int source[], int sink[] )
{
int i;
sink [0] = 1;
for (i=2, i<size; i++)
   sink [i] = sink [i] - source [i]* sink [i-1];
}
```

The value of the i*th* iteration of sink depends on the value of sink calculated in the previous iteration. If a previous iteration value is kept in a machine register, then it can be used directly instead of having to gain addressability to the sink array, calculate the address index of element (i-1), form the absolute address, and then load this value from real through virtual memory.

Instruction scheduling

Instruction scheduling rearranges the order of machine code instructions to exploit the concurrent execution possibilities of the fixed-point, floating-point and branch processors. Scheduling is performed twice, before and after register allocation, using dependence graph techniques.

5
Programming environments

UNIX systems have always provided leading-edge programming tools. Early versions of UNIX led the way and provided programs like *make* and *SCCS* as tools to enhance programmer productivity and software management. AIX continues this trend and provides an enhanced set of CASE tools in the form of the AIX software development solution. This is designed to deliver a new generation of professionally managed and developed applications. AIX also provides state-of-the-art communications programming interfaces and debugging tools. Finally, AIX encourages the design of modular applications using its dynamic linking facility and ability to ship applications with embedded performance tracing components. These aspects are covered in detail in this chapter.

5.1   Program management

AIX provides the standard UNIX tools for program management. For example, the following standard UNIX tools (and more) are available:

cb   C beautifier (*cb*) reformats a C language source program into a consistent format that uses indentation levels to show the structure of the program. Unfortunately *cb* does not produce such beautiful code, and it certainly does not measure up to the code formatting standards used within IBM. My personal opinion is, do it yourself!

cflow   The C flow diagram generator generates a diagram of the logical flow of a C language source program.

ctage   Builds a relationship matrix between the multiple source files and library sources required for an application. This information can be used by the *vi* editor to edit a multifile application more easily.

cxref   C cross-reference list generates a list of all external references for each source language program, including where each reference is resolved.

indent   Reformats a C language program by indenting it to the options
            specified by a user.

lint   Checks for syntax and data type errors in a C language source
            program. It performs more detailed analysis than the IBM XL C
            compiler with particular emphasis on producing portable, machine-
            independent code.

make   Allows an applications developer to specify a set of dependencies for a
            program in terms of what object files need to be compiled and linked
            to form an application. *make* looks at the dependency list typically
            contained in the specification file makefile. It then rebuilds the
            target application by just relinking and/or compiling the modules
            that have changed to form the most current version of the application.

SCCS   The source code control system allows the storage of historical versions
            of source code in a library. Using simple creation (*admin*), storage
            (*delta*), and retrieval (*get*) commands, particular revisions of modules
            or projects can be accessed. For development projects shared by
            several people, SCCS helps perform automatic source code control by
            locking modules taken out of the library for modification and unlock-
            ing them when they are returned. SCCS also maintains a history file
            with comments, allowing the systems administrator or project coordina-
            tor to view the history of changes to source files.

5.1.1 *imake*

A makefile is a file containing a list of programs and dependencies which
enable an applications developer to automatically compile an application from a
list or source modules. For example, a large project containing, say, 250 000 lines
of C program source code, split into 500 source files, needs to be compiled and
linked into an executable file. The makefile specifies the dependencies between
the various source modules and the compiler options required to translate the
source code into object code and to be linked into the executable application.

However when working in a multivendor environment, an applications
developer soon discovers that different UNIX systems need different compiler
options and hence a different makefile for each UNIX system. *imake* is a
program that works with a higher level, machine-independent imakefile that
is suitable for all environments. The applications developer can therefore write a
single imakefile that will build an application for all environments. *imake*
takes the imakefile, combines it with a machine-specific template file (usually
called imake.Template) and produces a makefile. *imake* then runs the
generated makefile with the *make* utility and generates the application.

imake is supplied as a sample program with the AIXwindows component of

AIX, since it is an industry standard component of X-Windows (see Chapter 6). A systems adminstrator is required to run *imake* at least once in order to build executables from the `/usr/lpp/Xll/Xamples` directory which contains the C source code to the X-Windows system sample programs.

Although a little difficult to master initially, *imake* should be used by applications developers to generate machine-independent `makefiles`.

5.2   Computer-aided software engineering

Computer-aided software engineering (CASE) is the application of computerized techniques and tools to automate software engineering. In today's environment the design of any serious software product involves a number of well-defined stages. This usually begins with the requirements and design analysis, proceeding through to functional specification. The functional specification leads to high-level then low-level design and then to the production of real code. As this code is written it is unit tested in isolation, then assembled and system tested as a complete product. The product can then be released, after which it must be maintained.

Using CASE technology means the automation of some or all of these stages. CASE tools are crafted in different ways. Some require rigorous (almost formally mathematical) functional specifications and produce pseudo-code then real code automatically. Others provide an enriched programming environment with tools to automate each programming stage and integrate the application build process electronically. AIX CASE falls into this latter category. In order for any CASE tool to be a positive addition to an application development cycle, developers must:

1   Have an existing process defined for software development. It is the process that the CASE tool will automate. Adding a CASE tool into a project that has no existing process or structure is unlikely to create one.
2   Ensure that the CASE tool is flexible enough to take over the existing methodology gradually. Developers do not like switching over *en masse* to a completely new set of rules and techniques. The AIX CASE environment allows the software professional to use existing UNIX-based tools and integrate them using a software integrator.
3   Be allowed time for learning how to use the new tools and technology. Just expecting the use of AIX CASE without allowing time for a development project learning curve may mean that developers reject use of CASE tools indefinitely.

5.2.1   The software development solution

The AIX CASE offering is known as the AIX software development solution (SDS). This is split into a number of constituent components which will be discussed further. They are:

- The software development environment (SDE) Workbench and Integrator
- The configuration management version control (CMVC) client and server.
- The library connector for the IBM RISC System/6000 and mainframe MVS operating systems

SDS is designed around the European Computer Manufacturers' Association and National Institute of Standards reference model.

Most of the Workbench and Integrator products are based on the Hewlett-Packard CASE offerings which have been licensed by IBM.

5.2.2   *The software development environment, Workbench*

The most fundamental component of the SDS is the SDE Workbench. This provides the basis for an integrated software development environment. The applications developer can use the Workbench with any or all of the programming languages C, C++, Fortran and Cobol. Eight basic toolsets in the following list can be used as they stand and applied to the development group's existing manual software engineering process. Later, when these tools have been accepted, the process itself can be automated.

- The *program editor* is the editor component, allowing the user to enter source code into the computer. The editor is either the *vi, GNU EMACS*, or *LPEX*, the live parsing editor. (Support for EMACS is included, but the editor itself must be purchased separately.) LPEX is a context-sensitive editor that understands the structure of high-level programming languages. It identifies reserved words, parentheses and code in different colours and also visually formats the source code that it edits.
- The *build manager* builds an executable program from a dependency file, identifying actions required to compile and link an application. This can use the traditional *make* tool if preferred.
- The *program debugger* provides the X-Windows development environment editor to allow a user to visually debug code.
- The *software static analyser* provides the ability to search visually and automatically through a series of source programs for function calls and global variables.
- The *development manager* provides a graphical interface to the AIX filesystem and allows the applications developer to assign actions to objects or classes of graphic objects.
- The *software configuration management tool* provides a visual interface to the source code control system. AIX, like any UNIX system, provides SCCS; also provided is support for the IBM code management version control system, described in Sec. 5.2.3.
- The *tool manager* allows developers to save the visual arrangement of their

programs on their 'visual desktop' and to manage the above described tools.

- The *integrated mail and transfer* component provides a visual front end to the AIX mail and TCP/IP file transfer facilities. For example, consider a 5-person project with 500 source modules. An individual may make a modification to a module and return it to the library. The build manager can rebuild the application based on this change and send all the team members a mail notification to say that the build has completed successfully.

The build manager, development manager, software configuration manager, tool manager and mail facilities are ports of the Hewlett-Packard Softbench CASE offering.

The software development environment integrator

The Integrator is a companion product to the Workbench and allows an applications developer to integrate existing tools so that they can use the Workbench services. As such, users can generate an OSF/Motif wrapper around an existing tool, without modifying that tool in any way. This is done by coding statements to the Integrator using the encapsulation definition language, or using the C, C + + languages.

The Integrator is also the tool required to build a basic process. For example, a *check process* could be defined so that after any user has put back a module to the source library, a test compile can be performed on that module. If the module does not compile cleanly then a note could be sent to that user informing that the module would break the 'build' of the application if it were to be made.

Since the Integrator is a port of the Hewlett-Packard CASE Integrator product, customers or vendors using the Hewlett-Packard Encapsulation format language can easily transfer their product to the IBM RISC System/6000.

5.2.3 Configuration management and version control

An alternative to using the native AIX SCCS version control system is to move up to the configuration management and version control (CMVC) component of AIX CASE. Aside from version control, CMVC allows a user to integrate problem-tracking and design changes into the software engineering cycle. Projects involving tens or hundreds of development staff can be catered for.

Using an OSF/Motif interface a project hierarchy is defined in an Informix, Sybase or Oracle database. This includes such elements as design drawings and documentation. Source code is stored in either SCCS or Intersolv's professional version control system (PVCS) revision control system with structure links to the hierarchy database. For example, consider an application which contains an error that is reported. Perhaps this is at a unit (module) testing phase, or while testing the application before launch (System test). The fault is reported and the test case used to reproduce the fault is entered into CMVC database. CMVC assigns a problem number to this report. For a coding and implementation error CMVC makes a record of the source changes required to correct the error. If the error is more involved and contained within the functional, or high- and low-level, specifications then CMVS records changes made to that design documentation and the corresponding source code changes. A customizable project-reporting mechanism can produce summary change management statistics.

The library connector

In some projects it may be necessary to access software stored on an IBM mainframe. The IBM mainframe version control system is called the software configuration and library manager (SCLM) and runs under the IBM mainframe operating system called MVS. The library connector provides an OSF/Motif application that operates on SCLM library members.

For example, in an international project within many IBM corporate customers, sites may be interlinked with high-speed IBM SNA communications between IBM mainframes. Instead of developing an international TCP/IP network it might be prudent to store internationally shared AIX source modules on a central mainframe. International development groups can use the library connector to retrieve and replace shared source modules into the host SCLM.

5.3   Communication programming interfaces

AIX provides a very full suite of intra- and intermachine communication programming interfaces.

5.3.1   Pipes

Pipes are one of the earliest UNIX communication programming interfaces. The concept of pipes has been adopted by other operating systems, for example OS/2 and DOS. A pipe provides a one-way flow of data between two programs residing in a single AIX system. Pipes are unidirectional, so programs normally open two pipes to enable a two-way conversation. Because these pipes are unnamed they are used from a parent program to a child program.

5.3.2   Named pipes

A named pipe or first-in first-out (FIFO) is similar to a pipe except that it is visible as a special file in the /dev directory. For example, a FIFO could be created with the *mkfifo* command called /dev/common. By knowing the name of the FIFO, two or more unrelated programs can exchange information by reading from and writing to the FIFO.

5.3.3 System V interprocess communication

Message queues, *semaphores*, and *shared memory* are collectively referred to as 'System V IPC' as AIX inherits them from USL System V. These three facilities provide the applications developer with three further mechanisms for programs within a single AIX system to exchange information. Again, many other operating systems such as IBM Operating System/2 also provide many of these same facilities.

Message queues

A message queue allows two or more processes in a single AIX system to send and receive arbitrary length data items to and from each other. Each participating process must first open a message queue using a numeric 'key'. The AIX kernel matches up requests in different programs using the same key.

Shared memory

Shared memory, as the name indicates, allows two or more programs running in a single AIX system to share a memory segment. This is considerably faster than other mechanisms which first send the information to the AIX kernel (where the pipe of FIFO, for example, is implemented) and then out to the program requesting the data.

Semaphores

Semaphores are a synchronization primitive. As a form of IPC they are not used for exchanging large amounts of data as are pipes, FIFOs or message queues. The main use of semaphores is to control access to a shared resource, usually shared memory. Two types of semaphore are common: exclusive (write lock) or shared (read lock). To obtain a resource that is controlled by a semaphore, a process needs to test its current value. If the value is greater than zero it decrements it by one. If the value is then zero, the process must wait until the value is greater than zero (that is, wait for some other process to release the resource). To release a resource that is controlled by a semaphore, a process increments the semaphore value. If some other process has been waiting for the semaphore value to become greater than zero, that other process is now able to obtain the semaphore and use the resource. That describes a write lock semaphore. A read lock semaphore works in reverse, that is, it is locked when the count is greater than zero.

5.3.4 Sockets

Sockets provide an excellent uniform way of implementing process communications. Sockets allow interprogram communication but unlike other IPC described so far, it can be between programs residing on separate AIX systems, or within a system. Once a **socket()** has been established between a client program and a server program, the applications developer can regard the socket as just another file. This is very convenient since programmers are used to dealing with files. To provide both intra- and intermachine communications, AIX allows the programmer to uses sockets with any of the following three underlying protocols:

- UNIX domain
- Internet domain
- Xerox NS domain

UNIX domain is used for intramachine communications, Internet and Xerox NS for intermachine communications. Sockets can use either connection-oriented protocols (more reliable but slower), or connectionless-oriented protocols (less reliable but faster). For Internet domain sockets AIX uses TCP or UDP protocols for connection/connectionless sockets respectively. The equivalents using Xerox protocols are the sequenced packet protocol (SPP) or internet datagram protocol (IDP).

AIX provides a rich set of socket programming interfaces and protocols. Recall that the socket interfaces were initially produced with the Berkeley 4.1c BSD UNIX; many vendors may not completely implement the socket interface and its three underlying protocols.

5.3.5   The transport layer interface

The transport layer interface (TLI) was introduced with USL Unix System V release 3.0. AIX provides the TLI with release of AIX 3.2 and later. Before TLI, sockets from Berkeley provided the main communications programming interface. TLI provides the same facilities as sockets but it is modelled after the ISO transport service definition standard. As with sockets, communications may be connection- or connectionless-oriented.

5.3.6   Streams

AIX 3.2 and later support streams. Streams provide a full duplex connection between a user program and a device driver. The intent is that streams replace the traditional method of accessing the device driver using **open()**, **close()**, **read()**, **write()** and **ioctl()** function calls. Instead, streams provide these calls and also the **getmsg()**, **putmsg()** and **poll()** calls. The principal advantage of streams is that they allow an AIX systems programmer to change the characteristics of a device driver dynamically. A user program talks to the system call interface for a driver (also called the stream head). The stream head then talks to the kernel device driver. Streams allow any number of modules to be pushed into the stream. That is to say, between the stream head and the kernel device driver, extra processing modules may be interposed. These 'pushed' modules make it considerably easier to write and modify network device drivers.

5.4 Device drivers

A device driver is a low-level component of AIX that forms the bridge between the AIX kernel and the real-world devices it needs, for example disk drives, terminals and printers.

Traditionally, when UNIX was ported from one machine architecture to another a number of nontrivial operations were involved. A C language compiler had to be written to generate code for the target machine architecture. Then the UNIX operating system written in C was compiled for the target platform. Finally, the low-level component of device drivers for the target system, usually written in assembler, needed to be written to interface the real-world devices.

On the RISC system there have been changes to device driver architecture and it is these changes that are explained here. The sophisticated POWER architecture of the RISC system makes it more difficult for a systems programmer to program in native assembler efficiently. Wherever possible, it is better to write drivers in C and leave the XL C compiler to schedule instructions for maximum concurrency. This is good news for a prospective device driver writer.

Changes to the overall structure of a device driver under AIX were made to enable a driver to be dynamically installable and to link this with the MicroChannel bus structure and the object data manager database.

5.4.1 Traditional UNIX device drivers

Under UNIX, special files are created by the *mknod* command. This creates a special file with a given name, usually in the /dev directory. This file has three special characteristics

- The major device number
- The minor device number
- A special file type: character or block device. (Actually the *list* command will also show other types such as directories, Berkeley sockets, Berkeley symbolic links or System V pipes.)

Here is a partial listing of typical devices in the /dev directory showing the entry for a printer (/dev/lp0) and console (/dev/hft):

```
crw-rw-rwT    1 root    system    19,    0 May 22 1992   hft
crw-rw-rw-    1 root    system    29,    0 Dec 24 21:23  lp0
```

Application programs access the device by name: for example, to print a file an applications developer could open /dev/lp0 and **write()** data to it. Inside AIX this is translated to a request to **open()** and **write()** to major device 29, minor device 0.

The major number identifies the particular device driver for the device, the minor number identifies particular characteristics of that device. For example, consider a tape drive /dev/rmt0 which can also be accessed using other device names:

```
crw-rw-rw-  1 root   system   16,   0 Sep 22 20:55 rmt0
crw-rw-rw-  1 root   system   16,   1 May 22 1992  rmt0.1
crw-rw-rw-  1 root   system   16,   2 May 22 1992  rmt0.2
crw-rw-rw-  1 root   system   16,   3 May 22 1992  rmt0.3
```

Using the /dev/rmt0.1 device the tape in the drive would not automatically be rewound after use, whereas if device /dev/rmt0 had been selected then the tape would automatically be rewound after use.

Types of UNIX device driver

UNIX has two classes of device driver: *character mode* drivers and *block mode* drivers.

The block mode driver is used for devices which deal in blocks of information. For example, a floppy or hard disk drive where the smallest addressable element is the disk sector. Another example would be a CD-ROM player. Block devices are capable of random access. For example, they could accept a request to read from block numbers 80 to block 100 in any order.

The character mode driver is used to access serial access devices a byte at a time. Examples of a character driver access might be to terminals, printers or networks devices. Usually a character mode interface is also provided for *block*. This is known as a raw device and, not surprisingly, it allows the programmer or operating system to perform raw unbuffered reads from and writes to that device.

5.4.2   AIX device drivers overview

AIX divides a device driver into two parts : a *device head* and a *device handler*, Fig. 5.1.

Device heads

A device head provides the link between the filesystem entry in the /dev directory and the entry point in the device driver. For example executing the **open("/dev/lp0")** tells AIX to call the **open()** entry point in the device driver for the printer **lp0**.

- Device driver HEAD
  - Predominantly pageable and pre-emptible
  - Runs in kernel mode of system

- Device driver HANDLER
  - Nonpageable
  - Runs in kernel mode of system

Figure 5.1.   AIX device driver components.

Overall, the device head performs the following functions:

- Converts from the file I/O request to a format known to the kernel handler
- Performs appropriate blocking and buffering
- Performs device management, for example, error logging and recovery

Since these routines do work in the process environment most of the code and data associated with the driver head is *pageable.*

Device handler

The device handler communicates with the actual physical device or adapter card. The device handler accepts requests from the device head. This part of the device driver executes in both the interrupt handler environment and in the environment of the calling process. Both the code and data for the device handler are pinned into real memory.

Table 5.1. UNIX device driver entry points

Driver type	config	open	close	ioctl	dump	read	write	select	mpx	strategy	evoke
Early UNIX	N	Y	Y	Y	N	Y	Y	N	N	Y	N
AIX char	Y	Y	Y	Y	Y	Y	Y	Y	Y	N	Poss
AIX block	Y	Y	Y	Y	Y	Poss	Poss	N	N	Y	Poss

AIX driver entry points

AIX has extended the number of device driver entry points that are defined. As Table 5.1 shows, the additional entry points **config**, **strategy** and **revoke** have been added.

- The **config()** entry point is an AIX extension to standard UNIX. When called it creates the /dev special file in the device directory. If the device driver is a block driver and supports a character interface to a block device then two entries will be created. For example, calling the config routine for a driver to hard disk 0 (**hdisk0**) creates /dev/hdisk0 and /dev/rhdisk0.
- The **open()** entry point makes a link from the requestor to the real device. In

so doing it verifies that the device is online and available.

- The **close()** entry point releases a user's right to access the requested device, flushing any associated buffers.
- The **ioctl()** entry point performs special I/O operations.
- The **dump()** entry point tells AIX that this device is the destination for system dumps. Some time later if AIX has reason to dump (see Sec. 15.4), that device will be sent the information.
- The **read()** entry point allows one or more bytes to be read sequentially.
- The **write()** entry point allows one or more bytes to be written sequentially.
- The **select()** entry point allows a user to poll a hardware device to discover whether specific events or conditions have occurred.
- The **mpx()** entry point allows multiple users to share a resource on a single device.
- The **strategy()** entry point is used to maximize I/O data transfer requests from a user to and from a device. The request is normally asynchronous. For example, consider a request for a read of 10 disk blocks. The request returns immediately so the application may continue. When the read is complete a callback function (one of the parameters passed via **strategy()**) is executed.
- The **revoke()** entry point is an AIX extension to support the AIX trusted computing path (see Sec. 14.8). This routine is normally involved when the secure attention key (SAK) sequence is detected to ensure that a secure path to a user's terminal is provided.

The device switch table

Within the operating system, the device switch table stores the device entry points for each device. Most UNIX systems allow kernel code direct access to this switch table. Under AIX this is a global data structure and since AIX has a pre-emptible operating system kernel (see Sec. 3.4.2) all global data structures must be protected. AIX therefore allows access only once the resource has been locked.

5.4.3 Dynamic device configuration

On traditional UNIX systems, device drivers are statically linked into the operating system. For example, consider the case when Ethernet network support needs to be added to such a system. The systems programmer would typically edit the makefile that tells the system how to rebuild the */unix* program, being careful to include the .o object code files that represent the new driver to be added. A configuration program would then be run to extend the size of the device switch table, making sure that the entry points to the new driver such as **open**, **close**, **read** and **write** from the new .o files were added successfully. Next, the makefile would be run using the *make* command, finally invoking the linker to

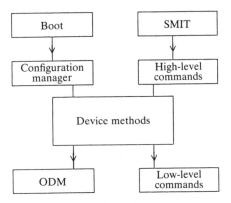

Figure 5.2.   The structure of the configuration subsystem.

rebuild /*unix*. After rebooting, the new drivers would be available for use.

AIX, however, allows for dynamic device driver loading either at or after system boot time. Device drivers are not statically linked to the /*unix* kernel. At system boot time AIX examines the installed configuration of the system and loads the required device drivers. In so doing it must first bring online installed MicroChannel adapter cards, soft configuring the cards' I/O port addresses, IRQ and DMA abilities so that there is no conflict. This is achieved via the *configuration subsystem* as shown in Fig. 5.2.

Either a system boot (which starts the configuration manager) or running the systems management interface tool generates high-level commands which in turn invoke device methods. Device methods invoke low-level commands and/or modify the object data manager database.

For example, at AIX boot time the configuration subsystem:

1   Scans each MicroChannel bus slot to determine the unique two-byte programmable option select (POS) adapter ID
2   Looks up the characteristics and capabilities of the adapter card via the ID in the object data manager database
3   Reassigns on-card resources for maximum performance without conflict of interrupt request (IRQ), buffer or I/O address, DMA levels, etc.
4   Calls the *configuration method* program for each device to be configured. The configuration method loads and initializes the device driver.

Device methods

Below the high-level commands that can be used to modify the state of a device are a set of *methods* (see Fig.5.3). AIX provides the following device methods:

define   Creates a device instance and places the definition in the object data manager (ODM). The state is set to *defined.*

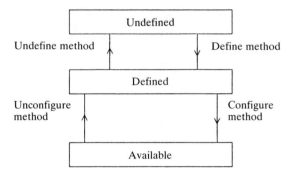

Figure 5.3.   Device states.

configure   A method that performs all operations to make the device
               usable then sets the state to *available.*

change   A method to change the characteristics of a device.

unconfigure   Stops the device from being usable but leaves the definition of
               the device in the ODM, setting the state to *defined.*

undefine   Deletes the definition of this particular customized device from
               the customized objects database leaving the device in the *unde-
               fined* state. (For example the systems adminstrator could unde-
               fine an 8 mm tape drive /dev/rmt0. AIX still stores the charac-
               teristics of 8 mm tape drives and can redefine another 8 mm
               drive at a later time without a problem.)

5.4.4   Dynamic kernel extension

Subsystems like TCP/IP and NFS are implemented in AIX as dynamic kernel
extensions to the operating system. That is to say, after they are loaded any user
program may call the additionally defined kernel functions that these subsystems
define.

   Adding a kernel extension can be done in AIX dynamically, while AIX is
running. It does not require the AIX /unix kernel to be rebuilt or for the system
to be rebooted. Figure. 5.4 is a simple example of adding a kernel extension that
simply adds two numbers together when called.

   The brevity of this example indicates how simple this is. First the program
comprising the kernel extension myadd.c is compiled making sure the entry
point **myadd()** is defined. Since AIX does not provide a command to load a
kernel extension, the above program myload.c loads it using the **sysconfig()**
system call.

```
/* --- myload.c --- */          /* --- myadd.c --- */
#include <sys/sysconfig.h>       int myInit (void)
main() {          {
struct cfg_load cfg;             /* initialization code here */
strcpy (cfg.path, "./myadd");    return 1;
cfg.libpath = NULL;              }

if    (sysconfig (SYS_KLOAD, &cfg, sizeof(cfg))) int myadd (int a, int b)
      perror ("sysconfig error");     {
}                                   return a+b;
                                    }
/* --- makefile --- */
all: myadd myload

myadd:          myadd.c
  cc -o myadd -e  myInit -bE:./myadd.exp -bI:/bin/kernex.exp myadd.c

myload:          myload.c
  cc -o myload    myload.c

/* --- myadd.exp --- */
#!/unix
myadd          syscall
```

Figure 5.4.   Loading a kernel extension.

5.5   Dynamic linking

Dynamic linking allows an application to be packaged as a main executable module and a number of separate 'link-libraries' of functions required by that application. When the application is executed it is loaded into virtual memory and it is the loader's responsibility to find and resolve any undefined subroutine references before the application starts. This is called *dynamic binding*. AIX also allows for *run-time binding* when unresolved subroutines are resolved while the program is executing, just before they are used. It is commonplace in both the IBM Operating System/2 and the Microsoft Windows operating systems to use the term *dynamic linking* to describe dynamic binding. Most modern operating systems including AIX use dynamic linking to their advantage as will be seen.

Traditional UNIX systems used *static binding*. Static binding or *linking* (Fig. 5.5) has the primary advantage of simplicity. With static linking one or more source C files are compiled to . o object modules using the cc compiler. The linker *ln* takes these files and if any external functions have been called, it resolves references to them by adding in the code for those functions. These functions may be defined in a development library, for example /usr/lib/libmouse. a, otherwise perhaps in one of the system libraries, for example libc. a. In the case of a system library special code called a *stub* is added to the application program to call a routine resident in the UNIX kernel. At run-time, the application makes calls to routines in the loaded code or via the stub routines to routines contained in the UNIX kernel.

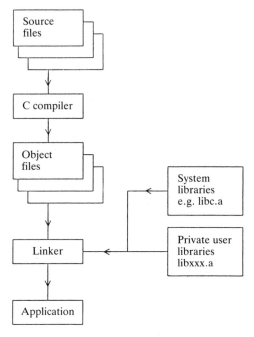

Figure 5.5. Static linking.

Before dynamic linking became commonplace some users became experienced enough to extend their UNIX kernel to include common routines, so that no matter how many programs they ran, each program did not have to include the common routines, only a stub. The stub routine was simply a pointer to call to the new shared routines contained in the kernel. This methodology had its drawbacks. For example, taking such applications to a similar machine without identical kernel extensions could cause the application or perhaps even UNIX itself to crash.

Dynamic linking provides the advantages of kernel extensions without the pain. With dynamic linking, applications are now composed of many modules instead of just one statically linked executable. Typically, this is a small executable file and subroutines located in dynamically loadable modules. Under AIX individually loadable modules can be placed in one or more libraries, so you do not have an application that comprises several hundreds or thousands of separate executable modules.

With dynamic linking, applications are smaller because common functions are placed in shared dynamic libraries and are not bound into each application. Smaller applications require less disk space. For example, this became 'graphically' clear to me when I wrote an initial X-Windows OSF/Motif application using the IBM RT PC system. The statically linked *trivial* 'hello world' program was over 650 kb in size. On the RISC system since the X-Windows library functions are dynamically linked, the same executable program is only about

30 kb in size. Smaller applications are faster loading; under AIX a function is usually brought into virtual memory only when it is used.

Finally, dynamic linking allows a user to upgrade applications more easily, without a user needing to recompile or relink an application. If a component of the application proves faulty, the application developer can send the user a new dynamic link library to cure the problem or to provide updates and enhancements to the product.

Of course, this increased flexibility involves a small and usually insignificant performance penalty over static linking. Calling a function in a dynamic link library costs in the region of an extra 10 clock cycles, to determine the address of the next instruction to be executed. This means an applications developer would be wise not to call a short function inside a dynamic link library from an applications performance or timing critical loop.

If a program has unresolved references after compilation and linking, then this must be stored in the object code format of the program. AIX uses an industry standard format called XCOFF (extended common object file format) to save this information. The breakdown of such a module is well defined. Some typical sections include:

- Module header
- Code section
- Loader section
- Debugger section

AIX added to the contents of the loader section, including in it an application's list of imports and exports of routines matched in dynamic link libraries. Here is a short program that demonstrates dynamic linking:

```
/* A dynamically bound (linked) program,   first.c  */
main()
{
    printf ("In the routine main() \n");
    printf ("Calling the routine shared() now \n");

    shared ("Hello mouse");

    printf ("Returned from shared() back in main() \n");
} /* main */

/* first.impexp,  the import file for first.c */
#! execode
shared
```

```
/* shared.c , the shared subroutine */
#include <stdio.h>
void shared ( char *string)
{ (void) printf ( "I got the argument **%s** \n", string);
}
```

Building the modules is a little more complex than for static linking:

1 Compile the `first.c` program with the unresolved reference to **shared()** function:

```
cc -b I: first. impexp -o first first. c
```

2 Compile the shared routine and place it in a default path that will be found by the `first` program at runtime:

```
cc -c shared. c
ld -b E: first. impexp -b M: SRE -o /usr/lib/execode
shared. o -lc
```

Typing *first* loads the program into memory and then before running the program resolves the reference to **shared()** by loading `shared.o` from `/usr/lib/execode`.

This works well but references are still resolved before any of the application is executed. If we had some functions that were infrequently executed, it would be better to load them just before they were required. This is shown in the following program `second`:

```
#include <stdio.h>   /* program second, source second. c */

extern int errno;
extern char sOverlay[];
extern int iOverlay;
extern int func1(), func2();
char *libpath= "/lib: /usr/lib:: ";

main()
{
  int (*pfunct) ();   /* pfunct is a pointer to an integer
      function */

  /* many lines of code not shown here */

  pfunct = load ("overlay", 0, libpath);

    printf ("Overlay string was \t \t%s \n", sOverlay);
```

```
printf ("Overlay integer was \t \t %d—n ", iOverlay);
funcl();                    /* call overlay function */

(*pfunct) ();               /* set using ld -e option */

unload (pfunct);            /* unload overlay */


} /* main*/
    /* ——————————————————————— */
/* this is the overlay. c file */
char sOverlay = "Make my day";
int iOverlay = (-69);
int funcl() { printf ("Inside function 1 \n"); }
int func2() { printf ("Inside function 2 \n"); }

# this is the second. imp file describing the imports to
second. c
#! overlay
sOverlay
iOverlay
funcl

# this is the overlay. exp file describing exports from
overlay. c
#! overlay
sOverlay
iOverlay
funcl
func2
```

1 In this example the program comes to a point where it needs to use
   functions contained in the source file overlay. c which has been compiled
   and placed in a shared object file /usr/lib/overlay using the command:

```
cc -c overlay. c
ld  -b  E:  overlay. exp  -b  M:SRE  -o  /usr/lib/overlay
overlay. o — lc -efunc2
```

2 The call load ("overlay", 0, libpath) dynamically loads in this
   module into virtual memory.
3 As proof of this the variables sOverlay and iOverlay can now be
   displayed.

4 Once the **overlay** has been loaded the `func1` can be called
5 Even the function **func2** can be found since it was made the default entry point for the module using the `-e func2` compiler option
6 As before an 'imports' file `second.imp` is required to compile `second.c` without error thus:

```
cc -b I: second. imp -o second second. c -lc
```

The current examples simply place an object into $LIBPATH which AIX will find automatically at execution. Larger applications however would place all shared objects into a library and place the library in $LIBPATH. The next example demonstrates this:

```
/* file third. c, compile to the program third */
main( )
{
  printf ( "About to call function sub() in library
  mouse \n" );
  sub( );
  printf ( "Returned from sub \n" );
}  /* main */

/* function sub, sourcefile sub. c */
/* compile with cc -c sub. c */
int sub() { printf ( "I am in the function sub \n" ); }
```

To explain what is happening here let us look at Fig. 5.6:

1 Initially programs `third.c` and `sub.c` are compiled.
2 The linker (invoked automatically by *cc* compiler) is informed that the function **sub()** is stored in the object `mouse.o` contained in the library `house.a`, by the `third.imp` file. This file contains the two lines   `#!`
     `house. a(mouse. o)`
     `sub`
3 The `sub.o` object is made into a shared object `mouse.o` using the command *ld -b:third.exp -b M:SRE -o mouse.o sub.o -lc.*
4 The export file (`third.exp`) telling the linker to export the function sub contains the lines
     `#! mouse. o`
     `sub. o`
5 `mouse.o` is then placed into a shared library `house.a` using the *ar* archiver command *ar vq /usr/lib/house.a mouse.o.*
6 The program `third` is now ready to run and when it does so it will automatically reference the subroutine `sub` stored in the archive library `house.a`.

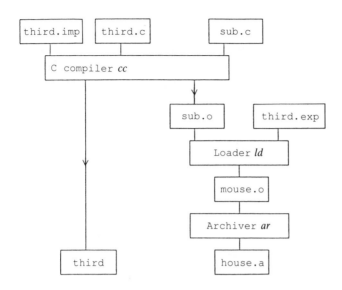

Figure 5.6.   Creating a shared library.

5.6   Debuggers

AIX provides four debuggers and a trace facility:

adb   From traditional UNIX

dbx   From Berkeley UNIX

xde   New to AIX

kdbg   The kernel debugger

trace   Low-level program trace

5.6.1   *adb*

adb is a very primitive debugger, so that it is now more commonly used just to examine, debug and repair executable binary files and to examine non-ASCII data files. As a debugger it suffers from the disadvantage of not having the ability to debug source code. To use a program within this debugger, the applications developer would need to compile a program with the assembly language listing option and use this as a guide as to where to set program breakpoints.

5.6.2   dbx

dbx is the principal debugger used with AIX. *dbx* is a capable yet simple to use product, as are many of the other Berkeley UNIX facilities. A basic help screen from the debugger shows some of the simple commands that will enable a developer to debug a program quickly after having compiled it with debugging information in the normal way (*cc -g* filename):

```
dbx version 3.3 for AIX.

(dbx) help
run                  — begin execution of the program
print <exp>          — print the value of the expression
where                — print currently active procedures
stop at <line>       — suspend execution at the line
stop in <proc>       — suspend execution when <proc> is called
cont                 — continue execution
step                 — single step one line
next                 — step to next line (skip over calls)
trace <line#>        — trace execution of the line
trace <proc>         —  trace calls to the procedure
trace <var>          — trace changes to the variable
trace <exp> at <line#>
                     — print <exp> when <line> is reached
status               — print trace/stop's in effect
delete <number>      — remove trace or stop of given number
screen               — switch dbx to another virtual terminal
call <proc>          — call a procedure in program
whatis <name>        — print the declaration of the name
list <line>, <line>
                     — list source lines
registers            — display register set
quit                 — exit dbx
```

While still a line-oriented debugger, *dbx* provides source level debugging as the norm. Besides being able to print and modify variables and structures, arbitrarily call procedures in programs and set breakpoints, *dbx* also has a number of advanced features. First, debugging can be carried out at assembler as well as source level for finer control. Breakpoints can refer to conditions, for example when variable a is equal to 10 in function **mouse()** stop execution. *dbx* also allows debugging a program which starts multiple processes. Finally *dbx* can debug an existing running program, not started under *dbx*, by 'attaching' to it.

Overall *dbx* is an excellent line-oriented debugger useful for source-level debugging regular characters as well as X-Windows programs.[1]

5.6.3   xde—the X-Windows debugging environment

X-Windows debugging environment (*xde*) is an X-Windows front end to the *dbx* debugger already described. The intention is to provide a multiwindowed front end to provide more effective debugging than under regular dbx. Figure 5.7 shows a typical *xde* session.

5.6.4   kdbg—the kernel debugger

The kernel debugger program helps locate errors in code running in the kernel. One important practical use of the kernel debugger is to help IBM software support resolve difficult AIX problems that you may have reported. In general, it will be required to help debug IBM or a user developer's kernel code. Why would an applications developer write kernel code? This may be part of a device driver, perhaps to interface a custom MicroChannel card. Or kernel code may be appropriate for some real-time software to avoid the context switch time of moving from a user to a kernel process.

A systems programmer uses the kernel debugger to set program breakpoints or to change processor memory and registers. Compare this with the *crash* program which allows a user to look at these items but not change them.

Under AIX, *kdbg* must be built into /*unix* by using the *bosboot -d hdisk0 -a -I* command. After rebooting, the kernel debugger is made available, in fact AIX will not boot to a login prompt without the user entering the *go* command at the debugger prompt. Sensibly, AIX does not allow a systems programmer to enter commands to the debugger on any high-function terminal console device. The kernel debugger displays its output to and reads its input from an asynchronous ASCII terminal attached to the planar serial port S1. It expects a fixed configuration of 9600 baud, 8 bits and no parity.

Normally, a kernel programmer would set a static debug trap (SDT) instruction at the code to be examined, or break into the debugger manually by pressing CTRL + ALT + NUMPAD4 and set a breakpoint. To try this procedure, use the ? command to display what help the debugger offers.

---

[1] Readers should perhaps also consider the *gdb* debugger available for AIX from Richard Stallman's US Free Software Foundation.

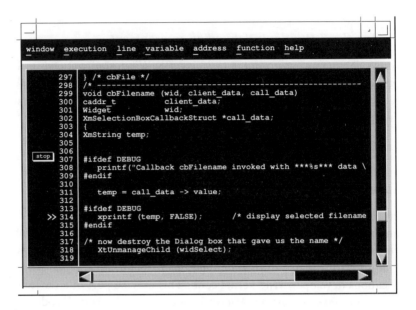

```
window   execution   line   variable   address   function   help

297   } /* cbFile */
298   /* ------------------------------------------------------------
299   void cbFilename (wid, client_data, call_data)
300   caddr_t              client_data;
301   Widget               wid;
302   XmSelectionBoxCallbackStruct *call_data;
303   {
304   XmString temp;
305
306
307   #ifdef DEBUG
308       printf("Callback cbFilename invoked with ***%s*** data \
309   #endif
310
311       temp = call_data -> value;
312
313   #ifdef DEBUG
314       xprintf (temp, FALSE);        /* display selected filename
315   #endif
316
317   /* now destroy the Dialog box that gave us the name */
318       XtUnmanageChild (widSelect);
319
```

Figure 5.7.   A sample *xde* run.

5.6.5   *Comparing debuggers*

Of all the debugging facilities discussed I have to admit to being disappointed
with those on offer. This is in no way a criticism of AIX, but more a general
UNIX criticism.

With experience of PC-based platforms I realize how elementary UNIX debugger technology is. Of all the debuggers, *xde* comes closest to IBM OS/2 *cvw*
(codeview) in terms of function, ease of use and reliability. But *xde*'s
multiwindowed nature really requires a 19 inch or larger X-Windows screen
for effective use. This should be borne in mind when planning a development
environment.

5.7 Tracing

When developing an operating system it is common to implement a low-level program tracing mechanism independent of any existing regular debugger or kernel debugging mechanism. AIX, like other IBM products (OS/2 for example), has a powerful, user-extensible trace facility that can be used as both a debugging aid and a tuning tool. As shipped, AIX includes tracing code throughout every kernel and program product. By turning on tracing, and selecting one or more categories for recording, the systems adminstrator can understand how an application interacts with AIX. An applications developer can add tracepoints into applications, with application-specific categories.

Care was taken in the design and implementation of *trace* to make it as noninvasive as possible so that switching on *trace* will not affect the performance of typical program flow. (I measured the overhead of an active *trace* hook to be about 15 microseconds.) Using *trace* is a two-part operation: collecting the data and then analysing it. The complete process is shown in Fig. 5.8.

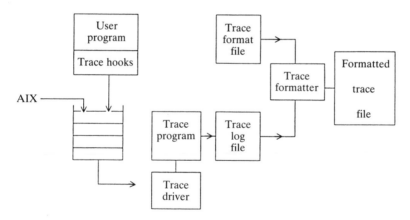

Figure 5.8. Trace collection and formatting.

5.7.1 Collecting trace data

Normally *trace* is started from the command line, the program of interest is run, then *trace* stopped. For example:

```
$ trace -a              ; start the trace
$ mycmd -arg1 -arg2     ; run command of interest
$ trcoff                ; stop the trace
$ trcstop
```

Initially the *trace* program saves the results into an 128 kb in memory buffer. If this becomes full then a default log file is written to, usually `/usr/adm/ras/trcfile`.

Before running the command, a user needs to edit the `/etc/trcfmt` file (or specify options using the *trace* command itself) and uncomment the classes of event that need to be traced. Uncommenting everything produces literally thousands of lines of formatted information per second, so some discretion is required.

There are alternative methods of starting the trace which include using the **trcstart()** subroutines within a program, though these have no advantages over the method previously outlined.

ID	PROCESS NAME-I	ELAPSED_SEC	DELTA_MSEC	APPL	SYSCALL KERNEL IRUPT
15B	cp	0.23839842	24.409600	open	/etc/trcfmt fd=3
15B	cp	0.00289384	13.433445	open	/tmp/mouse fd=4 RDONL CREAT TRUNC mode=rw ---
15B	trcstop	0.09958348	55.873436	open	/usr/lpp/msg/En_UK/ cmdtrace.cat fd=5
15B	trcstop	0.10498329	5.392358	open	/usr/lpp/msg/En_UK/ lic.cat fd=6
15B	trcstop	0.39504448	2.742352	open	/tmp/lapin fd=7

Figure 5.9.   Output from the trace command.

5.7.2   Formatting a trace

Once the *trace* has been collected the *trcrpt* command formats the *trace* ready for printing or viewing. The `/etc/trcfmt` file specifies formatting rules for each event. Figure 5.9 is an example of a trace output.

5.7.3   Adding trace hooks

Adding trace hooks is simply a matter of placing macro statements in source programs. If tracing is on, the macro writes a hook word (mandatory), 32-bit timestamp (optional) and up to five 32-bit values to the trace file. If tracing is off, the macro has no effect.

The format of the *trace* record is shown in Fig. 5.10. The corresponding macros defined in `<sys/trcmacros.h>` (for timestamped events) are:

TRCHKL0T (HW)

TRCHKL1T (HW, D1)

12-bit hook ID	4-bit type	16-bit data field
D1 Optional data word 1		
D2 Optional data word 2		
D3 Optional data word 3		
D4 Optional data word 4		
D5 Optional data word 5		
Optional timestamp		

Figure 5.10.   The format of a trace record.

TRCHKL2T (HW, D1, D2)

TRCHKL3T (HW, D1, D2, D3)

TRCHKL4T (HW, D1, D2, D3, D4)

TRCHKL5T (HW, D1, D2, D3, D4, D5)

The HW stands for the 'hook word' and is usually an offset from the base HKWD_USER defined in the file `<sys/trchkid. h>`. It is quite normal for a single event ID to be used for an entire application; clearly for use within an organization any event IDs may be used for testing. However, if an application is shipped with tracing code (a good idea) then a hook word event ID should be registered with IBM.

AIX also contains additional tracing tools. Here is a selection from an extensive list:

traceson   Turns tracing of a subsystem on. For example, to start tracing of the SNA subsystem with the command *traceson -l -d sna.* The problem is recreated with the tracing on, then turned off with the complementary command *tracesoff -s sna.* Finally, the trace output can be viewed with the command *vi /var/sna/snalog.1.*

iptrace   Provides an interface level packet tracing for TCP/IP Internet protocols. For example, to trace *telnet* traffic on a token ring LAN: *iptrace -i tr0 -p telnet /tmp/logfile.ip.* Next, formatting the trace ready for viewing: *ipreport /tmp/logfile.ip > /tmp/logfile.fmt.*

trpt   Performs protocol tracing on TCP sockets. The *trpt* command queries the buffer for TCP trace records, which is created when a socket is marked for debugging using **setsockopt()**. The *trpt* command prints out a description of these trace records.

tprof   Estimates where the processor spends its cycles of execution by periodically sampling the profiled program 100 times a second. Usage information can be generated on a global basis, for example, time spent in the profiled program and any program or subroutine referenced by that program. For more detail *tprof* will report time spent within source lines of the profiled program.

6
End user interfaces

The X Window System is the *de facto* windowing environment under UNIX.[1] AIXwindows is the graphical end user environment under AIX. AIXwindows, however, provides much more than the traditional X-Windows windowing system, OSF/Motif Window Manager and the IXI Desktop Manager combination. It includes capabilities to display concurrently Silicon Graphics GL, Display PostScript, graPHIGS and PEX applications. And, of course, it provides programming toolkits and libraries to write applications based on these interfaces. We will start first by examining the history of X-Windows, then move on to OSF/Motif and the Desktop Manager.

6.1   X-Windows and Motif

X-Windows began life as System W, a windowing system developed at Stanford University. Bob Sheifler and Jim Gettys began development for the X-Windows System at MIT in 1984 with Project Athena. Athena was a project mainly sponsored by IBM and DEC.[2] The first release of X-Windows was X10, similar to the Andrew Windowing system developed at Carnegie-Mellon University. X10 was originally developed for DEC VAX computers, and may have remained relatively obscure had not Gettys and Sheifler ported it to a variety of Sun workstations during their Christmas 1985 holidays.

From X10 came X11, making it a fully networked Windowing system using TCP/IP (or Digital's DECnet) as the transport mechanism. At the time of writing, the latest release of X-Windows is X11.5, a level which IBM has been shipping since December 1992. Since 1988, the development of X-Windows has been handed to the X Consortium. This is a nonprofit-making organization whose members are most leading computer vendors and large corporate users. IBM is a member of the X Consortium.

---

[1] The X Window System will be referred to by its more usual and readable name, X-Windows, throughout this chapter.

[2] Many DEC employees were seconded to this project. Many of the research papers were therefore written by DEC employees. IBM contributed AIX systems.

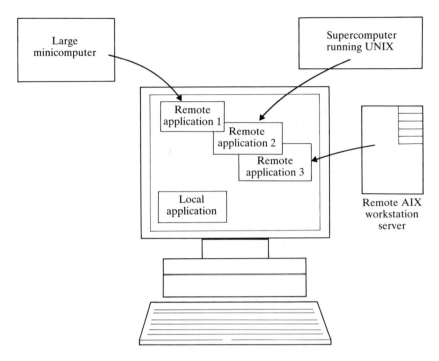

Figure 6.1.   Running network programs.

A networked windowing system means being able to run programs on one machine and display them on another. So at a local workstation a user can run both local client programs and programs from remote systems. For example, in Fig. 6.1 the X-Windows screen displays local programs as well as the output from programs running on a personal computer, supercomputer and a large minicomputer.

The development of a networked windowing system was only possible with the prerequisite development of:

- Bit-mapped graphics screens with graphics hardware accelerators
- Mouse technology
- Local area network (LAN) technology to enable high-speed interworkstation data highways
- Reliable high-speed protocols (TCP/IP and DECnet) to enable structured communications across a LAN.

Even so, most other vendors chose to develop an integrated windowing system, for example Microsoft Windows or IBM OS/2 Presentation Manager. Why is X-Windows different, and how can it be networked? The answer is that X-Windows is composed of three separate components, as shown in Fig. 6.2.

System menu ————————— ┌———— Minimize button

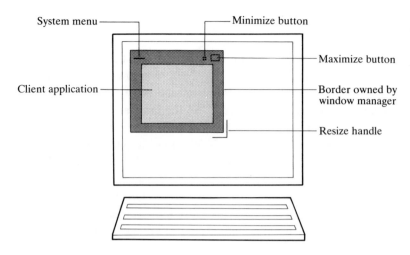

Maximize button

Client application ————————

Border owned by
window manager

Resize handle

Figure 6.2. X-Windows architecture.

The X server   The program that controls the display of the graphics
screen at which the user works. It interprets network
messages, for example to draw on screen graphics,
and acts on them. It passes keyboard and mouse
input *events* to the program that owns the window.

The X client   The user's application program, for example, a
spreadsheet, database or office system program. This
application does not know that it is displaying its
output in a networked fashion.

The Window Manager   A special client program that enables a user to move,
iconify and resize windows on the X server. In Fig. 6.2,
the Window Manager has surrounded the client application with a border with a number of features. For
example, resize handles, maximize, minimize and
system menu buttons. In such interaction, communication is from the user to the Window Manager and
then to the user application. For example, in resizing
the size of the applications window, communication
is initially to the Window Manager which passes on
the request to the application. The Window Manager
can reject the request, for example, the user may
have previously indicated that the application should
not be smaller than a certain size, in which case the
request will not be passed on.

6.1.1   Supplied utilities

Arguably the most useful client utility program supplied with AIXwindows is
aixterm, which is a terminal emulator for the X-Windows environment. Running
aixterm displays a rectangular window on the screen, which behaves like a
standard console display session to AIX. So the familiar command prompt ($) is
displayed and waits for the user's AIX commands to be entered.

With just *aixterm* and no specific X-Windows applications, a user can use
X-Windows as a way of viewing and executing multiple character-based applications on a single screen. *aixterm* is to X-Windows what the windowed DOS
prompt is to Microsoft Windows, or the windowed OS/2 session is to IBM OS/2
Presentation Manager. *aixterm* is based on the MIT sample program *xterm*,
but is enhanced to provide additional terminal emulations and also
internationalization.

AIXwindows also comes complete with a large set of sample X-Windows
games and utilities. It includes the entire OSF/Motif and UIL sample program
set. One of the first tasks an AIX systems administrator should perform after
installing AIX is to compile the sample programs. When compiled, these examples
will occupy about 20 Mb of space.

6.1.2   X-Windows security

Since the move to X-Windows version 11, release 4, X-Windows security has
been much improved. The key improvement is the use of the X-Windows Display
Management control protocol (XDMCP) and its associated cookie sample
program using the MIT-MAGIC-COOKIE-1. This replaces the now obsolete
xhost command which allowed any user on a named host to display programs on
an X-server screen. However, this was any user on the AIX system, enabling any
user on a given AIX system to start programs running on the X-Windows screen
of another user on the same system. The current magic cookie scheme actually
works well. While starting an X-Windows connection to an X-Windows display,
be it an X-station or console connection, the X-Windows Display Manager (see
Sec. 8.2.8) hands the X-server a hard-to-predict random number called a magic
cookie. Consider a single AIX system with two X-station users called Louie and
Douie. After Louie has logged on, a file in Louie's home directory called
.Xauthority is created. Any program that needs to display upon Louie's X-
server screen needs to pass the server Louie's magic cookie number. X-
Windows applications automatically reference the .Xauthority file and so
start correctly. If Douie wants to start an application running on Louie's
screen he needs access to Louie's .Xauthority file. For this to happen
Louie would have to make this file accessible to Douie explicitly, thus by
default Louie will be protected.

6.1.3 *Traditional character-based programming*

Traditional UNIX character-based programming differs substantially from AIXwindows graphical user interface (GUI) programming and this is often a source of great confusion to programmers new to GUI environments.

The structure of a 'regular' character-based program is called a straight-line program. Such a program may typically display a menu, allow a user to select an option and then act on the response. Complex applications have several menus normally linked in a hierarchical fashion. Eventually the user selects a quit option and the program terminates. In this scenario the program constrains the user to a tight set of choices defined by the applications developer.

A GUI program works in a different way. Usually a window is generated with a menu bar of options. A user selects options from the menu-bar by moving the mouse pointer to the menu option and clicking on it. This reveals a pull-down list of options. Here the user is driving the program, not the reverse. The internal structure of such a program is internally more complex because the user can select most options at any time.

The next difference the GUI programmer has to contend with is the change from character-based to pixel-based coordinate systems. An ASCII terminal normally displays 24 lines of 80 characters. X-Windows, however, deals with pixels. Worse still, several different styles and sizes of font are available, and fonts are usually proportionally spaced, so it is more difficult to know the width and height in pixels which will be occupied by even a simple text string.

Traditional UNIX programs use a terminal-independent programming interface called curses to display character, menus and line graphics on ASCII screens. AIX of course provides curses via the terminfo terminal capability database for character-based programming. But X-Windows deals only in pixels, and even if an application deals only with character output it is up to the applications developer to map the pixel coordinate system into one with lines of characters.

Another change that confronts the potential X-Windows programmer is the varying size of the program's display window (called the client area) which changes as the user uses the OSF/Motif Window Manager to resize the window. X-Windows responds by sending a message to an application indicating that the size of its client area has changed, and the programmer's code must take appropriate action. This may be to add scroll bars to the displayed area, or to adjust the size of the displayed fonts so that the information still fits in the resized window.

Lastly, consider what happens when an application's window is iconified or covered by another on screen window. What happens when that window is uncovered? X-Windows sends the application a message indicating that a specified region of the program's window needs repainting. The program must be able to redraw the exposed region. That is to say, under X-Windows the programmer must include code that is prepared to refresh any or all of an application's client

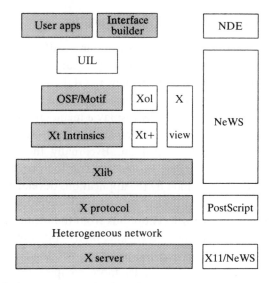

Figure 6.3.   X-Windows programming interfaces.

area when requested. This implies that an intimate knowledge of the pixel locations of all screen objects is required for each X-Windows screen panel.

All of these considerations make GUI programming an involved task. Depending on the programming interface, X-Windows may offer some degree of assistance with the above challenges. Over the years, X-Windows has developed several programming interfaces as shown in Fig. 6.3. The programming interfaces supported by AIX are shaded in this figure and are now described in detail. For completeness Fig. 6.3 also shows programming interfaces not supplied with AIX. Components not available under AIX include the Sun-style components: the NDE interface builder, the Network extensible Windowing System (NeWS), built upon the Display PostScript protocol and the merged Sun X11/NeWS display server.

6.1.4   The X protocol

The X protocol is the bottom protocol layer in the X-Windows system model. It presents a set of primitives, for example, **CreateWindow** or **GetKeyboardMapping**. These are used by all the higher X-Windows layers. The protocol specifies four types of messages: requests, replies, events and errors. There are over 100 different protocol verbs.

6.1.5   Xlib programming

X library (Xlib) is the lowest available programming interface to AIXwindows. The advantage of programming at this level is that Xlib software is compatible across a vast range of machines. Any manufacturer that offers X-Windows, and either OSF/Motif or Open Look, must by definition offer the lower programming layer Xlib. There have been very minor changes and extensions to the Xlib programming interface between X11 release 3 and release 5 but these are small compared to the differences at other API levels. There are over 200 function calls.

The best way to understand the level of programming is actually to look at a simple working program, such as that shown in Fig. 6.4. This program simply displays the message 'hello world' on the screen in a window. When the mouse button is clicked in the client area of the window the string changes to an alternative greeting. This program demonstrates a number of important points that are valid in the general AIXwindows programming environment:

Lines   *Description*

1–75   Defines variables to the program and parses the command line entered by the user.

76–81   Makes a network connection from this client program to the server screen that the user is using. This is the only point where programmers are explicitly aware that they are programming in a networked environment.

95   Sets some global data that may be read by a participating Window Manager program to decide where to place the program's window on the screen. The Window Manager is at liberty to ignore these requests however.

119   Once the program's window has been created and made visible, a program enters the traditional Xlib *event processing* loop. This is a key difference between traditional character-based programming and Xlib programming. The program simply sits in a tight loop and looks for three classes of events:
   1   ButtonPress—according to the button pressed either change the displayed string or exit.
   2   ConfigureNotify—for a window size change, clear the window and redisplay the 'hello world' greeting centred in the window.
   3   Expose—if the window is covered, then uncovered, redraw the text on the window.

6.1.6   Widgets

To increase the speed of X-Windows' development MIT decided to provide a higher level programming interface called *widgets*. A widget is, crudely speaking, a subroutine that creates a user interface element, for example, a scrollbar, a dialog box, or a pull-down menu. Instead of building the widget set directly on top of Xlib, an intermediate library called the *Xt intrinsics library* was created.

```
1:    #include <X11/Xlib.h>        /* structure and C sub definitions */
2:    #include <X11/Xutil.h>       /* various X11 utility functions */
3:    #include <stdio.h>           /* standard UNIX include file */
4:    /* --------------------------------------------------------- */
5:    /* DEFINITIONS */
6:    #define        BORDER      1
7:    #define        HEIGHT      100
8:    #define        MAXLINE     132
9:    #define        STARTX      10        /* window start coord */
10:   #define        STARTY      20
11:   #define        WIDTH       160
12:
13:   /* --------------------------------------------------------- */
14:   /* FUNCTION PROTOTYPES */
15:     void DrawText();
16:   /* --------------------------------------------------------- */
17:   /* GLOBALS */
18:   Bool              bFirstTime = True;
19:   char*              sent[] = {
20:                        " Hello World",
21:                        " Bonjour le monde",
22:                        " Hallo die Welt",
23:                        NULL
24:                     };
25:   char             *string;
26:   char             sFontName [MAXLINE];
27:   Display          *pDisplay;
28:   GC               gc;
29:   int              nScreen;
30:   unsigned int     ustringWidth;
31:   unsigned int     ustringHeight;
32:   unsigned int     uHeight = HEIGHT;
33:   unsigned int     uLength;
34:   unsigned int     uWidth = WIDTH;
35:   Window           window, winRoot;
36:   XColor           foregroundColor, backgroundColor;
37:   XEvent           report;
38:   XFontStruct      *pFontInfo = NULL;
39:   int              strindex = 0;
40:   XSizeHints       size;
41:   /* --------------------------------------------------------- */
42:
43:   void main (argc, argv)
44:   int argc;
45:   char **argv;
46:   {
47:      char           *pDisplayName       = NULL;
48:      Colormap       cmap;
49:      Font           fontID;
50:      unsigned int   uNewHeight;
51:      unsigned int   uNewWidth;
52:
53:   /* ----------- Parse command line width ---------------- */
54:   if (argc >4)
55:   {
56:      (void) fprintf (stderr, "Syntax %s: %s width height\n",
57:                      argv[0], argv[0]);
```

Figure 6.4.   An elementary Xlib X-Windows program. *Continues.*

```
58:          (void) fprintf (stderr, "Syntax %s: width height are optional\n",
59:                          argv[0]);
60:          exit (1);
61:       }
62:
63:       /* take window width from command line if specified */
64:       if (argc == 2)
65:          uWidth = (unsigned int) atoi (argv[1]);
66:       if (argc == 3)
67:       {
68:          uHeight = (unsigned int) atoi (argv[2]);
69:          uWidth = (unsigned int) atoi (argv[1]);
70:       }
71:
72:       /* you change this next line if you want a non English greeting! */
73:       string = sent[0];
74:
75:       /* ----------- Connect to X Server ------------------- */
76:          if ( (pDisplay = XOpenDisplay(pDisplayName)) == NULL)
77:          {
78:            (void) fprintf (stderr, "%s: cannot connect to X server %s\n",
79:                            argv[0], XDisplayName (pDisplayName));
80:            exit (2);
81:          }
82:
83:          nScreen = DefaultScreen (pDisplay);          /* our screen number */
84:          winRoot = XDefaultRootWindow(pDisplay);      /* root window */
85:          cmap = DefaultColormap (pDisplay, nScreen); /* default colormap */
86:
87:       /* ----------- Create top-level window --------------- */
88:
89:          /* create a window with a black border and white background */
90:          window = XCreateSimpleWindow(pDisplay, winRoot, STARTX, STARTY,
91:             uWidth, uHeight, BORDER, BlackPixel(pDisplay, nScreen),
92:             WhitePixel (pDisplay, nScreen));
93:
94:       /* ----------- Set hints to window manager ------------- */
95:          size.x   =           STARTX;      /* set window manager hints */
96:          size.y   =           STARTY;
97:          size.width       =           uWidth;
98:          size.height =        uHeight;
99:          size.flags       =           PSize  PPosition;
100:         XSetStandardProperties (pDisplay, window, argv[0], argv[0], None,
101:                            argv, argc, &size);
102:         uLength  =  strlen(string) + 1;  /* length of string to print */
103:
104:      /* ----------- Setup Graphics Context ----------------- */
105:         gc = DefaultGC(pDisplay, nScreen);
106:
107:         strcpy(sFontName, "Rom10.500");  /* font to display */
108:         pFontInfo = XLoadQueryFont (pDisplay, sFontName);
109:         XSetFont(pDisplay, gc, pFontInfo -> fid);
110:
111:      /* ----------- Select Input event types to monitor -------- */
112:         XSelectInput(pDisplay, window,   StructureNotifyMask |
113:                                          ExposureMask | ButtonPressMask);
114:
115:      /* ----------- Map Window ----------------------------- */
116:         XMapWindow(pDisplay, window);    /* make window visible */
```

Figure 6.4.   An elementary Xlib X-Windows program. *Continues.*

```
117:
118:    /* ------------ Event Loop ---------------------------- */
119:       while (True)
120:          {
121:          XNextEvent (pDisplay, &report);
122:          switch (report.type)
123:             {
124:
125:            case ButtonPress:
126:                 switch (report.xbutton.button)
127:                   {
128:                   case Button1:
129:                      if  ((string = sent[++strindex]) == NULL)
130:                         {
131:                         strindex = 0;
132:                         string = sent[0];
133:                         }
134:                      XClearWindow(pDisplay, window);
135:                      DrawText(argv);
136:                      break;
137:
138:                   case Button2:
139:                      XFreeFont(pDisplay, pFontInfo);
140:                      XDestroyWindow(pDisplay, window);
141:                      exit(0);
142:
143:                   case Button3:
144:                      break;
145:                   }
146:                break;
147:
148:             case ConfigureNotify:
149:    #ifdef DEBUG
150:             printf("ConfigureNotify\n");
151:    #endif
152:                uNewHeight  = report.xconfigure.height;
153:                uNewWidth   = report.xconfigure.width;
154:                if ((uNewHeight != uHeight) || (uNewWidth != uWidth))
155:                   {
156:                   uHeight  = uNewHeight;
157:                   uWidth   = uNewWidth;
158:                   XClearWindow(pDisplay, window);
159:                   DrawText(argv);
160:                   }
161:                break;
162:
163:             case Expose:     /* get rid of all other expose events */
164:    #ifdef DEBUG
165:                printf("Expose\n");
166:    #endif
167:                while (XCheckTypedEvent(pDisplay, Expose, &report));
168:                XClearWindow(pDisplay, window);
169:                DrawText(argv);
170:                break;
171:
172:             } /* switch */
173:          } /* while */
174:    } /* main */
175:    /* ---------------------------------------------------- */
```

Figure 6.4.   An elementary Xlib X-Windows program. *Continues.*

```
176:   void DrawText()
177:   {
178:       int                 n, nFontHeight, nLines, xpos, ypos;
179:       short int           ascent, descent;
180:
181:       ascent   = pFontInfo->max_bounds.ascent;
182:       descent  = pFontInfo->max_bounds.descent;
183:       nFontHeight = ascent + descent;
184:
185:       ustringWidth = XTextWidth(pFontInfo, string, uLength);
186:
187:       nLines = uHeight / nFontHeight;
188:       if (nLines == 0)
189:          {
190:          printf("Window too small to display any text\n");
191:          return;
192:          }
193:
194:       xpos = (uWidth - ustringWidth) /2;
195:       ypos = ascent;
196:       for (n=0; n<nLines; n++)
197:          {
198:          XDrawString(pDisplay, window, gc, xpos, ypos, string, uLength);
199:          ypos += nFontHeight;
200:          }
201:
202:   } /* void DrawText */
203:   /* ------------------------------------------------------ */
```

Figure 6.4.   An elementary Xlib X-Windows program. *Concluded.*

The Xt toolkit instrinsics are used firstly by Widget writers to develop their widget library and to a lesser extent by an applications developer. For example, when OSF created MOTIF they used the Xt layer and the Xlib layer to create the MOTIF widget layer. However, the applications programmer still needs to access the Xt, Xlib and MOTIF layers to write a complete OSF/Motif program.

Before the advent of the OSF/Motif widget library, vendors wrote their own. Each vendor's widget library had a different programming interface and also a different look and feel from the other. So for example, developers writing applications to run on Hewlett-Packard and DEC platforms would use the H-P or DEC widgets accordingly. IBM's RT PC system was shipped with the Athena widgets which are the standard MIT widget library. Initially, Athena did not include any graphics widgets but was otherwise quite capable.

The situation changed with the advent of OSF/Motif, which at last provided a widget set that nearly all vendors were prepared to adopt as a standard.

6.1.7   OSF/Motif

OSF's first product (see Sec. 16.1.2) was OSF/Motif, a GUI interface for users of X-Windows. As a result of OSF's vendor neutral selection process (see page 269), MOTIF draws on GUI components from a number of vendors thus:

- Hewlett-Packard's 3D appearance
- Microsoft and IBM's look and feel
- DEC gadgets and user interface language (UIL)
- MIT based X-Windows and Xt Intrinsics

AIXwindows supplies the full MOTIF user interface package which contains four main parts:

1   The style guide
2   The Motif Window Manager
3   The Motif programming toolkit
4   The user interface language (UIL)

The style guide describes how applications should be written. It describes the user interface in terms of both appearance and user interaction. It is a guide for application writers, for people writing extensions to the Motif toolkit and for Window Manager writers. For all practical purposes the Motif style guide conforms to the IBM systems application architecture, common user access (CUA) definition. CUA is IBM's user interface standard for all new developments on all micro-, mini- and mainframe computer platforms. Like the style guide, CUA describes how applications should be written. For example, the style guide recommends that an application should have a main window. The main window should have a menu bar with a number of options. The help option, if present, should be placed on the right of the menu bar and be selected using the keyboard accelerator ALT. + H.

The Motif Window Manager

The *Motif Window Manager* (*mwm*) is the default Window Manager under AIXwindows. This is a particularly sophisticated product with many features. First, it provides a Microsoft Windows (CUA) 'look and feel' to existing X-Windows applications by surrounding each client window with a border that includes a system menu, minimize and maximize buttons and resizing borders. By using the mouse the user can therefore change the size of an application window or, using the system menu, move or dismiss the application.

A second important feature of the Motif Window Manager is the provision of a keyboard interface to Window Manager functions. Thus a user who starts AIXwindows without a mouse can still use an application using just the keyboard.

The AIXwindows Motif Window Manager also provides a pop-up menu system that is invoked when the mouse is clicked outside any application window. This menu presents a list of programs that may be run, from which a choice can be made.

The keyboard interface, the menuing system, and many other user preferences are user customizable. This is another key difference between the configurable architecture of X-Windows compared with the preset nature of, say, Microsoft Windows.

Motif programming

Motif programming has the same aim as Xlib programming, that of producing an X-Windows-based application. However, the higher level Motif toolkit is designed to be easier to use and more productive than Xlib. The Motif toolkit provides a library of 3D Motif widgets all consistent with each other, for example, the main window, scrollbar and dialog widgets. By following the rules outlined in the Motif style guide, Motif widget applications have a well-defined 'look and feel' which is immediately familiar to any existing user of MOTIF. Additionally, since that look and feel conforms closely to SAA it will also be familiar to Microsoft Windows and IBM OS/2 Presentation Manager users.

The best way to show the reduction in complexity of Motif programming over Xlib is a simple example. The following program displays a pushbutton in a window with a message. It is similar in output to the Xlib program shown before but much simpler in concept. Fig. 6.5 shows how the program displays within AIXwindows.

Figure 6.6 (on page 95) is the source for the program. Notice how much shorter it is than the equivalent Xlib X-Windows counterpart. Notice also how the structure of the program has changed dramatically:

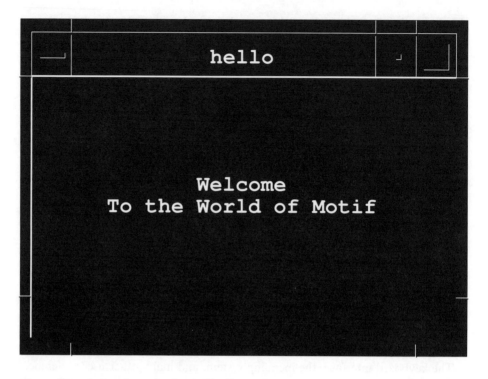

Figure 6.5.   Output from the simple Motif program.

1   X is now initialized using the **XtInitialize()** Xt intrinsics toolkit call. Already
    we see that a Motif programmer needs to know not only Motif, but also the
    Xt intrinsics programming layer! There are over 200 Motif-specific calls.
2   An argument array of properties is set and a pushbutton widget created with
    these properties.
3   In line 30 the callback function **cbCallback()** is associated with the created
    pushbutton. When the user presses the pushbutton the function is called by
    X-Windows.
4   The infinite **while** loop seen in Xlib is replaced by a call to **XtMainLoop**. This
    automatically reads events from the queue and dispatches them to the correct
    widget, in this case to the single pushbutton widget.
5   When the pushbutton is pressed the callback function is invoked which quits
    the program.

If the user resizes the program's window, the text is automatically repositioned
and centred. If the user covers then uncovers the window, the text is automatically
repainted. For Motif, all text-based widgets are able to cope with exposure
events; most also handle resizing.

With Motif, programming is at a higher level than for Xlib or, for example,

```
1    /* STANDARD EQUATES                                          */
2    #include <stdio.h>
3    #include <X11/Intrinsic.h>
4    #include <Xm/Xm.h>
5    #include <Xm/PushB.h>
6    /* ----------------------------------------------------------*/
7    /* FUNCTION PROTOTYPES */
8    void cbCallback();
9    /* ----------------------------------------------------------*/
10
11   void main (unsigned int argc, char **argv)
12   {
13   XmString     sButtonText;
14   Widget              widButton;
15   Widget              widRoot;
16
17   /* -------- Initialize Toolkit ----------------------------*/
18   widRoot = XtInitialize ("pbutton", "PButton", NULL, NULL, &argc, argv);
19
20   /* -------- Create compound string for the button text -------*/
21   sButtonText = XmStringLtoRCreate ("Push Here",
22                       XmSTRING_DEFAULT_CHARSET)
23   /* -------- Create Button with Arguments ------------------*/;
24   widButton = XmVaCreatePushButton (widRoot, "PushButton",
25               XmNlabelString, sButtonText,
26               XmNwidth,       200,
27               XmNheight,      200,
28               NULL);
29
30   XtAddCallback    (widButton, XmNactivateCallback, cbCallback,"Button");
31   XtManageChild ( widButton);
32   XmStringFree ( sButtonText);
33
34   /* -------- Realize the widget and start mainloop -----------*/
35   XtRealizeWidget (widRoot);
36
37   XtMainLoop();
38
39   } /* main */
40   /* ----------------------------------------------------------*/
41   void cbCallback(wid, client_data, call_data)
42   Widget   wid;
43   caddr_t client_data;
44   caddr_t call_data;
45   {
46       printf("Pushbutton was selected\n");
47       exit(0);
48   } /* cbCallback */
```

Figure 6.6.   A simple Motif program.

IBM OS/2 Presentation Manager or Microsoft Windows. These windowing architectures make use of an explicit event-processing loop and a lesser concept of widget object orientation.

6.1.8   UIL

User interface language (UIL) is a high-level presentation language. UIL originally comes from DEC-Windows, DEC's early implementation of X-Windows.

UIL allows the applications developer to specify a list of widgets and their characteristics in an ASCII file (`.uil`). A UIL compiler then takes this ASCII definition and compresses it into a run-time binary file (`.uid`). As before, the developer writes an OSF/Motif widget program but, instead of creating widgets dynamically make a series of **Mrm...()** calls to retrieve the widget hierarchy specified in the UIL files. This may seem like extra work for the programmer, and the user is left with two required binaries at run time instead of one. What are the advantages?

First, that the `.uil` file stores the screen format, resources and messages for the application. So if a screen's panels size or attributes need to be changed all that is required is a recompiled `.uil` file and not a complete rebuild of the application. Also, it is possible to have multiple-source UIL files. One would store the screen design, and the other the internationalized strings used by different language versions of the application.

Overall, UIL goes only part way to solving the fundamental problem of screen design. None of the methods allow the developer to perform any sort of interactive screen design of an application. This is a real shortfall for X-Windows and MOTIF and is really only addressed by buying a separate component called an interface builder.

6.1.9   The AIX Interface Composer

The AIX Interface Composer (AIC) is an interface builder. It is not part of AIXwindows but a separate product. In fact, it is really the UIM/X interface builder from Visual Edge Software Limited, specially packaged for the AIX environment. This is a very flexible product and takes much of the pain out of developing MOTIF applications. It provides improved productivity for both new and experienced GUI developers.

The AIC first allows a developer to design an application's panels on screen interactively. This is accomplished by a full-screen design tool that creates a top-level shell widget and allows interactive placement of child and peer widgets. The developer can use the *property editor* to edit widget resources. Next, the developer uses the *declaration editor* to declare global variables and then the *property editor* to add behaviour to the declared widgets.

At this point the visual interface is complete and the developer can select the 'test mode' to test the behaviour of the interface. The AIC includes a C interpreter which can interactively test the visual interface of an application together with developer-written program logic in C. Therefore, most aspects of program development can be carried out from within the AIC environment.

Once an application is developed it is saved as a project. The AIC offers a flexible set of code generation options. With the Ux output option C code is generated with calls to the Ux, Xt, Xlib and Xm (Motif) subroutine libraries. Ux is the native AIC specific library. For portability, the Xt output option generates C code using only the Xt, Xm and Xlib libraries. The AIC also supports the import of UIL source files.

6.2   Silicon Graphics GL

AIXwindows provides the graphics library (GL) programming interface from Silicon Graphics. This provides a simplified porting path enabling GL-based applications to run in the X-Windows environment under AIX. In conjunction with any RISC system 3D graphics adapter, GL can provide a high-performance, high-function graphical interface for the 3D graphics applications developer. An example of some of the facilities that are available include:

- Retained and nonretained mode interfaces
- Pick correlation—the ability to identify what object the user has clicked on or near
- Gouraud and constant shading, anti-aliasing lines
- Hidden line surface removal
- Support for proportional fonts and also multibyte character sets

With the integrated AIXwindows interface it is possible to produce an integrated OSF/Motif and GL application. X-Windows calls may be used to open a window and drawn into using GL subroutine calls. This implies that X-Windows and GL subroutines can be part of the same executable, which is not possible on many other vendor systems.

6.3   Display PostScript

The Display PostScript (DPS) interpreter is an extension to the basic X-Windows server program that the reader will recall drives the user's graphics screen, being driven from commands sent from a client program. IBM extended the standard X-server to include a PostScript level 1[3] interpreter. This ability is available only on native AIX workstation X-Windows sessions, that is to say it is not available on IBM X-stations for example.

The interpreter allows the definition of a DPS window to which PostScript commands can be sent directly, enabling the same PostScript graphics to be used for display and printing (upon a PostScript printer of course!). This is therefore device and resolution independent. To write a device independent program, parts of the X-Windows application are coded in PostScript. These *wrap definitions*

---

[3] Adobe, the originator of PostScript, defines Levels 1 and 2.

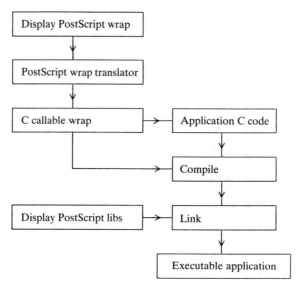

Figure 6.7.   Using display PostScript in an X-Windows application.

and are translated to C language callable functions using the *pswrap* program. The process is shown in Fig. 6.7.

6.4   graPHIGS and PEX

Although X-Windows is an industry standard end user interface, it starts to fall short when the display of sophisticated 2D or 3D graphics images is required. Recall that the lowest level of X is the X protocol and that this contains a number of drawing and other commands to be sent from a program (the X client) and performed at a workstation screen (X-server).

Even so, displaying 3D images is very graphics intensive and normally involves representing the object under scrutiny by hundreds and probably thousands of shaded triangles or simple polygons. Sending the drawing instructions to create and move such an object simply takes too long; creating the image at the workstation end and then sending it as a bitmap to the X-Windows screen would take even longer since X-Windows sends each bitmap pixel by pixel.

A far better option is to identify the collections of drawn polygons as an object and ask for operations on that object, e.g. rotation, enlargement, transformation. Programmer's Hierarchical Interactive Graphics System (PHIGS) provides this ability. IBM includes PHIGS support with AIXwindows with two components: graPHIGS and PHIGS Extensions to X-Windows (PEX).

graPHIGS was IBM's first implementation of PHIGS, and predates PEX. It includes the standard 2D graphics programming interface Graphical Kernel System (GKS). Under graPHIGS, X is one of the many workstations supported by the graPHIGS API. This implies that a graPHIGS application does not need to recognize that it is running within X-Windows, that is to say, it need not be event driven in the X-Windows sense.

Currently, graPHIGS works best on a local workstation although graPHIGS programs can be transmitted to a remote X-Windows server. A remote X-Windows server, however, cannot display 3D capabilities because drawing instructions are converted to Xlib calls and sent to the remote X-Windows server. For this reason remote performance will be very slow and perhaps unacceptable.

With the latest release of AIXwindows the preferred way to write and display PHIGS applications is with PEX. Using PEX, an applications developer creates and manipulates an object by calls to the PEX API to PHIGS. This is translated down to an X protocol request and sent to the Xserver.

The X server on a workstation running AIXwindows has a special PEX extension that enables it to recognize and act on these high-level commands. PEX is MIT's PHIGS implementation and as such is a standardized and non-proprietary protocol. This means that PEX is freely distributed with the X-Windows system software. PEX therefore is not hardware vendor dependent and supports mixed vendor environments. (The implementation of PEX specified by MIT is an initial release and not complete. Some areas such as Z buffering and lengthy operations have not been standardized yet.)

A graPHIGS application has to be ported to run under PEX. The porting requires major recoding, although the logic of the program and the logical structures in the graphics are the same. The calls are not portable and graPHIGS calls need to be ported to PEX calls. Therefore, unless existing graPHIGS applications are being enhanced, PHIGS applications should perhaps now be written using PEX.

6.5   AIXwindows Desktop

AIXwindows Desktop is a port to AIXwindows of the X.desktop version 3, a product from IXI Limited. IXI is a company founded by Ray Anderson, and is based in Cambridge, England. AIXwindows Desktop provides an X-Windows, graphical, and iconic view of files and programs on the filesystem. Fig. 6.8 shows a sample of desktop session.

A user can run programs and carry out file management activities such as deleting, copying, etc., without needing to know the AIX command language. At the simplest level the AIXwindows Desktop provides the facilities of the Microsoft Windows or the IBM Operating System/2 File Manager. The reason that AIXwindows requires X.desktop is that the underlying windowing system X-Windows has only a basic desktop metaphor. This is lacking in a number of important respects and it is this shortfall which AIXwindows Desktop attempts to make up. For example, using IBM OS/2 Presentation Manager version 2.1, users may directly manipulate program icons on their desktops. Consider a program that is represented as a printing icon. The user may drag an icon of a

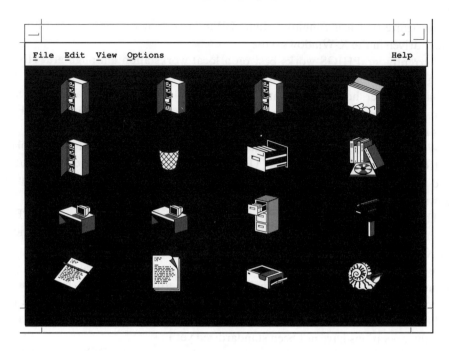

Figure 6.8.   A typical AIXwindows Desktop.

file and drop it on the printer icon. The printer icon is able to recognize this action and print the file. Icon manipulation outside the AIXwindows desktop window cannot be handled in this way and dropping the icon of an edited file on top of another will have no effect!

6.5.1   *Using the AIXwindows Desktop*

The AIXwindows Desktop is started using the *xdt3* command. The user is presented with one or more OSF/Motif windows showing an iconic view of that user's programs and files. The Desktop was written as a standard OSF/Motif 1.2 application and includes configurable menu bars, pull-down menus on all windows and a single status line help at the bottom of each window. At the simplest level a user can view and manipulate files: for example, opening two directory windows from the Desktop and moving files from one directory to another by first selecting the files with the mouse pointer, and then *dragging* the selection to the destination window. This is known as *direct manipulation.* Whereas the icons in X-Windows can only have two colours, a user can define multicoloured icons to represent files or programs on the Desktop. An icon editor is supplied for this purpose. By using a set of specification files based on the extension name of the file, icons can automatically be recognized by type. For example, C source programs can have their own special icon and are recognized because they have filenames ending with `.c`. The Desktop also supports animated icons. For example, dropping a file onto the printer icon causes the file to be printed. While printing, the printer icon shows a sheet of paper moving through the printer.

The Desktop has a backdrop option, where it covers the background or root window, allowing a user to work entirely from within Desktop. The Desktop also provides a configurable help system. Aside from the status line at the bottom of each Desktop window, the user may classify themselves as a general, power or administrative user, receiving different levels of assistance accordingly. The Desktop has links to InfoExplorer for full context-sensitive hypertext help.

6.5.2 Programming AIXwindows Desktop

The Desktop includes a rule-based programming language called *Deskshell*. The user or systems administrator can associate actions to icons. For example, an icon named 'compress' could be created and a set of rules written so that when a file icon is dropped onto the compress icon, the initial file is replaced by a compressed version of the file, generated by using the AIX *compress* program. Deskshell can be described as the command interpreter for the Desktop. It provides the same basic functions as the Bourne shell but with a simplified syntax and more consistent semantics. Internally, Deskshell scripts execute as 'threads' within the AIXwindows Desktop process avoiding the cost of starting separate processes for each task. IXI, who owns the Desktop product, has published the definition of its drag-and-drop protocol as well as the source code for its drag-and-drop handlers and donated its work to the X consortium in the hope that they can promote a standard in this area.

6.6   Open Look and XView

AIXwindows is not supplied with XView or any Open Look tools or products but an appreciation of Open Look is still very useful. The controversy over GUI superiority and eventual dominance is not easily resolved, but an appreciation of both the MOTIF and Open Look standards should enable the reader to at least express a considered opinion.

In 1987, Jon Kannegaard, Tony Hober and user interface experts from Sun, Xerox and AT&T began work on Open Look, a graphical user interface designed by Sun for AT&T. Open Look is independent of hardware, operating systems, and windowing systems. It standardizes the visual user interface but *does not* specify the programming interface. Open Look is therefore a functional specification, not a user interface with an assigned programming interface.

The designers of Open Look indicated that they wanted to create an open standard that could be implemented across many vendor systems, including

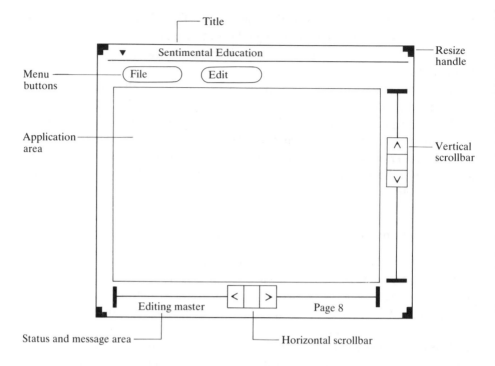

Figure 6.9.   A top-level Open Look window.

UNIX and non-UNIX platforms. A typical Open Look application has one main window and several pop-up windows for manipulating data. Like OSF/Motif the main window has some characteristic features. Figure 6.9 shows a typical top-level window.

The UNIX world has traditionally strongly supported high-quality, public domain software (for example X-Windows), and Sun decided to make their implementation of Open Look for X-Windows called *XView* freely available. By donating it to MIT, it is automatically packaged with MIT's X-Windows tape containing the X-Windows server, sample clients and free *widget sets*. By making XView public domain, Sun hoped to make XView the widget set of choice for GUI developers.

XView comprises an X-Windows object-oriented set of *packages*. Internally, XView is implemented directly on top of the Xlib and X protocol layers of X-Windows. That is to say, it does not require the Xt toolkit layer used by most other object-oriented widget sets. This makes the programming interface cleaner, though different in some ways from most widget sets. Because the Xt toolkit layer is required by some government customers, the *Xol* widget set and *Xt+* intrinsics can be used as an alternative to the regular XView programming interface. Sun designed the programming interface of XView (which you will recall is not specified by Open Look) to be close to that of one of its former windowing systems called SunView. This allows previous SunView applications to be ported to XView with minimal difficulty.

6.6.1 The future of Open Look

Open Look is a good product. Visually I do not see that it offers any advantages over OSF/Motif but I admit that the XView programming interface to Open Look is certainly cleaner than that of OSF/Motif. This is achieved, however, by not implementing the Xt intrinsics compatibility layer, which makes it nonstandard.

However as an applications developer I would prefer a single, common programming interface to develop a GUI-based application. Consider the case of the IBM CUA standard with which, for the most part, OSF/Motif is compliant. To produce such a CUA standard program that looks and feels the same in OSF/Motif, Microsoft Windows and IBM OS/2 Presentation Manager is certainly possible. Unfortunately, programmers and designers would have to be familiar with three totally different programming environments, which is extremely difficult. Open Look compounds this problem and provides the ability to produce an Open Look application for a single hardware architecture in several different ways. Programmers such as myself want both a programming and look and feel standard, not just the latter.

In the summer of 1993 significant developments took place to rationalize GUI standards under X-Windows. This was under the guise of the common open software environment (COSE), described in more detail in Sec. 16.1.5.

6.7 Professional Graphics Tools

AIXwindows now includes a component called the Professional Graphics Tools collection. This comprises three products, namely:

1 The AIX Computer Graphics Interface toolkit.
2 The Graphics File translator which allows computer graphics metafile (CGM) files to be viewed, manipulated or output to a printer or plotter.
3 The Graphics Plotting system provides a programming interface to enable programmers to create applications which display business graphics that can be displayed on X-Windows or on a hard copy device.

6.7.1 The computer graphics interface toolkit

This is not part of AIXwindows but a separate program that provides an applications developer with a set of primitives allowing C (or Fortran/Pascal) programs to create device-independent graphics code. This provides a migration path for users of the IBM RT PC system graphics development toolkit.

IBM has extended Xlib with routines to allow device-independent graphics and therefore to allow the developer to draw metafiles on the screen and then translate them to another CGI device, such as a printer, automatically.

7
Information strategy

This chapter examines the IBM information strategy for the IBM RISC System/ 6000. Information strategy means a lot more than online help text available at the touch of a button. It means giving full customer support on all aspects of IBM's products. In addition, IBM is committed to providing relevant information in paper and electronic form to enable customers to facilitate smooth implementation of their computer systems.

The IBM systems engineer has traditionally been responsible for making customers fully aware of IBM's products and services. In recent times, this has been assisted by new methods of information retrieval and distribution. In fact, IBM's overall position as an information provider has been greatly enhanced through its sophisticated electronically based help system. For example, with the purchase of an IBM RISC System/6000 comes a complete package of information called *InfoExplorer*. InfoExplorer is a hypertext help system with online copies of IBM RISC system commands, user and programming manuals. We will look at the principal features of InfoExplorer and then describe *InfoCrafter* which allows applications developers to create their own hypertext databases. An electronic publications strategy is matched by an equally effective way for customers to communicate with IBM. *Electronic customer support* (ECS) allows a customer electronic access to IBM personnel and worldwide IBM databases. We will look at what the customer stands to gain from ECS. For instance, how does ECS help customers to run their businesses more effectively? Lastly, IBM offers a broad range of training and customized education for the RISC system. We will look at a range of solutions that IBM provides, from self-study education to bespoke, onsite customer courses.

7.1   Documentation strategy

The new documentation strategy for the RISC system is very simple. All publications are shipped in the form of electronic books readable by the InfoExplorer help system. The only exception to this environmentally friendly policy is a small number of paper manuals shipped to enable basic hardware and software installation. To exploit this strategy fully a user needs a RISC system workstation with local or LAN access to a database stored on a CD-ROM disk. The CD-ROM version of the help system contains not just command-specific text but full copies of RISC system publications including artwork. The CD-ROM is updated quarterly.

Why is this the publications strategy for the IBM RISC System/6000? First, the RISC system is designed to be a production UNIX system. Many RISC system customers will be office professionals running standard applications. They do not want to accommodate the approximately 12 feet plus of shelf space required to hold the major publications for the RISC system. Users or administrators of such systems can use the hypertext help systems for general-purpose help. Applications developers have different requirements, but again there are clear advantages in using an online command and programming reference. UNIX has always been supplied with the traditional manual or *man* pages. AIX does not have a duplicate man pages database but extracts the man information from the InfoExplorer manuals for programming commands and subroutines and displays it in the traditional format. As with man pages, InfoExplorer is accessible from ASCII or X-Windows graphics terminals by any user. The electronic search facility of InfoExplorer is much more comprehensive than a paper index. Even with these and other advantages many developers still want some paper documentation. Paper copies of online books are therefore available as a chargeable item from the IBM Technical Publications department.

7.2   InfoExplorer

InfoExplorer is the hypertext help system supplied with the RISC system. Before describing this in more detail let us review exactly what is *hypertext*. Within a displayed article keywords are highlighted visually. By clicking the mouse pointer on this text (or using the text cursor on ASCII screens) the document window changes to information on the selected hypertext link. This new document can have embedded links too and a user can follow links recursively as required. InfoExplorer operates best under X-Windows and the rest of this discussion concentrates on this version. Readers only familiar with InfoExplorer in an ASCII environment are strongly encouraged to move up to X-Windows for all of the following advantages.

As InfoExplorer loads a *Welcome to InfoExplorer* screen appears. As this logo suggests, InfoExplorer is a product written by KnowledgeSet Corporation. The main InfoExplorer screen is then displayed. At the bottom of this *navigation window* (Fig. 7.1) is a set of 11 buttons which indicate the top-level functions available to the user. Pressing one of these buttons replaces the information in the navigation window with information on that topic, for example the list of commands. Although the InfoExplorer application is surrounded by an OSF/Motif Window Manager border, the reader should deduce from the style of the

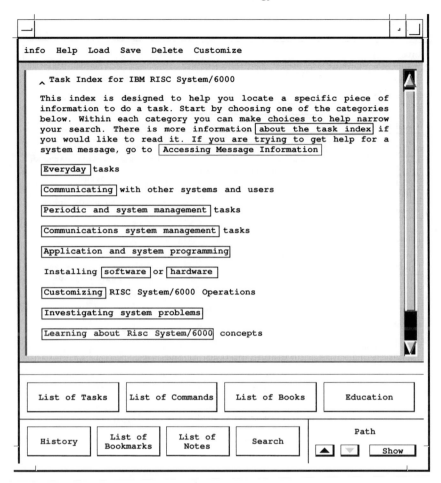

Figure 7.1. The navigation window.

buttons that InfoExplorer was not written using OSF/Motif. In fact it was written using the IBM and Carnegie-Mellon developed, Andrew Toolkit (ATK) widget library. This accounts for some slight differences in user interface behaviour as compared to regular OSF/Motif applications.

7.2.1 *Listing commands*

The *list of commands* button leads to an alphabetical list of commands. This is the preferred replacement to the traditional UNIX *man* command. Information is presented on each command with the same sections as for the *man* command, but with the advantage of hypertext links. Users can still use the *man* command from a full screen or windowed character session, but it does not present as much information as InfoExplorer.

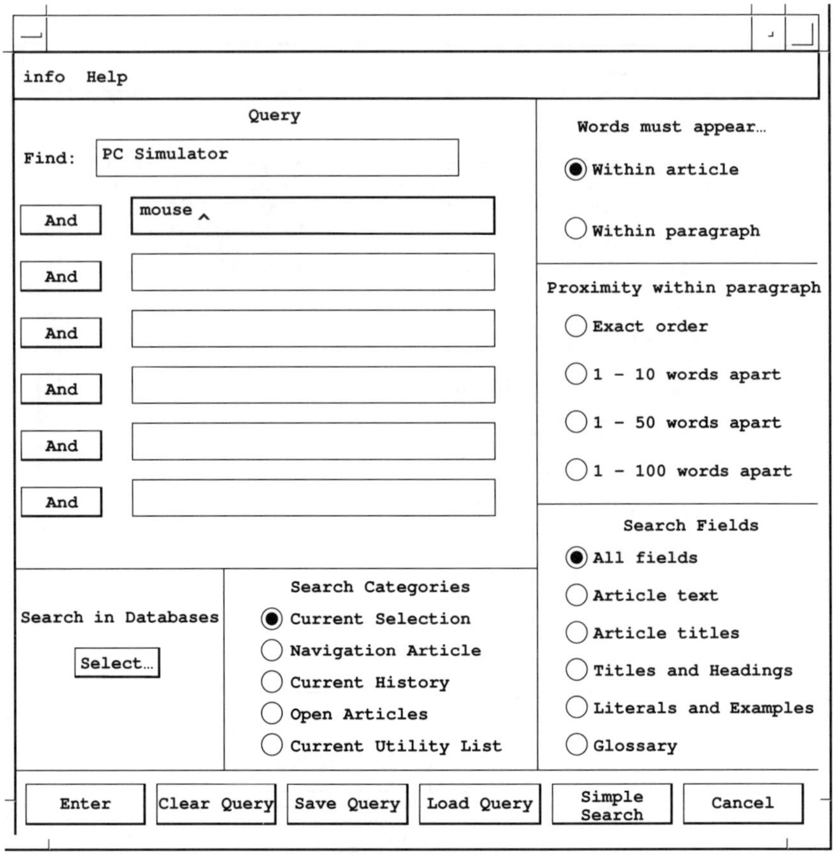

Figure 7.2.   The compound search window.

7.2.2   Searching for information

The *search* button allows a user to search part or all of the online databases for one or more phrases. The compound search screen is shown in Fig. 7.2. This shows how flexible the search can be, since it can be made for combination of terms in a sentence, paragraph or in a complete document or book.

Figure 7.3 shows the results of a search on the words 'PC simulator' and 'mouse'. The result is an example of a *reading window*. InfoExplorer by default allows only one reading window unless a user clicks on the hold button at the top of the client area. This pins this reading window to the screen and InfoExplorer automatically creates another reading window when presenting additional information. Using this method a user can perform complex searches (or indeed any InfoExplorer function) and pin a variety of related pages on an X-Windows screen.

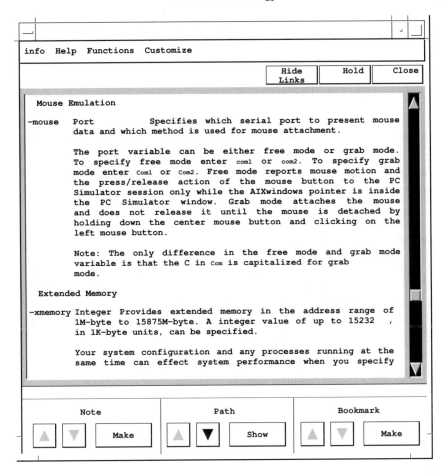

Figure 7.3. The results window.

7.2.3   Browsing a book

The *list of books* command presents a list of online AIX hardware and software manuals that are available. Unless the online CD-ROM database is being consulted this list will be almost empty. (In a network of AIX systems it is typical for the entire contents of the CD-ROM to be copied onto the hard disk of a dedicated help server RISC system. This requires about 200 Mb of space. Since the access time to hard disk is considerably faster than for CD-ROM this is the recommended configuration for a network help server.)

7.2.4   Retracing a path

InfoExplorer automatically keeps a record of the articles which have been selected and viewed during that session. Users wishing to view information previously selected may retrace their paths using the *history* button at the bottom of the navigation window.

7.2.5   Artwork

Articles can have links to other text or *illustrations.* Using the optional CD-ROM, these artwork diagrams will be presented in the *artwork window.* Since the diagrams are stored in a high-resolution graphics format they may be resized on screen without loss of resolution and even printed, typically on a PostScript printer.

7.2.6   Bookmarks and notes

The *bookmarks* function allows users to save the current state of information so that they can retrace the set of articles that was being viewed and come back to it at a later time. Bookmarks are often set to create learning paths for new users. Individual bookmark lists may be constructed to guide new users through a particular task. A bookmark is created simply by marking text and then selecting the *make* button at the bottom of the reading window.

Additionally, InfoExplorer allows a user to create private and public notes which add information to the InfoExplorer database. Since InfoExplorer uses an encrypted and read-only set of files, these notes are in files in a writable /usr/lpp/info directory.

7.2.7   Printing

InfoExplorer allows a user to print sections of articles of displayed help text. Artwork too may be printed although usually only to a PostScript printer. It is possible to print out an entire book by selecting the *print references* option while browsing a book, though this option is not recommended, because much of the formatting and all of the artwork and diagrams will not be printed, and the cost of the manual from IBM publications is probably cheaper than using a local printer.

7.3   InfoCrafter

InfoCrafter allows an information developer to create an InfoExplorer hypertext help database. It does so with much less effort than if the developer had to design their own system from scratch.

Traditional UNIX led the field early with the concept of the *man* online documentation. This was of course a document with a number of well-known

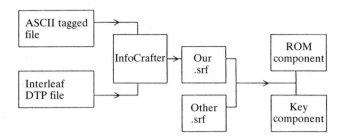

Figure 7.4. Generating InfoExplorer files with InfoCrafter.

sections, for example purpose, synopsis, description etc. The document was usually written with the native UNIX typesetting utility *nroff* and formatted on the fly for a user's ASCII terminal when required. Unfortunately the 'early lead' that UNIX systems showed with online help fell far behind in the age of graphical user interfaces. Since X-Windows does not have a standard way of displaying help text, InfoCrafter fills that gap. AIX is thus one UNIX system that can compete against workstation operating systems such as Microsoft Windows which have offered hypertext help for years now!

The fundamental process of converting a text to an InfoExplorer ready format is shown in Fig. 7.4. To generate InfoExplorer documents, text is generated using either Interleaf 5.0, Framemaker 3, maker interchange format (MIF) or any ASCII text editor in the SGML tagged format. This is combined with artwork in Interleaf, tagged image file format (TIFF) or computer graphics metafile formats. The *icft* program takes these raw files and produces special `.srf` files. (Standard record format (SRF) is a KnowledgeSet Corp. vendor format.) The separate preprocessed files are then combined into a single database `.srf` file and then into the traditional pair of InfoExplorer database files. That is to say, a single `databasename.rom` file containing the encrypted readable database, and a `databasename.key` paired key file. Several databases (that is filename pairs) can be combined to form a library.

Hypertext links are represented by *anchors* and *targets*. Each anchor, that is, a source hypertext link, can have at most one target. Using Interleaf, anchors and targets are represented by special index entries which are translated by the *icft* program. Links may be from one position to another in the same article, from one article to another in the same database, or from one database to another in the same library.

7.3.1 Available CD-ROM databases

Aside from the CD-ROM containing the InfoExplorer hypertext help system,

IBM also offers the Technical Library/6000.[1] This is a repository of comprehensive AIX documentation and service/support information on CD-ROM. Some examples of the contents of this library include: 'How-to' items, technical articles, sample programs, fix information on closed software problems and InfoExplorer system documentation. The technical library is updated quarterly.

7.4   BookManager

IBM vendor operating systems such as VM or MVS have traditionally provided a 'tag' and 'format' based document preparation system. In this scheme of things a document is prepared using a standard text editor. Text is 'tagged' with formatting codes, for example the code :p. for a paragraph, or :h1. for a Level 1 heading. After tagging the text is input to a formatter and output to a suitable printer. The original versions of this formatter were called *script* or generalized markup language (GML), these have now been superseded by a product called *BookMaster*. BookMaster provides a superset of script facilities and the product is well suited to the production of entire publications (as opposed to short documents). This book was originally produced as a manuscript using this product. Within IBM, practically all publications are written using BookMaster. IBM now provides an almost painless way to transform a document written in BookMaster into a soft copy publication that may be viewed and browsed on line. The result is *BookManager*. BookManager Read/6000 allows you to read publications composed with BookMaster.[2]

BookManager provides hypertext links to information through user-selectable cross-references found in tables of contents, indexes, lists, figures or glossaries. Because information is presented electronically, BookManager is able to offer the user sophisticated linguistic search capabilities which are considerably more effective than for a paper publication. Lastly, as with InfoExplorer, users may append margin notes to topics or lines in the soft copy book, or view the notes of others.

For users with large libraries of documents written in BookMaster, or BookManager versions of IBM publications, BookManager Read/6000 is a powerful and cost-effective assistant.

---

[1] At the time of writing this database was not available worldwide. Check with your IBM Marketing Representative for details.

[2] At the time of writing the RISC system product allows reading not composition of BookManager documents. BookManager documents must be prepared using VM, MVS or OS/2 hosts. Alternatively, a BookManager document can be created using WordPerfect or Microsoft Word as input to IBM SAA BookManager BUILD/2 under DOS.

7.5   IBM information sources

One of the first things that any new IBM employee learns is that very probably someone, somewhere, has already written a similar report, or carried out a similar study to that about to be undertaken. Instead of repeating work that has already been carried out it is more efficient to consult IBM's global database to make use of existing information. To enable IBM customers to become more productive, IBM makes a subset of this information available. Customers access this information using electronic links to IBM.

The rest of this chapter details the major service offerings that IBM provides. The list is not of course exhaustive, the message is that the reader should ask their IBM marketing representative or value added reseller first. IBM often has the service or can provide the information you need.

7.6   Electronic customer support

To improve its level of support to customers, IBM now makes available a sophisticated electronic bulletin board service. In the United States and Canada this is known as *IBMLink*. In other national areas it is known by other names, for example in the United Kingdom it is called *DIAL IBM*. This section will refer to facilities provided under the generic name—electronic customer support (ECS).

ECS benefits both the RISC system customer and IBM. The customer gains free access to a 24-hours-a-day, 7-days-a-week link to one of the largest and most sophisticated international databases. As will be demonstrated using actual screen captures of it in action, the service enables a user to find out detailed product specifications and pricing. It can determine the status of software orders with IBM and even order publications, and has the capability in the future to be used by customers even for software and hardware ordering.

In a real attempt to be open to the customer, ECS is in fact a subset of the actual internal IBM information systems used by IBM worldwide marketing and technical professionals. IBM gains when the customer uses the database facilities, since customers' questions and answers are recorded in databases, which build up a repository of useful information for future reference. ECS electronic mail facilities enable IBM and customers to communicate efficiently. The ECS service can be divided into five areas of operation:

- InfoLink—enquires of IBM hardware and software product information and price databases. Uses electronic tools to build valid IBM RISC System/6000 configurations ready to order.
- Orderlink—enquires of the IBM hardware and software customer databases for installed and ordered equipment.
- SupportLink—searches the international IBM database of questions and answers of known technical bulletins or announcements.

```
            DIAL-IBM - A component of IBMLink

Enter a selection or any Fastpath Name (LOGOFF will exit DIAL-IBM)

    1. PRODUCTS      - Product, publications and education information
    2. ORDERING      - Prepare, submit or query an order
    3. SUPPORT       - Technical support for an IBM product
    4. CONTACTIBM    - Communicate with IBM other than to ORDER
    5. NEWS          - News and general information from IBM
    6. USERTOOLS     - Guidance and tools for the DIAL-IBM system
    7. CONTENTS      - List of applications available on Dial-IBM
    8. EDITPERSONAL  - Edit your own personal menu




===>
PF 1=HELP
```

Figure 7.5.   The ECS top-level signon screen.

- ServiceLink—communicates with **IBM** customer service to resolve software and hardware problems. Allows for software test cases to be uploaded to customer service and software fixes to be downloaded.
- UserLink—allows a user to send electronic mail to known **IBM** personnel.

The ECS main menu is shown in Fig. 7.5.

7.6.1   Configuring software

The software configurators are a set of programs written in the language APL and they allow a user to generate an order for **IBM** software. Although the example that follows focuses on AIX, as one would expect, any software product from **IBM** DOS to **IBM**'s mainframe operating system MVS can be configured in this manner. In the following pages some intermediate screen captures are not shown for brevity.

   IBM allows the customer to order software in two ways (Fig. 7.6), through either a full BASIC licence or a distributed systems licence option (DSLO). The DSLO is a reduced cost option for customers on second and subsequent system orders, and does not ship any documentation. For a RISC system of course this does not have much effect since little paper documentation is shipped with a full order. Notice that a valid customer and system number is usually entered. In this way the internal **IBM** database containing current customer information is consulted and helps to form a valid order. For example, consider trying to order the 3D component of AIXwindows which provides GL and PEX programming interfaces. The configurator could warn a user that base AIXwindows would also be necessary if it detected that it was not currently ordered.

```
                   Customer Inventory Specification
EXEC
Specify desired licences for this configuration and the designated
customer system for which the selected software is to be ordered and
checked against and press Enter.

Prepare configuration for . . . .1    1. BASIC licences
                                      2. Derived licences (e.g. DSLO)

Customer inventory 1    1. Take customer inventory into account
                           (country, customer and system number needed)
                        2. Do not take customer inventory into account

Country . . . . .  866

Customer number .  123456

System number . .  FZP97   (leave blank if you want to select from list)

Force display of customer or system details :      N (Y=Yes, N=No)

===>
PF   1=HELP    2=       3=END     4=        5=          6 =RETURN
PF   7=        8=       9=        10=EXEC   11 =STEP     12 =EXIT
```

Figure 7.6.   Specifying customer details.

```
                        Language Selection
EXEC
Program . . . . . . :      5750-AET    RISC SYSTEM/6000
Confirm or correct the language selection and press Enter.

Type S=Select next to the desired language:
                                        ┌─────────────────────────────
                                        │               More:
 ┌──────────────────────────────────────┴─────────────────────────────┐
 │ S   US English  _     German     _    French                        │
 │ _   Italian     _     Spanish    _    Norwegian - Bokmal            │
 │ _   Swedish     _     Hebrew     _    Belgian Dutch                 │
 │ _   Arabic                                                          │
 └─────────────────────────────────────────────────────────────────────┘
Type DEFAULTS to view or change your language defaults
Invalid input. Select one of the listed language codes.

===>
PF   1=HELP    2=CHANGE  3=END     4=        5=          6 =RETURN
PF   7=        8=        9=        10=EXEC   11 =STEP     12 =EXIT
```

Figure 7.7.   Selecting the primary language.

Once this panel is completed the user answers some more screens (not shown) to select the particular version of the program to be configured.

Next the desired language needs to be specified (Fig. 7.7). An international customer may have RISC systems in many different locations, hence this panel enables a truly international order to be built. The language code will, for example, determine the language of any shipped installation and 'readme' instructions.

The next stage involves selecting the software components to be ordered (Fig. 7.8). Since the customer number was entered, notice that the orders database recognizes that the base AIX system and some programs have already been installed (marked with a 'P' in the left-hand column). This order adds the AIXwindows and PC/AT simulator programs to the existing installation.

Now the software media is specified (Fig. 7.9). We chose 8 mm data cartridge in this example.

To generate a configuration successfully, the configurator has determined that it needs extra information from the user (Fig. 7.10). In particular whether the DOS simulator will be used within X-Windows and whether DOS programs will be run on the PC hardware simulator (of course—what else!). Using this information the configurator realizes that this will require the customer to purchase the IBM DOS operating system too. Therefore another screen (not shown) will ask whether the customer wants to order IBM DOS also. The user can (I)gnore the relation, indicating that they already have a spare copy of DOS that can be used, or they can (R)emove the conflict by cancelling the order for the AT simulator. The configurator will not proceed until the conflict is resolved. This shows the ability of the configurator to suggest helpfully software that the user might not have considered. Clearly both IBM and the customer would be embarrassed if only part of the software needed for the job was ordered.

Next the size of the processor running the software is entered. Figure 7.11 is an example for a RISC system model 560. The cost of IBM software varies according to the size of the machine on which it is running. Additionally the software may be purchased outright (a 'one time charge'), or using a small 'initial' charge and a recurring 'monthly' rental charge. If the customer's cash flow could benefit from a series of monthly payments instead of an initial total charge then the 'monthly' payment option may be preferable. (Note that in some countries the monthly rental may not be offered, the reader should check with their IBM marketing representative.)

All questions are now answered, the program continues execution and produces a report of all the software that needs to be ordered, software part numbers, subpart numbers called 'feature codes' and, most importantly, pricing information. This is not shown here, since actual prices are liable to change and are expressed in local currency.

Using the software configurator a valid and tailored software order is generated. The user can play *what if* games at any time and alter any of the input options by pressing the change, function key 2. So for example, if at this late stage the user remembers that they had also wanted to order the mainframe communications program HCON, they would press the PF2 key and go back to

```
                        Component Selection
EXEC
Program . . . . . . :        5750-AET    RISC SYSTEM/6000

Type an action code next to the desired component(s) and press Enter.
Valid action codes    : S=Select.
Possible indicators   : S=Selected before, C=Custom built, P=Installed,
L=Language conflict. You cannot select components with code P and L.

                                    Available        Announced
Act    Component description        Rel.  End date   Rel.  CA date
       AIX V3 MUST BE SELECTED
P      AIX V3.2.1          5756-030  02.01
       PRELOAD
P      PRELOAD                       02.01
       MAINT. SUBSCRIPTION - ONE MUST BE SELECTED
_      MAINT: ON DEMAND ONLY         02.01
_      MAINT: AUTO SHIP NEW REL      02.01
_      MAINT: NEW REL AND PTFS       02.01
P      MAINT: NEW REL/PTFS  URGENT   02.01
       TOOLS TO MIGRATE FROM 3.1.5 TIL 3.2
P      TOOL TO MIGRATE FROM AIX 3.1.5  02.01
       OPTIONAL COMPONENTS TO BE SELECTED
_      AIX V3.2.0 DES      5756-030  02.01
P      AIX V3.2.0 INFOEXP  5756-030  02.01
_      AIX V3.2.0 HANFS    5756-030  02.01
_      AIX V3.2.0 FDDI     5756-030  02.01
_      AIX V3.2.0 BLK. MPX. 5756-030 02.01
_      ESSL/6000      2.1.0 5765-042 02.01
_      PASCAL RUNTIME 1.1.1 5601-251 02.01
_      NETWORK MGT    1.2.0 5601-253 02.01
_      PASCAL COMP.   1.1.1 5601-254 02.01
_      3270 EMULAT.   1.2.0 5601-256 02.01
S      AIXWINDOWS     1.2.1 5601-257 02.01
S      AIXWINDOWS 3D  1.2.0 5601-257 02.01
_      COBOL COMPILER 1.1.1 5601-258 02.01
P      COBOL RUNTIME  1.1.1 5601-259 02.01
_      3270 HOST CON  1.3.0 5601-260 02.01
S      PC/AT SIM.     1.2.0 5601-263 02.01
P      SNA SERVICES   1.2.0 5601-287 02.01
_      GRAPHIC TLKT   1.2.0 5601-386 02.01
_      XSTATION MGR   1.3.0 5601-457 02.01
_      INFOCRAFTER    1.1.0 5696-108 02.01
_      NETWARE        1.1.0 5696-236 02.01
_      ADA COMPILER   1.3.0 5706-291 02.01
_      ADA RUNTIME    1.3.0 5706-294 02.01
_      AIXW INTF COMP 1.1.0 5756-027 02.01
_      GRAPHIC PLOT   1.1.0 5765-004 02.01
_      GRAPHIC FT     1.1.0 5765-005 02.01
_      FORTRAN COMP.  2.2.1 5765-018 02.01
_      FORTRAN RTE    2.2.1 5765-019 02.01
       OPTIONAL DOCUMENTATION
_      AIXWINDOWS  GRAPHIGS PUBS      02.01
_      AIXWINDOWS  GKS PUBS           02.01
_      AIXWINDOWS  PEX SI PUBS        02.01
_      ADD COPY OF CLIENT KIT         02.01
       HEBREW AND ARABIC SUPPORT FROM APRIL 92
```

Figure 7.8. Selecting software components. *Continues.*

```
_      SECONDARY LANGUAGE ARABIC              02.01
_      SECONDARY LANGUAGE HEBREW              02.01
       SECONDARY LANGUAGE SUPPORT
_      SECONDARY LANGUAGE US ENGLISH          02.01
_      SECONDARY LANGUAGE FRENCH              02.01
_      SECONDARY LANGUAGE GERMAN              02.01
_      SECONDARY LANGUAGE SPANISH             02.01
_      SECONDARY LANGUAGE ITALIAN             02.01
_      SECONDARY LANGUAGE NORWEGIAN           02.01
_      SECONDARY LANGUAGE SWEDISH             02.01
_      SECONDARY LANGUAGE BELGIAN DUTCH       02.01




===>

PF     1=HELP      2=CHANGE   3=END    4=TOP      5 =          6 =RETURN
PF     7=BACK      8=         9=       10=EXEC    11 =STEP     12 =EXIT
```

Figure 7.8.   Selecting software components. *Concluded.*

```
                              General Medium Selection
EXEC
Program . . . . . . :         5750-AET   RISC SYSTEM/6000

Confirm or correct the medium selection and press Enter.
Type S=Select next to the desired medium:
                                        ┌─────────────────────────────┐
                                        │                   More:     │
  ┌─────────────────────────────────────┴─────────────────────────────┤
  │ S    8mm Data Cartr          _    1/4" DC QIC120                   │
  └────────────────────────────────────────────────────────────────────┘

If one or more components of this program are not available on the
General Medium selected, you can specify an Individual Medium later.

Type DEFAULTS to view or change your medium defaults


===>
PF     1=HELP      2=CHANGE   3=END    4=TOP      5 =          6 =RETURN
PF     7=BACK      8=         9=       10=EXEC    11 =STEP     12 =EXIT
```

Figure 7.9.   Specifying output media.

the panel shown in Fig. 7.8 and enter an 'S' in the HCON column then press the
PF10 to re-execute the configurator. The customer can of course save the
configuration questions and answers in a named response file for later reference.

```
                         Technical Relations - Questions
EXEC
Program . . . . . . :      5750-AET   RISC SYSTEM/6000

The following selected program component has triggered (a) question(s).

Component . . . . . :      PC/AT SIM.  1.2.0 5601-263     02.01

Please resolve the question(s), type Y=Yes or N=No and press Enter.
                                                      Page __1 of 1
                    Question
              y    RUN AIX PC SIMULATOR/6000 WITHIN WINDOW?
              y    EXECUTING THE PC APPLICATION?



===>
PF    1=HELP     2=CHANGE   3=END    4=         5 =         6 =RETURN
PF    7=         8=         9=       10=EXEC    11 =STEP    12 =EXIT
```

Figure 7.10.   Software relations.

```
                         Terms and Condition Defaults
EXEC
Complete following fields and press Enter.

Save option . . . . . .  2   1. Keep across configuration
                             2. Keep for current configuration only

Machine type / model . . 7013 / 560      OR   Processor group . . __
                                       ┌─────────────────────────────┐
                                       │              More:          │
Preferred charge options:    ┌─────────┴───────────────────────────────┐
(type 1,2,3 for priority)    │  1 Monthly (and Initial)                │
                             │  _ One Time Charge                      │
                             │  _ Primary/Recurring                    │
                             └─────────────────────────────────────────┘
Offer upgrade possibilities for selection . . .   N     (Y=Yes, N=No)
Update marketing offerings defaults . . . . . .   N     (Y=Yes, N=No)
Machine type / model or processor group must be specified


===>
PF    1=HELP     2=CHANGE   3=END    4=         5 =         6 =RETURN
PF    7=         8=         9=       10=EXEC    11 =STEP    12 =EXIT
```

Figure 7.11.   Software terms and conditions.

If a customer, for example, performed the above configuration and was happy
with the result, they could send the configuration file electronically to the IBM
representative asking them to confirm that it was suitable. They could indicate
that if it was, the IBM representative should call on the customer's manager to

discuss the upgrade, perhaps sending the manager an electronic note beforehand to schedule the meeting. Of course, the IBM representative could be based in London and the customer and manager in Kowloon but the mail system will handle the routing automatically.

7.6.2   Configuring hardware

The easiest way to configure an IBM RISC System/6000 reliably is to use a character-based program called the *visual configurator*. This DOS program, *vc* was written by Jim Bishop of IBM Austin Development using object-oriented Turbo Pascal. The program may be obtained from the IBM customer's local IBM marketing representative. Four principal windows are generated by the program:

- Physical layout of cards and disks in the machine
- Dollar priced output including hardware feature numbers
- Cabling information
- Configuration errors

vc has the advantage of being free, with the only pre-requisite a DOS personal computer on which to run.

A more sophisticated way to configure hardware is to use the ECS hardware configurator called *CFRS6000*, see Fig. 7.12. Again some screen captures have been removed for brevity.

```
CFRS6000 (Execute)

7855)              Set configurator default values for all products
DEFAULTS    0____       Select default values to be CHANGED.
                        0=No change 1=Power(1-phase)      2=Power(3-phase)
                        3=Languages 4=Nomenclatures       9=All
                           Separate entries with blanks or slashes (/).
                           Press the HELP PF key for additional information.

The country default values are:
ORGANIZATION:      EMEA
POWER:             (1-PHASE) - 50HZ/240V
                   (3-PHASE) - 50HZ/415V
LANGUAGES:         1ST OPTION- ENGLISH (U.K.)
                   2ND OPTION- ENGLISH (U.K.)
NOMENCLATURES:     1ST OPTION- ENGLISH (U.K.)
                   2ND OPTION- ENGLISH (U.K.)
If zero is selected, country default values will be used. For all other
selections, a question will offer available values. U.S. English will
be configured if the selected language or nomenclatures are not
available on a particular device.

===>
PF    2=EDIT                            10 =EXEC   11 =STEP  12 =MGR
```

Figure 7.12.   Country hardware defaults.

```
CFRS6000 (Execute)

5A)*              Type an 'X' in the SEL column to select a model
     SEL  MACH.MOD  STD.MEM  MAX.MEM  STD.DISK  MAX.DISK  SLOTS  MHZ
  1) _   7013-52H    16       512      400       6000       8     25
  2) _   7013-53H    32       512      400       6000       8     33
  3) _   7013-550    64       512      800       6000       8     41
  4) X   7013-560    64       512      800       6000       8     50
  5) _   7013-540    64       256      640       2571       8     30
  6) _   7016-730    16       512      355       2571       8     25

            Press HELP PF KEY for field descriptions.
===>
PF    1=HELP  2=EDIT                       10 =EXEC   11 =STEP   12 =MGR
```

Figure 7.13. Selecting the hardware system.

After the initial application signon screen which allows the user to restore a previously saved configuration, an initial series of screens need to be completed to specify the user's environment. This includes information such as:

- Voltage and power requirements
- Country information
- Default cabling lengths

This flexibility enables international customers to configure systems for worldwide use. These defaults determine the choice of keyboard, and national language instructions.

The next stage is to select the type of IBM RISC System/6000 that is to be ordered (screen not shown), that is a diskless workstation, desktop, deskside or rack-mounted model. Based on the choice of deskside, Fig. 7.13 displays the selected choice as model 560. At a glance the user can determine that this has 64 Mb standard memory, expandable to 512 Mb, is categorized as a high-perform-ance machine and can have up to 6000 Mb hard disk (DASD) installed in the system unit.

The aim of the hardware configurator is to generate a valid hardware order based on the features and cards that the customer requires. As with the software configurator the user can play a what-if game and rerun the configurator until a suitable configuration is produced. This may be a configuration with the exact features required, a configuration at a price that is within budget, or a configura-tion that tests the ability to add a new card to the user's existing configuration (for upgrade). This panel also shows that it is possible to configure older RISC systems that are no longer marketed, for example, configuring a model 530 to determine how to upgrade it to a model 560 class of machine.

The configurator contains a number of rules on the valid cards that can be placed in each RISC system. The user can use this facility to see if a desired configuration is possible.

```
CFRS6000 (Execute)

*** Selections for attachment to the 7013 Model 560 ***
2102)           (Enter 'X' beside one or more categories)

              System Memory and SCSI Devices


MEMORY      X           Additional Memory
DASD        _           Internal Fixed Disk Drives
INTERNAL    X           Internal Devices
                        Includes SCSI tape drives and other media.
EXTERNAL    X           External Devices
                        Includes 9333 and 9334 drawers, fixed disk
                        drives, tape drives, and other media.
CONT.CABLE  _           SCSI I/O Controllers and Internal Cables


===>
PF        2=EDIT                          10 =EXEC   11 =STEP  12 =MGR
```

Figure 7.14.   Selecting hardware devices.

Once the base model has been specified additional features may be added by selecting one or more categories from Fig. 7.14. Figure 7.15 shows an example of the selection of the internal and external devices categories. In Fig. 7.15 the user has selected an internal 3.5 inch drive, CD-ROM and 8 mm tape drives. Also an external $5\frac{1}{4}$ inch disk drive. The configurator checks all relations automatically, so for example the external diskette drive could not be ordered without the necessary cable.

For multiuser commercial systems it may not be necessary for users to work at individual RISC systems, or using X-Windows terminals. The screen in Fig. 7.16 allows the user to configure ASCII terminal devices and other asynchronous communications devices.

After this screen is completed the configurator checks and cross-checks the configuration. An important part of the checking verifies that there are enough slots in the machine for all the cards selected. The configurator makes this decision based on the cards selected and using a screen (not shown) that allows the user to reserve space for your own IBM or OEM vendor MicroChannel cards for the RISC system.

Should an error occur the user is returned to it and is required to enter a correction. If the user needs assistance at this, or indeed at any time, it is available by pressing the function key F1 for context-sensitive help. When the configuration is complete a series of output screens shows the precise cost of the total order broken down by each part ordered, and the cost of maintenance. As before this configuration may be saved or forwarded to interested parties for comments.

```
CFRS6000 (Execute)

*** Selections for attachment to the 7013 Model 560 ***
2216A)*          Internal Devices and Attachments
        FEATURES  QTY MAX  DESCRIPTION
    1)    9221    1__   1  Standard 3.5-Inch Diskette Drive
    2)    2600    1__   1  Internal CD-ROM Drive
    3)    6146    1__   1  2.3 GB Internal 8mm Tape Drive

    1)  4869-502  1__   1  External 5.25-Inch 1.2 MB Diskette Drive
    2)  7203-001  0__      External Portable Disk Drive
    3)  7204-320  0__      External Disk Drive Model 320
    4)  7207-001  0__      150 MB External 1/4-Inch Cartridge Tape Drive
    5)  7207-011  0__      525 MB External 1/4-Inch Cartridge Tape Drive
    6)  7208-001  0__      2.3 GB External 8mm Tape Drive
    7)  7210-001  0__      External CD-ROM Drive
    8)  9348-012  0__      Magnetic Tape Unit (1/2-Inch 9-Track)
    9)  9333-500  0__   4  Deskside High-Performance Subsystem
   10)  9334-500  0__   3  Deskside Expansion Unit

    1)    9220    1__   1  Standard SCSI I/O Controller
    2)    2615    1__   1  External 5.25-Inch Diskette Drive Cable
    3)    2835    0__   4  SCSI External I/O Controller
    4)    2915    0__      SCSI Controller Passthrough Terminator Cable
    5)    2829    0__   1  SCSI Internal I/O Controller
    6)    2832    0__      SCSI Controller Cable
    7)    3130    0__      SCSI Device-to-Device Cable
    8)    6210    0__   1  Disk Drive Subsystem Adapter

===>
PF    1=HELP     2=EDIT      3=END        10=EXEC      11=STEP      12=MGR
```

Figure 7.15.   Selecting input/output devices.

```
*** Selections for attachment to the 7013 Model 560 ***
2104)           (Enter 'X' beside one or more categories)

            Asynchronous Communications

ASCII        _        ASCII Display Stations (Terminals)
PRINTERS     _        Printers
PLOTTERS     _        Plotters
DIGITIZERS  _         Digitizers
ASYNC.ADAPT _         Async Communication Adapters
ASYNC.CABLE _         Async Communication Cables

The adapter and cable selection screens will be presented automatically
if any async devices are ordered. Wide-area network adapters and cables
appear on a following menu. Categories that are pre-selected with N (if
any) are not available in your country.

===>
PF   2=EDIT                          10=EXEC  11=STEP  12=MGR
```

Figure 7.16.   Completing a hardware configuration.

```
                    Publication Enquiry System Main Menu

Type an option number, complete related fields as desired and press Enter.

   Option          1      1. Free format search (also type search words)
                          2. Direct search (also type form number)
                          3. SLSS (also type product number)
                          4. Translation (also type form number)
                          5. Ordering information (also type form
number)

   Search words       aixwindows and aix_____

   Form number       _ - ___ - ____ - __

   Product number    ____ - ___

For descriptive information; select the data base to be searched.
   Data base       1      1. International  2. United Kingdom  3. Germany
                          4. Italy          5. Netherlands



===>
PF    1=HELP                   3=END                        12 =EXIT
```

Figure 7.17.   Searching for a publication.

7.6.3   Publications

IBM publications are shipped and sold by the IBM Technical Publications
Centre (TPC). Each country normally has a separate TPC, though actual publications are shipped from a centralized store. For example, in Europe all manuals
are shipped from Copenhagen. Anyone can have an account with TPC though
IBM customers automatically become account holders.

There are two ways of ordering AIX manuals, on a once-off basis and by
subscription. The latter means that TPC automatically ships updates (technical
newsletters) to any subscribed manuals.

The recommended procedure for ordering an IBM manual is thus:

1 Find the telephone number of the reader's country TPC. Contact the local
   IBM marketing branch if unsure.
2 If the manual number, known as the form number, is unknown, use ECS to
   find the correct manual and price.
3 Choose to order manual on subscription or on a once-off basis.

Figure 7.17 shows an example screen from the ECS publication support
system. The user selects the most appropriate search method from the five

```
                          Announcement Letters

Type your search words or dates and press the ENTER key. ENTER with no
search words or dates will list all documents added in the last month.

SEARCH WORDS AIX_AND_NCS_____
                         (Search words can be connected with 'and , 'or' etc.
                         Hit PF1=Help for more information.)

DATE FROM    910201      (documents added to database since  yymmdd)
DATE UNTIL   _____      (documents added to database before yymmdd)

TITLE ONLY   N           y = search only the title of the document
                         n = search entire document
HITLIST SORT Y           y = sort the hitlist by date
                            (Only first 800 hitlist documents will be sorted)


===>
PF    1=HELP      3=END                    8=NEXT            12=EXIT
```

Figure 7.18.   Searching for an announcement.

options. A variety of databases is available to international users. After the
search category is entered one or more document *hits* are displayed as one-line
title entries. In this example, there were 14 document hits. Further screens show
more detail such as the publication abstract and the publication price.

7.6.4   IBM products and services

Every time IBM announces an AIX product or service, IBM development
produces a customer document, called an *announcement letter*, describing the
offering. For large announcements this may be accompanied by a summary
overview announcement document. An IBM customer can use the announcement
letter to appreciate more fully the relevance of the announcement to their
business. For example, an announcement letter may specify a new hardware
product allowing cost-effective expansion of the customer's existing RISC system
installation. The letter includes hardware and software prerequisites and availability information.

Figure 7.18 shows a search for the announcement letters relating the network
computing system (NCS) and its availability under AIX. The results of this
search (not shown) found seven documents, including the one being searched for,
that of NCS under the mainframe AIX/ESA platform.

7.6.5   Technical queries

AIX, like any UNIX computer system, is a complex operating system. There

```
                  Question and Answer Main Menu

Type an option number and press Enter. If you choose option 1 you must
also type search file or search words.

          1       1. Find an Answer / Ask a Question.
                  2. View and maintain your Questions.
                  3. Maintain your search files.
                  4. View Question and Answer Guide.

Search file  _____

Search words AIX AND NCS_____
        For HELP with searching, move cursor to Search words and press PF1.
                  Search words can be connected with AND (default), OR, etc.

Specify period OR date fields if you want to limit your search.
Period          __        0-99 DAYs
Start date   _____     DDMMYY
End   date   _____     DDMMYY



===>
PF    1=HELP    2=        3=END   4=       5 =        6 =
PF    7=        8=        9=      10=      11 =       12 =EXIT
```

Figure 7.19.   Searching the answers database.

will be times when RISC system customers need technical help or configuration assistance. The function of the AIX Support Centre is not only to support hardware and software defects, but also to answer questions.

These questions and answers are stored in an online database and it is usually more efficient for the customer to search this database directly for the answer. For example, Fig. 7.19 is the panel from ECS, searching for information on the NCS component of AIX. A list of documents containing these keywords is displayed and may be browsed for the answer to the query. If no answer can be found, a question may be entered into the database and this is processed in turn by IBM staff at the AIX support centre, or, for more challenging problems by the IBM Field or Technical Support Centre.

7.7   IBM training

To help users get the most from the RISC system, IBM offers five principal sources of education. These are online electronic education, in-depth education broadcast by satellite, learning centre courses, classroom courses and bespoke education.

7.7.1 System-delivered education

Every AIX system is shipped with a set of hands-on training exercises as part of InfoExplorer. The exercises are known collectively as InfoTrainer. These should be the first point of reference for users new to AIX or to end user computing in general. Here are some of the topics available:

- Working with AIX—a multistep course designed for users new to UNIX or AIX
- Using AIXdesktop—using the IXI X.desktop product

7.7.2 The field television network

Many larger IBM marketing and development locations participate in the IBM field television network (FTN) programme. Each participating site receives a live satellite transmission of a talk, usually presented by an IBM development group. For example, in early 1992 there was an FTN programme regarding issues in converting from the then current level of AIX version 3.1.5 to version 3.2. Telephone links to the presenter allow two-way communication with the attendees. IBM marketing staff are responsible for making known the dates and venues of FTN sessions and distributing a paper copy of the foils shown to interested parties. FTN sessions are free.

7.7.3 Learning Centre education

Most IBM marketing branches have dedicated self-study courses available to customers which are performed in the IBM Learning Centre. Their courses usually rely on multimedia and software simulation exercises.

7.7.4 Classroom courses

IBM has a number of internal education centres throughout the world that work just to provide IBM internal and customer education. In the AIX world, many of the courses originate from Dallas, Texas, and are then replicated and distributed throughout the world. Some countries may be too small to have their own IBM education facilities, in which case two options exist. If the customer has the IBM AIX systems required, an IBM education professional can teach this course at the customer site directly. Alternatively, students can journey to the most appropriate IBM education location, for example, many customers of IBM Turkey use IBM UK education for AIX.

For a listing of course times and prices IBM customers need to receive and consult the IBM education catalogue, or preferably use ECS. Figure 7.20 shows the online education catalogue search screen. In this example eight courses were found that matched this description (screen not shown).

```
ECAT

Type your search words and press the ENTER key. ENTER with no
search words will list the last 40 documents added.

SEARCH WORDS AIX_AND_(_'TCP/IP'_OR_ADMINISTRATION_)_____
                     (Search words can be connected with 'and , 'or' etc.
                     Hit PF1=Help for more information.)

TITLE ONLY    N      y = search only the title of the document
                     n = search entire document



===>
PF    1=HELP         3=END                                  12=EXIT
```

Figure 7.20.   Searching for an education course.

7.7.5   *Bespoke education*

IBM offers customized courses to meet special customer requirements. An IBM
marketing representative usually calls to discuss these requirements and then
searches internationally for the most suitable people to deliver the education. At
the simplest level this can take the form of a one-company course. This is a
rework of an existing IBM classroom course taught at a customer site, for
example, systems administration, with the focus on high availability in the
financial dealing systems environment. Occasionally, there is no existing
classroom course which covers a customer's requirement so IBM will (for a fee)
design a completely new course. For example, IBM could work with your
computer staff to produce executive-level education aimed at showing the real
benefits of implementing a distributed UNIX workstation environment in your
organization.

8
New technology

The release of one vendor's technology is invariably superseded by a release from another vendor claiming greater sophistication, speed and precision. This chapter examines some of the high-technology components that establish the IBM RISC System/6000 as state-of-the-art minicomputer system. If you have been in the computing industry for more than a decade you probably recall the days of the punched card and core memory; I am sure you will be impressed by the new technology that we will discuss in this chapter. But if your first experience of computers was the IBM PC or perhaps a UNIX workstation will you still be impressed? I think so. A well-equipped IBM RISC System/6000 may well support 10 Gb of disk, have at least 256 Mb of memory, use several gigabytes of tape storage and run several hundred times faster than the original IBM PC. This is surely impressive!

We will examine some of the key technology changes that demonstrate the technological leadership that IBM has employed with the IBM RISC System/6000. The topics covered are:

- The 9333 serial link disk drive
- The IBM X-station 150
- Diskless workstations
- Optical disk and digital tape technology
- MicroChannel
- Optical networking
- High-performance graphics
- The POWER visualization system
- Parallel processing

8.1   Serial link disk technology

The IBM 9333 serial link disk family allows the external expansion of disk storage on an IBM RISC System/6000 to over 50 000 Mb (50 Gb). Although the 9333 subsystem uses fewer MicroChannel slots or interconnecting cables it is

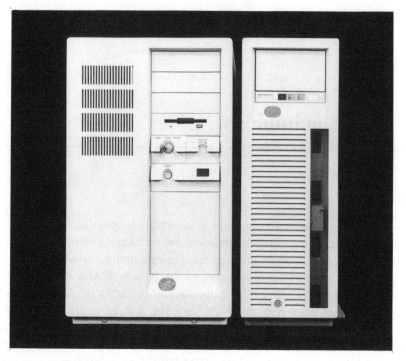

Figure 8.1.   The deskside IBM 9333 model 500.

significantly faster and more reliable than previous disk technologies. (A discussion of earlier hard disk interfaces is presented in Appendix 2. This includes a discussion about SCSI, the entry level disk interface for the RISC system.)

Figure 8.1 shows 8 Gb of external storage housed by a single 9333-501 subsystem. Rack-mounted enclosures are available to store over 100 Gb of serial link disk.

8.1.1   Connecting a serial link disk subsystem

Figure 8.2 shows how a serial link disk subsystem connects to a RISC system. A MicroChannel adapter card plugs into any available MicroChannel slot on the planar board. Each adapter card has four serial link sockets. Each socket connects to a 9333 subsystem, and each subsystem contains up to 8 Gb of disk storage (4, 2 Gb drives).

Within each subsystem each hard disk drive is housed in a removable (and lockable) self-docking package. This allows for individual disks to be quickly removed (without powering down) for security storage or replacement purposes.

The serial link disks may be attached to any model 300, 500 or 900 series RISC system.

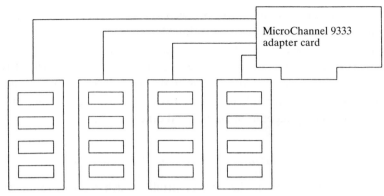

Four deskside 9333 housings, each containing four 2.0 Gb drives
and a deskside subcontroller electronics board

Figure 8.2.   Attaching the serial link disk subsystem.

8.1.2   What is serial link technology?

Serial link technology is simply the conversion of a set of parallel command and
data signals (found on other hard disk interfaces) into a serial data stream. This
is passed onto an 8 Mb per second full duplex interface from the RISC system
controller to the 9333 subsystem. Each link uses only five physical wires,
comprising two differential pairs and an earth wire. The AIX operating system
commands read and write data from system processor memory to the MicroChannel 9333 controller card. The data or control information (e.g. write block, select
drive) is serialized over the link. Each packet contains addressing information
allowing a single serial link to support concurrent operations of the four hard
disks it manages without any of the overheads for selection, disconnection or
reconnection.

The commands sent from the MicroChannel controller conform to the SCSI-2
(see Appendix 2) standard. The SCSI commands are passed from the serial link
to an inboard microprocessor controller card in the 9333 subsystem. From there
the command is passed to the correct serial link disk drive. It is important to
understand that a serial link disk drive does not understand SCSI commands,
though it is the same drive mechanism that is used in the SCSI bus interface
version of the drive.

8.1.3   Designing for performance

Performance of the 9333 easily meets and exceeds previous external disk technologies for the IBM AIX family of computers. A single 32-bit MicroChannel
adapter can control up to 4 disk subsystems, that is 16 drives. Oncard electronics
include an IBM RISC processor, 4 full duplex serial links and 32 DMA channels.
Because the card operates the data streaming mode of the MicroChannel, it can

sustain a bus transfer rate of 28 Mb per second (per adapter) with a burst rate of 80 Mb per second in full MicroChannel BusMaster mode.

The hard disks used are high-performance 3.5 inch drives. The disks have a latency of just 6 ms and an average seek time of only 11 ms. The drives are capable of a maximum burst data transfer rate of 3 Mb per second and, when used in this subsystem, are able to deliver a sustained average transfer rate of 2.1 Mb per second taking account of latency and other delays.

The read-ahead buffer

The 9333 subsystem contains its own controller which receives serialized SCSI commands from the MicroChannel controller in the RISC system. The subsystem controller contains a dedicated processor and over 1 Mb of track cache memory. When data is read from a device, subsequent sectors to those requested are stored in a read-ahead buffer. Subsequent sequential reads that request data can usually be satisfied by returning data from this cache (a cache hit), cache data being transferred at an average rate of 7.7 Mb per second (over three times the speed of the hard disk).

If a cache hit occurs as a result of a read ahead, the subsystem controller automatically initiates a further device read ahead command to repopulate the cache.

Back-to-back reads and writes

Reads and writes for a contiguous set of blocks are aggregated wherever possible. For example in Fig. 8.3 the multiple reads for sectors 10 to 35 are aggregated into a single read as an *extend order* command and a single acknowledgement is sent back to the MicroChannel controller.

Split reads and writes

The latency of a disk is the average time spent waiting to read or write the requested data. Consider a hypothetical case, where a track on a hard disk contains 36 sectors and a request is made to read sectors 10 to 30. If the disk head is positioned at sector 5 when the request is actioned then reading begins immediately when the disk head passes over sector 10. However, if the disk head is currently over sector 14 then traditional disk subsystems would wait nearly an entire rotation until the head is over sector 10. Using the 9333 subsystem, however, in this example sectors 14 to 30 would be transferred immediately and then in the next revolution sectors 10 to 13.

8.1.4   Reliability

One of the key design goals of the 9333 subsystem was to maximize reliability. This rationale is clearly supported by serial link technology because only five wires (one serial link) are required to support four disk drives. Fewer wires

Back-to-back reads/writes

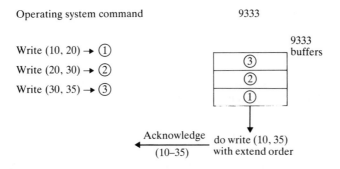

Split reads/writes

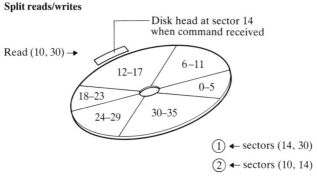

Figure 8.3. Maximizing disk performance.

means much greater reliability, so in a 64-drive configuration there are still a sensible number of interconnects. Disks can be separated from the MicroChannel controller by up to 10 metres.

Information is transmitted on the link in packets of 128 bytes. Should electrical noise corrupt packet information, subsystem controller microcode automatically retransmits packets without having to inform AIX or the user.

Media errors are reduced using error correction code (ECC) technology. Each disk sector is accompanied by a six-byte ECC capable of correcting a double byte error. Additionally, should sector framing information become corrupted, this is automatically interpolated. For example, every sector has a sector preamble containing the sector number. If the sector ID becomes corrupted, because the sector CRC does not match, the controller will read the ID of the previous and next sectors and determine the ID that way.

The subsystem uses *sector reassignment* to provide AIX with a disk that is logically free of errors even though some sectors may be defective. Owing to the nature of their manufacture, hard disk platters are not expected to be always error free. Usually defective sectors are listed at the head of a hard disk or maybe found during low-level formatting. In the 9333 subsystem one per cent of the disk sectors are allocated as spares at manufacture. They are allocated across the surface of the disk so that in operation, should a sector become unrecoverable, only a one sector time loss will occur in accessing the replacement sector.

8.2   The IBM X-station 150

Broadly speaking, an X-station is a graphics terminal that displays X-Windows programs running on a remote computer system.

8.2.1   Running multiple clients

As explained in Chapter 6, X-Windows is a networked windowing system. This enables an X-station to display multiple programs running on one or more RISC systems. In fact, the X-station will display X-Windows programs running on any remote TCP/IP connected system. This includes IBM mainframe computers running VM or MVS and most other UNIX vendors' systems if they use X-Windows.

8.2.2   X-stations vs. PCs vs. diskless workstations

It is important to understand the distinction between an X-station and a diskless workstation. An X-station has a dedicated graphics processor enabling it to run an X-Windows server program. The processor is used to display the program running on a remote machine but not to run that program itself locally.

A diskless workstation is a machine with local computing capabilities, a screen and an operating system. Such a workstation will typically provide an X server display just like an X-station but also has the capability of running programs locally. A diskless workstation is thus more expensive than an X-station.

A PC X-station is a computer, typically running the DOS or OS/2 operating systems. To provide an X server display the PC runs an X server emulator program, either on top of the native operating system or more usually integrating X-Windows into the native windowing system (for example, integrating X-Windows into Microsoft Windows or IBM Operating System/2 Presentation Manager). At first glance this would appear to be an ideal solution, that is, to be able to run from a single PC, Microsoft Windows and X-Windows applications and have them all appear together upon a single screen. However, there are disadvantages:

- Poor graphics performance of PCs
- Limited support for 19 inch or larger screens

as well as advantages:

- Able to access native operating system
- Workstation useful when network down

Table 8.1. Choosing an X-station

	Graphics	Cost	Applications processing
PC X-station	low–med	low–med	No
X-station	med–high	low	No
Diskless workstation	med–high	med	Yes
Workstation	med–high	high	Yes

A dedicated workstation is the ultimate platform to run and display X-Windows programs. It does not have the complex boot requirements of a diskless workstation and can operate standalone. However, a personal workstation requires the personal systems management and maintenance not required for an X-station.

The characteristics of the various machines are summarized in Table 8.1.

8.2.3 When to choose an X-station

An X-station should be chosen for the user whose needs can be satisfied by running remote X-Windows applications. Therefore users who need to transfer data from other AIX or DOS systems on diskette would not be good candidate X-stations users. The case for X-stations over ASCII or AlphaWindows terminals is more difficult to argue, but as the desire to use a graphical end user interface grows and the cost of X-stations falls, the gap is certainly narrowing.

8.2.4 Inside the X-station model 150

X-stations have been in production from IBM since 1990. Improvements and enhancements have been made on IBM's earlier X-stations, models 120 and 130, resulting in model 150. The IBM X-station 150 is IBM's third-generation X-station. The key asset of this X-station is not only performance, but also price and flexibility in areas useful to the customer. In this discusssion the features and facilities of model 150 will be compared against the earlier members of the IBM X-station family to emphasize these points.

Using industry standard benchmarks, the IBM X-station 150 is now a fast performer, functioning at over 115 000 Xstones on the Xbench benchmark test.

Figure 8.4 represents a schematic view of the X-station. The key to the significantly higher performance of the IBM X-station 150 over earlier X-stations is the use of a 64-bit reduced instruction set Motorola 88110 processor combined with a high-performance planar.

System memory between 6 Mb and 22 Mb is used to run the X server. Additional memory is used for backing store and save under areas. Two megabytes of double-ported video memory is used to support displays with a resolution up to 1280 pixels wide, by 1024 pixels high, with each pixel displaying any one of 256 colours.

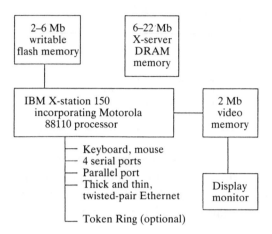

Figure 8.4.   Inside the IBM X-station 150.

8.2.5   X-station networking

The initial IBM X-stations, models 120 and 130, were designed with integrated Ethernet LAN adapters on the planar board with the option to support Token Ring networking via the MicroChannel planar slot. This provided the flexibility of sitting on two LAN networks concurrently. Unfortunately, this option was not cost-effective in terms of design and packaging costs and was rarely used. Therefore the IBM X-station 150 has rationalized networking support. It now provides either Ethernet *or* Token Ring network support. The Ethernet support provided is IEEE 802.3 or Ethernet version 2. The IBM X-station 150 does not have a MicroChannel bus. In addition to the four serial ports, a single Centronics parallel port is provided. AIX supports the IBM X-station using the Xstation Manager program and, using this software, AIX printer and plotter queues may be defined to any RISC systems that are physically rerouted to the printer or plotter connected to the X-station.

8.2.6   Attaching screens

The IBM X-station model 130 provided an impressive list of supported screens, from interlaced PS/2 style screens to large workstation noninterlaced displays. Table 8.2 summarizes the characteristics of many IBM screens. The IBM X-station 150 supports any screen capable of displaying 1024 × 768 pixels or greater operating in a noninterlaced display mode.[1]

---

[1] Interlaced displays take two passes to draw a screen image. In each pass they fill in every alternate line. For example, scan lines 1, 3, 5, . . . on the first pass, and 2, 4, 6, . . . on the second. This can give rise to more perceived flicker than for noninterlaced displays, hence the preference for the latter.

Table 8.2. IBM graphics screens

Model	Type	Resolution	Noninterlaced
1091–051	16" Colour	1280 × 1024	Y
6091–16	16" Colour	1280 × 1024	Y
6091-19i	19" Colour	1280 × 1024	Y
6091-23	23" Colour	1280 × 1024	Y
8503	12" Greyscale	640 × 480	N
8507	19" Greyscale	1024 × 768	N
8508	19" Greyscale	1280 × 1024	Y
8512	14" Colour	640 × 480	N
8514	16" Colour	1024 × 768	N
8518	12" Colour	640 × 480	N
9515	14" Colour	1024 × 768	N
9517	17" Colour	1024 × 768	Y
9518	14" Colour	640 × 480	N

The reduction in flexibility is to support only those screens useful to the workstation user. The IBM X-station 150 supports large graphics screens only; this results from the (im)practicalities of using a 640 × 480 pixel screen under X-Windows which is so small as to be quite frustrating. The support for only noninterlaced displays is also in line with the move to comply with the ISO 9241 ergonomic standard.

8.2.7 Booting the IBM X-station 150

When the IBM X-station 150 is powered on for the first time, it does not know its Internet address for TCP/IP communications, nor the address of the machine from where a login window will be displayed. Yet it needs both these items to be able to display X-Windows programs. Let us take a closer look at the boot process. It follows this sequence of events:

1 Power on the IBM X-station 150.
2 Execute diagnostics.
3 Request Internet addresses of host and self.
4 Start X-Windows server contained in flash memory.
5 Wait for host to start up log in window.

When the IBM X-station 150 is powered on it executes a power-on self-test (POST) which verifies that all the installed memory (up to 22 Mb) is working correctly.

Next a progress screen appears.[2] This shows the progress of an X-station booting request specified by the TCP/IP protocol BOOTP. BOOTP enables the X-station to determine the primary host's network address, its own network

---

[2] The IBM X-station 150 can also operate over a dedicated serial line using the Serial Line Interface Protocol (SLIP).

address and the gateway address if any. On second and subsequent boots the X-station knows the host network Internet number because it is saved in flash memory. If this fails, or if this is the first ever X-station boot, then a broadcast BOOTP will be attempted again. Now the X-station knows the Internet address of the host it can communicate with it using the TCP/IP networking support stored in flash memory.

Also stored in flash memory is the X server. The IBM X-station 150 is the first IBM X-station to store the X server locally in this manner. Models 120 and 130 had used a version of the TCP/IP trivial file transfer program (*tftp*) stored in a local ROM to retrieve the X server from the AIX host and store it in volatile X-station DRAM memory. However this was not a good idea for the following reasons:

- It precluded customers who did not have AIX from purchasing the X-station since the X-station needed to download the X server to boot.
- Each time the X-station was powered on it had to download the X server again, which was unnecessary.
- At times when large communities of users began to power up their X-stations, perhaps at the beginning of the day, or after a power failure, significant network X server download traffic was created. This could lead to erratic response times for the user which did not create a very favourable impression.

8.2.8   X-Windows display management

When an ASCII, serial port attached terminal is defined, AIX initiates the **getty()** process to look for activity on each terminal port. In the X-Windows world the equivalent program is called *xdm* (X-Windows Display Manager). *xdm* needs to run on at least one AIX system in a network to which the X-station is connected. The objective is for the X-station to receive a login window on its X server screen; this login window is produced from an *xdm* program running on a RISC system and from then on the user is able to log on. The sequence of events is as follows.

For the process to work, at least one AIX system is running the XDM daemon waiting for requests, and the X-station has successfully booted its X server from this or any other AIX server. The X-station sends out a broadcast request to the network using the X display manager control protocol (XDMCP). At this point all interested hosts return a *willing* response. If more than one response is returned, the X-station displays a list of hosts and the user chooses from the list. That host is then sent a *request* packet to indicate that a conversation is desired. *xdm* receives the request packet and needs to send back to the X-station either an *accept* or a *decline* packet. One reason for the latter is that the system may not be able to cope with any new logins. Otherwise, the X-station receives an *accept* packet and in response the X-station sends back a *manage* request. When *xdm* receives the manage request it switches from the XDMCP protocol to the X protocol and attempts to use the Xlib programming call **XOpenDisplay()** to connect to the X-station's X server and open a window, usually with the request to enter a login name and password. The user answers the prompts and thence logs in.

One last point is that normally *xdm* checks that the X-station is alive every couple of seconds by issuing an **XSync()** call to the terminal. Additionally, the X-station sends *keepalive* XDMCP requests to *xdm* to indicate that it has not hung. This enables an AIX host to terminate session programs if an X-station fails.

8.2.9 The AlphaWindows terminal

Positioned midway between a traditional ASCII terminal and an X-station is the AlphaWindows terminal. This terminal enables a user to display up to six character-based sessions running on an AIX host. Like a traditional ASCII terminal it displays character-based sessions and communicates to the RISC system using a serial interface. But like an X-station it supports a colour screen and a mouse, and enables the user to display and interact with multiple terminal sessions. In fact, the AlphaWindows terminal has many components in common with an IBM PS/2, including its IBM PS/2 8518 colour display, its IBM PS/2 keyboard and its two-button IBM PS/2 mouse. Software support for the AlphaWindows terminal is via JSB Multiview Mascot, the product that multiplexes the concurrent terminal sessions and displays them in movable and sizable windows on the terminal screen.

The AlphaWindows terminal is a low-cost alternative to the X-station for users who require concurrent, windowed terminal sessions which are character-based only.

8.3 IBM diskless workstations

The traditional diskless workstation is a computer without a hard disk drive that loads its operating system from a LAN server computer and has a filesystem on that or another remote server. Other than that it behaves as a typical personal workstation and, using X-Windows, it is able to display local and remote programs. The concept of diskless workstations is not new; Sun Microsystems, the pioneers and leaders in that field, have had diskless workstation technology for years. So why include it in this chapter on new technology?

From an IBM viewpoint, diskless workstation technology is new. Though the concept is well understood, until recently within IBM the idea of the diskless workstation has not been popular. The IBM RISC System/6000 model 220 represents IBM's first diskless AIX workstation, announced in early 1992, about two years after the very first IBM RISC System/6000 announcement.[3] A diskless workstation is, however, a sensible idea. The dedicated RISC system processor gives the user good applications performance, providing the workstation has enough local workstation memory to avoid having to perform paging across the network. As a diskless workstation, all filesystem backup and maintenance is handled by the systems administrator who maintains the IBM RISC System/6000 server. Also, since the workstation has no moving parts (save possibly a cooling fan and the keyboard) it should be very reliable and quiet. The rest of this section describes model 220 in more detail.

Operationally, the IBM RISC System/6000 model 220 can operate in one of three modes:

- As a *workstation* it behaves as a standalone, entry-level computer system. It runs and displays programs locally. It is distinct from the IBM X-station 150 which, although it has two onboard processors, only uses them to display programs running on machines elsewhere in the network.
- As a *diskless workstation* it can behave as a workstation with no disk drive. Boot images, paging space and all filesystems reside on one or more remote servers. Programs run locally and display locally or remotely using X-Windows.
- As a *dataless workstation* it is a machine with both local and remote file systems. The local disk may be used for boot images, paging and some local filesystems, relieving the burden placed on remote server machines. However, a dataless workstation cannot boot without the help of one or more remote servers and is thus not a true workstation.

Model 220 is *the* diskless workstation in the IBM RISC System/6000 family or, if configured with floppy and hard disk drives, an entry-level traditional workstation.

8.3.1   Model 220 hardware specifications

Model 220 represents a significant advance in RISC system technology. It uses the first single-chip implementation of the RISC system POWER architecture which, as we saw in Chapter 4, was based on a three-processor design on three separate chips. This POWER architecture processor is implemented in CMOS technology and runs at a clock rate of 33 MHz. The processor has a combined 8 kb data and instruction cache. In order to produce this single-chip POWER implementation certain other compromises were necessary. For example, certain instruction times are extended: the multiply and add instruction executes in two cycles on this processor, compared with a single cycle for the three-chip

---

[3] IBM has had a range of diskless PC products that can boot IBM DOS or IBM Operating System/2 from a remote server, but not AIX, until now.

processor implementation. As a result of this, model 220 achieves a performance of 16.3 SPECint92 and 26.7 SPECfp92. (See Sec. 16.5.1 for more performance details.)

The planar board includes all of the following components:

- IBM PS/2 keyboard port
- Mouse port
- SCSI disk interface
- Thick Ethernet LAN
- Parallel port
- Two serial ports
- Graphics tablet input port
- NVRAM
- Eight single inline memory module (SIMM) system memory slots
- Video RAM slots
- Video graphics slot
- Two MicroChannel bus slots

Memory is installed in pairs of IBM PS/2, 85 nanosecond memory SIMMs. The choice of this technology allows the customer to expand the default 8 Mb configuration to the maximum of 64 Mb memory inexpensively, using the 8 available SIMM slots. There is room for a single 3.5 inch hard diskette drive and therefore up to a 2 Gb hard disk drive may be installed. In addition, a single 2.88 Mb, 3.5 inch floppy drive can also be accommodated.

The I/O bus is MicroChannel, as with the rest of the RISC system family. However, because of space limitations inside the 16 inch square case, only the smaller IBM PS/2, type 3 cards can be accommodated.

A special slot on the planar board allows the addition of an entry-level graphics card called the *Gt1* that will drive any noninterlaced monitor from 1024 × 768 pixels to 1280 × 1024 pixels in size. The list of attachable screens is therefore a subset shown in Table 8.2 (see page 137). Like the X-stations, models 120 and 130, video RAM may be plugged into the planar board to take the default mono screen output (1 bit per pixel) right up to 8 bits per pixel for a 256 colours per pixel display. The performance of this graphics card is good, being driven directly from the RISC system processor, achieving performance of 50K characters per second, 184K vectors per second. Customers can achieve higher graphics performance by installing a standard Gt3i graphics card in a MicroChannel I/O bus slot.

8.3.2   Model 220 software support

AIX 3.2 or later supports diskless workstations such as the IBM RISC System/ 6000 model 220 or the Sun Sparcstation 2. On a server AIX system is a set of directories under /export called the *shared product object tree* (SPOT), that

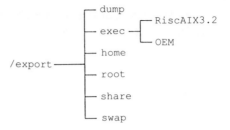

Figure 8.5.   A shared project object tree.

maintains the necessary files for each diskless workstation. A typical SPOT is shown in Fig. 8.5.

The /export directory is used as a common point for systems administrators to set up the directory tree for their diskless clients. A diskless server can export six kinds of disk space:

/export/exec	This contains directories that each client mounts over its own /usr directory. If all diskless work stations are AIX then some simplification of /export/exec is possible. Additional savings can be made if the diskless AIX workstation simply mounts a server's filesystem (for example /usr) instead of allocating a SPOT resource for it.
/export/swap	For a diskless client the paging space is located as a file, named after the client's host name, in /export/ swap on the server.
/export/share	This contains data that can be shared across AIX architectures.
/export/home	This contains user directories grouped by client host names.
/export/root	This contains the root directories for diskless clients. Each diskless workstation must have its own copy of the root file tree, it cannot be shared among machines.
/export/dump	Where a diskless workstation will dump to in the case of an operating system error.

The boot process for model 220 is similar to the IBM X-station 150 except that instead of loading a local X server from flash memory, the RISC system model 220 must use the trivial file transfer program to download a bootfile into its memory. This contains a network bootstrap that then requests the full AIX operating system from an AIX host. Once the workstation boots the AIX kernel it follows a boot process similar to a regular IBM RISC System/6000. That is to say, it configures devices using the *cfgmgr* command, varies on the root volume group, paging space and merges the temporary RAM filesystem with the remote NFS shared client's root directory. The **init** process executes the inittab file and allows the user to log in.

It is worth noting however that the model 220 read-only storage (ROS) which begins the boot process is an enhanced version of that found on the rest of the original RISC system family. Extra code in this ROS allows for diskless boot, and in fact this updated ROS is also present in the later members of the RISC system family, namely models 340 to 375. This means that although models 340 to 375 are normally operated as standalone or network-connected workstations, they may also be configured to use a remote SPOT for dump /usr/share filesystems as necessary. This configuration can save disk space on these worksta- tions and leave more room for applications and user data. It is especially beneficial if users spend most of their time in locally resident applications, not using system applications on the shared /usr.

8.4 Optical disk and digital tape technology

These two peripheral categories complement the high-capacity disk subsystems already described.

8.4.1 *The optical disk*

The CD-ROM player is quite simply an SCSI-connectable CD-ROM drive update. It is available in two forms, internal and external; the latter is shown in Fig. 8.6.

Operationally, a disk is put into a caddy then placed into the player. (The caddy is just like those used in Blaupunkt car CD-ROM players and helps keep the disk protected from surface damage and dust.) The player has a 380 ms access time and a 150 kb per second data transfer rate. This may not seem particularly

Figure 8.6. External CD-ROM drive.

fast when compared to a hard disk (11 ms access time and, say, 2 Mb per second transfer rate), but this is a limitation of CD-ROM media rather than gross inefficiency of the player. The reader may know that some PC CD-ROM players offer average access time figures well below 380 ms; this is achieved via a large on-player cache. The RISC system CD-ROM player has a 64 kb cache and further caches the data read from the CD-ROM in virtual memory.

The capacity of the CD-ROM player is 600 Mb of data. The player's large capacity and moderate access time lends itself to accessing large read-only databases of information. Currently, customers are encouraged to order the SC23-2163 part comprising the InfoExplorer help text (described in more detail in Chapter 7) on a CD-ROM disk.

Aside from data storage there is an audio jack and volume control on the front of the player. IBM does not supply a CD player program; however, it is relatively easy for applications developers to write their own player programs. Of course, when the CD player is set to play audio disks it does not require supervision from the RISC system and thus does not take any processor cycles. Clearly, if the user makes significant use of the CD player then two may have to be installed on a single system.

For customers who require read/write optical storage, IBM markets a 595 Mb rewritable optical disk drive. Available as in an external package only, this drive attaches to the external SCSI port. The drive has an average access time of 70 ms and a data transfer rate of 612 kb per second.

8.4.2   Digital tape products

To meet the needs of backup for high-capacity workstations, IBM offers two types of digital tape storage. The entry-level digital tape drive connects to RISC systems models 200, 300 and 500. It comprises an external digital audio tape (DAT) cartridge tape drive, sometimes called the 4 mm tape drive, since this is the width of the tape in a DAT cartridge. The native data capacity of this system is 2.0 Gb written to the 90 m tape cartridge at 183 kb per second. However, the unit includes inbuilt data compression, increasing the capacity to between 4.0 Gb and 8.0 Gb written at a rate of up to 732 kb per second.

The next drive to consider is the 8 mm digital tape drive. This is an SCSI connected device, available as an internal or external package. The internal device is cheaper, more compact and has the advantage that it cannot be removed unexpectedly. Alternatively, a portable 8 mm tape drive can be connected to any machine in a group of systems for emergency backup and restore. Figure 8.7 shows the external 8 mm drive. This is considered the backup medium of choice. Two models are available, with native data capacities of 2.3 Gb or 5 Gb on a single 8 mm tape cartridge. The latter model includes improved data recording capability (IDRC) data compression hardware in the tape unit, boosting the typical data capacity to between 10 Gb and 20 Gb.

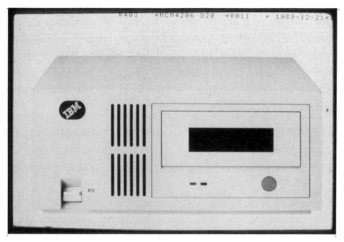

Figure 8.7. The external 8 mm tape drive.

Data is transferred to the tape at 245 kb per second for the 2.3 Gb model which is significantly faster than the entry-level $\frac{1}{4}$ inch tape drives which transfer data at 90 kb per second. The data compression model achieves significantly better, achieving 500 kb per second without compression, or between 1 Mb and 2 Mb per second with compression. The data transfer rate enables users to perform nightly backups of their personal workstation /home user file tree, say of about 500 Mb nightly. The 8 mm cassette is simply a computer-certified version of a standard 8 mm video cassette, as used in a standard 8 mm video camera. This user-friendly medium means that nightly offsite backups can be delegated to the user. An 8 mm drive enables the user to practise sensible backup procedures with convenience.

8.4.3   The datawheel tape library system

An individual workstation user is unlikely to require more than 10 Gb of disk space, but a large RISC system, model 980B for example, serving as a compute server could have attached over 160 Gb of hard disk storage. How can this easily be managed? The answer is to use the LAGO Systems 8 mm tape library system. This is an SCSI-2 attached, 8 mm tape carousel available from IBM, with a 270 Gb tape capacity. The drive comprises an autoloader with a 54-cartridge carousel together with two 5 Gb capacity, 8 mm cartridge tape drives. Two drives are supplied for better performance and availability; if one drive or loader mechanism fails, the other will continue to function without operator intervention. Since the carousel is removable (though it is electronically lockable), the entire 270 Gb storage can easily form part of an organization's centralized offsite backup strategy.

The recommended software to support the tape library is Legato Networker, from Legato Systems. This is a client–server companion product, that is, it supports not only a single machine with hundreds of gigabytes of disk storage, but also backup for a network of AIX workstations, each of which would run the client component of Networker. Individual AIX clients talk to the Networker server (and thence to the LAGO systems tape library) using the remote procedure calls programming interface (see Sec. 12.3.1). Some of the facilities provided by the Networker and LAGO combination include:

1   Automatic media handling—media is automatically labelled by the Networker Jukebox component. User-requested file recovery is automatic if the file is contained within any one of the loaded cartridges or with prompted operator assistance if not.

2   High-performance operation—the concurrent devices component of Networker is optimized for performance without compromising reliability. This component allows both tape mechanisms to perform independently of each other, allowing for simultaneous file recovery and backup. Backups are typically performed significantly faster than when using traditional remote dump utilities, for example the Berkeley UNIX command *rdump*.

3   Convenience—users can take advantage of the tape library's large 270 Gb capacity to make backups for them without the effort of media handling. Alternatively a systems administrator can set up a network backup strategy. For example, daily at midnight, an automatic, incremental network backup of the 100 workstations connected to the network can be performed. When each backup has completed a summary report can be produced and emailed to the systems administrator.

8.5   MicroChannel

The forerunner of the IBM RISC System/6000, the IBM RT PC system, used an IBM PC AT bus for I/O and so it was a small logical step for the IBM RISC System/6000 to use MicroChannel as its I/O bus. MicroChannel is IBM's strategic bus for its current and future micro-, mini- and even low-end mainframe computers. In plain terms, IBM wanted to create a general-purpose bus that was powerful enough to extend beyond the PC marketplace. Using a common bus across a variety of IBM computer systems rationalizes the design effort required to produce cards for these systems, thus reducing cost and time to market. Designers of systems software benefit too, because low-level driver software can be reduced to supporting the same or similar cards in systems with different system processors. Indeed, if some of the driver software is written in a high-level language such as C then it may be possible to share or reuse code across the different platforms. That was the theory, but is MicroChannel up to the task of covering these different environments? Let us take a closer look at MicroChannel and its implementation on the IBM RISC System/6000.

8.5.1   What is a computer bus?

A computer bus is crudely speaking, a printed circuit board called a *backplane*, with a number of connectors upon it. (A more precise definition is a connection highway interconnecting data, control, timing, power or other signals. A bus may be externalized with explicit cards and connectors, or internalized on the tracks of a PCB or even within an IC. Most people use the word 'bus' in the external/ explicit case.) The connectors are called 'bus slots' in IBM terminology since they allow expansion cards to be slotted into the bus. Early bus designs were 'passive' and the backplane contained no electronics. All computer components such as the processor, memory and I/O control circuitry needed to be plugged into bus slots. This was an expensive design because all computers require at least a processor and some memory. Later designs therefore put this and other common features onto the backplane, which was renamed 'motherboard', or to use the IBM term, *planar*. The next stage of development was to move from a passive bus, which is just a series of connectors, to a bus which was *active*. The MicroChannel is an example of an active bus. The planar contains electronics dedicated to regulating and controlling the bus, for example, selecting and deselecting individual cards, or deciding (that is, arbitrating) which card should control the bus.

Overall, deciding how much electronics, if any, to place on the planar, depends on a balance between expandability, functionality, performance and cost. At the most basic level, any bus provides a way for the component parts of a computer to talk to each other. Defining the pins, voltage levels and agreed procedures enables different manufacturers to compete for a customer's business as the supplier of option cards for a given system. Designing a bus well should take into account today's needs and allow for growth tomorrow. The design should include features that make the total operation of the bus-based computer as reliable as a hardwired system.

The IBM RISC System/6000 is a good example of a balanced design, using explicit buses where appropriate, but also integrating electronics on a planar to reduce costs and enhance reliability. The basic design consists of three planars:

1   A CPU planar with the POWER architecture processor(s) on it, base cache and timing circuitry, slots for the optical connection, the engineering support processor connection and explicit memory bus slots. It makes sense to put the memory on the planar rather than to use a general-purpose I/O bus for system memory. This allows a very short and wide connection between the system processor and memory and reduces traffic on the remaining busses. The RISC system memory architecture is arranged so that each 32-bit memory word is represented by 40 bits in real memory. This is composed of 32 bits of data, 7 check bits and 1 spare bit. This, combined with hardware bit remapping, can detect and correct any single bit per word memory error and detect any double bit error.

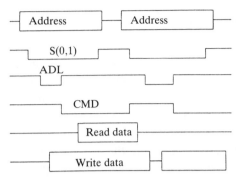

Figure 8.8. MicroChannel basic bus cycle.

2 An I/O planar connecting to the CPU planar, comprising a MicroChannel I/O bus and MicroChannel support circuitry. As the name suggests, the MicroChannel bus is used for I/O devices, so for example a Token Ring or Ethernet LAN card would plug into the MicroChannel bus. An SCSI disk controller card would also plug into the MicroChannel bus.

3 A standard I/O planar connecting to the I/O planar, with support for standard I/O devices, including the parallel printer, diskette drives and serial, tablet, mouse and keyboard ports.

The rest of this discussion concentrates more closely on MicroChannel. Figure 8.8 is a short example of a typical basic bus cycle. The lines represent the activity of various signal lines on a MicroChannel bus. This example shows a basic write cycle where the *master* (the RISC system processor) is writing something into the *slave* memory stored on an option card (let us say, a buffer in the Token Ring adapter card):

1 The master places the 32-bit address on the address bus.
2 Line − S0 is lowered and line − S1 is raised to indicate a memory write cycle.
3 The master lowers − ADL (address decode latch) to indicate that the slave should read the address now.
4 The master places the 32 bits of data on the data bus.
5 The master raises − ADL and lowers − CMD to indicate data signals are available and stable on the bus.
6 The slave reads the data.
7 The master raises − CMD to end the cycle.

This basic data transfer cycle is capable of transmitting (that is, it has a 'bandwidth' of) 20 Mb per second. The IBM RISC System/6000, however, was the first IBM computer system to make use of the 32-bit streaming data transfer cycle, transferring data at 40 Mb per second. For the RISC system models 580, 970 or 980, this has been enhanced to 80 Mb per second. This is usually known as MicroChannel XIO. The data transfer modes are shown in Fig. 8.9.

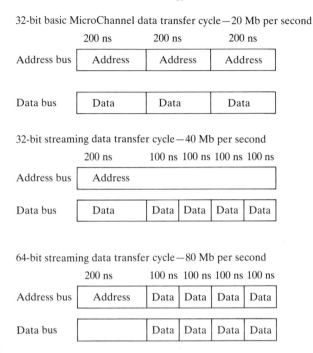

Figure 8.9.   MicroChannel data transfer modes.

8.5.2   Physical bus

Figure 8.10 shows a plan view of the five types of bus connector for MicroChannel.

- 16 bit (58-way edge connector)
- 16 bit with video extension (58-way edge connector and 10 connection video extension)
- 32 bit (89-way edge connector)
- 32 bit with matched memory extension (89-way edge connector plus 4 connections for matched memory)
- 32 bit with video extension (89-way edge connector plus 10 connections for video extension)

The RISC System uses only 32-bit slot connectors since it does not need to support the video or matched memory extensions. (The matched memory extension enables a bus-connected processor to access bus connected memory more quickly. The system processor on the IBM RISC System/6000 stores its programs in system memory on a separate system bus and not on MicroChannel and so does not need matched memory. The video extension is used to attach higher than VGA resolution cards such as XGA-2 to the PS/2 bus. The IBM RISC System/6000 has its own series of graphics adapter cards that do not require this extension.)

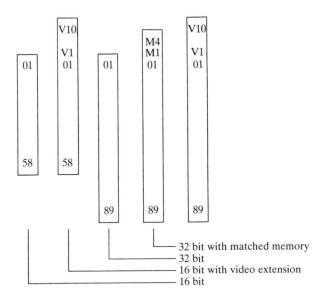

Figure 8.10.   MicroChannel card connectors.

However, RISC systems have slots equipped with extended MicroChannel physical connectors with appropriate signal terminators so that cards equipped with these features can be used at a reduced functional level.

Each connector position has two contacts, to connect with each side of the MicroChannel card. Thus RISC system cards have 178 connections per card.

The entry-level 220 series has two free MicroChannel slots. The desktop model 320H has three free MicroChannel slots, and other 300 series machines four, whereas the 500 series deskside systems have seven free MicroChannel slots. Physically, IBM calls MicroChannel cards for the RISC system type 5. A type 5 card is 13.1 inches in length and 4.825 inches in height. The smaller type 3 cards may be used on the RISC system too, and must be used in model 220. A type 3 card is 11.5 inches in length and 3.475 inches in height. Initially, the Micro-Channel design was to be type 3 only, but a type 3 card's reduced surface area (known as 'real estate') makes it difficult to accommodate the necessary circuitry, so type 5 design was devised.

8.5.3   Active logic

MicroChannel uses an active logic design which means that certain functions are provided on the RISC system I/O board and are available for use by any MicroChannel card. These functions are provided by the I/O channel converter (IOCC).

The IOCC is a single-chip device that links the RISC system branch, FX and FP processors to the MicroChannel. The IOCC provides a set of facilities including:

- The direct memory access controller
- Dynamic random access memory (DRAM) refresh circuitry
- Programmed I/O mapping
- Endian mode conversion

The DMA controller

Direct memory access (DMA) is used in the traditional sense to mean the transfer of data between MicroChannel devices or between MicroChannel and system memory. DMA is accomplished without the utilization or intervention of the system processor or any processors on MicroChannel.

The DMA controller is programmed by an IOCC program comprising a number of tags. Readers familiar with IBM system/370 mainframe technology will realize that these are similar in concept to the channel control words (CCWs) used there. Each tag contains information such as real source and destination addresses, control information and a pointer to the next tag. Tags are sent to the IOCC from the system processor and executed by the DMA controller in the IOCC.

The IOCC is also responsible for allowing the *bus master DMA* facility of MicroChannel. On an IBM PS/2, a transfer from one MicroChannel card to system memory would be performed by MicroChannel cards themselves, that is, the card is mastering the bus. However, in the RISC system, MicroChannel to system memory bus mastering must clearly pass through the IOCC. In order to send from MicroChannel-based memory to system memory (one of the channel status) registers in the IOCC must be set. As data passes through the IOCC, it goes through one of the sixteen 64-byte buffers then across the 8-byte-wide system bus to real system memory. Unlike DMA transfers, bus master transfers are made to system virtual addresses and need to be transferred to real addresses to reach actual system memory. This is achieved by the translation control Words (TCWs) translate table stored in the IOCC.

Programmed I/O

Most computer systems have two distinct address spaces, that is, the system processor can read from and write to, two quite different areas. The first area is regular processor memory used to store programs and data. (Actually some designs create separate address spaces for data and programs. This is not the case for the RISC system.) Secondly, there are ports which, when written to or read from, cause certain actions on a particular card. For example, the 16-terminal serial I/O card may support 16 attached ASCII terminals. Each terminal attaches via an RS232 interface and may be seen by the IBM RISC System/6000 to be three ports: a write data to terminal port, a read data from terminal port and a control/status port. Other typical uses of ports may be, for example, the hardware that interfaces a floppy disk controller or SCSI port. Floppy disk commands to seek to a certain track or read a sector may be sent to particular ports. The controller performs the function sent on the command port then, when it has completed the operation, it generates an interrupt to the RISC system and transfers the data to system memory using DMA.

As discussed in Sec. 4.2, a programmer uses a 32-bit address in an AIX program. The upper four bits of this address represent a segment which is mapped to either an I/O port request or a system memory address. An I/O port request is translated into a request to send/receive information to/from a MicroChannel card. If the I/O request is for an address in the hexadecimal range 0x0000 to 0xFFFF then this is taken to be a request to a MicroChannel port. If the request is above this 64kb area then this is translated into a read from or write to MicroChannel bus memory. This leads to the restriction that MicroChannel cards should not enable any on card ROM or RAM at the lowest 64kb area if they want it to be accessible from the RISC system.

In the current design the system processor may transfer up to 128 bytes of programmed I/O (PIO) at a time. To protect invalid PIO transfers from writing into unauthorized memory, each PIO transfer may only write into system memory between two bound registers previously loaded into the IOCC. If a system memory address outside of these bounds is specified, an error is set in a channel status register within the IOCC.

Endian modes

Like most IBM systems (save the IBM PC) the IBM RISC System/6000 uses the big-endian[4] mode of data storage. However, MicroChannel uses the little-endian mode. This means that the ordering of bytes within a 32-bit word is different:

- In a little-endian format, the least significant digit has the lowest number and is stored at the lowest address.
- In a big-endian format, the most significant digit has the lowest number and is stored at the lowest address.

The IOCC then needs to reorder bytes correctly so that memory transferred between system memory and MicroChannel memory is in the correct format.

8.5.4   The future of MicroChannel

IBM initially designed MicroChannel as much more than a replacement to the system bus in its range of microcomputers. It was to be an active bus structure,

[4] The term 'endian' comes from Jonathan Swift's *Gulliver's Travels*. Gulliver found that in Lilliput inhabitants were required to eat eggs by breaking them at their little ends. Some rebels of course broke eggs at the big ends resulting in civil war.

first destined for volume production in the personal computer market with the IBM PS/2, but also to permeate IBM's other families of computers including minicomputers and workstations. Hence its use in the IBM RISC System/6000 and small mainframe systems, for example the 9370.

However, unlike the introduction of the PC bus, IBM has not had an easy task in the market second time around. When IBM introduced the IBM PC in 1981, the then S100 or IEEE-696 standard bus for microcomputers was soon displaced and rendered obsolete. The market had a new standard, that of the PC-XT bus now often referred to as the ISA (industry standard architecture). When IBM announced the IBM Personal Computer Advanced Technology (AT), again the industry enthusiastically welcomed the new technology. In April 1987, however, when IBM introduced MicroChannel, the vendor marketplace was less enthusiastic because initially IBM wanted royalties for any vendor who designed MicroChannel machines. Other vendors, it seemed, would be quite happy to use MicroChannel but only if it was free. For the most part, PC users have decided to reject the preferred IBM strategy of replacing their typically AT bus system with MicroChannel ones. Non-IBM vendors believed that most customers would select a gradual upgrade strategy, something allowing them to use old cards in a new machine. This attitude led to the development of the extended ISA (EISA) bus architecture which is physically a superset of the AT bus architecture. (In fact, today most PC users are staying firmly put with their ISA architecture machines, rejecting both EISA and MicroChannel.)

The considerations of card reusability are less important to minicomputer users who benefit more from the reduced space, higher performance and reliability factors of MicroChannel over its predecessors than saving a few pounds on card reusability. In fact, MicroChannel is more up-to-date in most respects to many other minicomputer bus architectures having the advantage of being one of the youngest.

The bottom line to all this is that internally the IBM RISC System/6000 design is modular. A deskside system comprises of three related boards as shown in Fig. 8.11:

1   CPU planar—containing processing chips, read only storage, system memory slots, optical slots
2   I/O planar—containing MicroChannel bus slots
3   Standard I/O planar—containing keyboard, mouse, table, serial and parallel circuitry

Should it be necessary to replace the MicroChannel bus structure with another, then from a technology viewpoint this is feasible, although politically this would be a tough decision. In response to customer demand, in late 1992 IBM announced its family of ValuePoint (VP) personal computers based on the ISA and not on the MicroChannel bus, so MicroChannel is by no means the only IBM bus standard for workstation format computers.

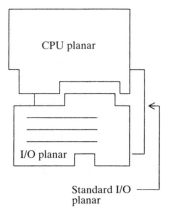

Figure 8.11.   Internal MicroChannel layout.

8.6   Optical networking

Widespread LAN technology currently interconnects IBM RISC System/6000 computers together at 16 megabits per second for Token Ring and 10 megabits per second for Ethernet. Though this is some 10 000 times faster than most asynchronous RS232 communications used in early UNIX systems, network congestion is an increasingly common occurrence. A partial solution is to divide a LAN into smaller independent segments, and even to add multiple LAN routes where appropriate.

A more forward-looking solution would be to use a much faster LAN. Optical LAN technologies can provide an effective LAN data transport speed of hundreds of megabits per second compared to the tens achieved to date.

The IBM RISC System/6000 offers two different optical network facilities: the *serial optical channel converter* (SOCC) and the *fibre distributed data interface* (FDDI).

8.6.1   Serial optical channel converter

All deskside and larger IBM RISC System/6000 computers have at least one SOCC slot. That is to say, the RISC system models 220 and 300 series have no optical slots, the deskside 500 series has one optical channel slot, and the 900 rack series two. Because of the speed of this interface it is necessary to locate optical slots on the CPU planar rather than on the I/O planar where MicroChannel slots are located. This design also ensures that large amounts of optical network traffic do not swamp the bandwidth of the MicroChannel I/O bus. Into each slot plugs an SOCC card. Each card has four unidirectional links (half duplex), with two links working together to form a port. Each port can be connected to a router manufactured by Network Systems.

The Network Systems router can be viewed as an optical junction box interconnecting the SOCC-connected RISC systems. The router also has an FDDI network output and, optionally, an IBM mainframe channel connection. Using the SOCC configuration actual RISC system to RISC system raw transfer rates of 220 megabits per second are possible. Architecturally, speeds of up to 400 megabits per second could be driven through the optical channel.

The software interface that sits on top of the physical SOCC is TCP/IP and provides the full range of TCP/IP commands and programming interfaces available to the user and programmer.

8.6.2   Fibre distributed data interface

The IBM RISC System/6000 can also attach directly to a fibre distributed data interface (FDDI) ring network. A RISC system requires a MicroChannel FDDI interface card to attach the workstation to the 100 megabits per second (125 megabits per second raw speed, with 1 error correction bit per 5 bits of data) optical network. The number of FDDI cards that may be installed in a single RISC system is only limited by the number of free MicroChannel slots available. The software support is by TCP/IP and supports the usual standard facilities such as network file system file-sharing. Also available is a 'dual attach station' (DAS) option for attachment to both a primary and a secondary ring. In the event of failure, the primary ring may be wrapped to the secondary ring for advanced network availability and problem isolation.

8.7   High-performance graphics

As with traditional UNIX computer systems, an IBM RISC System/6000 may be configured with only ASCII terminals, that is to say, with no graphics or LAN-attached graphics screens. These configurations may be appropriate in some low-cost, multiuser configurations; however most users today expect to work in a GUI environment. It is certainly more difficult to cost justify a business solution comprising only ASCII displays in terms of function delivered; such systems today are competing against low-cost PC-based network solutions which can offer multiuser shared business solutions working in a user-friendly GUI environment such as Microsoft Windows or IBM OS/2 Presentation Manager. Therefore IBM provides a comprehensive set of graphics facilities across its family of RISC system products. These divide into three areas:

- Standalone graphics terminals—the IBM X-station 150
- Mid to high-end MicroChannel graphics adapter cards
- A high-end dedicated graphics engine

The first of these options, the IBM X-station 150, has already been discussed in this chapter. Recall that the IBM X-station 150 has built-in graphics hardware integrated onto its planar board. The entry-level IBM RISC System/6000 model 220 provides a dedicated planar slot for the Gt1 graphics processor.

Most IBM RISC System/6000 systems purchased today will use one of four graphics adapter cards: the IBM Gt3i, Gt4, Gt4e or Gt4x. These form a family of increasingly higher performance graphics cards. Note that IBM's strategy is wherever possible to place graphics functionality on a plug-in MicroChannel card. This contrasts with many vendors who offer graphics hardware integrated onto the system planar. IBM's strategy is designed to allow a customer to choose exactly the right graphics hardware for the required application; this also allows upgradability should needs change. This results in slightly slower performance and a higher cost than placing the equivalent technology on the planar, because graphics must be routed via the MicroChannel bus, and this is more expensive due to card rather than planar packaging costs.

The high-end graphics subsystem, the IBM 7235 POWERgraphics Graphics Terminal Option (GTO), is described later in this section.

8.7.1   The Gt3i, Gt4 and Gt4e range of graphics cards

The Gt3i graphics card is implemented as a single MicroChannel card and is the lowest cost adapter in the Gt family. The card drives a screen of up to 1280 × 1024 pixels. Each screen pixel is stored as an 8-bit colour number, allowing for any one of 256 colours to be displayed. The colours are selected from a table of colours, called a *colourmap*. The colourmap is 256 entries long and 24 bits wide: this allows for any pixel on the screen to be one of a set of 256 colours, that set being any of 256 colours from a palette of 16 million (2^{24}). In fact, the Gt3i card contains two hardware colourmaps. One is shared by all running X-Windows applications, the other is free for use by other applications, for example graPHIGS. This means that both types of application can be simultaneously displaying colours without conflict.

The card is also known as a '2D' card because it has hardware support for the following two-dimensional graphics primitives/features:

- Depth cueing and anti-aliasing
- Ellipse, spline and triangle primitives
- Polyhedron and line grid primitives

Like all Gt series cards, the output drives any 60 Hz noninterlaced screen. This card can be used in the IBM RISC System/6000 Model 220 for better graphics performance than the planar in entry graphics Gt1 hardware.

The Gt4 graphics card provides all Gt3i facilities and more. It is packaged as two MicroChannel cards, and uses two Texas Instrument TMS320C30 digital signal processors and a custom high-speed VLSI MicroChannel bus interface chip. The Gt4x provides hardware support for three-dimensional graphics and is thus known as the 3D card. This is achieved using a 24-bit Z buffer. Each bit that is written to the screen has not only a colour but a depth (Z) value. Consider an example where a blue triangle is drawn onto the screen where there is already displayed a yellow square. The blue triangle will only overlay the existing square if the Z values of all the pixels indicate it is in front of the square. The Gt4 also provides a dual-screen frame buffer. Therefore the system processor can be writing to one buffer while the Gt4 card displays the contents of the other. By switching buffers and by the system processor writing to the buffer that is not displayed, animation effects can be achieved. The Gt4 also includes:

- Five hardware colourmaps
- Hardware assist for Gouraud and flat shading and lighting effects

The Gt4 graphics card is suitable for many diverse applications requiring medium-level graphics performance, for example, design automation, architectural design, visualization and animation.

A space saving alternative to the Gt4 card is the Gt4e adapter. This provides the facilities of the Gt4 card, but in a nonupgradable, single-card format. This may be important when adding this adapter to RISC system models with fewer available slots, such as the model 220.

The last member of the Gt family is the Gt4x, which is an extension of the Gt4 cardset. This is implemented as three MicroChannel cards which include an extra six Texas TMS320C30 signal processing chips. The Gt4x has a 24-bit screen frame buffer. This means that each screen pixel can be any of 16 million (2^{24}) colours. Users can start with the Gt4 card and upgrade to the Gt4x card.

8.7.2 The IBM 7235 POWERgraphics GTO

The POWERgraphics Graphics Terminal Option (GTO) is the highest performing graphics adapter available for the RISC system. Physically, the GTO comprises two components, a single MicroChannel card and an externally boxed graphics accelerator. Prior to the availability of the GTO alternative, for customers with high end graphics requirements IBM sold a special version of the IBM RISC System/6000 called the model 730. This was housed in a special wide-bodied deskside case which incorporated not only the traditional planar and I/O boards, but also an additional card cage containing the graphics accelerator. However, this combination was inflexible and the GTO option allows any model of the IBM RISC System/6000 family (save the entry-level workstation model M20) to be upgraded to the very highest graphics performance levels. The GTO is available in two versions, one using an 8 bit colour frame buffer, the second using a 24-bit buffer. This gives the ability to display either 256 or 16.7 million colours simultaneously, for the 8-bit and 24-bit models respectively. The 24-bit GTO also includes a shading processor. This is utilized by writing GL programs which automatically take advantage of features such as constant and smooth colour shading, line removal and depth cueing.

Table 8.3. Graphic card specifications summary

	Gt1x	Gt3i	Gt4e	GTO
10 pixel line (K lines/second)	622	702	708	948
10 × 10 rectangle (K rect/second)	331	275	278	96
Char in 80 char line 6 × 13 (K char/second)	402	95	125	102
77 Hz noninterlaced output[1]	Yes	Yes	Yes	Yes

[1] In this mode cards comply with ISO 9241 Part 3, Ergonomic Display Standard for reduced flicker displays, an important standard in Europe.

Table 8.3 is a summary of the **X11perf** benchmarks for the different graphics cards discussed so far.

8.8   The POWER visualization system

The POWER visualization system is a response to the needs of many professional engineers and scientists, who analyse and extract meaning from vast quantities of raw data. For example, in the oil industry large quantities of geophysical data have traditionally been fed as batch jobs to large mainframe or supercomputer systems. With the POWER visualization system IBM has designed a cluster processor with ANSI standard interfaces to the RISC system and supercomputer, together with a software package called Visualization Data Explorer/6000. Data Explorer contains a number of realization and rendering techniques which can be applied in isolation or in sequence to produce results in real time. There are facilities to add user-coded programming techniques into the system.

The processor technology that forms the heart of the visualization system is a significant advance in technology. Figure 8.12 shows a typical visualization system. The heart of the visualization server is a paired set of 40 Mhz Intel i860 processors. Two, four or eight processing cards can be accommodated in the visualization server. Each processor card contains 4 processors and 16 Mb per processor local memory. The processors also have access to between 128 Mb and 256 Mb of global memory. The server is connected to the IBM RISC system/ 6000 by a MicroChannel visualization video controller card. This has a single bidirectional high-performance parallel interface (HIPPI) port. The output from the controller is an RGB output to a standard RGB colour monitor. This monitor can be displaying regular X-Windows program output as well as visual data and real-time images from the visualization server. The video controller has up to 32 Mb of memory and can display animation of up to 15 frames per second from the visualization server without data compression. Using compression, up to 100 frames per second can be displayed.

Compression is important because instead of the RISC system HIPPI port just connecting with one server, the server can feed several RISC systems, daisy-

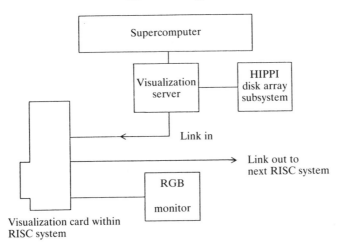

Figure 8.12. The **IBM POWER** visualization system.

chained from a single visualization server. Here the HIPPI output from the server connects to the HIPPI input of the RISC system video controller. The HIPPI output of the video controller is fed to the HIPPI input of the next RISC system until finally the HIPPI out of the last video controller connects back to the visualization server.

The visualization server has two bidirectional HIPPI ports. One is used to connect to the IBM RISC System/6000, the other typically connects to an IBM supercomputer such as an IBM ES/9000 with vector processing facilities. To provide data storage for the visualization server, up to 230 Gb of IBM disk array can be connected.

The hardware technology used in the visualization server is state of the art by most objective standards. The sheer processing power and high-speed interfaces (100 Mb per second for HIPPI, 640 Mb per second memory to processor) enable real-time visualization of problems that could previously take hours on multiuser mainframe computers. Combined with the IBM RISC System/6000 and the Data Explorer/6000 software, it provides a rich environment for professional engineers and scientists to work within.

8.9   Parallel computing

While the current individual IBM RISC System/6000 processors represent a very powerful range of computers, with individual processor ratings of over 100 million floating-point operations per second (MFLOPS) there is still an increasing marketplace for yet more powerful computers, for example:

- Financial institutions and investment houses for arbitrage, stock pricing and opportunity calculations

- Engineers and scientists working with large scale nonlinear modelling, fluid interaction, chemical modelling and various types of simulation
- Corporate clients requiring a centralized computer-intensive resource for general business computing
- Traditional UNIX workstation users requiring vastly more powerful and parallel computational facilities without recourse to traditional mainframes

Many of these types of user will be attracted to IBM's range of POWER-parallel computer systems, systems based upon the IBM RISC System/6000 POWER processor family, systems which run an unmodified version of IBM's AIX.

8.9.1   POWERparallel hardware platforms

The POWERparallel system comprises from eight to sixty-four 62.5 MHz IBM RISC System/6000 rack-mounted processors in up to four physical cabinets. This provides a parallel processing environment with a peak processor performance of up to eight gigaFLOPS for a 64 processor configuration.

By convention, all processor nodes should have the same memory and disk storage as their peers. Hard disk capacity is to 2 Gb per processor. In the case of a 0 Gb disk (that is, diskless) a processor would require an external network-attached disk for environment, temporary and paging storage. A Network Dataserver (see Sec. 12.3.3) is an example of a suitable network-accessible disk subsystem.

The POWERparallel uses a distributed memory architecture to provide memory for each processor. In fact, two memory architectures are commonly used in parallel processing. In a *distributed memory* architecture such as POWERparallel, each processor has its own local memory. That is to say, there is no shared memory. Interprocessor communication is using an interconnection mechanism. This could be via a LAN or via a custom point-to-point link often known as a switch. Distributed memory systems can be easily expanded in terms of numbers of processor nodes.

The alternative architecture uses *shared memory* between multiple processors. This has the advantage of using memory very efficiently, and allows faster interprocessor communication using shared memory. However, complexities (known as 'cache coherency') begin to dominate these designs for anything more than a small set of multiprocessor nodes. This design is best for multiprocessor systems with, say, less than 10 nodes.

Since POWERparallel systems are designed to be scalable to 64 nodes today and more in the future, a distributed memory architecture was chosen. Currently, each processor may have between 64 Mb and 256 Mb of storage.

By definition, parallel processing involves running a task on multiple processors, and, for any nontrivial application, information will be exchanged between concurrently executing program components. Parallel applications are therefore classified into one of two categories:

- Coarse grain—where each parallel application component executes with little or no communication from another.
- Fine grain—where each parallel application component requires frequent data interchange between executing elements.

The optional high-performance switch forms a point-to-point, any processor-to-processor communications path with a 40 Mb per second bandwidth. In most environments where the POWERparallel processor is more than lightly loaded, and running a variety of coarse- and fine-grain applications, a significant number of simultaneous and statistically random interprocessor communications will be required. In such an environment, the POWERparallel system will be most effective when the switch is installed.

POWERparallel has two Ethernet LANs. The first Ethernet is used by each processor for initial system booting, and, if the processor node is diskless, for paging when AIX has loaded. The second Ethernet is used as a TCP/IP connection between workstation users and other individual POWERparallel processors.

Just as a traditional IBM mainframe makes use of a system console, POWERparallel systems require a control workstation. This can be any IBM RISC System/6000 model 220 or larger. A RISC system model 220 is normally included with the POWERparallel order unless customers elect to provide their own systems. The control workstation is required for POWERparallel initialization, hardware monitoring, maintenance and administration. For example, a serial RS232 connection connects the control workstation with each POWERparallel's rack environmental status electronics. An OSF/Motif program displays the information, for example: the status of the individual AC and DC power supplies, the hardware and software logging status, and the per processor keyswitch position (normal, secure or service).

8.9.2 The POWERparallel operating system

Each of the 64 POWERparallel processor nodes runs a full version of AIX version 3.2.3 or later, just like any other regular RISC system. This was a conscious design decision for the POWERparallel series of computers. By utilizing standard AIX, POWERparallel customers have access to the large existing domain of AIX applications and applications development tools. This enables users at the simplest level to take existing binary applications unchanged and run them on the POWERparallel systems and, using the power of X-Windows, to display them through the network on their LAN-connected workstation.

8.9.3   Using POWERparallel

The POWERparallel systems do not represent a series of specialized parallel processing computer systems. Rather, they can be used in a number of ways to appeal to a very wide variety of users.

Cluster-based processing

Using the POWERparallel system support program users can regard the entire POWERparallel system as a single processing resource. This program gives the user a single account on whatever processor they log on to, automatically mounting their normal home directory and file systems as appropriate (see Sec. 12.3). The system support program also takes care to route printing and other service requests transparently to the devices normally used by that user.

In this way a user community can use the POWERparallel system as a centralized yet 'personal' high-performance computing resource.

Batch processing resource

The POWERparallel system may also be used as a high performance batch processor by using the IBM LoadLeveler program. This provides a job-scheduling service to users by means of resources divided into classes. Users submit their program for execution and LoadLeveler matches the users' stated requirements for the jobs against the available resources in the POWERparallel system. Users have the normal batch-scheduling abilities, being able to query, submit, resubmit and otherwise manipulate their current and prospective jobs.

Parallel applications enablement

The easiest way to benefit from parallelized applications on the POWERparallel systems is to purchase POWERparallel enabled applications. Some of the enablers who have announced intentions of support include the Livermore Software Technology Corporation, Fluid Dynamics International and Transvalor. Other products, for example the FORGE 90 product from Applied Parallel Research, provide tools to assist with the parallelization of currently serial programs, in this case written in Fortran.

Parallel development environment

To realize the full potential of the POWERparallel environment, the applications developer should consider developing applications using the AIX Parallel Environment. This product comprises components to develop, debug and analyse parallel applications. Applications are coded in the languages Fortran, C or C + +, making calls to the 'Parallel API'. They are debugged using the parallel debugger *pdbx*, and profiled using modified versions of the UNIX execution profilers *prof* and *gprof*. Applications are monitored using the 'graphical visualization tool'.

Moreover, an applications developer can start a parallel applications development on a single, TCP/IP networked cluster of RISC systems. Then when the applications have been developed sufficiently, move them without effort to run in the POWERparallel environment.

8.9.4 *Typical costs*

To give the reader an idea of the cost of the POWERparallel series of systems I configured several POWERparallel systems using the IBM ECS link. The costs of POWERparallel systems ranged from around £275 000 to £5 million.

9
Systems administration

Sophisticated graphical end user interfaces, distributed file systems and access to several thousand megabytes of data all increase the need for capable systems management tools. So exactly what does an AIX systems administrator do? Here are a few examples:

- Software ordering and installation
- Error logging, tracking and resolution
- Regular backup/restore
- End user administration
- Machine, network configuration and housekeeping
- Performance monitoring

Do any of these concern you? Well, the chances are, yes. In the world of workstations it is now unusual for systems administration and management to be solely the concern of a 'datacentre glasshouse'. It is more likely that the user's workstation is part of a group, which is partly or wholly managed and maintained by staff from within that user group. Any sceptic who believes that any computer system 'just runs' without any maintenance should talk to those individuals who have to administer their personal workstations. They know only too well that systems administration is vitally necessary, although traditionally a time-consuming business.

The design point for AIX therefore was not only ease of use, but also installability and manageability. AIX supplies several tools and techniques to ease the traditional administration tasks. The main systems management interface tool (SMIT) provides a user-friendly, menu-driven interface to all aspects of administration. Accountable software installation, update and maintenance allow the systems administrator to install software components selectively and, most importantly, to track an installation, update and fix history. The rest of this chapter concentrates on these issues.

9.1   Systems management interface tool

On most traditional UNIX systems, systems management tasks are performed with a combination of editing flat ASCII format files and executing one or more UNIX commands at the command line prompt. This method is not very effective, for a number of reasons:

- In a manual process there is little opportunity for automatic checking. If a menu-driven system were in operation it could attempt to provide a degree of checking on the actions of the systems administrator.
- Simple systems administration tasks are mundane and tend to become automated by writing dedicated shell command scripts. If this happens in a large community of machines it can easily result in a varying and inconsistent environment with many nonstandard commands valid only at particular sites.
- In a complex administration task it is all too easy to miss out a step. For example, adding a new device driver into the kernel of the operating system is a procedure which, if bungled, could cause a UNIX system not to reboot at all.

The systems management interface tool (SMIT) is a menu-driven, task-oriented interface to AIX systems management. SMIT is available in two versions: *smitty*, a version suitable for ASCII terminals (and thus also a windowed command session under X-Windows); and *msmit*, which provides an OSF/Motif version of the same program. The two programs are functionally the same, and since the character-based version is considerably faster than the OSF/Motif version it is used by most systems administrators.

SMIT presents complex system management tasks in an organized manner and leads the user through the desired task using a series of menus and dialogs. The principal functions of SMIT are many, the major ones include:

- Installation, update and maintenance of software
- Backup and restore
- Physical and logical filesystem maintenance
- Management of users and groups
- Configuration of hardware devices
- Configuration of communications devices and subsystems
- Printing devices and spooling
- Problem determination and diagnostics
- Management of system environments

Here is an example of an actual SMIT panel arrived at by selecting SMIT, using the up and down cursor keys to traverse the hierarchy of menus: devices, communication devices, Token Ring adapter, adapter, change characteristics of adapter. Finally, the panel of Fig. 9.1 is displayed.

```
                Change/Show Characteristics of a Token Ring Adapter

Type or select values in entry fields.
Press Enter AFTER making all desired changes.

                                          [Entry Fields]
Token Ring Adapter                        tok0
Description                               Token-Ring High-Perfor>
Status                                    Available
Location                                  00-07
RECEIVE DATA TRANSFER OFFSET              [24]                        +#
TRANSMIT queue size                       [20]                        +#
RECEIVE queue size                        [10]                        +#
STATUS BLOCK queue size                   [05]                        +#
RING speed                                4                           +
Receive ATTENTION MAC frame               no                          +
Receive BEACON MAC frame                  no                          +
Enable ALTERNATE TOKEN RING address       no                          +
ALTERNATE TOKEN RING address              [0x]                        +
Apply change to DATABASE only             no                          +


F1=Help             F2=Refresh        F3=Cancel         F4=List
F5=Undo             F6=Command        F7=Edit           F8=Image
F9=Shell            F10=Exit          Enter=Do
```

Figure 9.1.   A sample SMIT panel.

The general format of a panel is a full-screen display, with function keys support as indicated at the bottom of the panel. Certain fields of a dialog need to be completed and a visual key is displayed on the rightmost column of the display to help the user. The symbol meanings are:

[ ]   A field to be completed

<   There is more text to the left of the field

>   There is more text to the right of the displayed field

        A numeric field

X   A hexadecimal field

/   A valid pathname needs to be entered

*   The field needs a value (cannot be left blank)

+   The systems administrator can select from a list of choices which is displayed by pressing the F4 key

These visual guide characters are helpful in guiding the systems administrator in the correct choice of values for a panel. If the systems administrator is at all unsure, help can be requested by pressing the F1 key. Dialog panels normally have context-sensitive help on all fields. This can be found for each panel from

```
                          CONTEXTUAL HELP

Press Enter or Cancel to return to the application.

Indicates the ring speed of the token-ring network to which the adapter
is attached. This attribute must be set to match the speed at which the
network is currently running. An incorrect value can cause the network
to become inoperable. Valid values are 4 for a 4-megabit ring and 16 for
a 16-megabit ring. The default value is 4.

F1=Help            F2=Refresh         F3=Cancel
F8=Image           F10=Exit           Enter=Do
```

Figure 9.2.   A sample SMIT contextual help panel.

```
                     SHOW COMMAND STRING

Press Enter or Cancel to return to the application.

    chdev     -l 'tok0' -a rdto='24' -a xmt_que_size='20'
              -a rec_que_size='10' -a sta_que_size='05' -a ring_speed='4'

F1=Help            F2=Refresh         F3=Cancel
F8=Image           F10=Exit           Enter=Do
```

Figure 9.3.   A sample SMIT command string panel.

the associated byte value index in the hypertext help database. When the F1 key
is pressed the database is searched to the referenced point and the help text is
displayed in a pop-up on the screen. In Fig. 9.1 pressing F1 in the 'RING speed'
question field caused the pop-up of Fig. 9.2 to be displayed.

When the main dialog panel has been completed the systems administrator can
press function key 6 (F6) and display the command that will be executed as a
result of this panel. Figure 9.3 shows the result of our example. Notice how
involved this command is. Clearly, executing it from the command line would be
prone to error. In most cases it is best to execute functions from SMIT. There are
some cases, though, where specific commands can just as usefully be entered
from the command line. The suggested learning procedure for the new systems
administrator is to use SMIT to perform the function and use the F6 key to
display the command prior to execution. Thus SMIT can be used as a learning
tool by the systems administrator, since if the command generated was a simple
one it can be remembered and entered manually in future.

SMIT also keeps a log of the panels selected, command strings executed, date
and time of execution and any output produced. A log of commands executed is
stored in the file smit.script and a log of the menus and dialogs visited
stored in the file smit.log.

SMIT is a program that makes frequent use of the object data manager (described in Sec. 3.2). All SMIT panels are stored in the ODM, and SMIT is written in such a way that option lists and selection values are, whenever possible, dynamically created from entries in the ODM database. For example, a hardware vendor who supplies a printer and associated software printer driver for AIX would include entries in the ODM for various device classes. When using SMIT to add a printer to a particular port the new printer type would automatically be detected and presented as a choice.

So SMIT significantly eases the task of systems management. It is invaluable to users with their own workstations who can now perform systems management quickly and in an error-free manner. This leaves the user more time to perform business-related work.

```
AIX stanza format
/usr/lpp/info:
    dev      = /usr/lpp/info
    vfs      = nfs
    nodename = superx
    mount    = false
    check    = false
    type     = nfs
    options  = ro, bg, soft, intr, retry=6, rsize=32384, wsize=33284

UNIX format
    /usr/lpp/info@superx:/usr/lpp/info:fo:0:0:nfs:bg,soft,nosuid:
```

Figure 9.4.   AIX stanza file formats.

9.1.1   Stanza formats

The initial port of UNIX Systems III to IBM PC/IX changed the format of configuration files within the system. AIX version 2 and AIX version 3 maintain this change of style. Consider Fig. 9.4. This shows the differences between the /etc/filesystems of AIX and the /etc/fstab of another typical UNIX system, in this case, DEC Ultrix.

In most UNIX systems, a configuration file contains a number of lines, each line containing information separated by colons. Colons are field separators and a line feed is a record separator. Under AIX, a stanza format is used, whereby a heading line is followed by one or more lines of the format *tag* = *value*. Blank lines are allowed, as are comments which begin with the (hash) character.

The AIX format has several advantages:

● Each entry is spaced over several lines and is therefore more readable. The colon format becomes difficult to read and edit as the lines get longer.
● Errors in a configuration entry, for example a bad tag name or value, will not affect other tag names or values.
● The tag/value format is forward and backward compatible. This is not true in

Table 9.1. Filesystem locations

Description	AIX	Early UNIX
Root filesystem	/	/
Devices	/dev	/dev
Configuration files	/etc	/etc
Password information	/etc/security	/etc/passwd
Client files	/export	
User file	/home	/u
Programs for booting	/sbin	
Temporary files	/tmp	/tmp
System information	/usr	
System binaries	/usr/bin	/bin /usr/bin
Configuration binaries	/usr/sbin	/etc
BSD conflicting commands	/usr/ucb	
SV conflicting commands	/usr/usg	
Fonts	/usr/lpp/fonts	
Libraries	/usr/lib	/lib /usr/lib
Program products	/usr/lpp/*	
Help	/usr/lpp/info	
X-Windows and samples	/usr/lpp/X11	
Arch. independent files	/usr/share	
Opsys images	/usr/sys/preload	
Variable per machine files	/var	

the traditional colon format. For example, should the meaning of the second field in Fig. 9.4 no longer be the mount point of the filesystem, then old configuration files would be incompatible. When AIX parses the tag/value format it discards unrecognized lines, so preserving compatibility.

9.1.2   The AIX file tree

AIX has a considerably different file tree structure from early UNIX systems. This is to be expected; these changes were made from AIX version 3.2 and later, to provide compatibility with the Open Software Foundation OSF/1 file tree. OSF/1 was changed to be similar to System V release 4.

In previous versions of AIX and other vendors' UNIX there had been much debate as to the correct place for some files to be located. This led to the placement of the same file in different places on different vendor UNIX systems; this was a problem. Another problem was that many different types of file were contained in the same directory. A remote AIX system could not share a server's /etc directory because although many of the files could be shared, this directory contained many machine-specific files, for example /etc/filesystems. The reorganized filesystem avoids these problems and is one unifying standard for the new generation of UNIX systems. See Table 9.1.

The root filesystem

The root file tree contains all of the information that needs to be present for AIX to start. It contains a device directory /dev and empty directories where other filesystems may be mounted,[1] that is /usr, /var and /home. The root file tree is as small as possible and contains information specific to that system. The /sbin directory in the root file tree contains system utilities needed to mount these other filesystems.

The /usr file tree

The /usr file tree contains commands, libraries and data that is not modified by users. Thus the /usr directory is sharable among IBM RISC System/6000 systems. Some notable directories in /usr include:

/usr/bin	Executable commands and scripts
/usr/ccs	C compiler directory
/usr/include	Programmers include .h files
/usr/mbin	Multibyte character set (MBCS) versions of /usr/bin
/usr/sbin	Systems administration commands
/usr/share	Machine independent sharables, e.g. manual pages
/usr/ucb	BSD specific commands with the same names as in /usr/bin

The /var file tree

The machine variable /var file tree contains files that tend to grow. Some of the directories in /var include:

/var/adm	Accounting result files
/var/spool	Print and mail spooler files

9.2   Software installation

IBM pre-installs the base AIX operating system on the hard disks of the IBM RISC system/6000 so that after unpacking a RISC system and cabling it together, AIX comes up just by switching on the RISC system. IBM has recognized that the IBM RISC System/6000 will be sold into environments where detailed UNIX

---

[1] Under UNIX a filesystem containing one or more directories and subdirectories may be mounted over an existing (and usually empty) directory. For an example see Sec. 12.3.1.

expertise may not be available. So can the user really just power up and go, or are there other installation considerations?

The ordered AIX system should arrive with all the necessary boxes and cables. One box contains an installation guide, a service guide, some diagnostics disks, and, for US customers, a VHS video tape. The video tape shows a systems administrator how to unpack, cable and start a system. For European customers (without the benefit of video recorders), the procedure is outlined on paper only.

AIX comes with the base AIX operating system already installed, that is, loaded and configured for a customer's personally ordered and built machine. However, optional components are *pre-loaded* not pre-installed. This means that compressed binary disk files, each containing an image of a licensed program product (such as the C compiler, the SNA services and so forth), are placed on the user's hard disk. This has two consequences. First, the user is required to install some or all of the selected components using SMIT. Secondly, the user will need more disk space during installation, since, as the images are unpacked and installed there will briefly be two copies of a licensed program on the hard disk.

9.2.1   Manually installing software

AIX may be installed in any one of five ways:

- From diskettes
- From tape
- From CD-ROM
- From a network
- From image

Since the AIX base is part pre-installed, is there ever a need to re-install? Of course! There are many environments where re-installation is the norm rather than the exception, for example, vendor application developers, where people use many different computer systems for short periods, the services department of most large AIX financial dealing rooms, where continuously available AIX systems are at a premium. In these and other environments it is important to provide a machine in a known state for a new user. When a workstation changes ownership, it is normally a better policy to clean all software from the machine completely, reformat the hard disks, and re-install the machine at the latest software levels to a known configuration.

Whatever the motivation for re-installation it is a practical process, so how straightforward is an AIX installation?

Diskette installation

Early RISC system customers may have noticed that the AIX operating system may be ordered on diskette. It costs no more (than for tape) and since the operating system is actually pre-installed, the diskettes are only needed for a re-install.

There are a number of drawbacks to this approach. First, a fully loaded AIX system may occupy in excess of 350 Mb of hard disk—over 200 diskettes. Creating, storage, indexing and, very possibly, reliability problems—not to mention the time required to insert all those diskettes—mean that IBM has withdrawn the option to order new AIX systems on diskettes. Even preventative or corrective service is now formally only shipped on tape.

Tape
start

| Bootstrap | Installation and maintenance | Table contents | Base OS | Extensions | COBOL | Ada | NetView | ⋯ |

◄---------------- Base AIX ----------------► ◄-- Optional products ⋯

Figure 9.5. The SIPO tape format.

Tape installation

Tape installation is now the standard method of re-installing AIX. Either two or three 150 Mb tape cartridges or a single 8 mm digital tape cartridge is required.

As supplied, the AIX software tape is supplied in the system installation productivity option (SIPO) format. This name, and indeed the format of the tape, is borrowed from IBM mainframe technology. The format of a SIPO tape is shown in Fig. 9.5.

To re-install AIX, the systems administrator turns the front keyswitch to the service position and reboots the system with the installation media inserted. Because the keyswitch is set to 'service', the RISC system uses the NVRAM service list of devices to boot from, in sequence. Unless changed, this will be from first the diskette drive, then from any attached and powered-up tape drive.

The built-in IPL ROM begins to read the bootstrap header on the tape. AIX then needs to determine what screen will be used for the installation so a message is displayed on all detected and available screens. The screen at which the administrator replies is used for the rest of the installation.

At this point the installer could change the installation settings. However this is not normally necessary, unless a change to the previous configuration is desired. This is because certain vital information, such as the hard disk that contains the root filesystem or the time zone and keyboard language information, will be available from the system NVRAM configuration.

So, after selecting a new install, or one that preserves the user (/home) directories, the base operating system will be installed. Once the base is installed it is then a simple matter to use SMIT with the *install* fastpath to install the remaining products stored on the SIPO tape. Overall, installing a full AIX system with over 300 Mb of licensed programs from $\frac{1}{4}$ inch tape cartridges takes about three hours with one tape change. That is a big improvement over previous AIX systems, and this time is reduced considerably if the installation uses a faster tape drive, for example an 8 mm tape, or installs using a faster processor, for example a RISC system model 970.

Installation from CD-ROM follows a similar process to tape. A better way of installing groups of AIX systems is using network installation.

Network installation

AIX now allows the systems administrator to install machines via a LAN, that is, via either a Token Ring or Ethernet connection to a specially prepared server machine. The server machines must have image files of the basic operating system (BOS) and licensed program products (LPPs) that the systems administrator wishes to install. A special network install user ID is set up on the server called *netinst* and a file `/home/netinst/db/choices` is created containing a list of directories in which the server image files reside.

It is now a simple matter to create some boot diskettes using the *bosboot* command and insert these into the target machine that is to be installed. With the front keyswitch set to the service position the target RISC system will boot from the inserted diskettes and the systems administrator simply selects the installation device as 'network'. Then, after entering the Internet network address of the installation server, the boot program retrieves a list of installable images. In the simplest case, the systems administrator then needs to transfer each of the required images across to the destination system and individually install each one. However, AIX provides a way to automate this procedure. It is possible to build up packages of files on the server in two ways:

- By a named class, where a class consists of a base operating system and named licensed program products. In this case the systems administrator selects the appropriate class, for example *sysprog*, *novice*, *poweruser* etc, and the desired group of programs is transferred.
- By a named client description file. This ties a particular installation set to a given Internet address, making it specific to a particular machine.

Typically, network installations can be further automated by also transferring all the image files and a special class or client package file. The package file is a shell script designed to perform all but the base operating system installation automatically. After installing the base operating system the systems administrator runs the package script file which installs the remaining products and then tailors configuration of the various systems like networking, mail and local hardware terminal configurations. In this way customers with large populations of IBM RISC System/6000 can perform effective and managed installations.

9.2.2   Software update strategy

An IBM RISC System/6000 customer purchases their system from either IBM or an accredited value added reseller (VAR). The VAR may be responsible for the user's software updates. Please bear this in mind in the following explanation.

IBM provides its customers with four classes of software update:

1   The selective fix package
2   The selective enhancement package
3   The preventative maintenance package
4   The selective subsystem update

All these packages are composed of one of more program temporary fixes (PTFs). PTFs are supplied in two forms. First, a single *code PTF* contains program code and data that add function or resolve a problem with AIX. Larger problems use *packaging PTFs*. A packaging PTF contains no code, only a description of the several dependent code PTFs, the order in which they must be applied, and to what software products they must be supplied in order to perform the update successfully. PTFs are built in IBM Advanced Workstations Division, Austin, Texas and distributed by IBM Software Publications Centre (SPC). For example, in Europe this means distribution by IBM Copenhagen.

A *selective fix* is a PTF that will correct a reported AIX problem. If more than a single PTF is required to solve the problem then a packaging PTF will be shipped. A systems administrator receives a selective fix in response to a software problem report to the Systems Support Centre. For example, a systems administrator may find a security-related problem regarding the automatic timed program execution facility named *cron*. The problem is reported and the Systems Support Centre and a customer- and system-specific selective fix tape is generated and sent to the customer. The customer applies the *cron* fix and if it resolves the problem, closes the problem with the Systems Support Centre. The Support Centre then *tclose* or temporarily closes the problem, and if after 30 further days no further problems are reported, the matter is finally laid to rest.

The *selective enhancement package* is a collection of PTFs that, when applied, provides a new function to AIX. For example, in April 1992, a selective enhancement package was released that provided support for the then new 1 Gb capacity 3.5 inch hard disk drives. A selective enhancement may require a selective fix to operate correctly. In this case the required selective fix is included automatically in the enhancement package.

The *selective subsystem update* (SSU) provides an update to an area of AIX, for example printer device drivers, raising that subsystem to the latest fix level. There are about 100 categories of SSU. The SSU was formed in response to customer suggestions that selective fix tapes were beginning to contain too many fixes, and that this could take an excessive amount of time to install. This is because before the SSU concept, the AIX Systems Support Centre could only assume that a customer had installed the most basic level of AIX at level 3.2, so a selective fix tape would contain tens or possibly hundreds of particular fixes to bring the RISC system to the correct software level. The position before SSU was:

$$\text{Required AIX level} = \text{initial AIX level} + \text{selective fix}$$

Each SSU contains a cumulative set of fixes for that entire subsystem. Not only do SSUs install very quickly, they (and PMPs described later) establish a new base level of code known to be resident on that RISC system by IBM. This means that once a SSU is installed, and known to be installed, subsequent fix tapes will be much more compact since:

$$\text{Required AIX level} = \text{Initial AIX level} + \text{PMP level} + \text{SSUs level}$$
$$+ \text{selective fix}$$

The *preventative maintenance package* (PMP) is, as the acronym suggests, a preventative software update. It contains those selective fixes which are used by the majority of AIX customers. It is shipped automatically from the Systems Support Centre and contains those selective fixes that are the highest priority and the most pervasive.

Let us assume that a selective enhancement package arrives from IBM. How easy is software updating? For a single or small set of systems then it is a simple matter to insert the update package tape and use SMIT to update an individual machine. The procedure works well and has many facilities, for example:

- Fixes can be applied in whole or in part. Normally, a selective enhancement package comprises a number of packaging PTFs. Systems administrators are normally instructed to apply just those selective enhancement PTFs or selective fixes that they require. For example, if the enhancement package contains five packaging PTFs, four of which relate to diskless workstations, of which the user has none, then normally only a single PTF is installed.
- The update can automatically extend the size of a filesystem if this falls short of space as the update proceeds.
- The update can be applied but not committed. This means that if the update causes problems it may be selectively backed out.
- The update stores information in the vital product database part of the object data manager; a precise log of what components of AIX were updated and when.

In my experience updates are fast and rarely fail if installed with care.

9.2.3 Enterprise software updates

Medium- and large-scale users of AIX need some way of automatically packaging, distributing and updating software packages installed on their AIX systems. In small or moderately sized companies this may not be an issue, but for a customer with a 100 strong community of RISC systems then updating all systems from, say, AIX 3.2 to AIX 3.3 may be an involved process.

Consider a countrywide supermarket chain installing a new version of their vendor Sybase database in each of 350 stores. How would this be achieved in an orderly, controlled and timely fashion? UNIX certainly has the basic tools to do this. This usually involves the use of the *cron* timer program in each remote system checking to see if any new updates have been applied to a master system. If they have, then they are shipped to relevant network machines using the BSD *rdist* command. Next, a sample update installation script program is sent to each machine to be updated, and, using TCP/IP remote command execution, the scripts are executed, thereby updating all the remote systems.

AIX could also use this method, but customers would be better advised to consider the licensed program AIX Software and Data Distribution/6000 (SoftDist/6000). *SoftDist* allows RISC system users to electronically ship the AIX base operating system, IBM licensed program products, OEM products or indeed any customer packaged software or data. Selected items may be checked for prerequisite software requirements, required filesystem space and requisite operating system level. If these criteria are met, the selected items can be electronically transferred and installed. A SoftDist user typically interacts via a user-friendly Motif graphics program, though an ASCII terminal interface is provided as an alternative.

SoftDist contains three main components as shown in Fig. 9.6:

- Server: the RISC system containing the repository of available packages. This is the focal point for SoftDist and all client transactions are processed on this machine. Logically, therefore, it also contains a list of authorized end users, machines and corresponding authorizations.

A special user ID is known to SoftDist for server administration. The Server administrator is responsible for building and testing distribution packages. Once validated, the server administrator needs to authorize access rights on a per package basis.

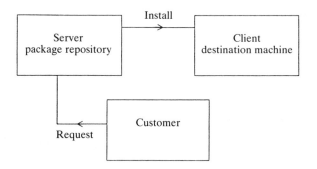

Figure 9.6.   AIX SoftDist/6000 components.

- End user: requests the software distribution.
- Client: the target of selections made by a customer. All selected packages will be installed on the client machine. SoftDist allows a customer to be the owner of several clients and to select a target for each transaction.

In the simplest of scenarios the server and client are the same physical machine; also, the server administrator and customer are users on that same machine.

A more typical scenario is that the server is one physical machine, and one or more client machines exist on an interconnected LAN. The server administrator is typically a user on the server machine; customers are users on client machines. For convenience (for example, you are not at your personal machine) a customer can perform their function from any machine in the administrative domain.

In a large user community SoftDist allows master and subservers. An example may make this clearer. A large AIX development site may be split across several physical sites. It may be convenient to have an individual subserver system at each site. Individual build, research and development and test groups may request software packages from their building subserver. Each subserver receives its packages from a single centrally maintained master server.

9.3 Performance management

Performance management is the art of configuring and tuning the RISC system so that it provides the very best response to the computing load presented to it. This is certainly a nontrivial process even if the RISC system is being used as a single user workstation, since by definition the nature of AIX means that several concurrent tasks will always be executing. Of course the task is made several times more complex if the RISC system is being used in a multiuser and/or real-time environment.

Performance management of course has an obvious prerequisite, that of performance monitoring. UNIX has always provided a traditional set of monitoring tools that have been used as the foundation for performance management of a complex multiuser, multitasking, virtual-memory-oriented computer system. But AIX also provides some monitoring tools that aim to provide more meaningful information, since they are specific to the RISC system and not just UNIX generic tools. For example, tools are provided to help determine bottlenecks in logical as well as physical resources, code bottlenecks, virtual memory and scheduling contention. So, every RISC system running AIX 3.2 or later comes complete with both the traditional and the extended AIX monitoring tools. Clearly, this is an involved area, but we shall consider the fundamental tools available to the systems administrator.

9.3.1   Traditional performance monitoring tools

AIX provides the standard UNIX performance monitoring programs:

gprof   Produces a call graph profile of CPU usage

iostat   Reports CPU and I/O statistics for terminal, disk and other media
            devices

netstat   Displays network traffic

nfsstat   Displays network file system and remote procedure call activity

ps   Lists the processes and their state

sar   Collects, reports and saves systems activity information

timex   Reports in seconds, the elapsed, system and user time for a program

vmstat   Reports on virtual memory usage

9.3.2   AIX performance monitoring tools

In addition to the AIX programming performance tools such as *trace* discussed
in Sec. 5.7, the RISC system comes complete with the following AIX-specific
tools:

svmon   Virtual memory: shows the pages allocated, locked in memory and
            allocated to paging space by program name.

rmss   Reduce memory system simulator: simulates the effect of a reduction
            of real memory to a RISC system without having to go to the
            trouble of physically removing memory cards. While *rmss* is running
            the systems administrator or applications developer can run applica-
            tions as normal in conjunction with other performance monitoring
            tools such as *svmon* or *trace* to determine the effect of the memory
            reduction.

filemon   Filesystem activity monitor: reports filesystem performance statistics
            for logical volume and physical volume input/output. It can also
            report on paging and logical file I/O.

fileplace   File placement display: shows the sequentiality of filesystems.

lvmake   Logical volume creation

lvextend   Logical volume extension

lvedit   Logical volume display

            These three programs allow more precise creation, modification and display of logical volumes under the logical volume manager than via regular AIX commands.

netpmon Network performance monitor: sometimes also known as *netmon*, runs as a background program while applicationsare executed. *netmon* monitors a trace of system events and network activity and performance during the monitored interval.

If, as a workstation owner or systems administrator, you believe there is a performance problem, where do you start? The first point of call is to contact IBM's team of technical professionals and marketing staff. Their systems consultants are skilled in analysing current RISC system configurations, working hand-in-hand with real users and the systems administrator to determine the source of the bottleneck. Is there too much work on too small a machine, is it a resource bottleneck in one area of the system, or perhaps a particular application software bottleneck? The consultant will probably follow an action plan similar to that shown in Fig. 9.7.

As systems administrators become more accomplished they will be able to perform most of these tasks themselves and perform regular capacity planning to spot the trend of resource exhaustion before it becomes critical, or will be able to identify bottlenecks deriving from errant or consuming applications.

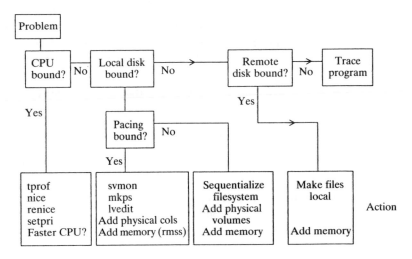

Figure 9.7. Performance monitoring strategy.

10
Storage

The traditional UNIX filesystem suffers from a number of shortcomings that limit its flexibility, reliability and recovery. The AIX journalled filesystem was designed to overcome these while maintaining compatibility with the original filesystem at the user and programmer level.

Many UNIX systems (including IBM's forerunner to the RISC system the IBM RT PC system) divided the systems' hard disks into a number of logical partitions. This had a number of consequences. An individual partition or minidisk could be up to the size of a physical disk, meaning that a single file could not be larger than the physical disk (the case where a single file resides in a single filesystem which is the size of a single physical disk). Moreover, the number of files that could be stored in a minidisk was governed by the number of inodes of filesystem, a parameter permanently set at the filesystem's format time.

In addition, a partition usually needed to be contiguous; if there was space elsewhere on the same physical disk it could not be used. Lastly, filesystem maintenance was via the program *fsck*, a program that was time consuming for systems with large hard disks. Worse still, some users now using UNIX workstations retain the expectation, usually gained by working under DOS on PCs, of being able simply to power off the computer without regard to an orderly shutdown. On early UNIX workstations (for example an IBM PC/XT running PC/IX) this behaviour was normally guaranteed to corrupt the data the user had been working with, and if the user was unlucky, a few critical files of the operating system too.

10.1   Benefits of the journalled filesystem

The journalled filesystem (JFS) is a new class of filesystem available for AIX hard disks (that is, not CD-ROM drives or diskettes). At the highest level of abstraction, this is handled by a logical filesystem, mapping onto a physical filesystem and at a lower level to the logical volume manager (LVM) layer.

Using the LVM layer, a filesystem (for example, a volume mounted onto the directory /home/voltaire) or even a single file (for example, /home/

voltaire/candide) may extend across more than one physical disk up to a maximum file size of 2 Gb. The size of a filesystem is also dynamically expandable, so that as the filesystem becomes full the systems adminstrator can use the *chfs* command to expand the filesystem on the fly,[1] and without even the need for an *unmount*. To enhance reliability, a filesystem may be mirrored, or double mirrored. Mirrored copies may be kept on separate physical disks for extra reliability.

Aside from mirroring, AIX includes a persistent storage manager (PSM) to enhance reliability. Key parts of a filesystem are journalled, for example, changes to directories, or disk block allocation maps. At system startup if *fsck* detects the filesystem is in an inconsistent state, it needs only to replay the journal log of changes to make good the filesystem's integrity. The recovery time in this instance is related to the number of changes made, rather than the filesystem size.

Let us first define some of the terms used by journalled filesystem technology and present the logical view of the old UNIX and new filesystems to the systems administrator, then discover how the JFS is implemented.

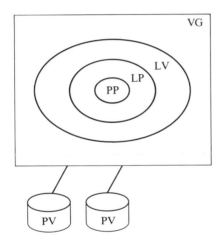

VG   volume group
LV   logical volume
LP   logical partition
PP   physical partition
PV   physical volume

Figure 10.1. AIX filesystem organization.

10.2   Filesystem organization

Refer to Fig.10.1 for a set-like description of the following terms. A *volume group* is a storage pool comprised of up to 32 physical disks. A volume group contains

---

[1] By comparison, a traditional UNIX filesystem cannot be enlarged. The systems administrator would have to bring the system down to maintenance mode, back up the the filesystem to be modified, unmount the filesystem, delete the filesystem, create a new larger partition and filesystem, and finally restore the data and bring back the system to multiuser mode.

up to 256 filesystems. The maximum size of a file within a filesystem is 2 Gb. In AIX terminology a filesystem is a logical volume. (Strictly, a filesystem is always contained in a single logical volume. However, the reverse is not always true. For example, some database packages prefer to work with a raw logical volume, e.g. /dev/lv01, rather than by placing files in a filesystem within a created logical volume.) A *logical volume* is composed of one or more 4 Mb (by default) *logical partitions* (LPs). A logical partition is made from one or more *physical partitions* (PPs). If mirroring is not used, then a LP maps exactly to a single PP; for single mirroring an LP maps to two PPs; for double mirroring an LP to three PPs. Let us look at a simple example to illustrate this.

A user wishes to create a filesystem called /home/sheela and needs it to be 80 Mb in size. Mirroring is not required, that is to say, 20 PPs of 4 Mb will suffice:

```
mklv -y'patra' rootvg 20
```

This creates the logical volume *patra* in the Volume Group *rootvg*.

```
crfs -v jfs -d'patra' -m'/home/sheela' -A'yes' -p'rw'
```

This command shows us that the file will be automounted and the entry in the /etc/filesystems file is now:

```
/home/sheela:
        dev             = /dev/patra
        vfs             = jfs
        log             = /dev/hd8
        mount           = true
        check           = true
        options         = rw
```

To give a user more flexibility the systems administrator has control over not only the degree of mirroring, but also its characteristics. From zero (no mirroring) to double mirroring may be selected. Additionally, the systems administrator may select sequential or parallel write policies. A *sequential write* policy means that a program that issues the write request is suspended until all mirrored writes have completed. For a *parallel write* policy the first successful write will allow the controlling program to continue. When reading from a mirrored system, the first successful read is returned to the program. Therefore, on average, a mirrored filesystem with a parallel write policy is at least as fast as a nonmirrored system for writing and reading data.

10.3   The traditional UNIX physical filesystem

In order to understand and appreciate the JFS it is necessary to understand the

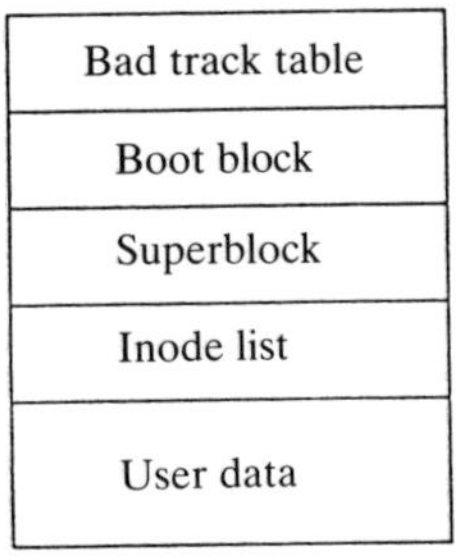

Bad track table
Boot block
Superblock
Inode list
User data

Figure 10.2.   Physical disk format.

traditional UNIX filesystem. Consider a physical hard disk drive. This is divided into a number of components as shown in Fig. 10.2.

The *boot block* occupies the first addressable sector of the disk and contains the bootstrap machine code read into the computer that boots the system. Although only one boot block is required (on the booting disk) typically every UNIX filesystem has a (possibly empty) boot block.

The *superblock* describes the rest of the disk, for example how large the inode area is, how large the filesystem is, etc. The *inode list* follows the superblock. Its size is fixed as listed in superblock and is decided when the filesystem is initially created with the mkfs command. Each inode contains a list of data blocks that make up a file. Data blocks start after the inode list and contain the data in the filesystem, including not only regular user data but also directories.

10.3.1   Inodes in more detail

The inode is the key storage element in the UNIX filesystem. It stores the list of blocks that constitute a file. An inode typically contains the following information:

- entries referring to this file
- Filetype (file, pipe, socket, . . .)
- permission (read, write, execute)
- User ID of owner
- Group ID of owner
- Size of file
- Number of blocks
- Time last modified
- Time last read
- Disk address 01
- Disk address 02
- Disk address 03
- Disk address 04

- Disk address 05
- Disk address 06
- Disk address 07
- Disk address 08
- Disk address 09
- Disk address 10
- Disk address 11
- Disk address 12
- Disk address 13

The disk addresses field is interesting. If a file is nine blocks or smaller (assume a disk blocksize of 4 kb) then these pointers give us the physical disk block addresses that make up the file. So, in this example, to find any file 36 kb or smaller, only a single inode entry need be read. For a file greater than 36 kb in size, the tenth inode pointer references a block containing block pointers as shown in Fig. 10.3.

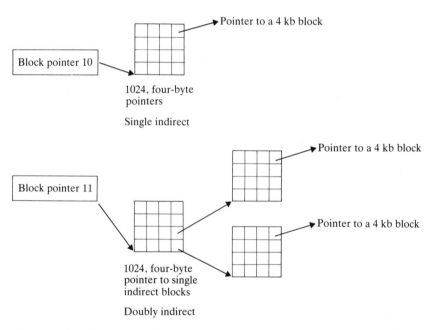

Figure 10.3.   Allocating space to files.

In our example, let us assume that the block addresses are 4 bytes (32 bits) in length. (This means block numbers can range from 0 to $2^{32} - 1$. This gives up to 4 G blocks.) If each block is 4 kb in size then the maximum size of a filesystem is total number of blocks × block size = 4G × 4 kb = 16 000 Gb. Since the block size is 4 kb we have room for 4096/4 = 1024 block pointers. And 1024 block pointers would point to 4096 kb of file. Add to this the original 36 kb to give

4132 kb, so files between 36 kb and upto 4132 kb are referenced by the first nine block pointers in the inode or the blocks pointed to by the pointers contained in the block, pointed to by the tenth block pointer. The tenth block pointer is known as the single indirect block. Files larger than 4132 kb are stored by a pointer stored in the eleventh block pointer. This is an extension known as double indirect. Here the eleventh pointer points to a block, whose contents are the pointers to 1024 single indirect blocks. As before, each indirect block is a block containing 1024 pointers to datablocks. This scheme caters for files up to 36 kb + 4096 kb + 1024 × 4096 kb = approx. 4 Gb. Larger files than this would be handled by the twelfth inode that had a further level of indirection called triple indirect. (Since single file sizes of 4 Gb are pretty academic, triple indirect may not need to be implemented. For example, under AIX the maximum size of a single file is 2 Gb.)

But how does UNIX find a particular file by name? Looking back at the contents of the inode, notice that the filename is missing. Each file has an inode number but this is not stored in the inode itself. Why?

Under UNIX any number of filenames may point to a single physical file. For example /usr/bin/vi and /usr/bin/vedit are both names referring to the *vi* screen editor. (The first thing the editor program does when loaded is detect its name: argv[0] in programming terms. It then changes its behaviour according to the name under which it was invoked.) If the filename was stored in the inode then a link would only be possible by replicating the inode entries for each filename. This would not be very efficient and would be error prone too. Instead, the first inode in the filesystem points to a directory file called root. In this directory there is an association between filenames (or indeed other directories) and inode numbers. So for example, to load /usr/bin/vi UNIX would read the top-level directory to find the inode that corresponded to the directory /usr. From that inode it would read the directory file for /usr to find the inode number for the directory file /usr/bin. Finally, it would read the contents of the /usr/bin directory file to determine the inode number for the *vi* which it would then load.

10.4   The AIX physical filesystem

The hierarchy of the AIX filesystem is as follows:

- Virtual filesystem
- AIX physical filesystem
- Virtual memory management
- Logical volume management
- Physical device driver
- Physical device

The AIX physical filesystem replaces the traditional UNIX physical filesystem described previously. From the hierarchy diagram notice that this layer sits directly below the virtual filesystem that allows for transparent access to local and remote files. For AIX however, the physical filesystem is shown as follows:

- Superblock
- Disk block allocation map
- Inodes
- Inode allocation map
- Inode extensions
- Inode extension allocation map
- Indirect blocks
- Directory segments
- User file segments

The *superblock* is a file located at block zero of the filesystem. The *disk block allocation map* is a bitmap used to indicate the use of each block in the filesystem logical volume. (Remember that a single logical volume may span more than a single physical disk.) This is stored as a file called .diskmap.

The *inodes* are stored in a file called .inodes. This file begins at block two of the filesystem. The *inode allocation map* is a bitmap maintaining the allocation map of inodes. It is stored in a file called .inodexmap. The *inode extensions* area stores additional information such as access control list (ACL) data. This is stored in a file called .inodex. ACLs are described in more detail in Chapter 14. The *inode extension allocation map* is a bitmap describing which entries in the inode extensions area are allocated. This is stored in the file 16.inodexmap.

The *indirect blocks* area stores indirect blocks used for storing files that are too large to be stored in just the inode (that is, files larger than 32 kb). The *directory segments* area stores all files (or objects) by name (Table 10.1). The first page of the root directory is stored at block number three of the filesystem.

The fundamental difference then between the traditional UNIX filesystem and the one outlined is that traditionally fixed sized and fixed placed entities like the inode table are now stored in . (hidden) files at a predefined inode number. (Note that these files cannot be seen using the *ls -a* command.) This means for example that the file .inodes can grow as required, and also that it can be spread out across the physical surface of the disk.

Another difference is the contents of an inode as a file grows from disk inode to single indirect. If a file uses more than eight disk blocks then it becomes single indirect. At this point the first eight block values become the first eight values in the single indirect block. The first eight disk inode values are maintained but not used again unless the file contracts to eight disk blocks or less. When a file grows from single to double indirect the first index of the doubly indirect block is the only singly indexed root. This ensures that if AIX knows the size of the file it need not read the disk inode for files greater than 32 kb to find the logical volume address contained in the inode.

Table 10.1. AIX file systems

Inode #	Description
0	Not allocated
1	Superblock
2	Root directory
3	.inodes
4	.indirect
5	.inodemap
6	.diskmap
7	.inodesx
8	.inodexmap
9	
10	

10.5   The persistent storage manager

The AIX physical filesystem talks through the AIX virtual memory management (VMM) layer to the logical volume manager device driver. For filesystems this means talking to the persistent storage manager (PSM).

10.5.1   Mapped files

AIX does not use the traditional UNIX buffer cache to store frequently used parts of files. In traditional UNIX an application reading or writing data makes a request to the UNIX kernel. For a read, the kernel reads part of the file from disk, then places this information in the kernel buffer cache. It then passes the requested data to the application. On subsequent reads if the part of the file requiring access is still in the buffer cache, a real physical disk read is not required and information is transferred directly from the cache to the application. A similar process operates for disk writes. However, AIX does not need this intermediate buffer and required bytes of files are read or written directly from the disk to the application buffer. This results in an average 300 per cent (or better) improvement in disk-to-application data transfer, clearly a very large performance advantage for AIX. How is this achieved? With AIX, access to files is done via the virtual memory management subsystem (as though a memory access) because all files are mapped.

When a file is opened, the kernel maps the whole file into virtual memory. This means that the file is now represented by an address range in the virtual memory space of the system. When a program issues a **read()** system call to access data from the file, the kernel converts this into a request for one or more pages from virtual memory. If the page is not in real memory then a page fault occurs. At this point the virtual memory management part of the kernel reads the required part of the file into real memory. The page remains resident subject to the normal rules governing reuse of real memory pages.

Currently the default memory page and disk block size is 4 kb.

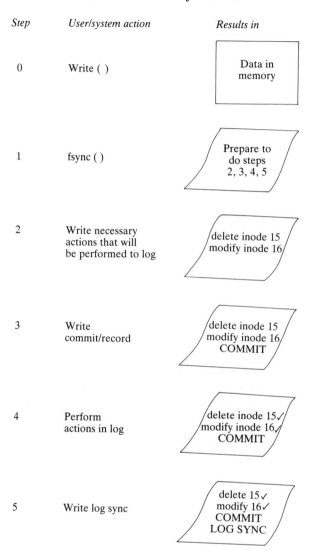

Figure 10.4. Filesystem journalling.

10.5.2 Operation of the PSM

The purpose of the PSM is to pass on data blocks to be written via the logical volume manager. It is also instrumental in logging certain critical filesystem entities that need to be journalled (for example, changes to inodes).

  Each filesystem component, that is directory, file and superblock, is mapped to a persistent storage segment (PSS). A PSS may be journalled, in fact all but the file's data is journalled by the PSM component called the log manager. The log manager writes out changes to a noncached log file. Let us look at this in more detail by referring to Fig. 10.4:

- The user works on a file.
- A background process called **syncd** (synchronization daemon) or a user causes a **fsync()** system call to flush out the changed data blocks from in-memory cache to the logical partitions (LPs) that form the filesystem in the volume group.
- The persistent storage manager instructs the device driver to write out changed and newly allocated data blocks to disk (step 1).
- A record of changes needed to be made to the critical filesystem structures such as the inodes is made in a log (step 2).
- A commit record is written (step 3).
- The actual changes to the inodes, indirect blocks, etc. are made (step 4).
- A log sync record is written to the log, indicating that changes written to the log have been carried out (step 5).

This process is designed to be atomic in nature and the reader should be convinced as to its reliability by considering the possibility of an instantaneous power failure between steps 1 and 4.

Step 1   A power failure after step 1 means that blocks have been written through the logical volume manager but no changes made to the critical filesystem entities (that is, inodes, directories, indirect blocks, . . .). Because of the latter, although the data is lost the filesystem is in a consistent state.

Step 2   When AIX boots it checks the consistency of filesystems. In particular it looks at the log records and rejects any changes that have not been committed. If no log records need be actioned then all data written before the crash would be lost, but again note that the filesystem is still in a consistent form since no critical filesystem entities have been altered.

Step 3   In this case the reboot of the AIX system would detect that a commit record had been written but not completed. AIX simply continues with step 4 and step 5 as outlined below to make good the changes to the filesystem. In this way no data is lost and the filesystem is consistent.

Step 4   Here is the very rare case that the commit actions were carried out but the log sync record not written. In this case AIX attempts to replay the log of changes as in the previous case. However, it will find that all changes have been made, so although the replay will succeed, the net effect will be zero since the filesystem was completely up to date as the system rebooted. In this case, as above, no data is lost and the filesystem is consistent.

Step 5   If a power failure were to occur after step 5 then upon reboot the system would find that there were no changes to be applied since the

last log sync record, so it would be as though the filesystem had shut
down gracefully. No recovery processing needs to be performed.

In all cases a consistent filesystem is maintained but the user may have lost
data. This can only be improved on in the traditional way, that is by using an
uninterruptable power supply.

10.5.3   *Physical volume recovery*

Because a single AIX file or filesystem may extend over one or more physical
disks, and may even be mirrored, special considerations are necessary to
recognize, tolerate and even recover from physical volume failure.

Consider the case where a user volume group is comprised of two physical
volumes. In the volume group there is one filesystem, that is, a single logical
volume. Suppose that when the system starts one of the disks has a catastrophic
failure (for example, a motor burns out). If the filesystem is spread across the
two drives it would be nice to be able to work with files that exist wholly on the
remaining good drive. Now consider the case where we have another two drives
in this volume group. Let us assume that we have a single mirroring set and
again a single drive has a catastrophic failure. This time any file will be contained
in its entirety on physical volumes that are still operational. So while IBM
customer service engineers are bringing the replacement drive parts, users can
continue to work on the mirrored copy of the file. The system is powered down,
the new hard disk motor is installed and upon reboot AIX will automatically
resynchronize the *stale* physical volume.

The key to recovery is the physical structure contained at the head of each
physical volume as shown in Fig. 10.5. Each physical volume contains four areas:

- 128 sector with DASD configuration information
- Area for boot IPL code
- Space for one or more volume group descriptor areas (VGDAs)
- Space for the user's data

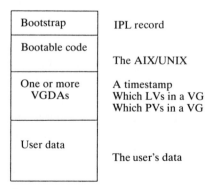

Figure 10.5.   The AIX volume group descriptor area.

The VGDA contains a complete description of how physical partitions of every physical volume in the volume group are allocated. It describes every logical volume, and the physical partitions allocated to every logical partition in that logical volume. Each volume group is bounded by a header and trailer timestamp. If the timestamps match then the volume group is considered valid.

If a physical volume becomes unavailable within a volume group then, for a mirrored disk, accesses to other good physical volumes will continue. On the disks that are still operational, physical partition entries referring to the offline disk are marked as stale. If, as in the previous example, the system is powered down and the disk fixed then, when the system is started, AIX will attempt to vary on this volume group. In this mirrored example the system would:

1 Find the most up-to-date volume group descriptor area in the volume group. (latest matching timestamps).
2 Update that VGDA with the repaired physical volume and the physical partitions contained in it.
3 Overwrite all other VGDA in the volume group with this VGDA.
4 Perform mirroring update to resynchronize the stale physical volume.

Even in the case when mirroring is not used, the VGDA gives the user the ability to work with files wholly contained on operational disks in a volume group, even when some of the disks in that volume group are temporarily unavailable.

10.6   Logical volume manager characteristics

The logical volume manager is in software terms directly above the physical device driver and uses this knowledge to try and optimize its disk operations. The LVM attempts to improve average access time for the filesystems based on parameters set by the systems administrator.

Consider the characteristics of a physical disk drive as shown in Fig. 10.6. The closer a given physical partition is to the centre of a disk platter, the lower the average seek time, assuming a uniform distribution of disk seeks. So it makes sense to position information that will be most frequently accessed close to this centre and to place less frequently used data towards the edge of the physical platter. The LVM defines a number of intraphysical volume allocation policies. These are edge, middle, centre, inner middle and inner edge. When logical volumes are defined within a volume group one of the options is to specify the allocation policy.

Not to be confused with this is the *inter*-physical volume allocation policy. This is a parameter that may be specified when creating a logical volume (instead of taking the default), telling AIX across how many disks to spread the logical volume. Currently choices are maximum or minimum. Clearly, if the destination volume group comprises a single physical volume (physical disk) then this choice is meaningless since the logical volume must be located on a single disk.

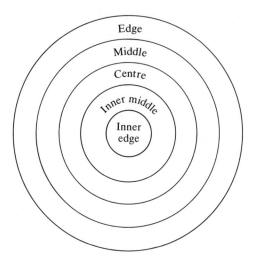

Figure 10.6.   Physical disk layout strategies.

Choosing 'minimum' tells AIX to create the logical volume on as few disks as possible. Maximum lets AIX place the logical volume on as many physical disks as possible. Maximum will be faster because disk writes are spread over more disk arms; however, if any disk becomes unavailable the logical volume is incomplete. It is a traditional tradeoff of speed versus reliability!

11
DOS

Recently I received a flyer announcing 'the extension of DOS into the 21st century'. This was a bit of a surprise because most PC software developers or hardware architects acknowledge that the microcomputer industry can move on from DOS to something better. To UNIX? To OS/2? To NT? There are many more choices, however indications are that the 40 million and growing worldwide base of DOS users will be staying with the DOS with which they have become familiar.

Ironically, in the UNIX world DOS is particularly relevant; over 80 per cent of UNIX sites make significant use of DOS. DOS is here, and here to stay. Certainly, we need to take account of users who want to run both DOS and UNIX programs from a single workstation, or who wish to migrate existing DOS applications to an AIX platform.

IBM has always had a close linkage between its DOS and AIX platforms. Indeed, recall that one of IBM's first UNIX platforms (described in Appendix 1) was the humble IBM PC/XT running PC/IX. When IBM announced its first minicomputer UNIX workstation its name—IBM RT PC system—gave the clue to its linkage with DOS. The IBM RT PC system enabled the workstation user to run DOS and AIX tasks simultaneously. Initially, an IBM PC AT form factor card performed the emulation. This plugged into the I/O bus of the IBM RT PC system. This card contained Intel 80286 and 80287 microprocessors and the necessary timer and interrupt support circuitry to provide a PC on a card. Using a program written by IBM and Microsoft called the PC Simulator, this card then became a hardware implementation of an IBM PC. Since there was no memory on this emulator, system memory from the IBM RT PC system was accessed by special circuitry built into the I/O channel controller (IOCC) on the planar of the IBM RT PC System. Accessing this system memory was a slow process since memory reads and writes had to be translated from real DOS addresses to virtual system memory addresses. Therefore the user had the option of installing regular IBM PC AT bus memory on the I/O bus which brought the real-time performance of the emulation to about that of an 8 MHz IBM PC AT. The user could also install AT graphics adapters and dedicate them to DOS. With all these options installed, a user could simultaneously run a DOS session on a physically separate EGA screen with little or no performance degradation to AIX. Within IBM this configuration was very popular with people who worked with AIX. IBM staff would run DOS-based IBM mainframe terminal emulators to enable connection to the IBM worldwide office system, and on the other native AIX screens run regular character- and graphics-based applications under X-Windows.

As the IBM RT PC system design developed, alternate methods of DOS emulation were considered; the results provided the basis for today's DOS emulation product on the IBM RISC System/6000. AIX software designers no longer considered a hardware emulation card necessary. Why not provide the entire IBM PC emulation in software, giving the user an extra bus slot and obviating the need for the purchase of an additional hardware processor and memory card? It sounds simple, however emulating an entire IBM PC in software was an extremely nontrivial task. It involved not only the fundamental emulation of the Intel 8086 processor in software, but also the emulation of the characteristics of the IBM PC, such as the programmable logic of the communications ports, the memory-mapped screen, the software BIOS and other standard ROMs. Nevertheless, the design went forward, and the first incarnation of the PC simulator (PCSIM), developed by Microsoft and IBM, yielded an entire software emulation of the IBM PC.

11.1   DOS emulation on the IBM RISC System/6000

On the RISC system PCSIM has been enhanced and is supplied as a standard part of AIX. PCSIM allows the RISC system to emulate an IBM PC AT running in real mode. On a performance test of PCSIM on a RISC system model 340, I measured the processor performance at about 30 times the speed of the IBM PC/XT using the Norton SI (systems information) utility. This is certainly faster than a 20 MHz Intel 80386DX based IBM PS/2. IBM officially rates the performance as good as or better than a 10 MHz Intel 80286 based IBM PS/2. As can be seen, in practice I achieved significantly better on what is now certainly only a modest RISC system (33 MHz clock speed) in performance terms. Of course, if multiple PCSIM sessions are started at the same workstation, or if significant AIX tasks are being executed, this performance metric will decrease.

Running DOS on the IBM RISC System/6000 has a number of advantages over running on a real PC hardware platform. First, it enables centralized storage of all DOS and UNIX software. This saves on the maintenance, cost and desk space required for the two separate machines (and associated screens) required to run both operating systems. Furthermore, both the external 5.25 inch and the internal 3.5 inch floppy drives are supported simultaneously by DOS and AIX.

In the process of installing PCSIM, the installation program copies the heart of the DOS kernel from the original licensed DOS disks (that needs to be purchased separately) and creates a bootable DOS kernel in a regular file in the AIX filesystem. This image is used subsequently on invocations of PCSIM.

PCSIM has two ways of emulating DOS hard disk drives. The first method creates a single, perhaps large (say 20 Mb), AIX file and dedicates it to PCSIM. In this example, PCSIM sees the file as a hard disk of size 20 Mb. While running, PCSIM owns the file completely and there is less interaction with the native AIX filesystem improving performance. The second method tells PCSIM that one or more AIX directories are to be mapped to DOS, for example, that the /home/dos/d file be mapped to the D drive. This is significant, because this AIX file can be local on the user's personal workstation or, perhaps, remote. That is to say, the directory could be imported to the local system executing PCSIM from another AIX system using NFS. If the AIX filesystem is used for files, file-sharing between multiple users or PCSIM sessions using files in the native AIX filesystem would be the preferred method of operation, because each PCSIM session can read from and write to the DOS filesystem simultaneously, based on the underlying AIX file permissions set on individual files and directories. If, however, a single AIX file is used to represent an entire DOS disk, second and subsequent users of this disk receive a read-only hard disk. This is the best that can be done in this mode because DOS has control of all the data within the file.

Executable files may be run from either the single file or mapped AIX filesystems.

A helpful modification made by PCSIM is to redirect the printed output sent to the DOS printer port to the AIX spooling subsystem. This can of course even include remote printer queues.

The screen resolution emulated using PCSIM varies according to the available hardware. Full VGA graphics are emulated when running in a window on an X-Windows display (local workstation or remote) or at an X-station. Monochrome display is possible in all other cases, that is:

- On a local console display (full screen)
- On a local console display in a window under AIXwindows
- On a remote X-Windows server display
- On an ASCII terminal display
- On a character-based *telnet* emulation

This flexibility is an advance over many competitive vendors' attempts to offer DOS emulation, which is normally limited to a high-function workstation graphics screen. True, this is the preferred environment but many IBM RISC System/6000 systems are destined for multiuser commercial use and occasional multiuser use of DOS from ASCII terminals.

Overall, PCSIM emulation is complete. For example, some of the simulated facilities include:

- I/O emulation on a per device basis. Devices included are IBM PC AT interrupt control, the interval timer, CMOS RAM, the real-time clock and speaker hardware.
- VGA graphics on local or remote graphics workstations.
- The Intel 8259A interrupt controllers as used on the IBM PC AT.

To test compatibility I made extensive tests using two very demanding DOS programs by running two instances of PCSIM simultaneously on the same X-Windows screen. The first program was Microsoft Flight Simulator. The second was Microsoft Windows (version 3.0 was used because PCSIM supports only real mode processor emulation).

PCSIM includes special drivers to emulate the Microsoft mouse when the mouse pointer enters the PCSIM window (outside the window it is controlled by X-Windows).

11.1.1   Supporting ASCII terminals

As indicated, users connected to the RISC system with only ASCII terminals can also make use of PCSIM. In general, PCSIM allows DOS applications running in monochrome display mode to be mapped onto an ASCII terminal screen. Even 'misbehaving' applications like Lotus 1-2-3 can be mapped to an ASCII terminal gracefully because machine code instructions that write directly to the PC hardware screen buffer are caught, batched and sent as a sequence of cursor positioning and write movements to the attached ASCII terminal.

Since up to 129 DOS sessions can, in principle, be started on each RISC system workstation, it is easy to understand how multiple occasional DOS users connecting via even simple ASCII terminals can run their screen-based, monochrome, character applications. To perform this and other character mapping, PCSIM needs to know the exact characteristics of the user's terminal. IBM supplies configuration files for its own and other popular terminals. Since the IBM PC screen is 25 rows by 80 columns in size, allowance is made to view output on a normal ASCII terminal whose screen size is typically only 24 rows by 80 columns. Allowance has also been made for the fact that while on a PC a program may write to the last character on the bottom line of the screen without side-effects, on an ASCII terminal this causes the whole display to scroll upward one line. A variety of other user-configurable features help users run unmodified DOS applications from an ASCII screen. To help diagnose character translation and configuration file problems, PCSIM is supplied with a *ttylog* utility to monitor all key-sequences passed to PCSIM and all data written from PCSIM to an ASCII terminal screen. By running this command the differences between the actual and expected data streams can be detected and appropriate diagnostic action taken.

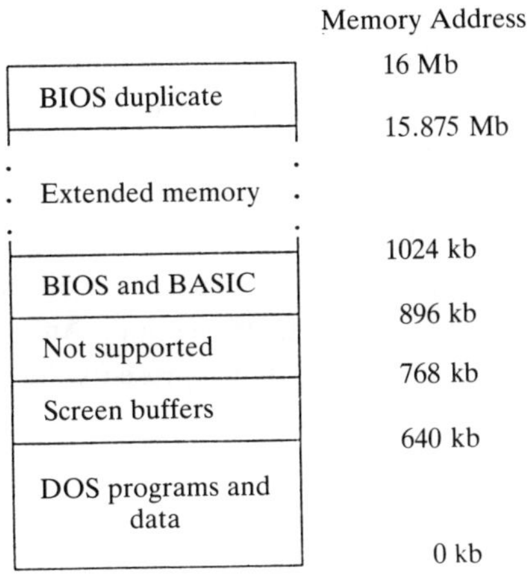

Memory Address

16 Mb

| BIOS duplicate |
15.875 Mb

.   Extended memory   .

1024 kb

| BIOS and BASIC |
896 kb

| Not supported |
768 kb

| Screen buffers |
640 kb

| DOS programs and data |

0 kb

Figure 11.1.   The emulated DOS memory map.

11.1.2   Memory capabilities

For its operation each PCSIM DOS session has allocated to it a 2 Mb virtual memory space. For users new to DOS the real-world PC memory map needs a historical explanation. The emulated DOS memory map is shown in Fig. 11.1.

When the IBM PC was first sold with 64 kb of RAM memory it seemed reasonable to locate the BASIC and low-level operating system read-only memory chips, such as the low-level machine-dependent drivers (called the BIOS), at 896 kb and above in the memory map. Similarly, it seemed that locating the screen buffers in the region 640 kb–768 kb in the memory map would also not present a conflict. After all, the previous standard of microcomputers used the control program for microcomputers (CP/M) operating system, and that had only a 64 kb space for programs—this new architecture allowed for 640 kb. Unfortunately, a ten-fold increase was not enough. Although the IBM PC AT used an Intel 80286 processor capable of addressing 16 Mb of contiguous program, compatibility dictated that the locations of the ROMs and screen buffers between 640 kb and 1 Mb could not be changed. The AT architecture did make one change, which was to shadow the BIOS and BASIC ROMs just below the 16 Mb line; this is of course accounted for by PCSIM.

Although PCSIM emulates the Intel 80286 processor, emulation is for real mode instructions only, that is generating addresses in the range 0 kb–1024 kb. However, there is BIOS support for up to 15 232 kb of extended memory.

11.1.3   DOS to AIX communications

The PCSIM provides a way for DOS and AIX programs to talk to each other. This enables an application developer to create a hybrid application that is part DOS and part AIX. This may be either from choice or, for example, while migrating a DOS application to AIX. Assuming an application is modular, parts of the application can be migrated to AIX, communicating with the remaining parts running under DOS. Of course, since potentially up to 129 separate DOS sessions may be running, there is a way of sending information to a particular DOS session, or for a DOS program to determine which invocation of DOS it is.

Facilities also exist for a DOS program to invoke any AIX system call or to send any known signal to a running AIX program. Conversely, an AIX program can send a software interrupt to a DOS session. An AIX program can also determine the global memory segment that represents the DOS session of interest and, if it has the appropriate authority, read its contents.

11.1.4   Device specific support

PCSIM (unlike AIX PS/2) does not provide any way to support dedicated hardware cards. This is a technical limitation due to the fact that PCSIM does not own the real hardware machine and is simply another program executing under AIX. Responses to interrupts cannot be guaranteed to be within a regular PC timeframe, for example, the PCSIM program may have been paged out to disk because of inactivity.

Conversely, AIX PS/2 uses the hardware virtual mode 86 (VM86) mode of the Intel 80386 (or better) processor required to run AIX PS/2 to enable device-specific cards to be supported. Under AIX PS/2 the exact interrupt level, on-board ROM and RAM of any particular card can be specified in the file called /etc/dosdev. A simulated DOS session can then be started and may own one or more of the specified cards with declared characteristics.

11.1.5   PCSIM performance

As previously indicated, running Norton SI gave me a CPU performance rating equivalent to faster than a 20 MHz powered Intel 80386 computer. However, there are many factors that need to be accessed if one is to contemplate regular use of PCSIM to replace an existing DOS computer. First, the responsiveness of the emulated DOS session. Real DOS computers are very attentive because, while waiting for input, the entire processor's attention is usually polling the keyboard. On the PCSIM emulation, PCSIM competes for RISC processor time with all the other running AIX tasks. A user can obtain the described perform-ance, but running multiple DOS tasks will noticeably degrade the performance of a system. PCSIM attempts to improve overall performance of AIX by sleeping DOS sessions that it detects are idly waiting for input.

Another consideration is the screen update speed. When running in VGA emulation mode on an X-Windows screen, DOS software usually writes directly to the DOS screen buffer located above the 640 kb user area in the DOS memory map. The RISC system needs to catch such a memory write, determine what

VGA screen mode the session is in, then translate this to an X-Windows screen write. This is not a trivial process and the current strategy is to study the state of the DOS screen buffer every 20 milliseconds and make changes to the windowed X-Windows screen at these intervals. Thus the screen update speed is noticeably slower than for a real PC.

Overall, the software emulation of the IBM PC AT is a processor-intensive task. However, I still believe it would be more efficient to have a hardware emulation, but that would require the design of another MicroChannel card that would be useful only to RISC system customers. Under AIX PS/2 the DOS emulation is provided using DOS Merge, a product that was written in conjunction with the Locus Computing Corp. By using the VM86 mode of the native Intel 80386 (or better) processor, almost 100 per cent real DOS performance is achieved without impacting the AIX performance to any noticeable degree.

If a user's need is primarily to run DOS programs with occasional AIX, it may be more appropriate to use a personal PS/2 running AIX PS/2 rather than the IBM RISC System/6000.

11.2   NetWare for AIX

Novell NetWare is the dominant operating system for PC LANs today, with an estimated 60 per cent plus market share. Initially, NetWare was a family of networking products running entirely on Intel-based computers. Today, NetWare can run on dedicated Intel PCs or on UNIX systems which support the Novell Portable NetWare system. The functions provided by NetWare include file- and printer-sharing among different types of computers on a network. Network connectivity is accomplished by client software residing on an individual user's DOS or OS/2 workstation, connecting to one or more NetWare servers. NetWare for AIX interoperates with:

- Other Netware for UNIX workstations
- Native PC Netware workstations
- DOS Windows Netware computers
- OS/2 Netware computers
- LAN attached print servers

AIX NetWare is based on Novell Portable NetWare, version 3.11. It allows the IBM RISC System/6000 to become a NetWare server that is accessible by DOS, DOS Windows or OS/2 NetWare clients attached via either Token Ring or Ethernet LAN networks. The product was ported to AIX by IBM working in conjunction with Novell. It runs as an application on top of the native AIX operating system and uses native AIX facilities to access the AIX server filesystem and perform memory management and scheduling.

11.2.1   NetWare file sharing

The principal use of NetWare is to enable DOS, DOS Windows or OS/2 NetWare clients to share files stored remotely on the AIX NetWare server. The AIX NetWare server stores its data in the AIX filesystem. Files residing on the AIX system appear as DOS or OS/2 files to the NetWare client user. Therefore the NetWare client users can manipulate regular DOS, OS2 or AIX files transparently. Because client files are stored simply as AIX files, centralized backup and management can be performed on a user's files using regular AIX commands. This also allows the NetWare client user to take advantage of the AIX logical volume management capabilities, such as mirroring, for enhanced availability and performance.

11.2.2   Access to AIX applications

AIX character-based applications can be accessed by DOS and DOS Windows NetWare clients using the Novell virtual terminal (NVT) protocol and a compatibile DOS terminal emulator. Using NVT the NetWare client can establish a logon session with the RISC system and log on as a standard user. This allows a user to run standard AIX applications from a remote workstation and take advantage of the superior processing power available at the RISC system. Furthermore, once logged on the user can make use of AIX connectivity facilities, for example, IBM mainframe emulation using the HCON terminal emulator, or file transfer and mail to other AIX users using TCP/IP.

11.2.3   NetWare printing

NetWare print services allow printers to be shared by users throughout the network. To NetWare clients, printing from a network station seems the same as standalone printing. However, NetWare redirects this printer output to a number of destinations, for example, to the AIX printer on the AIX NetWare server, or to a printer on a remote AIX machine (which need not be running NetWare). The output can even be directed to another NetWare client's printer, enabling a small user department with NetWare clients to share the printer resources of a particular NetWare client with a printer.

11.2.4   When to use NetWare

NetWare client and server functions were initially written in Intel assembly language and optimized for PC networks. In a PC-only environment my experience is that a dedicated high-performance IBM PS/2 (for example a 33 MHz Intel 486 model 95) will outperform the AIX NetWare server. The message therefore is that AIX NetWare should not be purchased purely for perceived performance reasons. It is an open, interoperable, network server allowing users to interoperate with the AIX environment. IBM also markets and services the full range of Novell products, so if a regular IBM PS/2 based NetWare server is more appropriate, this can be obtained from IBM.

11.3   AIX access for DOS users

AIX Access for DOS Users (AADU) allows DOS systems to have access to RISC system resources. It provides the same types of facilities as the Novell NetWare client and server technology but is more suitable for customers who do not already have NetWare or who have only small numbers of workstations that need AIX access. The product is comprised of two parts: some server code that is always included with AIX, and some client code that resides on the DOS PC. It includes specific support for IBM PCs, PS/2s and compatibles. AADU is available from IBM or from Locus Corporation, since AADU is simply a licensed version of the Locus PC interface product.

Several services are provided. First, terminal logon to the IBM RISC System/ 6000. AADU users can log on and emulate either a DEC VT100 or DEC VT220 terminal. Secondly, users can view some or all of the AIX filesystem under DOS (depending on the standard AIX file access permissions). For example, users in a workstation group running DOS computers with DOS 3.3 have access to 'virtual' hard disks physically located on the IBM RISC System/6000, in excess of hundreds of megabytes in size. The *on* command allows the AADU user to execute AIX commands while not specifically logged on to AIX, and return the results to the PC screen. Output from an AIX command may even be intermixed and sent to a DOS process. Lastly, AADU enables a DOS user to share AIX printer facilities, remapping a user's local `LPT1:` device and other ports to the AIX spooling subsystem.

Overall, AADU is a low-cost yet flexible package. PCs can connect via Ethernet, Token Ring or even async connections and share the resources of the AIX host and/or run AIX applications using the built-in terminal emulation.

AADU competes in the marketplace with various other TCP/IP based products enabling the same facilities such as AIX logon and disk sharing using NFS. The user should find, however, that AADU provides a higher level of integration in a lower cost and easier to use package.

11.4   TCP/IP for DOS

TCP/IP for DOS is an excellent implementation of TCP/IP for Personal Computers (see Sec. 12.2) using the DOS 3.3 operating system or later. The latest version was part written by the University of Maryland, located in Washington DC. Within the limits of the DOS operating system this product provides many facilities. Users can log on to remote TCP/IP systems using the *telnet* command

and transfer files using *ftp*. Remote command execution and printing are also supported. Disk-sharing to a remote NFS server is made possible using the provided NFS client support. Physical connections to remote systems can be made using Token Ring, Ethernet, IBM PC network or RS232 asynchronous connections. Finally, this product can operate concurrently with Microsoft Windows.

11.5   X-Windows servers for PC users

The whole rationale for providing good DOS support under the IBM RISC System/6000 was so that users did not have to resort to using a separate DOS workstation to perform DOS tasks, fragmenting their data, practically taking up more desk space, and reducing the user's overall productivity. However, some users turn the solution to the interoperability problem around. They see it like this: Why can't I access AIX from my DOS system rather then access DOS from my AIX system? There are a number of cases where the user is not being awkward, but where the facilities provided by the RISC system DOS emulation simply do not meet their needs. Some examples might be the need to run Microsoft Windows 3.1 or later, or the need to run OS/2 full-screen or OS/2 Presentation Manager programs.

In these cases the user's solution would be to make a link from the AIX system to their native DOS or OS/2 PC-based workstation. The usual requirement is normally more than can be satisfied by a straight character-based AIX host emulation. What the user typically requests is the ability to concurrently run DOS Windows or OS/2 Presentation Manager software *and* their X-Windows AIX applications.

The only way to do this, currently, is to run an X-Windows server under the DOS or OS/2 operating system. This is a fairly thankless task made difficult by the following limitations of the PC architecture:

- Users will require significant processing power if they expect to run X-Windows concurrently with other DOS or OS/2 applications. Practically, this means an Intel 80386 based computer or better.
- X-Windows makes great demands of a workstation's graphics hardware. A VGA display and adapter card are acceptable practical minimums. But beware, many specialized 'go faster' PC graphics accelerator cards may not be supported at all nor run to their full potential with the X-Windows server emulator.
- Under DOS, running X-Windows is particularly painful due to the limitations of the DOS operating system. Most X-Windows for DOS emulators run under the Microsoft Windows environment which, in principle, allows the use of Windows and X-Windows applications simultaneously from the same workstation. However, maintaining communications links under Microsoft

Windows is difficult for a software designer and almost inevitably leads to the utilization of a dedicated terminate and stay resident (TSR) program. Recall that X-Windows needs underlying TCP/IP networking software, and the user may find their DOS Windows and X-Windows server enabling TSR programs monopolizing low DOS memory. This will leave a user running Microsoft Windows unable to run anything but Microsoft Windows and X-Windows programs concurrently (that is, no separate DOS programs for example).

Overall I do not recommend running X-Windows on a DOS system. Although acceptable for demonstration purposes, I find response too slow if DOS, Microsoft Windows and X-Windows are mixed together.

X-Windows and IBM Operating System/2 is a usable combination however, since although the underlying hardware may be identical to that used with DOS, OS/2 is able to make significantly better use of resources. Additionally, for some time now, a number of enthusiasts working at IBM in Cambridge, Massachusetts, have been working very hard to produce a workable X-Windows environment under OS/2. The product that IBM retails is called simply TCP/IP for OS/2 and represents one of the most complete and value-for-money packages I have seen. It includes all of the following:

- TCP/IP
- Network driver interface support (NDIS)
- NFS
- X-Windows server
- Kerberos security
- Simple mail transfer, remote printing
- NCS, NFS and both RPC programming interfaces
- Optional source code

The implementation of X-Windows here is usable; I use it daily from my OS/2 systems desk to my AIX systems desk. Since these are in physically different places it is convenient for me to be able to log on to AIX from my OS/2 system or vice versa, share disks from AIX to OS/2 or vice versa, and run the X-Windows program on my OS/2 workstation.

Architecturally, the product makes use of NDIS, which allows this product to co-exist with other network protocol stacks such as SNA or NETBIOS, on the same card. Although the display of X-Windows is still slower than I would like, it is robust and usable.

12
Networking

This chapter deals with UNIX-to-UNIX networking as implemented by AIX. Traditional UNIX systems have always provided a set of utilities that are used to interconnect UNIX computers using asynchronous RS232 connections. This connection is only normally used today (if at all) to connect AIX systems between different sites using slow-speed analogue telephone circuits.

The traditional utilities have been superseded by transmission control protocol/internet protocol (TCP/IP). This allows a set of computers, each running TCP/IP and usually physically connected on a LAN, to send files, mail and log on to each other's systems.

IBM's open systems connectivity strategy is TCP/IP. For example, to enable file transfer between an IBM RISC System/6000 to an HP, Sun or MIPS workstation, the answer would be TCP/IP. It would also be the preferred connectivity product to link AIX systems to IBM's traditional range of computers. Because of this, IBM now sells TCP/IP for DOS, OS/2, AS/400, VM and MVS platforms.

12.1   Basic networking utilities

UNIX-to-UNIX copy program (UUCP), is a facility built into UNIX systems particularly suited for dial-up lines. It can be used to send automated, person-to-person electronic mail messages using wide area networks (WANs), peer-to-peer file transfer and remote execution.

Before the advent of LANs, the basic networking utilities (BNU) were the traditional form of inter UNIX-system communication. This could be between systems separated by only a few metres, or systems in different countries linked by a dial-up telephone line. The physical intermachine connection can be just a three-wire (transmit, receive and ground) RS232, serial port connection. Setting the software component of BNU is, however, nontrivial. In most systems administrators' experience it either works first time, or only works with a lot of effort. AIX UUCP is no better and no worse than other UUCP implementations in the marketplace. With high-speed LAN connections now in existence, BNU is now rarely used; TCP/IP (described shortly) is now the favoured communications mechanism. A strong contributory factor is that it is easier to set up.

AIX offers the HoneyDanBer version of UUCP. The name comes from the three logons of the original authors: Peter Honeyman, David Nowitz and Brian Redman.

BNU has a number of commands intended primarily for users, although systems administrators can use these commands to perform basic systems management in a WAN environment. Some of the important ones are:

ct   Instructs the local computer to call a modem attached to the remote system and then allows a remote user to log on to the local system to perform tasks.

cu   Connects a local user to a remote system and executes commands and transfers files interactively.

uucp   Copies a file from one system to another. *uucp* creates command and data files then calls the *uucico* daemon to do the work.

uulog   Displays the activity log for transfers.

uustat   Displays the status of *uucp* transfers.

AIX has extended the basic BNU communications protocols to accommodate the TCP/IP networking protocol (described shortly). Therefore, with BNU the systems administrator can use the following communications mechanisms:

- Dial-up WAN
- Leased line WAN connection
- Ethernet LAN
- Token Ring LAN
- X.25 WAN

12.2   TCP/IP

Transmission control protocol/internet protocol (TCP/IP) is the primary means of allowing AIX systems to talk to other UNIX systems or to any other vendor system running TCP/IP, for example, talking from an IBM RISC System/6000 to a SUN Sparcstation or to an IBM mainframe running TCP/IP. Physically, participating TCP/IP systems are normally interconnected via a LAN; for the IBM RISC System/6000 this means Ethernet or Token Ring. TCP/IP also provides for point-to-point TCP/IP communications using asynchronous serial lines using alternative protocols.

What really differentiates TCP/IP from many other networking protocols (including IBM's Systems Network Architecture, SNA) is that TCP/IP includes numerous actual programs built on top of the protocols that allow the user to become immediately productive. So for example, once the TCP/IP component of AIX is installed users immediately have available the following TCP/IP commands (and many more not listed):

Network management

ping   Test network communications

netstat   Network traffic statistics

File transfer

ftp   File transfer program

rcp   Remote copy program

Host or peer logon

telnet   Remote logon

rlogin   Remote logon

rexec   Remote execute a program

rsh   Remote shell

talk   Talk to remote users

Mail

sendmail   Set up mail routeing

mail   Send and receive mail

Like ISO Open Systems Interconnect, or IBM's SNA, TCP/IP is a layered protocol. Figure 12.1 shows the breakdown of TCP/IP within AIX. The diagram

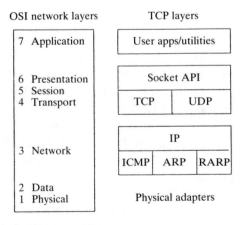

Figure 12.1.   AIX TCP/IP protocol layers.

shows the TCP/IP layers and where they are implemented in AIX and compares this with the Open Systems Interconnect (OSI) protocol networking reference. The highest level of protocols is the *application layer*. This represents the programs supplied as part of AIX TCP/IP, or applications written by users using TCP/IP lower level programming interfaces. Most TCP/IP programs make use of the BSD programming interface called *sockets* since it is simple and efficient.

The *transport layer* protocols are transmission control protocol (TCP) and the user datagram protocol (UDP). TCP provides for the reliable transmission of data. At the lower layers, all transmissions are divided into individual packets. TCP provides both error-checking and the correct sequenced disassembly/reassembly of packets to and from applications. The programs *telnet, simple mail transfer protocol* (SMTP), *ftp* and others use the TCP protocol. UDP provides the delivery of datagrams without guaranteed delivery or ordering. Programs using UDP must implement their own methods of checking for errors and delivery, and if necessary request retransmission. Many TCP/IP application programs use UDP over TCP, because such applications implement application-specific checking and packet-ordering routines which are more efficient than the general-purpose TCP ones. For example, TCP/IP uses UDP for X-Windows and file-sharing with NFS.

The *network layer* protocols are the Internet protocol (IP), Internet control message protocol (ICMP), address resolution protocol (ARP) and reverse address resolution protocol (RARP). IP is responsible for routeing packets between networks and between systems on each network. This includes providing packet processing rules and defining the precise contents of packets. ICMP allows for the exchange of control and error messages between IP layers of individual hosts. ARP is responsible for the translation of Internet addresses to hardware addresses, whereas RARP provides the reverse operation.

12.3 Directory and file sharing

When using workstations it would be very convenient to be able to share files centrally from a server machine to one or more AIX client workstations. In essence this is exactly what the Network File System (NFS) component of AIX enables a user to do. Consider Fig. 12.2. By using NFS, the client workstation

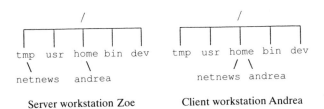

Figure 12.2. Sharing files with NFS.

named Andrea believes that she has /usr, /home/andrea and /home/
netnews directories. User Andrea sitting at her personal workstation can *cd*
(change directory) into these parts of the file tree, execute programs in /home/
andrea or read network news stored in /home/netnews. In practice though,
these directories are not local but shared from the machine Zoe. The NFS server
simply marks these directories as exportable and machine Andrea imports these
directories to user-defined places on her own filesystem. This is done by user
Andrea using the *mount* command to 'mount over' an existing (and usually
blank) directory. (If the local directory that is mounted over contains any files,
these will not be visible to any user while the mount is active. This is the
traditional way of hiding selected files with AIX.)

12.3.1   Network File System

NFS is the *de facto* standard system for sharing of files and directories for
machines in the TCP/IP and thus AIX environment. Developed by Sun
Microsystems, NFS is now implemented by all major suppliers of UNIX-based
systems. In addition, NFS is available on IBM vendor operating system platforms
such as VM and MVS.

NFS is based upon the remote procedure call (RPC) package which allows
communications between programs on different machines and the external data
representation (XDR) standard, which describes protocols that allow dissimilar
machines to exchange data via RPC. NFS itself is merely an application that
defines the NFS protocol on top of RPC and XDR and uses these programming
interfaces to provide its functions. The NFS protocol is used by the daemons and
programs supplied with the NFS product.

NFS on AIX is an implementation of Sun NFS version 4.0 plus. NFS provides
transparent remote access to remote directories in networks of heterogeneous
machines. Remote directories can be mounted over local directories or empty
local directory stubs and accessed by local programs as if they were local
directories. Hosts that mount directories from other machines are called client
hosts; hosts that allow other hosts to mount their directories are called server
hosts. A host may be a server for one or more clients and at the same time be a
client for one or more servers.

Early implementations of NFS used a stateless protocol. This was designed to
avoid complex crash recovery—a client would just send requests until a response
was received.

Today the design of NFS is not stateless, though some of the design points
have been carried over. For example, whenever a service is required (for example,
reading the next bytes from a remote file), the RPC issued from NFS carries all
information required to identify the function requested and the data required.
This goes well with the connectionless UDP which NFS uses for transport
services.

Today's NFS implementation includes a duplicate server cache. This stores the last several hundred, nonidempotent[1] requests made to the server. If a nonidempotent request fails at the server, the server checks its duplicate cache, and if it finds it is a duplicate request, returns a success. For example, if a client sends a request to erase a file, and the server receives the request, acts upon it, and sends a response, but the response gets lost, the client will timeout and retry. The server gets the second request, finds the entry in the cache and returns a success to the client.

NFS depends on the use of virtual filesystem inodes called *vnodes*. Whenever a directory is mounted the inode defining that directory is linked to a vnode, and every request belonging to the mounted directory is directed over the network to the remote host. Before a given directory on a server can be mounted on a client, the filesystem or directory where that directory belongs must be exported by the server. Since AIX uses version 4.0 of NFS, exports are allowed at the directory level. An exported directory allows a client to access that directory and any subdirectories.

One important aspect of the AIX implementation of NFS is support for remote file locking. AIX supports remote locking using the system V function advisory locking functions **lockf()** and **fcntl()**. NFS lock requests go to the NFS lock daemon process *lockd*. They are also registered in the kernel.

12.3.2 File-sharing comparisons

Many other computer architectures allow file resource sharing. Under IBM PC DOS or IBM Operating System/2 a family of client/server file-sharing products are available, for example, the IBM DOS LAN Requestor and the Microsoft or IBM OS/2 LAN server programs. With these products a PC fileserver has one or more hard disks to be shared. This physical disk is divided into a number of *resources* within a named *domain*. A user workstation uses the *net use* command to assign a LAN resource to a local hard disk drive letter. For example, the command *NET USE V: PVCSFILES* would assign the drive V: to the LAN resource named *PVCSFILES* on the client machine. The client machine automatically contacts the network *domain controller* to determine which server provides the *PVCSFILES* resource. On the LAN server the resource *PVCSFILES* may be a subdirectory on an existing drive, for example C: \SOURCES.

IBM mainframes allow resource-sharing too, though usually only between users of the same centralized mainframe. Under the IBM VM CMS operating system a user has a number of named disks from A to Z (rather like IBM PC DOS in fact!). When a user logs on, some of these disks are reserved for the CMS

---

[1] 'Idempotent' means that a request can be executed one or more times without error: for example, asking a server the network address for another user. An example of a nonidempotent request could be erasing a file.

system files, the user also has an A disk where personal files are stored. The system defines other disks by server user names and a command in a user startup profile file links to these files. So for example, the command *cp link internet 191 555 rr* in the user startup file PROFILE EXEC A allocates the server user called *internet*s disk number 191 to be seen by the client as disk number 555, read only. The disk is then accessed as a specified letter, for example, *access 555 i* would allocate the disk number 555 as the I filemode. In this way the mainframe allocates special server user IDs which have disks containing shared information. Users or groups of users then share these disks as required.

Overall, the AIX or UNIX ability to mount directories over waiting stub directories is more flexible than for the DOS or VM equivalents, since the AIX view of the filesystem is a single file tree. Under IBM PC DOS or VM, a user can share disks from remote systems or server users respectively, but ends up with a set of disks from A to Z, each of which contains a complete hierarchical set of files and directories.

12.3.3   The POWER Network Dataserver

Using NFS, many large corporate businesses are evolving large distributed networks of interconnnected PCs and workstations. In the earliest days of distributed computing, the trend was very much for individual workstations to have purely local data, with building, country or corporate-wide network links the exception rather than the rule. Today, while it is recognized that without personal data your workstation may be but a terminal, there are distinct advantages to holding some, or perhaps the majority of a workstation's data in one place. For example:

- Easier file-sharing
- Delegated backup/recovery (from workstation owner to shared data administrator)
- Easier and cheaper upgrading

The POWER Network Dataserver provides such a high-performance, high-capacity file server that individual workstations access using NFS. Up to 144 Gb of disk storage can be provided, communicating via up to 8 Ethernet LANs to up to 200 NFS attached workstations.

Network Dataserver design

Figure 12.3 shows a schematic of the Network Dataserver. It is organized as a set of independently functioning units working together to provide performance with reliability. As Fig. 12.3 indicates, the Dataserver contains:

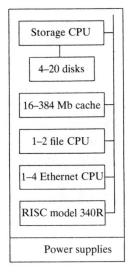

Figure 12.3   The POWER Network Dataserver.

- A storage processor
- A memory cache
- A file processor
- An Ethernet subsystem
- A control processor

Following the dataflow of a typical NFS request from a client workstation will explain how these various parts interact.

Consider a client workstation connected via an Ethernet LAN to the Dataserver. The user of the client workstation makes a request for data contained on the Dataserver. This request enters via the Ethernet subsystem, which performs the NFS protocol processing. Up to four Ethernet subsystems can be contained in a single Dataserver, and, with two Ethernet connections per subsystem, this gives a connectivity to up to eight Ethernet networks. The user's request is analysed by the Ethernet subsystem based on destination address. If it is for the Dataserver the request is passed to the file processor.

The file processor consults the disk cache of up to 384 Mb contained on one or two storage cards. If the data requested is in the cache, the cache location is passed to the Ethernet subsystem which retrieves the data and sends it to client requestor. If the data is not in the cache, the request is passed to the storage processor.

The storage processor can be viewed as a highly parallel disk controller. Each storage processor contains 10 parallel SCSI buses, each of which connects one or two physical SCSI devices. A single Dataserver can contain up to three storage processors. Hence, the maximum disk capacity that can be handled, using 5.25 inch form factor 2.4 Gb hard disks, is 2.4 × 20 × 3 = 144 Gb. (The 2.4 Gb 'drive' is actually two 3.5 inch 1.2 Gb hard disk drives, contained in a close-fitting frame.) To house this maximum amount of disk storage, the main Dataserver cabinet (containing 48 Gb) is attached to a single expansion cabinet containing the remaining 96 Gb. In our example the read request is retrieved from the hard disk and sent to the Ethernet subsystem for transmission to the requesting workstation.

When a client workstation writes data to the Dataserver, the Dataserver should not return a 'successfully written' indication to the client until it has physically stored the information on a reliable medium, for example hard disk (rather than into cache memory). Otherwise, should there be a power failure after a successful write status is returned to the client caller, but before the data has been flushed from cache onto the disk, data loss will occur. In order to combat this problem, the Dataserver can be fitted with up to 1 Mb of nonvolatile memory. Writes to the dataserver are buffered through this memory, and a successful write may be returned to the caller as soon as the data is stored in nonvolatile memory. Subsequent power loss will not lose data as automatic recovery is initiated when power is restored.

Lastly, the functionality of the Dataserver is enhanced by the integrated IBM RISC System/6000 model 340R. This is, as the name suggests, a rack-mounted version of the standard RISC System model 340. It therefore runs a standard, unmodified copy of the AIX operating system. This system is responsible for initializing the Ethernet, file and storage processors at power up. Additionally it is in an ideal position to run supervisory Dataserver care applications such as network administration and storage management.

12.4   High availability

High availability computers improve upon the reliability of regular computers, which fail if just a single subsystem fails, by employing replicated hardware and software. The IBM RISC System/6000 has two high availability offerings that could be classified as mid-range, fault-tolerant solutions. IBM already offers the System/88 nonstop computing system. This strives to achieve 100 per cent continuous availability by duplicating all hardware components. It is discussed in Appendix 1. The solutions provided by AIX cannot compete with System/88 availability, but they cost correspondingly less.

The two high availability options for the IBM RISC System/6000 comprise:

- Highly available NFS (HA/NFS): this is a system that uses two RISC systems to provide access to shared and mirrored disk storage. Should one server computer fail, the backup system will take over the role of server automatically.
- High Availability Cluster Multi-Processing/6000: this is a software and hardware solution that enables a database application to continue, even though perhaps the machine on which it was initially running, fails.

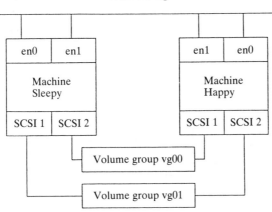

Figure 12.4. Highly available NFS.

12.4.1 Highly available NFS

Figure 12.4 shows a typical configuration. A pair of RISC systems form an NFS server to other RISC systems on the network (not shown). If machine Happy fails then Happy's server disk vg00 will automatically be taken over by the backup machine Sleepy. A single RISC system may be a backup and a server, so after Happy fails, machine Sleepy automatically begins to export the vg00 disk. HA/NFS does not require any special hardware components, only that the participating RISC systems be suitably configured to include redundancy. As such, each RISC system needs two network adapters and two SCSI controller cards controlling two sets of external disks.

Consider a situation where a user executes an application on a local RISC system connected to machines Happy and Sleepy. An application is reading from and writing to files within volume group vg00 served from machine Happy which suddenly fails. Server and backup machines communicate with each other each second using a 'heartbeat' message. After 30 missed heartbeats Happy's backup machine Sleepy becomes suspicious and attempts to contact Happy with the TCP/IP network command *ping*. If it determines that Happy is unavailable, Sleepy reconfigures its second LAN adapter (en1) to the Happy's primary network address and then uses the *varyon* command to access the shared disk volume vg00 of Happy which will then be exported.

12.4.2 High Availability Cluster Multi-Processing/6000

High Availability Cluster Multi-Processing/6000 (HACMP) is an implementation of loosely coupled multiprocessing for the IBM RISC System/6000. This is similar in concept and operation to the DEC VAX Cluster. Figure 12.5 shows a typical HACMP configuration. This shows a number of user workstations

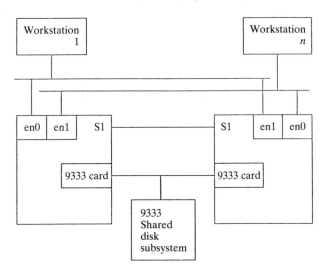

Figure 12.5.   High availability cluster multi-processing.

connected to two IBM RISC System/6000s that form the highly available cluster system. HACMP offers three levels of fault tolerance:

1   Mode 1 is a traditional redundant hardware configuration. Here a standby system stands idle waiting for the server to fail. If the server fails, the standby takes control of the shared resource, then restarts the highly available applications. This configuration is also known as the *hot standby* configuration.
2   Mode 2 is also known as the partitioned workload mode. Here there are two server machines, each running applications. The shared disks are divided between the servers. If one processor fails, the other one takes over the disks and restarts the highly available applications belonging to the failed server.
3   The third mode of operation is the third party takeover configuration. It provides the highest level of fault tolerence. It allows a cluster to balance its workload between two processors and not suffer undue performance degradation should a single processor fail. Here an idle standby system sits between two active server RISC systems. Should either server fail it can take over the failing machine's resources. In an emergency situation it can take over both servers' resources should both servers fail.

The hardware requirements for HACMP are more demanding than for HA/ NFS. Participating workstations must be connected to two separate networks. Each RISC system has two network cards (en0 and en1 in Fig. 12.5). This configuration ensures that any single network card or cable problem cannot provide a single point of failure. The RISC systems in the availability cluster must have at least one point-to-point connection. This must be at least an

RS232 serial line (shown in Fig. 12.5 as S1 to represent the planar serial port), and at best this and a serial optical network connection.

Furthermore the shared filesystem ought to reside on external serial optical link disk drives (the 9333 subsystem) which are connected using a special twin tailed cable ('twin tailed' means a single disk subsystem connects to two RISC systems). The choice of the 9333 enables both systems to concurrently access information on the shared disk, whereas a valid but not as robust configuration using multiple external SCSI disk subsystems shared between two systems would not.

An applications developer may choose to develop highly available applications in the traditional manner, making allowances for the use of shared resources as described in the next section (the cluster lock manager). However, it would be more usual to make use of special multiprocessor versions of vendor data base management systems (DBMSs). Currently supported DBMSs include Oracle, Sybase, Ingres and Informix.

The cluster lock manager

In the simplest scenario (Mode 1, hot standby configuration) the 'shared' external disk is used by at most one RISC system at a time. That is to say, it may be used by different machines, though not concurrently.

For partitioned workload and third-party takeover modes the situation is more complex. The external shared disks may be accessed concurrently by two computer systems. Consider the result of individual applications both writing to the same named file on the external shared disk. The result will be data corruption if both applications write to the same parts of the file.

This problem is resolved using the cluster lock manager (CLM). This provides advisory locking services allowing concurrent applications running on multiple nodes to coordinate the use of shared resources. Advisory locking means that the system does not enforce locking. Instead, applications running on the cluster must cooperate for locking to work. An application wanting to use a shared resource is responsible for first obtaining a lock from the CLM before attempting to access it. To the applications developer CLM provides two programming interfaces, each representing a locking model. They are either the CLM lock model, or the UNIX System V lock model. The two locking models are implemented separately and an application could therefore use both types of locks concurrently. In practice, the CLM locking model is superior in terms of granularity, for example, it provides six increasingly restrictive locking modes, compared with UNIX System V's two. And, since even the Unix System V locking needs to be accessed through an HACMP programming interface, the CLM locking model and associated API would be recommended for applications developers.

12.4.3   UniTree

Designed to operate on either a single RISC system or more usually under workstations running HACMP file system manager, UniTree provides system-transparent, file archival and retrieval facilities. UniTree copies automatically modified user data onto lower level backup media, for example 8 mm digital cassette tape, then recalls the file from the storage device automatically when the file is requested. By specifying site-specific parameters, UniTree provides the user with an apparently unlimited amount of online storage. When used with HACMP UniTree allows concurrent access to shared data in a cluster of processors. In this scenario, UniTree maintains multiple copies of the data, and each processor has access to at least one copy of any file that a user on that client machine may try to access. Whenever data is modified, modifications are propagated automatically through the cluster, either instantaneously or when the copies are made available on line (some time later, in the event of a failure for example).

12.4.4   Other high availability considerations

It is important to realize that simply using either HA/NFS or HACMP will not just magically increase total system availability. Other factors must be considered, for example:

- Separate power supplies to server and backup machines and also to disk subsystems
- The effect of the loss of air conditioning
- Network failure for LAN-connected users
- Switching of ASCII terminals for direct connect users

12.5   Network Computing System

NFS enables a user to share disk resources between computers. Network Computing System (NCS) is oriented to share application services between participating computer systems. NCS is a fundamental building block of the OSF/1 distributed communications environment and as such IBM sees NCS as the preferred method for sharing processor resources between its RISC systems.

12.5.1   NCS users' and administrators' perspectives

Users should not need to know or care that their applications use NCS. Users may of course benefit from the advantages of a distributed application, for example, performance and reliability may be vastly improved. The user may be working from a very small workstation, yet processing vast databases or performing highly numeric-intensive calculations, which an intelligent user can sensibly deduce is more than the capability of the local RISC system. Reliability may be enhanced because if there are several providers of a remote service that is needed (for example high-speed mathematical matrix manipulation) then only a single remote matrix provider machine need be working for the user's application to succeed.

The administrator's perspective is that the NCS environment is significantly more complex than the traditional one. In the NCS environment an application running on a user's workstation may make calls to programs on other machines. This implies that network connections between these machines are available and that the service provider machines are also available. Additionally, two programs (described in the next section) called the local location broker and the global location broker need to be running on other machines in the network. Recall from Sec. 3.1.2 that NCS is one of the subsystem components that is started automatically by the systems resource controller at AIX startup.

12.5.2 The NCS programmer's perspective

An applications developer wishing to create an NCS application divides an application into a main program called a client and a set of remote subroutines that will execute on one or more servers. Calling a remote subroutine is the process of making a remote procedure call (RPC). One of the fundamental concepts of RPC is that RPC functions are called in exactly the same way as local functions. Exactly how is outlined soon, but for example suppose the following C language is defined:

```
Boolean invert ( int input [5] [5], int output [5] [5]);
```

That is to say, a function called **invert()** with two array parameters each of which is a 5 × 5 array, one of input values, the other of output values. The powerful facility that RPC provides is that there is practically no difference in the programmer's code for calling a remote subroutine as for calling a local subroutine. For example:

```
result = invert (              inarray, outarray);
/*local call*/
result = invert ( handle, inarray, outarray);
/*RPC call*/
```

This is important because existing applications can be analysed for bottlenecks, and if these occur in areas which can be distributed, these areas can be migrated to faster remote systems. The application can be *distributed gradually* and the original C source code to the application will require only minimal changes. This is in contrast to many other program-to-program communications methods. For example, applications using IBM's advanced program-to-program communication (APPC) protocol know very intimately that they are running in a distributed

```
%c
[
uuid (48e1a3fcce4a.02.09.03.01.39.00.00.00.00),
version(1)
]
interface product {
[idempotent]
void multiply (
    handle_t        [in]    h,
    unsigned long   [in]    num1,
    unsigned long   [in]    num2,
    unsigned long   [out]   *result
);
}
```

Figure 12.6.   A simple NIDL definition.

environment; this makes gradual distribution possible only with many source code changes. This is not the case with NCS.

How is an application distributed?

Within an NCS application the user benefits, the programmer's code is practically unaltered and the systems administrator has tools to help them. How is this possible? A good way to prove how easy it is to write an NCS application is to work through a small but complete example. This example also describes local and global location brokers.

The first step in writing a distributed NCS application is to define the name and parameters of the remote function that will be called. This is done using the network interface definition language (NIDL). The language has a C-like syntax. Figure 12.6 is an example of . idl definition file describing the function **multiply()** that multiplies two numbers together and returns the result in third integer pointer. The rather long number after the letters uuid is the universal unique identifier and is created by the *uuid_gen* program automatically (actually from the name of the machine and the time of creation, among other values). The interface is idempotent, because the multiply request can be requested any number of times and the same result will be returned without error. After running this definition (file multiply. idl) through the *nidl* compiler, four files are generated. The basename of the file is taken from the basename of the source idl file thus:

- multiply. h—a common header file
- multiply_cstub. c—the local client stub
- multiply_cswitch. c—the local client switch code
- multiply_sstub. c—the remote server stub

To write a complete application, the programmer needs simply to write a program that makes a call to the **multiply()** function. This call is intercepted by

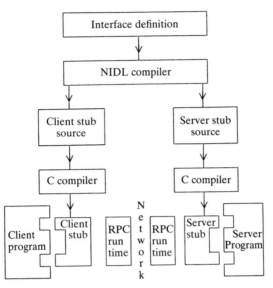

Figure 12.7.   NCS stub relationships.

the local client stub, sent across the network to the server stub and then to the server program. The whole procedure looks something like Fig. 12.7.

For completeness, here are the client and server programs that are actually used. For brevity, the error-checking has been removed; real programs need to check the return codes on the calls to the NCS RPC library. Figure 12.8 shows the client calling program; Figure 12.9 on page 221 shows the server program.

In this example a user runs the client program by simply typing ncsmult 3 4. If all goes well the request is transmitted across the network to the server program and the number 12 is returned to the user. But how does the client know where to send the request? The answer is that NCS defines two special programs called the *local location broker* and the *global location broker*. Each AIX computer that runs one or more server programs needs to run a local location broker. When the server program is started it registers its service by class, object and type with the global location broker and/or the local location broker. When the local client application runs, it makes a call to a known broker to find the location of the named service it requires. In our example, there is only one server, but in a large network it would be possible to choose from a number of servers and the global location broker would return a list of services that match the class, object and type requested by the client program. Once the client has the location of the server it corresponds directly with the server machine. In future correspondence the client program can contact the server directly or ask the global location broker again for the location of the best service (which may have changed). That is all it takes to generate a very simple NCS program. NCS, like AIX in general, has great appeal to real applications developers, principally because it is simple and effective.

```
/* Client program 'ncsmult'. Calls server program 'ncsmultd'     */
/* via NCS. Syntax: ncsmult number number (Ex. ncsmult 12 32)     */
/* 'ncsmultd' returns the product of the two numbers to 'ncsmult'. */
/* Johnny Lauridsen, Mar 1991                                      */
/* Compile with -I/usr/include/ifl/c -lnck                         */
#include <stdio.h>
#include <base.h>
#include <ncsrpc.h>
#include <lb.h>
#include "multiply.h"

extern uuid_$t uuid_$nil;

main(argc, argv)
int argc;
char *argv[];
{
    handle_t rhnd;
    lb_$entry_t lbentry, *lbentry1;                    /* Broker entry   */
    lb_$lookup_handle_t lh = lb_$default_lookup_handle;   /* Start search
    */
    socket_$addr_t loc;                                /* Socket address */
    status_$t st;                                      /* Return status  */
    unsigned long number1;
    unsigned long number2;
    unsigned long end_res;
    unsigned long num_res;
    unsigned long max_res = 1;

    number1 = atoi(argv[1]);
    number2 = atoi(argv[2]);

    lb_$lookup_interface (&product$if_spec.id, &lh, max_res, &num_res
                    &lbentry, &st);

    lbentry1 = &lbentry;

    rhnd = rpc_$bind(&uuid_$nil,&lbentry1->saddr,lbentry1->saddr_len,&st);

    multiply (rhnd, number1, number2, &end_res);

    printf("Result: %ld * %ld = %ld\n",number1,number2,end_res);
}
```

Figure 12.8.   A sample client NCS program.

Network licensing

Besides enabling developers to write distributed applications, NCS has a
component called the network licence server. This provides control of software
product licenses in a LAN environment. For example, a business could purchase

```
/* NCS server program 'ncsmultd'. It receives two numbers from a client */
/* calculates the product of the numbers and sends the result back to   */
/* the client. Syntax: ncsmultd&                                        */
/* Johnny Lauridsen, Mar. 1991                                          */

#include <stdio.h>
#include <lb.h>            /* location broker functions   */
#include <signal.h>        /* signalling functions        */
#include "multiply.h"      /* header file created with NIDL */

uuid_$t uuid_$nil;
lb_$entry_t entry;


main()
{
   /* Declarations */
   void cleanitup();
   lb_$lookup_handle_t lh = lb_$default_lookup_handle;
   socket_$addr_t loc;
   status_$t st;
   char name[256];
   unsigned long family;
   unsigned long llen, port, namelen = sizeof(name);
   unsigned long num_res;
   unsigned long max_res = 1;
   /* signals that will invoke cleanitup function */

   signal(SIGHUP, cleanitup);
   signal(SIGINT, cleanitup);
   signal(SIGTERM, cleanitup);
   signal(SIGQUIT, cleanitup);

   family = socket_$family_from_name("ip", (long) strlen("ip"), &st);
   rpc_$use_family(family, &loc, &llen, &st);

   rpc_$register(&multiply$if_spec, multiply$server_epv, &st);

   lb_$lookup_interface(&multiply$if_spec.id, &lh, max_res, &num_res,\
   &entry, &st);
   if (num_res != 0)
      lb_$unregister(&entry, &st);

   lb_$register(&uuid_$nil, &uuid_$nil, &multiply$if_spec.id, (long) 0,\
   "multiply interface\0", &loc, llen, &entry, &st);

   rpc_$sockaddr_to_name(&loc, llen, name, &namelen, &port, &st);

   printf("Registered with LB. Name='%s', Port=%ld\n", name, port);
   rpc_$listen((long) 5, &st);
}


/* Multiplying function */
void multiply (handle_t h, unsigned long num1,
```

Figure 12.9.   A sample server NCS program. *Continues.*

```
unsigned long num2, unsigned long *res1 )
{ *res1 = (num1 * num2); }

/* cleanitup routine - Unregisters interface from LB and RPC */
void cleanitup()
{
   status_$t st;
   lb_$unregister(&entry, &st);
   rpc_$unregister(&multiply$if_spec, &st);
}
```

Figure 12.9   A sample server NCS program. *Concluded.*

a five-user CADAM computer-aided design application. This allows for any five
users to run CADAM and display the output on their machines. This is a so-
called 'floating licence' since this could be any five LAN-connected users. When
a user starts the application it registers it with the licence server. If it succeeds,
the application continues, otherwise it fails, printing a message that the maximum
number of licensed users are already using the application. This is a good
security facility and prevents users from unintentionally breaking their software
agreements. In IBM, the acronym NLS, however, is synonymous with national
language support, so IBM renamed network licence server as the resource licence
manager (RLM) to avoid acronym confusion!

12.6   Network management

Network management is the process of monitoring network activity. It involves
detecting, responding to and correcting user problems caused by network situations. Here are some examples of typical user problems which could be solved
using network management tools:

- 'My remote printer queue is not emptying. Has the printer jammed or run out
  of paper?'
- 'I can't reach my remote AIX systems for logon or file transfer. Are the links
  to that system down?'
- 'When I *telnet* to my remote AIX system the logon prompt appears but it is
  not responding to my keystrokes to it. What's wrong?'
- 'I've lost access to some of the files in my /home/joseph directory, though
  they can be displayed with the *ls* command. Is this a network problem?'

12.6.1   *AIX NetView/6000*

The primary tool for network management in the AIX or UNIX environment is
AIX NetView/6000. This provides network management configuration management, fault detection and performance monitoring using a set of X-Windows
applications. In addition to standalone distributed network management, AIX

NetView/6000 also provides a bidirectional connection to IBM's mainframe-based NetView product to enable central management of the enterprise from the IBM System 370 and 390 mainframes running mainframe NetView.

The ability to perform this level of network management rests on the use of the TCP/IP network management protocol called SNMP.

Simple network management protocol

The simple network management protocol (SNMP) is a protocol used by AIX and other TCP/IP network hosts to exchange information used in the management of networks, such as line up or down, number of packets received or number of packets in error. SNMP network management is based on the familiar client/server model used in TCP/IP-based network applications. Each host that is to be managed runs a program called an *agent*. The agent is a server that maintains a database of network information (such as packets sent, received, in error, etc.) for that host in a management information base (MIB). The host that is to manage the network also runs a program called a *monitor*. A monitor is a client application that periodically requests information from the MIB database of other machines on the network running the SNMP agent. In addition, a monitor may send requests to agent servers to modify MIB information (for example, reboot machine, bring line up or down, etc.) of other machines.

12.6.2   Configuration management

The configuration section of AIX NetView comprises a graphical display of the network connections. This display is produced automatically using a *discovery* process which generates and maintains a network topology database. Discovery need not be completely automatic; the systems administrator can create known topology files containing lists of connected nodes if desired. Clearly this aids in the reduction of total network discovery time.

Once a database of managed network elements is established, AIX NetView is ready to detect, determine and, if possible, recover automatically from problems with network devices.

12.6.3   Problem detection

Problem detection is handled in two ways, *interrupt notification* or response from *polling*. Interrupt notification is defined as an asynchronous event, for example an SNA alert or an SNMP trap sent from a managed device to AIX NetView. SNMP defines generic trap conditions for all device types and allows new classes to be added. AIX NetView can also monitor the AIX system hardware and software error log using an SNMP subagent. The subagent and other trap conditions result in messages being sent to the *status window* of the AIX NetView main window. Polling involves AIX NetView sending out requests for status to known network devices. Since clearly a totally failed device will not be sending interrupt notifications to anyone, a degree of polling is always necessary. Polling is accomplished by using the ICMP protocol to send *ping* requests to network devices.

12.6.4   *Problem determination*

After an error has been detected the NetView operator will be notified and this individual must use their experience and a number of AIX NetView tools and techniques to determine the exact source of the problem and finally correct it. The first tool that the operator may use is selective polling of the failing device using IP, TCP or SNMP. In some cases AIX NetView can be used to obtain detailed network information about a device, for example for remote AIX workstations, the TCP/IP physical addresses, routeing tables or the TCP/IP services supported by the workstation.

Additionally, the operator can use the MIB browser. For example, by selecting a particular network device by TCP/IP address, the operator can query the MIB values from a list of discovered MIB object IDs. By using the MIB graphing tool these values can be compared against historically 'good' data to discover any anomalies.

If the cause and necessary corrective action are still unclear, the operator will probably attempt to log on to the troubled device. This normally involves using SMIT on the remote AIX workstation and running online diagnostics/tracing as appropriate. (For non-AIX workstations, the NetView operator would probably use the remote TCP/IP logon command *telnet* and use the equivalent UNIX family systems management or diagnostics tool.)

The initial release of AIX NetView does not attempt to perform automatic error recovery. However, AIX NetView is extensible so that user-written shell script programs can be incorporated into AIX NetView. When NetView operators detect the error they can trigger the execution of the required script to automate recovery.

12.6.5   *Performance management*

The key to good performance management is usually proactive performance monitoring. For example, on non-AIX systems, too heavy CPU utilization may cause the system arbitrarily to kill processes to reduce system load.[2] Real-time device monitoring can help detect and thus prevent potential problems from occurring. AIX NetView provides the MIB application builder. The MIB

---

[2] AIX changed the scheduling policy in line with the revised virtual memory management to prevent this as described in Sec. 4.5.

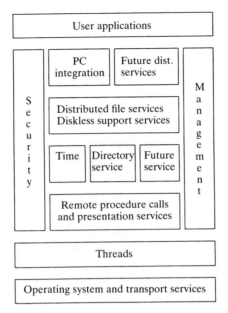

Figure 12.10.   The OSF distributed computing environment.

application builder generates an application that monitors a network device in real time. The NetView operator selects one or more MIB variables that need to be periodically monitored and graphed. The application is then saved under a user-definable name which is then dynamically added to an AIX NetView menu. AIX NetView is based on technology developed from Hewlett-Packard's Network Node Manager.

12.7 The OSF distributed computing environment

The distributed computing environment (DCE) was first made available in early 1993, with an enhanced DCE product in mid 1993. UNIX International has announced support for DCE and the European Community (EC) has endorsed DCE as their strategy for distributed computing.

DCE is OSF's standard for distributed computing. Figure 12.10 shows DCE's principal components. DCE allows computers from a variety of vendors to communicate transparently and share resources such as computing power, files, printers and other objects in the network. As with other OSF components, DCE was the result of an OSF vendor neutral request process. As with other chosen selections (for example, OSF/Motif) DCE combines the best of technologies submitted to OSF. The principal components are now described.

Remote procedure calls

This was provided by the Hewlett-Packard and DEC submission of Network Computing System (NCS) already discussed in this chapter.

Distributed filesystem

Like the industry standard distributed filesystem NFS already described, the purpose of the DCE filesystem (DFS) is to allow users and applications to use files on remote computers as though they were locally based. OSF chose the Andrew filesystem (AFS) version 4.0 from Transarc. AFS provides some advantages over NFS including *uniform name space*, meaning that every file available on the network has a consistent and uniform name, regardless of computer. Like the IBM journalled filesystem, DFS is a log-based filesystem, giving rise to high reliability even after a DFS server machine failure. DFS also includes support for AIX filesystem security extensions such as access control lists. AFS is implemented using a client-to-server programming approach using underlying RPCs coded with OSF DCE.

Naming services

The naming services provide a consistent name for resources throughout the distributed environment. This allows applications to make use of resources such as files, disks or print queues in a consistent manner and without needing to know their precise network location until runtime. DCE supports the directory services programming interface from X/Open called XDS. This is based on ISO 9594, 1988, or equivalently CCITT X.500.

Authentication and authorization

DCE chose Kerberos[3] version 5 from MIT. Kerberos is an encryption-based third-party authentication mechanism for network security. Version 5 includes an authentication interface to RPC.

Time services

DCE chose DEC's DECdts time services. The purpose of a time service is to synchronize the clock of a local computer with universal time, coordinated (UTC). DECdts includes tracing and management tools and interoperates with

---

[3] In Greek mythology Cerberus (its Latin name) was the three-headed hound of Hades and guardian of the chasm which led to his master's kingdom. Cerberus was brought back from the underworld by Herakles.

the current industry standard network time protocol from Transarc (which was not chosen by OSF).

PC integration

This component allows PC-connected users to share files on a DCE-based machine and to send printing to attached printers on that system. OSF chose two components. First, PC/NFS from Sun Microsystems allowing DOS PCs file-sharing. Second, the LM/X server from Microsoft allowing any PC having software using the server message block, LAN protocol to access the DCE server. It is important to remember that these two products are server-only products running on the AIX host. It is the user's responsibility to provide the client implementation products that run on the typically DOS systems.

13
The IBM bridge

For existing IBM customers the natural method of network connection is provided by IBM's systems network architecture (SNA). Probably the largest and most complex SNA network in use today is that of IBM itself. This allows any IBM employee to send and receive files, notes and messages to over 300 000 other users. For *any* new IBM product to be accepted therefore, either internally by IBM, or by IBM's existing customer base, it must include good SNA support.

However, the UNIX world too has its own set of network standards, based on TCP/IP. To be a credible UNIX computer system, then, the RISC system had to support TCP/IP at least as well as other UNIX vendors. So the RISC system designers had to satisfy both SNA and TCP/IP requirements. This chapter begins by explaining some basic IBM mainframe concepts terms and technology. It then moves on to see how the RISC system interoperates by way of mainframe terminal emulation, and the associated programming interfaces that allow RISC system to IBM mainframe and minicomputer connectivity.

13.1   Fundamentals

Many large computer vendors, including Unisys, ICL and IBM, have retained a vendor set of communications protocols or character encoding standards to talk between their traditional computer systems. First, let us consider EBCDIC, the character-encoding system used by IBM mainframe and IBM minicomputer systems.

13.1.1   Extended binary coded data interchange code

Extended binary coded data interchange code (EBCDIC) is a character-encoding standard that takes characters represented by the English language and assigns them an 8-bit binary value. Its counterpart is the ASCII coding standard used in the PC and UNIX world. Since EBCDIC is an 8-bit code there is room for 256 possible characters, so it has room for a full set of punctuation characters and special symbols. Traditional ASCII is, by comparison, only a 7-bit encoding scheme.

Since the encoding schemes are different, if data is transferred from a RISC system to an IBM mainframe it must clearly be translated from ASCII to EBCDIC using a suitable conversion program. The reverse conversion needs to be made when downloading host information to the RISC system.

13.1.2   *SNA, logical and physical units*

SNA is an architecture that enables IBM computers to talk to each other over a variety of physical connection media, be they telephone lines, Ethernet, Token Ring or X.25 connections. Like the ISO OSI and TCP/IP architectures, SNA is split into a number of layers. Also, like ISO and TCP/IP, SNA is *open* because all its interfaces are openly documented. The principal layers of SNA are shown in Fig. 13.1.

Any SNA network contains one or more host systems known as system

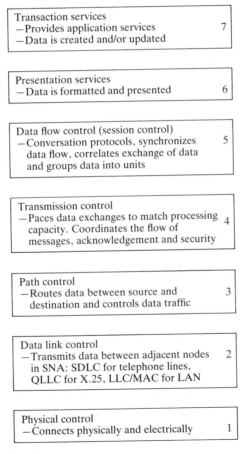

Figure 13.1.   SNA architectural layers.

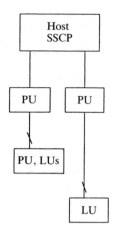

Figure 13.2.   SNA domain structure.

services control points (SSCPs). The SSCP activates and controls the network. An SSCP manages a portion of the network known as a domain. The SSCP talks to the user via a hierarchy that normally includes a *physical unit* and a *logical unit*. This is shown in Fig. 13.2.

The physical unit (PU) controls the physical resources of the node. A PU must be able to implement the lowest three SNA layers. PUs are classified by capability:

Type 1 (PU T1)   Peripheral node (old terminal node)

Type 2 (PU T2)   Peripheral node, e.g. cluster control unit 3174

Type 2.1 (PU T2.1)   Cluster control unit and/or peer node

Type 4 (PU T4)   Communications controller, e.g. 3745

Type 5 (PU T5)   Host node

The logical unit is an end point in SNA terminology. That is to say, the end point for data sent across the network. Here are the types:

LU0   Customer-defined session, raw API programming interface

LU1   Remote job entry (RJE) applications

LU2   3270 type terminal using the 3270 data stream

LU3   3270 terminal printers

LU6.2   Advanced program-to-program communication (APPC). This is a peer-to-peer session-oriented protocol, that is, it is between LU6.2 devices and the first stage in communication involves establishing a communications path between devices between the participating systems.

13.2   What is an IBM mainframe?

In the sixties most computers were used in scientific applications; IBM's range was no exception. IBM, however, began development of a new range of general-purpose computers that could be used for more general-purpose data processing. These systems introduced the concept of the 'balanced design' point whereby a computer could manipulate all forms of data effectively without a particular preference for high-speed mathematics. Additionally, the various subsystems of the computer such as the processor, disk, communications, were of similar capability, so they were in balance with one another. So in 1965 the System/360 system was born, the number 360 representing the the 360 degrees of a circle to indicate a balanced all round design.

System/360 (named S/360 for short) improved, and thus was born System/370. System/370 was then developed to include extended architecture (XA) and then progressed to System/390. Table 13.1 shows the principal advances in IBM mainframe architecture to the present day.

Table 13.1. Mainframe machine architecture advances

Year	Name	Attachment	Instruction set
1964	S/360		
1970	S/370	Block multiplexer channel	
1972			Virtual storage
1980		Data streaming channel	
1981	370-XA		
1985			Vector facility
1986	ESA/370		
1989			Move page
1990	ESA/390	ESCON channels	Sysplex timer, security
1991		Extended distance feature	Enhance move page, subsystem storage protection, processor availability facility

13.2.1   Mainframe operating systems

IBM has four mainframe operating systems:

VSE   Virtual storage extended

VM   Virtual Machine

MVS   Multiple Virtual Storage

AIX   Advanced Interactive eXecutive (see Appendix 1)

VSE is the cheapest, simplest and least capable of the four, with MVS the most capable of IBM's vendor systems. VM is an operating system in its own right but it is also commonly used as a Hypervisor. In this mode it presents one or more virtual machines' environments, which can contain a 'second level' operating system, e.g. MVS or VSE. Today each of these operating systems has a preferred version orderable in the /ESA form. For example, MVS/ESA, meaning the MVS operating system for the Enterprise Systems Architecture (/ESA), that is to say, exploiting the latest in IBM mainframe technology.

13.2.2   Connecting the RISC system to an IBM mainframe

The fundamental concept in IBM mainframe connections is the *channel*. The channel is a high-speed block-oriented communications path that connects peripherals to the mainframe. Figure 13.3 shows the most important connection methods from an IBM RISC System/6000 to an IBM mainframe. Working from left to right in the diagram: from a regular *parallel channel* output a 3174 local cluster controller connects IBM terminals. AIX1 shows that an AIX system with a MicroChannel 3270 connection card (having a coax output) can connect to such a controller and, with suitable software, provide RISC system users with IBM mainframe terminal emulation on their attached ASCII or X-Windows screens.

If the mainframe is not local but perhaps several thousand kilometres distant, the user will need to connect to a remote cluster controller (AIX2). In this example the parallel channel has an attached model 3745 communications controller which communicates via two modems and a telephone line with the remote 3174 cluster controller. As before, the RISC system will require a 3270 connection adapter.

For RISC system to mainframe communications using TCP/IP, a cluster or communications controller cannot be used, as this is designed to support SNA communications.[1] Connection needs to be via a 3172 interconnect controller. The 3172 controller connects to a mainframe parallel or ESCON channel and has output of Ethernet and/or Token Ring LAN and/or FDDI. The RISC system can then connect in the conventional way to this LAN, as shown in AIX3, AIX4. The 3172 can also connect to other IBM systems running TCP/IP, for example, IBM PS/2 systems running the IBM products TCP/IP for DOS or TCP/IP for OS/2.

Finally, the RISC system may be running SNA communications software, for example, participating in a program-to-program communication from mainframe

---

[1] Strictly, a communications controller can be used for TCP/IP in two cases: using a 3745 with an Ethernet adapter and NCP version 6, or using a 3745 with an X.25 link and NPSI. Additionally, it is possible to encapsulate TCP/IP within SNA. These topics are beyond the scope of this discussion.

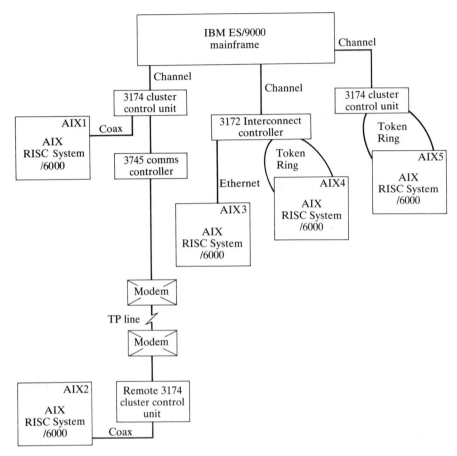

Figure 13.3.   IBM mainframe connections.

to IBM RISC System/6000. Such SNA communications would be connected as shown in AIX5. A 3174 cluster controller connects to an IBM mainframe. Downstream this model has a Token Ring LAN output instead of the more usual coax. This then connects the RISC system. Of course other participating SNA communications from other IBM systems such as DOS or OS/2 may also be attached.

The IBM mainframe family

In an effort to provide an easier migration path for users, IBM is rationalizing its mainframe offering onto a single model family called *Enterprise System/9000* (ES/9000). This family replaces other well-known model numbers, for example the 3081, 4381, 9370 and 3090 families.

The ES/9000 includes:

- Support of the System/390 architecture
- Multiway processors
- Vector processing
- Hardware partitioning using PR/SM
- Faster channel support via Enterprise Systems connection (ESCON) and ESCON/XDF

13.2.3   Why use a mainframe?

Certain computer applications cannot be distributed easily and are best suited to mainframe processing power. The banking and airline industries make significant use of large IBM mainframe systems, each system serving thousands of online users. The economies of scale mean that the real cost per user for a mainframe providing a distributed transaction processing application is very low. From a systems viewpoint, mainframes offer centralized control, management and backup. Upgrading mainframe systems is, of course, much easier than upgrading distributed minicomputer systems. Large corporate IBM mainframe computer users typically run applications written in-house, perhaps using the IBM transaction processing system CICS. Applications typically display on character-based screens, though Graphical Data Display Manager (GDDM) graphics is possible. Applications are typically written in COBOL, PL/I, C or a number of other languages.

13.3   IBM mainframe communications

Existing users connect to IBM mainframe systems in one of two ways: terminal emulation or program-to-program communication. In the first case the objective is to allow a user sitting at a RISC system console, X-Windows-attached or ASCII terminal to view an IBM mainframe screen and interact as though they were using a genuine IBM 3270, fixed-function terminal or better.

In the second case, the objective is for there to be a communication between a RISC system and the IBM mainframe. This may be simply to download data stored on the IBM mainframe, or it could be that a program on the IBM mainframe is cooperatively processing with a program on a RISC system.

AIX allows both these functions to be performed, typically using native UNIX TCP/IP or using IBM SNA.

13.4   IBM mainframe terminal emulation

Because of the differing user requirements for interconnecting a RISC system to an IBM mainframe, IBM provides more than one IBM mainframe terminal emulation package.

13.4.1 AIX 3278/79 terminal emulation

The most simple form of terminal emulation is provided by the AIX 3278/79 terminal emulation program. As the program name suggests, it allows the user sitting at a high-function terminal (HFT) or windowed *aixterm* session to emulate IBM 3278 and 3279 terminals. These are base function terminals, the 3279 supporting colour. Physically, the connection is made between the coax output of the 3270 connection adapter installed in the RISC system and a 3174 cluster control unit. The control unit can be either the SNA or the non-SNA version, be local or remote to the host, and must operate in the control unit terminal (CUT) mode.

This emulator really does provide base function indeed, but it is very simple to install and use.

13.4.2 Host connection terminal emulation

Host connection (HCON) is the name given to the high-function IBM mainframe terminal emulator. With HCON a user has a great deal of flexibility as to the connection of the RISC system to the IBM mainframe and also the type of RISC system terminal screen on which the IBM mainframe terminal emulation screen will be displayed. Figure 13.4 shows the connection options.

The connection from the RISC system to the IBM mainframe may be via any one of the following:

- An X.25 WAN (SNA connection)
- A local or remote 3174 cluster control unit (SNA or non-SNA)

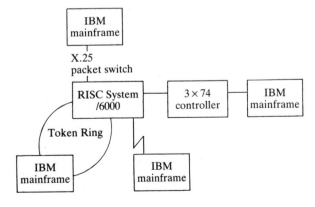

Figure 13.4.   HCON connectivity.

- A locally attached Token Ring (SNA connection)
- A remote SDLC line (SNA connection)

If an SNA connection is used then the RISC system emulates a 3174 cluster control unit and therefore appears to the host as an SNA PU T2.1 connection. This means that SNA Services/6000 must also be installed as a prerequisite product. In practice this is not a problem, but it does require a good degree of setup.

Once installed, the user may run HCON from even an ASCII terminal, and of course from an X-Windows or HFT display. A user can have multiple sessions, and be logged on to multiple hosts.

HCON also allows file transfer between a RISC system and an IBM mainframe. This enables a user to work with files locally and then to transfer them to the IBM mainframe (or vice versa). Various options allow for the translation of data between ASCII and EBCDIC formats and the creation of blocked records on the IBM mainframe.

13.4.3 TCP/IP terminal emulation

If a user is fortunate enough to have TCP/IP installed on the IBM mainframe then mainframe terminal emulation is an easy process. A user can enter standard TCP/IP commands to perform file transfer and terminal emulation. For example, using the *ftp* command a user may transfer files from the RISC system to the mainframe and vice versa, translating from ASCII to EBCDIC datastream as required. Using the RISC system *telnet* command a user will perform IBM mainframe terminal emulation to the TCP/IP-equipped mainframe host. The *telnet* program on the RISC system has a component that allows it to perform full-screen emulation so that mainframe applications that use cursor addressing (and most do) work correctly. The advantage of this configuration is that *any* LAN-connected RISC system can use the RISC system as a gateway, by using the *telnet* command twice—once to log on to the gateway RISC system and the second time to log on to the host. IBM mainframe terminal emulation is available even though HCON is not installed on the local RISC system.

The user can of course run a *telnet* session from an *aixterm* window on an X-Windows screen and so produce a windowed IBM mainframe terminal session under AIXwindows. However, IBM now has available a separate program *x3270* called the AIX X-Windows Emulator that performs this more efficiently. This emulator is a native OSF/Motif program and therefore must be run under X-Windows. The physical connection requirements are the same as for the previous *telnet* method.

The AIX X-Windows Emulator offers advantages over using *telnet* or any other mainframe terminal emulator discussed so far. First, it is a native OSF/ Motif application and supports cutting and pasting from other X-Windows and

MOTIF applications to the emulator screen, or vice versa. Most importantly, the emulation provides Graphical Data Display Manager (GDDM) graphics. GDDM is the standard for IBM mainframe graphics. For example, the IBM mainframe application system (AS) makes use of GDDM to display data graphically in the form of charts. Various IBM host printing utilities allow previewing of documents containing graphics by using GDDM.

If the reader is considering adding an IBM RISC System/6000 into an existing IBM mainframe network, IBM mainframe terminal emulation is probably a requirement. But which emulator to choose? Although the AIX X-Windows Emulator provides the highest function, it also requires that TCP/IP be running on the host VM or MVS mainframe computer. And recall that to make the TCP/IP connection requires the RISC system to IBM mainframe connection to be made via a 3172 interconnect controller and not the traditional (and inexpensive) 3174 control unit. In an IBM SNA network-managed environment this may be unlikely, so the bottom line is that terminal emulation is normally enabled by using the HCON terminal emulator.

13.4.4   Express 3270 terminal emulation

Systems Strategies market a family of products called Express 3270 which also provide IBM mainframe terminal emulation (and more) for RISC systems. The software comes in four basic flavours:

- SNA (systems network architecture): the software emulates terminals connected via a 3274 cluster control unit and connects physically using the SDLC protocol from the multiprotocol adapter.
- BSC (binary synchronous communication): the software emulates terminals connected via a 3274 BSC (non-SNA) cluster control unit.
- QLLC (qualified logical link control): the software emulates a terminal connected via a 3274 cluster control unit but the physical connection is via the X.25 card.
- RJE: the software allows emulation of the IBM 3770 remote job entry workstation.

At the time of writing, these products cannot be used concurrently with IBM SNA Services/6000 or any product that depends on it, for example, AIX NetView Service Point.

13.5   AIX to IBM mainframe programming interfaces

The most popular form of programmed communication from the IBM RISC System/6000 to the IBM mainframe involves the use of a programming interface that is part of the HCON emulator. (The 3278/79 emulation program does not provide any programming interfaces, only terminal emulation.)

HCON provides a number of programming interfaces. The first is similar in concept to the IBM HLLAPI (high-level language application programming interface)[2] in that it allows a program to act as a programmable operator to an IBM mainframe. It is called *API/3270*. Program function calls can be coded to send keystrokes to the HCON terminal session or to examine the contents of the screen buffer (called a 'presentation space' in SNA terminology). As an example, an applications developer could write a simple program that automatically checks the IBM mainframe response time when the user is otherwise idle. Such a program might operate in the following way.

Do the following actions for the whole duration of the program:

- If the operator information area (OIA) below the bottom enterable line on the screen indicates link failure then terminate program.
- If the bottom right-hand corner of the screen has a message of HOLDING and user is idle then send a clear key to the host.

This is the program flow:

1   Establish that the user has logged on.
2   Take a capture of the presentation space.
3   Wait the time limit and take another capture of the presentation space.
4   If the two compare then user is idle.
5   If the user is idle then send an Enter keysequence to the host and monitor the time for the busy indicator in the OIA.
6   Print the result in a window on the X-Windows screen or write results into a logfile.

HCON also provides an additional API interface called HCON *API_T*. This is another API interface designed for program-to-program communication. A RISC system program uses this API to talk to a program running on the IBM mainframe. API_T also has additional programming calls that can perform HCON API/3270 facilities such as automatic logon and the ability to start a program running on the IBM mainframe. A typical HCON API_T program flow is:

1   Start emulator if not running and log on to it.
2   Start program on IBM mainframe host
3   Send message to host program.
4   Host program replies.
5   Repeat above steps 3 and 4 as necessary.
6   Close down host program and if necessary log off host.

---

[2] In a recent announcement HCON now provides the real HLLAPI programming interface allowing migration of customers' existing non-AIX, HLLAPI applications.

The advantage of using the HCON API/3270 or HCON API_T is that their programming and configuration requirements are small. Using API/3270 an AIX interface to an existing IBM mainframe program can be quickly developed. Using API_T cooperative processing applications can be easily developed.

Both of these programming interfaces use the LU2 (logical unit 2) method of defining the entity at the RISC system end. This is an imbalanced configuration. It would be far better for the RISC system to communicate with the IBM mainframe on an equal basis. This is achieved using IBM APPC, described in Sec. 13.7.

13.6   What is an IBM AS/400?

The IBM AS/400 is *the* established IBM minicomputer family. A business can start with the entry level AS/400 model D02 capable of supporting fewer than six users and grow their requirements to a D80 system with several hundred users.

The AS/400 system, designed in Rochester, Minnesota, is an evolution from the IBM System/38 and the result of a development of the IBM Future Systems group. In the seventies IBM set up the Future Systems group with the object-ive of developing a replacement to the mid-range System/370 architecture. The architecture was designed to overcome some of the limitations of classic IBM mainframes. As such, the System/38 and AS/400 were designed to operate in office environments and not require maintenance by computer-skilled personnel.

Some of the extensions in the AS/400 architecture may have influenced the RISC system design including *single level storage*—the ability to map files into memory—and some aspects of the journalled filesystem.

The AS/400 usually drives character-based terminal screens using a twinax cabling system. Twinax cable is similar in concept and construction to the Ethernet LAN coaxial cable. Twinax, however, as the name suggests, has two internal core cables surrounded by a braided shield, instead of one for coax.

13.6.1   Physical IBM AS/400 to RISC system connections

Local terminals have twinax cables that connect directly to a card in the AS/400 called the workstation controller. IBM does not supply a MicroChannel adapter with twinax output, so physically the RISC system connects to an IBM AS/400 in the following ways:

1   From a serial port on the IBM RISC System/6000 to an IBM link protocol converter and thence to a twinax port on the IBM AS/400. The IBM link protocol converter models 5208 or 5209 convert from ASCII to twinax protocol, therefore the IBM AS/400 believes it is talking to a native IBM AS/400 screen.

2   Directly to the ASCII ports provided by ASCII workstation controller card in the IBM AS/400.

3   To a remote IBM AS/400 by an SDLC communications line to a modem, telephone line, remote modem and into the SDLC communications port of the remote IBM AS/400 system.

4   Via an X.25 network, where both the IBM AS/400 and the IBM RISC System/6000 have X.25 adapter cards installed.

5   To a LAN such as Token Ring or Ethernet. The IBM AS/400 now has integral Token Ring or Ethernet adapter cards.

Of the five methods described, the last, LAN connection, is the preferred option.

As with IBM mainframe connections, connecting the IBM RISC System/6000 to the IBM AS/400 can be divided into two categories: first, emulating the standard AS/400 terminal (called the 5250); and second, making AIX to AS/400 program-to-program communications.

13.6.2   IBM AS/400 terminal emulation

In the first two methods described above the RISC system can connect its ASCII serial ports to an IBM AS/400 via the protocol converter or ASCII workstation controller. Using either of these options the RISC system does not need any additional software, it can use standard UNIX terminal emulation software to make the connection. In all other cases however, it is necessary to use the IBM AS/400 Connection Program/6000.

The IBM AS/400 Connection Program/6000

The IBM AS/400 Connection Program/6000 allows an IBM RISC System/6000 to communicate with the PC/support component of the OS/400 AS/400 operating system via SNA or TCP/IP. When an SNA connection is used the RISC system users can:

• Log on to the AS/400 and have a full-screen emulation session to the AS/400.
• Transfer files between the AS/400 and the RISC system. (This requires PC support at the AS/400 end.)
• Execute commands remotely on the AS/400 from the RISC system.
• This is possible with Token Ring, Ethernet, X.25 and synchronous data link control (SDLC) physical connections.

The AIX IBM AS/400 Connection Program can also be used with the AS/400-based TCP/IP connectivity utility which allows the IBM AS/400 TCP/IP functionality. These two programs working together allow:

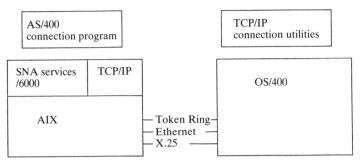

Figure 13.5.   IBM RISC System/6000 to IBM AS/400 communications using TCP/IP.

- File transfer to any remote TCP/IP system including AIX.
- RISC system to IBM AS/400 mail exchange via the simple mail transfer protocol.
- Telnet: AIX users have full-screen access to IBM AS/400 applications, and IBM AS/400 users full screen access to AIX applications.

The connection of an IBM RISC System/6000 to an IBM AS/400 is shown in Fig. 13.5.

13.6.3   AIX to IBM AS/400 programming interfaces

Since there are no specific AS/400 terminal emulators, there are no equivalent programmable operator interfaces from AIX to the AS/400 as there were with the IBM mainframe. Instead, applications developers wishing to maintain program-to-program communications should use APPC, which is the subject of the next section.

13.7   AIX SNA transaction programs

Several different application programming interfaces (APIs) are available to the AIX SNA transaction programmer. Each API is composed of a set of C language function calls, that provide the necessary communication between transaction programs (TPs) and logical units (LUs). An applications developer must choose among them, according to the LU type used, the requirements of the application and the style of coding you prefer. *AIX SNA Services/6000* provides the following APIs:

- Operating system subroutines limited interface (LU type 6.2 support)
- Operating system subroutines extended interface (LU types 1, 2, 3, 6.2 support)
- Library subroutines (LU types 1, 2, 3 and 6.2 support)
- Generic SNA interface (special-purpose SNA functions)
- LU type 0 facility interface

The most commonly used interfaces are the extended interface and the library subroutines.

The extended interface consists of the following functions: **open()**, **close()**, **readx()**, **writex()**, **ioctl()** and **select()**. The purpose of this interface is to provide TPs with access to and control of SNA functions, but yet not to depart from the well-known AIX programming context. The library subroutines, however, provide a more SNA-oriented programming context. From a functional viewpoint, these two interfaces are equivalent.

The library subroutines consist of the following functions: **snaopen()**, **snalloc()**, **snaread()**, **snawrit()**, **snactl()**, **snadeal()** and **snaclse()**. Here is a brief overview of what these functions provide:

snaopen()   Open a connection

snalloc()   Create (allocate) a conversation on the opened connection

snaread()   Receive data from the remote TP

snawrit()   Send data to the remote TP

snactl()   Control and monitor conversation

snadeal()   End (deallocate) conversation

snaclse()   Disable access to a connection

These subroutines are provided through the `libsna.a` library.

To show the simplicity of coding a small sample application, Fig. 13.6 shows a sample *source transaction program* and Fig. 13.7 shows a sample *target transaction program*. These programs are sample AIX SNA APPC programs, using the LU type 6.2 protocol. Think of a source TP as the program initiating (allocating) a conversation and the target TP as the program receiving an allocate request. Somewhat like the client/server relationship we know so well from the TCP/IP applications. However the client/server relationship between APPC TPs often 'changes direction', making the client a server and vice versa, by means of different levels of flow control, not usually seen in the traditional client/server relationship.

Note the `luxsna.h` include file. This file defines all the error codes specific to AIX SNA Services/6000. It also defines all the necessary C structures used by AIX SNA TPs.

The program flow is:

1 Source TP opens a connection and a *cid* is returned. This is an identifier, identifying the *connection*.
2 Source TP allocates a conversation and an *rid* is returned. This is an identifier, identifying the *conversation*, also called the *resource identifier*.
3 Source TP sends two numbers to the target TP, using **snawrit()**.

```
/* snamult.c:  LU 6.2 Source Transaction Program */

#include <luxsna.h>

long               cid = -1;    /* SNA file descriptor   */
long               rid = -1;    /* SNA resource ID       */
struct allo_str    allo_str;    /* allocate structure    */
struct write_out   write_out;   /* write structure       */
struct read_out    read_out;    /* read structure        */

main(argc, argv)
int argc;
char *argv[];
{
        char buf[512];
        int i;

        if (argc != 4) /* check input = conn_name + numbers */
        {
                printf("Usage: %s conn_name number number\n",argv[0]);
                exit(0);
        }

        sprintf(buf,"%s %s",argv[2],argv[3]); /* build buf */

        if ((cid = snaopen(argv[1])) == -1) /* open connection */
        {
                perror("snaopen");
                exit(1);
        }

        memset(&allo_str, 0, sizeof(struct allo_str));
        strcpy(allo_str.tpn, "snamultd"); /* transaction program name   */
        allo_str.type = MAPPED_CONV;      /* conversation type: Mapped  */
        if ((rid = snalloc(cid, &allo_str, "M")) == -1)  /* allocate    */
        {
                perror("snalloc");
                if (snaclse(cid) == -1) perror("snaclse");
                exit(2);
        }

        /* ---- clear write structure and send transaction ------- */
        memset(&write_out, 0, sizeof(struct write_out));
        if (snawrit(cid, buf, strlen(buf)+1, rid, &write_out, "M") <= 0)
                perror("snawrit");
        else
        {
                /* ---- read server response and display it ------- */
                if ((i = snaread(cid, buf, sizeof(buf), rid, 0, &read_out,
                                                           "M")) == -1)
                        perror("snaread");
                else
                        printf("%s\n",buf);
        }

    if (snaclse(cid) == -1) perror("snaclse");
}
```

Figure 13.6.   snamult source transaction program.

```
/* snamultd.c:    LU 6.2 Target Transaction Program */

#include <luxsna.h>

long            cid = -1;              /* SNA file descriptor    */
long            rid = -1;              /* SNA resource ID        */
struct allo_str allo_str;             /* allocate structure     */
struct deal_str deal_str;             /* deallocate structure */
struct write_out write_out;           /* write structure        */
struct read_out read_out;             /* read structure         */

main(argc, argv)
int argc;
char *argv[];
{
    char buf[1024];
    int a, b, i;
    rid = atol(argv[3]);              /* Get resource ID        */
    if ((cid = snaopen(argv[2])) == -1)    /* open connection   */
    {
        perror("snaopen");
        exit(0);
    }

    memset(&allo_str, 0, sizeof(struct allo_str));
    allo_str.rid = rid;               /* Put resource ID in structure */
    if ((rid = snalloc(cid, &allo_str, "M" )) = -1)
    {
        perror("snalloc");
        if (snaclse(cid) == -1) perror("snaclse");
        exit(2);
    }

    for (;;)

    {
        /* ---- clear receive buffer and read message ---------- */
        memset(buf, '\0', sizeof(buf));
        if ((i = snaread(cid, buf, sizeof(buf), rid, 0, &read_out, "M")) = -1)
        {
            perror("snaread");
            break;
        }
        else
        {
            sscanf(buf,"%d %d",&b,&a);
            if (b*a == 0) break;
            sprintf(buf,"%d * %d = %d",b,a,b*a);
            /* ---- clear write structure and send response ---- */
            memset(&write_out, 0, sizeof(struct write_out));
            if (snawrit(cid, buf, strlen(buf)+1, rid, &write_out, "M") <= 0)
            {
                perror("snawrit");
                break;
            }
        }
    }
}
```

Figure 13.7.   snamultd target transaction program. *Continues.*

```
memset(&deal_str, 0, sizeof(struct deal_str)); /* clear dealloc structure */
deal_str.rid       = rid;           /* specify resource ID */
deal_str.deal_flag = DISCARD;       /* type discard */
deal_str.type      = DEAL_FLUSH;    /* deallocate flush */

if (snadeal(cid, &deal_str, "M") == -1) /* deallocate conversation */
        perror("snadeal");
if (snaclse(cid) = -1) perror("snaclse");
}
```

Figure 13.7.   snamultd target transaction program. *Concluded.*

4   Target TP reads these numbers using **snaread()**, multiplies the numbers and returns the result to the source TP, using **snawrite()**. The source TP reads the result using **snaread()** and displays the result.

Here is an example of how to use the program:

```
snamult CONNECTION_NAME  10 5
10 * 5 = 50
```

The CONNECTION_NAME is the name of an AIX SNA SERVICES/6000 *connection profile*. To make AIX TPs work, a systems programmer needs to set up some profiles describing local LUs, TPs and the location of the remote system.

Several programs are available for the RISC system, that use the mentioned APIs. If you need additional source sample code for APPC programming, a sample file transfer application comes with AIX SNA Services/6000. This is located in the /usr/lpp/sna/samples directory.

13.7.1   *Common programming interface-C*

Common programming interface-C (CPI-C) is not yet available for the IBM RISC System/6000[3] but because of its strategic importance to APPC the reader should understand it.

As APPC developed, distinct APIs for APPC platforms on different IBM platforms emerged. Each API had unique characteristics and usually a different function call interface. CPI-C was developed to avoid platform dependencies. Although the actual implementation of CPI-C over APPC may vary from platform to platform, the API is consistent. A distributed applications developer can utilize CPI-C without needing specific knowledge of how the interface is implemented on a specific platform. Portability is also clear. Since the programming interface to APPC is standardized with CPI-C, applications may be moved from one CPI-C platform to another. Also note that the CPI-C function call interface has adopted as an X/Open standard, though X/Open will not necessarily

---

[3] Not available directly, but it is available using the Encina Transaction Processing subsystem, see Appendix 3.

use APPC as the underlying transport protocol. This means that the CPI-C
programming interface is likely to be used by even non-IBM systems wanting to
communicate with each other.

13.8   Network management

The concept of network management has already been explained in Sec. 12.6,
where the AIX NetView/6000 product which enables a suitably configured IBM
RISC System/6000 to perform Network Management of a TCP/IP network using
SNMP was also discussed. The choice of the name 'NetView' for this product
might be regarded as confusing however, since NetView has traditionally been
the term used to describe tools that IBM uses to manage networks of systems
interconnected via SNA. The rest of this section therefore describes the relationship and interconnection of AIX NetView/6000 and the host SNA NetView
facilities available on an IBM mainframe running either the MVS or VM
operating systems.

Within SNA, network entities are divided into four categories for network
management as shown in Fig. 13.8:

- The *focal point* provides the final level of network decision making and
  centralizes the network management task. Skilled operations staff are hence
  required only at the focal point and not throughout the system.
- The *entry point, service point and collection point* transport network management information from particular devices to the focal point.
- The collection point simply forwards information collected by other entry
  points The entry point provides network management for itself and attached
  devices and must be an SNA physical unit.
- The service point provides network management of non-SNA devices outside the entry point, for example from SNMP (see Sec. 12.6.1). The service
  point converts the information into SNA format and sends it to the focal
  point.

The product that links AIX NetView/6000 to the host by providing the service
point function as described above is IBM AIX NetView service point. Of course
this runs on top of SNA Services/6000 which they use to communicate with the
IBM mainframe focal point.

13.8.1   NetView service point

Recall that the service point function means acting as a relayer or bridge between
an IBM SNA subsystem and a non-IBM subsystem, such as TCP/IP. The idea of
using the Netview service point (NSP) package then is to forward any machine or
network problems back to a centralized NetView focal point where an operator
can use NSP or NetView management facilities to resolve the problem. This is

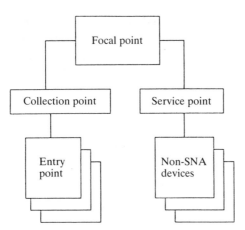

Figure 13.8.   Network management structure.

done by writing a user-written event-driven application (see Sec. 6.1.5) program using a programming toolkit. The application interface library has two programming interfaces:

- Function-specific functions: high-level functions (may use)
- Toolkit interface: low-level functions (must use)

An example of a function-specific function would be 'send error sense data to IBM mainframe NetView'. An example of a toolkit interface function might be 'create object'. Although a supplied toolkit is used to write event-driven programs, these programs neither require nor use any component of the X-Windows event-driven programming environment or the Motif toolkit. The programming facilities available fall into five functional areas:

1 Alert processing facilities: allow the programmer to send notification of detected problems to the host.
2 Common operator services: allow the programmer to receive commands from and send commands to the NetView command processor.
3 Asynchronous communication facilities: allow programs to establish sessions with asynchronous TTY ports.
4 Host data facility: provides an LU 6.2 protocol-based file transfer utility.
5 Distribute application support: provides remote procedure call interface for communications between AIX systems.

Here are some examples of NSP applications:

- Check the hardware and software error log on a IBM RISC System/6000 and send any major failures to IBM mainframe NetView for operator notification.
- Check disk space left on all AIX logical volumes. If space is short inform

IBM mainframe NetView and wait for an IBM mainframe NetView
RUNCMD which triggers a local AIX program to increase the size of the
filesystem dynamically using the AIX logical volume management facilities.

- Use TCP/IP SNMP commands to retrieve TCP/IP network status and relay
this to IBM mainframe NetView.

14
Security

Computer manufacturers are to an extent victims of their own success. In early mainframe systems, relatively few people had access to computers, and such access may well have been via terminals in physically secure areas. Additionally, the sheer complexity of early mainframe systems discouraged unauthorized access.

Today, the situation has changed radically and personal computers and workstations permeate even the smallest businesses. For example, within IBM there is a policy that employees should have access to their own personal computer or workstation and be connected to the worldwide IBM mainframe network. Without implementation of proper security measures, an employee could inadvertently or maliciously alter sensitive data or programs, or gain access to restricted information. AIX implements an impressive array of security features designed to protect a user's data from unauthorized access. This chapter explains these features in detail.

14.1   Complying with security standards

The American National Computer Security Commission (NCSC) is the driving force behind developments in computer security. In 1983, this organization published the US Department of Defense (DOD) Trusted Computer Systems Evaluation Criteria (TCSEC). This work is commonly known as the 'Orange Book', an understandable abbreviation since this was the colour of the cover of the original report. The Orange Book became a US military standard in 1985 and today offers the central role in the specification of secure computer systems.   An up-and-coming standard perhaps better suited to the requirements of commercial users is the Minimum Security Functionality Requirements for Multi-User Operating Systems (MSFR). However, discussion of MSFR is beyond the scope of this book.

The Orange Book defines a trusted system as 'one which offers its users and administrators an assurance that a particular, well-defined level of security is attained'. The computer's hardware and software must incorporate security

A1 Verified design		
B1 Labelled security	B2 Structured protection	B3 Security domains
C1 Discretionary security protection	C2 Controlled access	
D No protection		

Figure 14.1.   Orange Book, levels of trust.

facilities that must pass a formal evaluation, and their purpose and use must be documented.

The Orange Book defines four levels of trusted systems, as shown in Fig. 14.1.

- C1 Discretionary security protection
  —User ID logon and authentication
  —Enforcing a need-to-know security policy
  —Separate execution domain for trusted computer base (TCB)
- C2 Controlled access protection
  —Limiting user access
  —Clear storage objects prior to use
  —Security auditing
- B1 Labelled security
  —*Mandatory access control (MAC)*
  —Labelling of human readable output
  —Process isolation through TCB controlled separate address spaces
- B2 Structured protection
  —*Device labels for all attached physical devices*
  —Trusted communication path
  —Modular kernel designed to enforce least privilege
  —Separate read/write attributes for segments
  —Covert storage channel analysis
  —Formal model of the security policy
  —Design top-level specification
  —Configuration management
- B3 Security domains
  —Discretionary access control
  —Administrative privilege

Features not implemented in AIX 3 are shown in italics. The current security classification is no better than C2 though most of the necessary features of the other levels have already been implemented. I believe it is just a matter of time before AIX reaches B1 and B2 security levels.

14.2   Physical security

The first level of security is physical security. Physically, the IBM RISC System/ 6000 is well protected against unauthorized access. All models have a three-position keyswitch on the front of the machines which has the states:

Normal   The usual position. The RISC system boots from any trusted device, which does not include the diskette drive.

Secure   This is as for the normal position but in addition the operation of the front panel reset button is disabled.

Service   In this position the RISC system will boot to standalone diagnostics stored on the hard disk. If not yet installed or corrupted then it is possible to boot from a diagnostics diskette placed in the diskette drive. Booting diagnostics is a restricted option since the program has the choice of starting a root 'superuser' privileged shell.

In addition a RISC system may not be dismantled unless the keyswitch is set to the service position.

14.3   Identification and authentication

Identification means logging on to AIX with a valid user name. *Authentication* is by default supplying the correct password that corresponds to the entered user ID. As with most other UNIX systems, an invalid user ID is not challenged by AIX, but after a password has been entered the error message 'name or password incorrect' is displayed. Thus the potential fraudulent user cannot determine which was in error. Also, the time to process the entered password and user ID has been deliberately extended so that it would take a user an impossibly long time to try and uncover a password to a known user ID by random attempts. Of course all incorrect logon attempts are logged, so the potential criminal may leave the systems administrator clues about their identity from the user IDs, locations and times of the attempted logons.

Normally, a single password is the only check required for a user logon. AIX extended this to allow the systems administrator to add one or more default authentication programs. Figure 14.2 is an example. This means that every user will also be subjected to the authorization program *TopSecret*. If this program returns a nonzero value then the logon will be rejected. Of course this test could be made more specific to a set of users instead of to all.

```
In the file /etc/security/user

default:
        auth1 = SYSTEM,NextCheck

and in /etc/security/login.cfg

NextCheck:
        program = /usr/bin/TopSecret
```

Figure 14.2.   Adding the Next Check authorization.

14.3.1   Resource control

Once a user has logged on AIX enables the systems administrator to limit a user's use of AIX resources. These limits include values for the amount of CPU time, real and virtual memory and stack that a user can legitimately use.

AIX also provides the control of disk storage on a user or group basis based on the Berkeley BSD 4.3 disk quota system. This includes the ability to set a normal (soft) limit on allowable disk allocations, a hard limit beyond which the user can not exceed, and a quota grace period, that is, the time the user can exceed the soft limit, which when exceeded causes the new hard limit to be set to the soft limit.

14.3.2   Users and superusers

Three types of users can be defined under AIX: root (also referred to as superuser), administrative and normal. The user identification (UID) is the factor which determines the type of the user. A UID of 0 gives a user complete access to all resources on the system; when the system is installed there is one user defined with a UID of 0 and a user name of root, however it is possible to create another user with the same UID but a different name—something you would only do for specific reasons such as creating a *shutdown* user to run the shutdown command immediately on logging on to the system. The second type of user is an administrative user who is assigned a UID in the range 1–199. Administrative users automatically belong to the system group and have access rights to many processes (performance monitoring commands, printing and spooling commands and accounting, to mention a few) unavailable to normal users. The third type of user is a normal user with a UID of 200 and above.

UNIX also defines the concept of a group identification (GID). A number of standard groups are defined under AIX at system installation; the default group for normal users is *staff* and for administrative users the default group is *system*. Another group defined at installation is *security*; members of this group have permission to run all the user and system group commands. Members of the security group are powerful users, they can add and remove users and groups and change user passwords. Being a member of the system group and a member of the security group is not mutually exclusive, in other words a user can be a member of either group or both. There is, however, an added bonus in making members of the security group also members of the system group—which is that only root can add, remove or change the details of users in the system group (administrative users). Thus, if there were two members of the security group on the system (in charge of creating new accounts and dealing with forgotten passwords), it would be wise to make them members of the system group so as to prevent them being able to administer each other.

14.4 The trusted computer base

The trusted computer base (TCB) enforces the security policy of the system. Basically this means that certain programs in the system are sensitive and should be accessible only to certain classes of user. AIX maintains a list of these programs (in the file /etc/security/sysck.cfg), and their required levels of authorization, therefore running the *sysck* checking program it is a simple matter to verify the TCB.

TCB programs fall into three categories:

- The operating system (kernel and installable libraries)
- Any configuration files that control the system
- Any programs that modify the above

Of course the systems administrator can modify the programs that are listed in the TCB and use this list for a variety of purposes. As an example consider the following entry stored in the sysck.cfg file:

```
/home/robert/bin/stepon
        class  = music
        owner  = robert
        group  = aixpeople
        mode   = TCB, rwxr-x---
        program = "/home/robert/bin/stepon"
```

This entry indicates that the program *stepon* has the class of *music*. There may be many programs that have this class, but by running the *sysck* the systems administrator can check the validity of all programs in the *music* class in one pass. By dividing programs into named classes, users can check program sets regularly, perhaps at logon time.

14.5 Modifications to password storage

In early versions of UNIX, encrypted passwords were stored in a publicly readable file called /etc/passwd. The *login* program simply encrypted the password entered by the user, compared it with the encrypted version already in

/etc/passwd and if a match was found logged on the user. Unfortunately, this also enabled any logged-on user to encrypt a number of 'common' passwords and compare them against entries in /etc/passwd. If any of the encrypted passwords matched any entry in the /etc/passwd file then that user's password was discovered. The key problem was that the password file was readable. AIX changed this and moved the password field in the password file into an AIX superuser-accessible-only file /etc/security/passwd. In general, many security files are stored in the /etc/security directory and these files are modifiable only by root and are not readable by anybody else.

14.6   Limiting user access

As originally designed, UNIX (unlike IBM PC DOS or OS/2) recognizes the concept of file ownership by a specified user ID. Any UNIX file has three sets of file permissions: read, write and execute. These are applied to the three classes: user, group and anybody. For example, in long list command in Fig. 14.3 the file shortpeople is owned by the user *snowwhite* who may read, write or execute the file. Any users who are in the *dwarfs* group can read from and write to the file. Finally, anybody may write to the file. The UNIX file permissions are classified at the C2 security level.

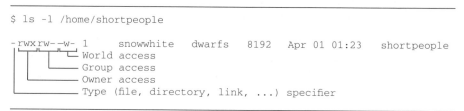

```
$ ls -l /home/shortpeople
```

Figure 14.3.   UNIX file permissions.

14.7   Discretionary access control

Discretionary access control (DAC) provides an extended set of file permissions that are used to augment or to replace the standard UNIX file permissions already discussed. These extended file permissions are known as access control lists (ACLs). For example, a file can be made totally inaccessible to anyone by issuing the following command:

chmod 000   /home/jane/topsecret

However the user *jane*, a member of the group *staff*, could still access her file provided the ACL information had been set thus:

permit rw- u: jane, g: staff

This information, retrieved using the *aclget* command says 'allow the read and write access to the user jane, when she is also a member of the group staff'. In general there are three allowable modes:

Permit   Grants the specified access modes for the users, groups or user/group combinations. This is in addition to any access rights granted by the regular UNIX filesystem permissions.

Deny   Explicitly restricts a type of access to named users, groups or user/group combinations. This restrictive mode overrides the permit and specify modes.

Specify   Allows the specified access modes for named users, groups or user/group combinations. This overrides any permissions granted by the regular UNIX file permissions.

The *aclget*, *acledit* and *aclput* commands manipulate the ACLs which are stored in the filesystem inode (see Sec. 10.4). Extending the previous example, assume the user jane's file topsecret is changed in the following ways:

```
permit   rw- u: snowwhite
deny     rw- u: grumpy
specify rwx u: sleepy, g: dwarfs
```

Now the file topsecret, in addition to its base UNIX file permissions, has three additional restrictions imposed on it. First, that the user *snowwhite* is allowed read and write access, as well as anything that the base permissions allowed her. Second, that the user *grumpy* is denied read and write access to the file, no matter what the base file permissions allow him. Third, that the user *sleepy*, while a member of the group *dwarfs*, is given read, write and execute access regardless of the state of the base file permissions.

This is clearly a powerful facility, and is particularly useful for sensitive information. A user can remove all accesses to a file by changing its mode to 000, then using the ACLs give only their own user ID access.

Another benefit of the ACL is that the set user ID (SUID) and set group ID (SGID) do not work with ACLs. In traditional UNIX, when a program is run it is executed with the privileges of the user's logon name. For example, I have a utility called *fm* (file manager) that allows me to manipulate my files. It is a program owned by the user ID *marcus*. When another user *jane* executes this program, she executes this program with the user ID *jane*, that is to say with the ID of the caller. However, if I set the SUID or SGID file permission bits on then *jane* executes the program with my authority, that is with the ID of the owner. This would seem to be necessary in some cases, for example, the tape drive in the AIX system should not be accessible by just anybody, but by giving the *backup, restore and tar* commands *root* ownership and setting the SUID bit on these commands, when I execute the *tar* program I become the superuser *root*. The user ID *root* has authority to access the tape commands so the tape manipulation commands can proceed without error. The SUID facility is useful here, but for my file manager program it would be a security loophole, because my program allows the user to run AIX commands from its built-in command line. Setting the SUID bit on my program would allow any other user to execute the program, and, while executing this program, allow the user the authority of the user *marcus*. From the built-in command line that user could, for example, delete all my files.

In fact, current releases of AIX now ignore SGID and SUID on any shell script. This means that a script program that needs access to a secure resource must use an ACL on that file to give the user the required access explicitly.

14.8   Trusted communication path

The trusted communication path allows for secure logons. Users invoke the trusted communication path by pressing a special key sequence known as the secure attention key (SAK). This is defined as a two-key sequence Control-X followed by Control-R. So in AIX to ensure a correct logon you should:

- Wait for the logon prompt to be displayed.
- Do not enter user ID, enter SAK sequence.
- If a new logon screen scrolls up you have a secure path and may log on with confidence. However if the trusted shell prompt appears, the initial logon screen was a fake program that was trying to steal your password.

14.9   Mandatory access control

AIX does not yet implement mandatory access control (MAC), which prevents the operating system from being classified to the B1 security level. In this scheme files are first tagged with a security classification. A user wishing to manipulate files must have a security tag at the same level or higher than the data being accessed. So for example, a user named *Sheela* with security clearance *secret* could try to manipulate two files, one tagged *top secret* and the other tagged *not secret*. MAC would prevent *Sheela* from accessing the *top secret* file. *Sheela* may be able to access the file tagged *not secret* depending on its regular UNIX file permissions (rwxrwxrwx). That is to say, the MAC permissions must be satisfied in addition to the standard UNIX file permissions for access to be granted to the user.

14.10   Accounting

While the accounting system was developed primarily to charge users for resources used, there are two spinoff benefits from setting up accounting— security and performance. Accounting records the users who logged on to the system, when and from what terminal, what commands they ran during their session and what resources were used by those commands.

AIX provides both traditional accounting systems, from BSD and USL. There are two main directories: `/usr/lib/acct`, where all the C programs and shell proceedures needed to run the accounting system are stored; and `/var/adm`, which contains the data, report and summary files. The accounting data files belong to members of the system group, and all active data files reside in the user *adm*'s home directory `/var/adm`.

The accounting package provides information in four areas: connect, process, disk and printer statistics. Connect data, entries for system startups, shutdowns and logons including date, time, user and port details are written to `/var/adm/wtmp`. Process data, user ID, group ID, name, elapsed time, memory usage and I/O to disk are written to `/var/adm/pacct`. Disk information, that is filesystem space per user, is written to `/usr/adm/dtmp`. Printer and queue information is written to `/usr/adm/fee`.

Once started the collection of data is on-going; the startup command `/usr/lib/startup` can be included in `/etc/rc`, so that on subsequent reboots accounting is automatically restarted. There are two shell script commands which create daily and monthly summary reports, *runacct* and *monacct*. These commands can be automated by the use of the *cron* timed command daemon facility.

In addition to the summary shell scripts, there are two 'interactive' commands: the *acctcms* command, which summarizes resource use by command name and can be used to produce long-term statistics on system utilization, providing information on total system usage and the frequency with which commands are used; and the *acctcom* command, which handles the same data as *acctcms*, but provides detailed information about each process. The commands include options to display all process accounting records or records of particular interest based on criteria such as time, name of command, user or group that invoked the process, and resources used.

14.11   Auditing

The auditing system provides a means of detecting potential violations of the system security policy by recording information about security-relevant events such as activities in the trusted computer base, changing system configuration information, modifying user accounts, or even circumventing the auditing system itself.

To audit an activity the command or process that initiates it, i.e., the audit event, must be listed in the `/etc/security/audit/events` file, otherwise it must be added to the file along with the message to be generated when that event occurs. Auditing events can be grouped into subsets, called *classes* which facilitate the selection of particular events for specific users.

In order to understand auditing issues the terms 'subject' and 'object' need to be defined. In general, subjects initiate actions, and objects receive actions; therefore processes can be defined as subjects and filesystem components (such as files, directories, devices and named pipes) and also interprocess communications (such as semaphores, shared memory and message queues) can be defined as *objects*.

Both user and object auditing can be configured: user auditing enables a specific user to be monitored, while object auditing allows for specific files, such as the password file, to be monitored.

There are two methods of collecting data: *bin mode* enables the long-term storage of a large amount of data for offline analysis; *stream mode* allows the system to process the data as it is collected. In a situation where both the long-term logging and the immediate reaction to security violations is required, both bin and stream modes should be configured.

There are two directories central to auditing: `/audit` is where the data files reside; and `/etc/security/audit` is where the auditing commands and configuration files reside. The files `objects`, `events` and `config` in `/etc/security/audit` determine the audit configuration: `objects` contains a list of files which when accessed in either read or write mode will generate an event; `events` lists all defined events and the format for the message generated; `config` specifies the event classes, the users who are to be monitored, and what mode auditing is to use—bin, stream or both. Figure 14.4 shows some sample configuration files.

Once the `config` file has been suitably edited the auditing system can be started with the command `/etc/audit start`. `/etc/audit shutdown` halts the audit program and all audit data is flushed from the kernel buffers into the audit bin.

14.12   Checking programs

AIX includes a number of checking programs that verify the consistency of system files. *sysck* has already been discussed. AIX also provides commands (*usrck, pwdck*) *to check the consistency of the user, password and group files.*

The virscan command checks that no executable program contains a binary string known as a virus. Typically this 'signature' string is machine code which, when executed, damages the user's files or environment. *virscan* checks the files specified against a set of signatures listed in `/etc/security/scan/virsig.lst`. For example, within many AIX development environments it would be prudent for each user's startup program to check all the executable files on the workstation or, for a shared machine, that user's directory. Also, any software that is to be installed on a machine has to be checked with *virscan* before execution. In this way the environment is kept clean.

```
A sample objects file

/etc/security/user:
   w = "S_USER_Write"

/etc/security/audit/config:
   w = "AUD_CONFIG_Write"

SAMPLE EVENTS FILE
   S_USER_Write = printf "%s"
   File_Write = printf "file descriptor = %d"

SAMPLE CONFIG FILE
classes:
   general   = USER_SU, PASSWORD_Change, FILE_Unlink, FILE_Link, FILE_Remove
   system    = USER_Change, GROUP_Change, USER_Create, GROUP_Create

users:
   root = system, general
   fred = general

bin:
   "info on bin filenames, sizes and commands"
stream:
   "info on stream commands"

start:
   binmode = on
   streammode = off
```

Figure 14.4.   Sample auditing files.

15
Diagnostics

IBM has traditionally produced systems with advanced diagnostics capabilities because of its long history with commercial computer systems; even the best of systems fail, perhaps because a component has come to the end of its useful life. For a commercial customer the cost of not having their IBM RISC System/6000 running their business application may be large, for example where RISC systems are used in the financial dealing systems marketplace. Whatever the problem or failure, a customer is first interested in getting their RISC system operational as quickly as possible. This chapter shows the excellent range of diagnostics facilities that the RISC system provides to help minimize system downtime and maximize user productivity.

One of the key innovations that the RISC system uses to enhance reliability has already been discussed in Sec. 3.1. Recall that the RISC system contains an on-card sequencer and dedicated test circuitry on the planar which thoroughly tests the electronics in a series of built-in self-tests (BISTs) and power-on self-tests (POSTs). Because these tests do not rely on the RISC system processors and drive a three-digit numeric LED display, they overcome the basic limitation of many other vendors' diagnostics, which run a diagnostic program under the control of the system processor, loaded into system memory. In such systems, a system processor or memory failure may lead to erroneous diagnostic results.

Another key innovation of the RISC system is that diagnostics can be performed online while the system is running. This is of great importance for the business user whose systems administrators can perform first-level diagnostics while a customer's business application is still running, perhaps at reduced functionality, and try and determine the cause of the problem. Therefore the SMIT systems management tool has a top-level option—*diagnostic routines.* This option runs the same diagnostic software as for standalone diagnostics. Because the panels are the same, the systems administrator has a consistent set of diagnostic tools in both online and standalone situations. Further, these diagnostic tools are the same as those used by the IBM Service representatives.

Clearly, some diagnostic routines cannot be run while the system is doing productive work, and in such circumstances the systems administrator can bring the machine down to maintenance mode and run the test again.

This chapter discusses both hardware and software diagnostics.

15.1   Hardware diagnostics

Aside from the BIST and POST processes already described, the main hardware diagnostics tool is an integrated set of screen-based programs run either from SMIT while AIX is running, or standalone from diskette.

For an error that cannot be detected while AIX is running, it may be necessary to change the *run level* of the AIX system from multiuser mode to maintenance mode with the *telinit* command, and rerun the diagnostics stored on the hard disk. Alternatively, for a complete system failure the same application needs to be loaded from diskette. This is performed by switching on the RISC system with the first diagnostics diskette in the floppy disk drive and the keyswitch set to the service position. There are four basic categories of diagnostics:

1   Diagnostic routines: test the machine hardware and detect any hardware problems. A problem will be indicated by an SRN (service request number). The SRN will allow a service representative to determine quickly what parts are required to repair the machine.

2   Service aid: will look at the machine configuration, exercise external interfaces, format media, look at past diagnostic results, control what resources are tested, check out media, etc.

3   Advanced diagnostic routines: will normally be used by the service representative. It comprises a set of extended diagnostic tests presented in the same format as for option 1.

4   System exerciser: tests resources running in an overlap mode.

Figure 15.1 is an example of a diagnostics screen from diagnostic routines menu, system verification submenu. In this example the user had tested the *hdisk0* disk and *rmt0* tape objects. Notice also the function key descriptions at the bottom of the panel; diagnostics are presented as a full-screen character-based application.

It is recommended that online diagnostics be run as part of a preventative maintenance schedule of the systems administrator.

The next sections of this chapter focus on software diagnostics and other AIX tools and techniques used for detecting errors.

15.2   Software diagnostics

Software diagnostics accessible from the SMIT menu allow:

1   *Verify an optional program product*   Since the *installp* and *updatep* installation and update programs record installation history in the ODM/VPD database, AIX can recheck if a program product has been installed correctly.

```
DIAGNOSTIC SELECTION                                              801006

An * in front of the resource shows that the test has been run.
Choose the test that you want to run.
     Object        Location        Description

     Base System 00-00             CPU, fpa, memory, I/O planar, op panel
     fd0           00-00-0D-00     Diskette Drive
     lp1           00-00-0P-00     Standard Parallel Port P
     lp0           00-00-S1-00     Serial Port
     tty0          00-00-S1-00     Serial Port
     tty1          00-00-S2-00     Serial Port
     ent0          00-04           Ethernet High-Performance LAN Adapter
     3270c0        00-05           3270 Connection Adapter Version B
     tok0          00-07           Token-Ring High-Performance Adapter
     scsi0         00-08           SCSI I/O Controller
   * hdisk0        00-08-00-00     670 MB SCSI Disk Drive
     hdisk1        00-08-00-10     1007 MB SCSI Disk Drive
     hdisk2        00-08-00-20     670 MB SCSI Disk Drive
     cd0           00-08-00-30     CD-ROM Drive
   * rmt0          00-08-00-40     2.3 GB 8mm Tape Drive
     rmt1          00-08-00-50     525 MB 1/4-Inch Tape Drive

 F3=Cancel         F10=Exit
```

Figure 15.1.   A sample SMIT diagnostics screen panel.

2 *Alert manager*   The concept of an alert has already been described in Sec.
   13.8.1. The alert manager gathers information from the AIX error log system,
   converts this to a format known by NetView and forwards this information
   to the IBM mainframe NetView via a PU-SSCP session. The error log in AIX
   has some flags related to errors. If a particular error has alert=1 and it is
   logged log=1, the alert manager will handle the error as described.

15.3   Error logging

The AIX *error logging* facility is a powerful nonintrusive tool that is a first line of
defence for the AIX systems adminstrator in detecting and tracking down errors.
The purpose of the error log is to save errors as they occur for later analysis. As
shipped the error log may grow to 1 Mb in size or 30 days in age before being
overwritten. Look at Fig. 15.2 to see how error logging works.

When an application or kernel component of AIX detects an error it writes the
error to a special file called /dev/error. Kernel programs (for example, a
device driver) use the functions **errsave()** or **errlog()**. The *errdaemon* which should
always be started (see Fig. 3.2 on page 17) reads /dev/error, time stamps the
message, and, using an error record template and information from the VPD and
ODM configuration database, places a compressed binary entry into the error
log. If AIX has been set to *concurrently notifiable* then the error is written to the
console as well.

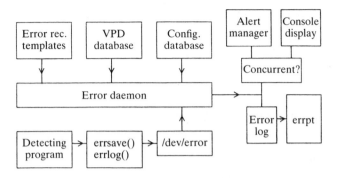

Figure 15.2.   Error logging.

At regular intervals the systems administrator[1] formats the error log. This is done using the *errpt* command which can produce both summary and detailed reports. In order to maximize the chances of detecting an error, the detailed AIX error log is *very* detailed so it is usually best to print out a summary listing first, then to use the appropriate flags on *errpt* to select just the events which are of interest. For example, Fig. 15.3 shows the key parts of a real summary report.

An applications developer designing an application may well choose to include error logging in their product. Do not forget that since the error log may be converted into *network alerts* this provides a good way to report and maintain a set of distributed applications centrally. The reader should distinguish clearly between error logging and trace logging. The trace facility enables a systems administrator to track the usage of AIX operating system and kernel facilities by applications. This was described earlier Sec.5.7.

15.4   Dump and crash

AIX provides powerful dump facilities that can be used to analyse the state of a RISC system at the time of an unexpected system failure. Of course, at that time it is too late to check whether the /dev/rhd7 dump device is large enough for the dump, so a good systems administrator should try creating and examining system dumps ahead of schedule. In order to prevent unauthorized dumping, the keyboard command to dump (*sysdumpstart*) needs root authority, and the dump keysequence (Control + Alt + NumPad1) will only be actioned if the front panel key is in the service position.

Once the dump is started it saves the following information:

---

[1] On my IBM RISC System/6000 workstation the systems administration, systems and applications programming is all down to one person—me! It is therefore in my interest to keep my system productive; I check the error log once weekly.

ERROR_ID	TIMESTAMP	T	CL	RES_NAME	ERR_DESCRIPTION
192AC07A	0310843291	T	O	errdemon	Error logging turned off
9DBCFDEE	0301044591	T	O	errdemon	Error logging turned off
0E017ED1	0303182191	P	H	mem2	Memory failure
038F2580	0304165291	U	H	scdisk0	Undetermined
AA8AB241	0304180191	T	O	OPERATOR	Operator notification

Figure 15.3   A sample summary error report.

- System variables and status
- Process, file and inode tables
- System buffers and TTY information
- Kernel stack
- User state areas
- Timer information
- Socket information

Once a dump has been produced it may be examined using the *crash* command. *crash* can also be used to examine an active system.

15.5   The IBM support system

No matter how reliable a RISC system is, hardware and software do fail. If they do, what does the RISC system customer do next? The support system does work but needs to be understood by both customer and IBM personnel. It only works well when both parties understand the ground rules, since a failure to do so can easily lead to misunderstandings and frustration.

15.5.1   *Good housekeeping*

There are a number of tasks an AIX systems administrator should do, and others that must be done to submit a problem successfully to IBM support. Being prepared before a problem develops will certainly save time.

Recommended tasks

Advisable but not essential tasks include:

- Regular checking of the error log
- Regular checking of the accounting system (if enabled)
- Periodic exercising of online diagnostics
- Familiarization with the contents of the IBM RISC System/6000 *Problem Solving Guide.*

Mandatory tasks

Before submitting a problem, the user must have the following:

- The telephone number of the AIX Systems Support Centre (SSC). For IBM mainframes separate numbers for software and hardware exist. For AIX however, usually a single number deals with both software and hardware. This means, therefore, the required number is usually neither the mainframe numbers, nor the number of the IBM marketing branch who have configured, received and processed the customer's order. Make a note of this number *before* it is needed!
- An IBM customer number. The SSC will not accept a call without one.[2]
- The system number of the failing system. Usually it is an alphanumeric sequence, for example FM0G9. Or if the failing component is software probably the AIX program number—currently 5756-030—and the level of the software that is running, discovered by typing the *lslpp* command.
- A description of the problem.
- A severity rating in the range 1 to 3. These ratings are classified in the following way:
  1 As a result of the reported problem my live system is down and my business function cannot proceed. This is the highest priority. IBM endeavours to fix severity 1 problems in 48 hours.[3]
  2 My system is down as a result of the problem but I may be able to manage without it (for example, I have a backup or alternative system). IBM endeavours to fix these problems within a few days.
  3 My system is affected by the problem but able to proceed (or for example, the fault occurs on a nonbusiness production system, say on a development machine). IBM endeavours to fix this problem in less than a working week.

Note that one should be very careful not to report all problems at severity level 1. In the real world there is only a finite amount of resource available to fix problems; artificially reporting at a high priority may adversely affect the resolution of other outstanding problems.

A subcategory of severity is priority. Priority ratings are either 1 or 2 and are issued internally by the Support Centre. So for example, a problem may be progressed as a severity 2, priority 1 problem.

---

[2] Readers who are IBM customers will be pleased to hear that this is especially true for IBM personnel reporting problems on internal systems. The cheerful phrase 'but I'm calling from within IBM' will cut little ice with the AIX Systems Support Centre unless the IBM employee knows their customer number.

[3] The times listed here are estimates only, they may vary from country to country but give the reader a feel for the kind of turnaround that IBM development or hardware customer support (CS) aim to provide to its customers via the Support Centre.

- A detailed description of the problem. For any problem this means an analysis of what machine configuration and sequence of events led to the problem. For hardware problems, this may also include information such as status of front panel LEDs. For software problems, ideally developers require a test case that will clearly reproduce the problem complete with supporting documentation. Other items that may be requested include a software dump, or error logs.

15.5.2 Reporting an AIX problem

The call to the SSC will follow the flow outlined in Fig. 15.4. When a user first calls the SSC, identification is required by way of the IBM customer number and the system number of the failing system (or software number of the failing AIX component). A brief description of the problem and the associated severity rating also needs to be given. In reply, the call-taker returns a problem reference

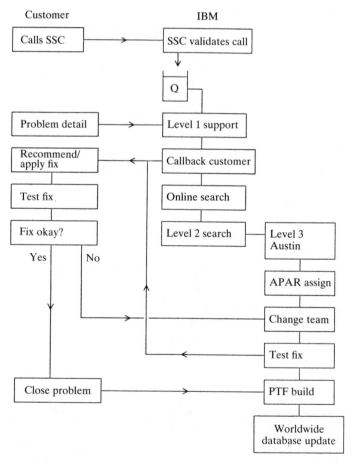

Figure 15.4.   Reporting an AIX problem.

number that should be used in further communications with the SSC until the problem is resolved.

The person who takes the call is not necessarily an AIX-skilled person and so a detailed problem description here is not required. The call-taker's function is simply to register the problem with the correct support group. This is level 1 support for software problems or customer services (CS) for hardware problems.

For a hardware problem the next stage in the process is the CS personnel telephoning to try and determine the problem. CS use the same diagnostics previously described, so an experienced AIX systems administrator who has already run diagnostics when a problem occurs may be able to indicate the failing item(s) directly by quoting the service request number (SRN) produced by diagnostics. In this case the CS technician will usually be able to call with the replacement part rather than having to make a visit to determine the cause of the problem. In some countries RISC systems are shipped with a modem that can be used by CS to run diagnostics remotely.

A software problem is usually more involved. Problems are passed to level 1 support and handled on a 'first come, first served' basis within their severity band. After a call is registered, level 1 support call back directly to ask for a more detailed problem description. If appropriate, level 1 support will make an on-the-spot search of the IBM worldwide Remote Technical Assistance Information Network (RETAIN) database. Hopefully this will identify the source of the problem and enable it to be solved. It may be classified as 'user error', or it may be that a fix to the problem has already been identified but that the failing system is not at the required software level.

If this does not resolve the software problem, the SSC will take the problem away for further level 1 or level 2 support analysis. This means a more extended search of various international databases for symptoms of the problem that have been outlined. Usually this will prove successful and the discovered fix will be shipped to rectify the problem.

If level 1 or level 2 support cannot resolve the problem, it is passed to level 3 support located in IBM AIX development labs in Austin, Texas. The problem and supporting document is received by development and receives an APAR number. Development labs have standards on resolution times of APARs. There is considerable pressure on development to turn around quality problem resolutions as soon as is practicable. When the fix is identified it is thoroughly tested and sent to the customer. Normally this involves electronic transmission from Austin to the country's SSC and then to the customer.

The fix should be applied and tested and, assuming the problem is cured, the SSC informed that the problem may now be closed. (If the problem is not resolved more communications to level 3 support will be required.)

At the end of a valid software problem resolution a new APAR will have been created and a problem fixed. At periodic intervals IBM collects pervasive APARs (that is to say, particular selective fixes to common problems) and combines these on a preventative maintenance package (PMP) shipped automatically by IBM to AIX customers. At interim times, however, it would be the task of the systems administrator to report the problem to the SSC, who can usually typically identify the selective fix necessary to cure the problem.

16
Standards and performance

The UNIX world is driven by standards—but whose standards and what do they really mean? This chapter concentrates on the larger and more popular standards. It describes the background on each standard and shows how AIX or the IBM RISC System/6000 participates in the standard.

To start with Table 16.1 is a performance summary of the IBM RISC System/ 6000. IBM has said that where there is a standards conflict it will try to comply with standards in the following hierarchy:

- ISO/IEC 9945-1:1990
- ANSI
- IEEE POSIX
- FIPS 151
- XPG3
- SVID issue 2
- BSD 4.3

16.1   Vendor standards

16.1.1   Berkeley Software Distribution

BSD (Berkeley Software Distribution) is the UNIX implementation developed by the University of California at Berkeley. The latest version of BSD is 4.4. AIX includes BSD 4.3 components with some additions from BSD 4.4, for example networking.

16.1.2   The Open Software Foundation

The Open Software Foundation (OSF) is an international nonprofit-making research and development company whose goal is to produce a leading open systems environment achieved through an 'open, vendor-neutral process'. The founders of OSF were major computer vendors such as IBM, DEC and Hewlett-Packard who each made million dollar investments into OSF.

Table 16.1 Summary performance figures for the IBM RISC System/6000

Model	220	32H	340	350	360	370	520H	530H	550L	560	580	950	970	980
Configuration	DT	DT	DT	DT	DT	DT	DS	DS	DS	DS	DS	RK	RK	RK
Clock speed (Mhz)	33	25	33	41	50	62.6	25	33	41	50	62.5	41	50	62.5
SPECmark	25.9	43.4	56.6	71.4	95.7	117	43.5	59.9	82.8	89.3	126.2	75.8	100.3	126.3
SPECint 92	15.9	20.9	27.7	34.6	48.4	59.8	20.9	28.2	40.7	42.0	59.1	N/A	47.8	59.2
SPECfp 92	22.9	39.4	51.9	65.0	97	118.2	39.6	57.6	83.3	85.5	124.7	N/A	101.0	124.8
LINPACK DP	06.6	11.8	15.0	18.8	22.2	25.9	11.9	20.5	N/A	31.3	38.3	25.6	31.0	38.1
TPC-A (OLTP) Local tpsA	N/A	N/A	N/A	N/A	N/A	N/A	29.0	42.0	N/A	61.0	N/A	48.0	100.9	N/A
TPC-B (server) Server tspB	31.4	41.4	56.4	66.9	N/A	N/A	44.7	52.6	N/A	80.1	N/A	74.2	N/A	N/A

DT—desktop; DS—deskside; RK—rack; N/A—not available.

OSF's first marketable product was OSF/Motif, a GUI environment for X-Windows. Spectacularly successful, Motif has become almost a *de facto* GUI interface for UNIX computers, much to the annoyance of Sun Microsystems whose Open Look products predate Motif.

Currently OSF is working in six major areas:

- The operating system, OSF/1
- The graphical user interface, OSF/Motif
- A distributed computing environment, OSF/DCE
- A distributed management environment, OSF/DME
- An object code distribution format, OSF/ANDF
- The interface specification, OSF/AES

OSF/1

OSF's main focus of activity after OSF/Motif was the development of OSF/1, which in plain terms is the main competitor to the principal mainstream UNIX product in the marketplace, USL Unix System V release 4. OSF/1 is a UNIX operating system with the following features (and more):

- MACH kernel and memory management
- Encore symmetric multiprocessing
- Dynamic system configuration
- AIX Logical Volume Manager, Berkeley File systems
- ANSI C
- Secureware B1 security
- X-Windows and MOTIF GUI
- OSF /DCE communications

OSF distributed management environment

The OSF distributed management environment (DME) product provides management of systems in an open system. OSF selected a number of technologies including:

- Tivoli's WizDOM, graphically enabled and object-oriented service manager
- Banyan Systems' network logger, actually developed by Wang
- Bull's consolidated management (CM) protocol programming interface
- Hewlett-Packard's Open View network management server
- Hewlett-Packard's and Gradient Technologies' software distribution utilities
- IBM's systems resource controller (SRC)
- IBM's Resource Data Engine, for monitoring and resource control
- Gradient Technologies' PC Agent and PC Event. These allow a systems administrator to perform management functions remotely, and to transfer

files from OSF/DME to the PC. The PC Event component forwards error notifications from the PC to a management system.

OSF architecture neutral distribution format

The OSF architecture neutral distribution format (ANDF) is a compiler intermediate technology that enables developers to develop and distribute applications in a format that may run on differing open systems architectures. The goal is to provide 'shrink-wrapped' software that can run on many differing systems, avoiding the extra manufacturing and tailoring costs of providing software for a specific vendor's architecture.

OSF selected a product from the Defence Research Agency in the UK.

OSF application environment specification

The OSF application environment specification (AES) provides a set of programming interfaces built upon POSIX, ANSI C, FIPS 151 and XPG3 (all covered in this chapter). Each OSF component, for example DCE or DME, has an AES component describing the systems administration, API interface, user environment and system environment for that product. The AES should be thought of as an enabling technology, enabling the building of portable and interoperable applications, rather than as a product.

OSF components are chosen using a four-step vendor-neutral process. These stages are:

- Vendor neutral request for technology (RFT)
- Selection of best technologies
- Development and snapshot program
- Full product delivery

In the request for technology, OSF publishes a list of requirements for a technology area that needs to be implemented, for example, distributed communications, or security. Any vendor may then submit proposals to satisfy this request. After an allotted time OSF makes a decision based on opinions from within OSF and from experienced external consultants. OSF's decisions usually result in selecting the best components from a variety of offerings.

IBM has announced its intention to support OSF/1 and other OSF components on its future UNIX platforms. Already we have seen the announcement of AIX/ESA which is a native OSF/1 port to the IBM mainframe architecture. We should expect IBM over time to integrate OSF/1 functionality into AIX on the IBM RISC System/6000.

However, what about ports of OSF/1 to other IBM platforms? A port to the PS/2 architecture would be politically sound, indeed a test port was performed over two years ago now, but running OSF/1 native on the IBM RISC System/6000 would be a difficult decision for IBM to make. If we look at the history of OSF/1, we see that things did not proceed according to IBM's initial expectations. Initially, OSF chose the AIX kernel as the foundation for OSF/1 and the other components as listed above. For a number of reasons though, this became an unacceptable choice and the kernel component was changed to Mach, a *microkernel* UNIX operating system from Carnegie-Mellon University. So IBM's internal plan of integrating OSF/1 into AIX went from possible to extremely nontrivial overnight. (Today AIX logical volume filesystem management, and some internationalization support is included in OSF/1. Also, AIX has already adopted the OSF/1 file tree naming standard.) It does bode well for the independence of OSF over its founder vendors, especially IBM who contributed financially more than most. Overall, I believe that IBM will incorporate OSF/1 and other components into future releases of AIX. The timescale for integration was to be in 1993 and beyond because IBM does not want to reduce the total function shipped with AIX. For example, some AIX facilities such as real time and fault tolerance will only be available in OSF/1.2, shipping in 1993, and so IBM cannot fully merge the base operating system component of OSF 1.x until that time.

16.1.3 SVID

SVID, the System V interface definition, is a vendor specification from UNIX System Labs (USL, formerly part of AT&T). SVID, like X/Open's XPG, is organized into two parts—base and extensions. SVID issue 2 defines System V release 3.2 compatibility; SVID issue 3 defines System V release 4 compatibility.

I have not been able to find any documentation to say that AIX version 3.2 and higher adheres to any SVID level, although as stated earlier IBM tries to comply with SVID issue 2 whenever possible so long as this does not conflict with compliance to other more favoured standards.

16.1.4 IBM'S systems application architecture

Systems application architecture (SAA) is one response from IBM to providing a coherent set of programming interfaces and a single look-and-feel specification across its entire line of vendor computer operating systems, namely:

- IBM Operating System/2
- IBM OS/400
- IBM VM/ESA
- IBM MVS/ESA

SAA is IBM's key strategy for integration of its non-UNIX offerings. The reader should appreciate that AIX and SAA are IBM's key architectures for the future. SAA interfaces consist of three related elements: *common user access*, *common communications support* and the *common programming interface*.

Common user access (CUA) is the definition of user interface components that should be common across all applications, for example, the placement of a menu bar with a number of options and that the help option should be the rightmost option in the menu bar. CUA is based on a set of generally accepted user interface design principles and is optimized for ease of use. CUA defines two interface models: entry and graphical. Entry is the recommended model for the nonprogrammable terminal environment and is best suited for data entry environments. The graphical model is recommended for workstation applications and makes extensive use of windows, action bars with pull down and stand graphical widgets such as pushbuttons and scroll bars.

The common programming interface (CPI) comprises a broad and consistent set of languages and services that programmers employ. Using these interfaces programmers can more easily move their applications from one SAA platform to another.

The common communications support (CCS) defines architectures and protocols that allow standardized communications between devices, application programs, systems and networks. CCS consists of IBM SNA protocols and selected OSI protocols to allow IBM and non-IBM systems to be connected. It now also includes TCP/IP.

16.1.5   *Common open software environment (COSE)*

The common operating software environment (COSE) is an attempt by six manufacturers, Hewlett-Packard, IBM, Santa Cruz Laboratories, Sun Microsystems, Univel and UNIX Systems Laboratories, to broadly deliver a common software environment for GUI development across their UNIX platforms. It is only a paper specification at the time of writing (late 1993) but when (and if) this standard is embodied in real products, it will offer hope for programmers who want to develop their applications just once for UNIX platforms. COSE is split into six sections which are described here:

Common desktop environment

This relates to the look and feel of applications and the necessary programming interfaces, technical and style guide documentation necessary to support the production of such applications. X-Windows version 11 forms the base technology upon which this will be built, with the programming interface for applications being provided by OSF/Motif, with inter-application communication using Sunsoft's Tooltalk. Other technologies which will be drawn from include HP's visual user environment and USL's desktop file manager.

Networking

The six vendors have agreed, in principle, to support the systems listed below for communication between their own and other vendor systems.

- OSF's DCE
- Sunsoft's Open Network Computing +
- Novell/Univel Netware

High performance graphics

Three levels of graphics will be supported. These are:

- Xlib for basic 2D graphics
- PEX for 2D and 3D geometry graphics
- X Image Extensions library (XIElib) for advanced imaging

Multimedia

The six vendors will submit a joint specification to the Interactive Multimedia Association's (IMA) request for technology. (The IMA, of Annapolis, Maryland, is an industry forum in which over 250 companies discuss the merits of proposed formats, protocols and technologies. It is the practical standards-setting organization for multimedia.)

Object technology

The six vendors will support the efforts of the Object Management Group (OMG) and the Common Object Request Broker (COBRA) for distributed management solutions.

Systems management

The six vendors will work together to provide common solutions and implementations to support user group management, software installation, maintenance and licensing, storage management, printer and filesystem management.

Of the six areas, the most clearly defined, and the most important is the common desktop environment. It uses components that already exist in the marketplace today, and establishes OSF/Motif as *the* programming interface (and look and feel) for GUI applications on UNIX and also AIX platforms. Significantly, OSF have agreed to submit the Motif specification and associated support materials to X/Open for incorporation into the influential X/Open portability guide during 1994. (X/Open is described in more detail in Sec. 16.3.5.)

16.2   US government standards: FIPS and NIST

The Department of Commerce agency of the US government sets standards for its procurement. NIST, the National Institute of Standards and Technology, develops product-level implementation standards for this department. Of particular interest are the Federal Information Processing Standards (FIPS) which are computing standards.

FIPS standards are important because the US government usually makes these a prerequisite to winning a government contract. The two standards that computer vendors are often required to meet are FIPS 151-1 and FIPS 158. In 1988, FIPS 151 simply stated that the computer system should comply with the IEEE POSIX standard draft 12.0 of IEEE P1003.1. In March 1990 this was updated to the now ratified POSIX standard 1003.1-1988. IBM's AIX meets and exceeds this standard.

FIPS 158 specifies the windowing interface. It dictates that the Windowing system should be X-Windows X11.3 or later; also that the vendor should supply the programming interfaces Xlib and the X toolkit intrinsics Xt. IBM meets and exceeds FIPS 158 with its AIXwindows component of AIX for the IBM RISC System/6000.

NIST is also involved in setting standards for CASE. The IBM, AIX CASE offering described in Sec. 5.2 conforms to the recommended NIST reference model for CASE.

16.3   US standards bodies

16.3.1   ANSI

ANSI, the American National Standards Institute, is a voluntary organization which coordinates US representation to ISO. The ANSI X3 committee defines standards for programming languages such as C, Fortran and Pascal.

The IBM RISC System/6000 XL series of compilers all meet ANSI standards.

16.3.2   IEEE

The US founded, Institution of Electrical and Electronics Engineers (IEEE) is the recognized voice of professionally qualified (to degree level and higher) electronics engineers in America. The IEEE also has members worldwide. The IEEE is very active and has been particularly so in standards setting. For many years, the IEEE has been the source of many of the hardware computer bus standards in the industry. Of late, the IEEE's Technical Committee on Operating Systems (TCOS) has established standards for a comprehensive set of operating system interfaces that support both portability and interoperability. The principal output so far has been the portable operating system interface called POSIX.

Over 25 committees are involved in defining POSIX standards and application environment profiles (AEPs), which can be applied against the base standards to define a particular environment. For example, the 1003.4 committee defines the interface extension for real time to 1003.1. The 1003.13 committee defines a profile that specifies the AEP. Table 16.2 is a summary covering the various standards.

When a systems or applications vendor ships a program they can classify in one of four levels of POSIX compliance:

- Nonconforming: this means that the application is not POSIX compliant at all.
- Conforming using extensions: a POSIX application built with some non-POSIX extensions, for example NFS, or X/OPEN extensions.
- Conforming: a POSIX application including some ANSI or ISO options.
- Strictly conforming: an application built using just POSIX and ANSI C.

16.3.3   Standard P1201.1

The IEEE P1201.1 has undergone many changes. Initially, it was to be a standard like POSIX but for GUIs. In this respect it was really to be a straight choice between OSF/Motif and Sun Microsystems Open Look. Unfortunately both Sun (the chief supporter of Open Look) and many other vendors dedicated to OSF/Motif were not prepared to see anything other than their GUI environment as a standard. The result? Neither GUI could be selected as 'the standard' so the long-suffering P1201.1 committee tried a different approach. This was the layered API (LAPI) approach. LAPI adds an additional layer above the GUI (as if there were not already enough layers!) and the programmer would write to that layer. Three organizations submitted LAPI technology to the P1201.1 working committee, namely XVT Software, the US Air Command and NASA. Of the three, only XVT has a working product, a high-level programming interface that allows C programs to be written in a GUI-independent fashion. Target windowing systems include OSF/Motif, Open Look, IBM OS/2 Presentation Manager and Microsoft Windows. Unfortunately the LAPI approach has many problems, for example, the programmer cannot use any GUI-specific features else portability is lost. No firm decision has yet been made.

On a closely related area, and partly because it seems P1201.1 now represents a higher level programming interface, the sponsor executive committee for POSIX submitted a project authorization request for a standard GUI for POSIX. As one might expect, OSF submitted a modular toolkit environment based on Motif, while Sun Microsystems and UNIX Systems Laboratories submitted the open toolkit environment based on Open Look. Once again Motif and Open Look fought to a draw, and the committee could not decide.

The bottom line is that there are two unofficial 'standards' in the GUI arena,

Table 16.2. IEEE POSIX 1003 standards

Standard	Description
1003.0	Guide to the POSIX open system environment
1003.1	Base system including system calls and utilities
1003.2	Shell and application utilities
1003.3	POSIX test methods
1003.4	Real-time extensions
1003.5	Ada binding to the POSIX base system
1003.6	Security
1003.7	Systems administration
1003.8	POSIX networking
1003.9	Fortran binding to the POSIX system
1003.10	Supercomputing application environment
1003.11	Transaction processing environment
1003.12	Protocol independent interface
1003.13	Real-time application environment profile
1003.14	Multiprocessing
1003.15	Batch services

Open Look and Open Software Foundation. With the announcement and implementation of COSE (see Sec. 16.1.5) this will undoubtedly change.

16.3.4   ISO

ISO, the International Organization for Standardization, is a body founded to encourage standardization. The members of ISO are the national standard bodies such as ANSI for the United States, DIN for Germany, and BSI for the United Kingdom.

Two ISO standards of note include the IEEE POSIX standard which in ISO terms is ISO/IEC 9945-1, and the character classification standard ISO 8859. AIX meets and exceeds ISO/IEC 9945-1 and also enables ISO 8859 standards to be used natively under AIX character-based and graphical windowing environments.

16.3.5   X/Open

X/Open is not strictly a standards body, but a consortium of international computer and software vendors who came together to encourage open systems. X/Open's objectives are to develop an open and multivendor common applications environment (CAE) based on international or *de facto* standards. The CAE that vendors need to adhere to is specified in the X/Open Portability Guide (XPG). The latest level of XPG is XPG3 which constitutes two sections. The base is built around POSIX 1003.1-1988 and includes specifications for the systems programming interface, commands, utilities and ANSI C. The extension has 12 parts:

- Fortran
- COBOL
- Ada
- Pascal
- ISAM
- Terminal interfaces
- Window management
- SQL
- X/Open transport interface
- PC networking
- IPC
- Source code transfer

IBM uses X/Open's VSX test suite to ensure that AIX conforms to XPG3 base brand, which in fact really means that AIX complies to POSIX!

16.4   Graphics bodies and standards

16.4.1   X Consortium

The MIT X Consortium was formed in January 1988 to further the development of the X Window system and promote cooperation within the computer industry of standard software interfaces at all layers in the X-Windows environment. There are two categories of membership: member (for large organizations like IBM) and affiliate (for smaller companies). The X Consortium publishes the Inter-Client Communication Conventions Manual (ICCCM) which describes the conventions that X client programs must observe to co-exist peacefully.

16.4.2   PHIGS

PHIGS is both an ANSI and an ISO standard. PHIGS defines a powerful API for both 2D and 3D graphics applications. IBM's version on PHIGS is called graPHIGS and is based on the following standards:

- ISO/IEC 9592-1 PHIGS part 1, Functional Description
- ISO/IEC 9593-1 Fortran Language Binding of PHIGS

16.5   Performance standards

Over the last few years the explosive growth in workstation computing power has led to an equally explosive growth in the claims of many workstation vendors each to have the 'fastest' performing UNIX computer system. Many performance benchmarks are now available, claiming to test thoroughly the all-round capabilities of the IBM RISC System/6000. This section discusses some of the more meaningful tests and the results.

16.5.1 SPEC

Standard Performance Evaluation Corporation (SPEC) is a nonprofit-making corporation initiated by the *Electronic Engineering Times*. SPEC's stated purpose is to design a suite of benchmarking programs that are effective and fair in comparing the performance of computer systems. SPEC's members include some of the foremost computer vendors in the industry. IBM joined SPEC in May 1989 and is a member of the SPEC steering committee. The benchmarks are so large that they cannot easily be 'optimized' and have long enough run times to minimize timing differences.

SPEC has announced two benchmark suites to date. The first benchmark suite SPEC suite 1 was released in October 1989. Its present revision is SPEC 1.2b, and focuses on CPU-intensive applications in a technical workstation environment. The result of this benchmark is a number called the SPECmark. A DEC VAX 11/780 has a SPECmark of 1.0. The SPECmark is computed by taking the geometric mean of the 10 individual ratios for the benchmarks (that is to say the 10th root of the product of the benchmark times in seconds). Two derived numbers are the integer SPECmark and the floating-point SPECmark which are the geometric means of the four integer and six floating-point benchmarks. In January 1992, SPEC introduced SPEC suite 2 comprising two benchmarks: CINT92 and CFP92. CINT92 extended the number of integer tests to six, and CFP92, floating-point tests to fourteen. As before, a geometric mean is calculated, this time for each set of results. Unlike SPEC suite 1 an overall measure of the 20 tests is not now computed since systems with a similar SPECmark rating could have widely different floating and integer performance characteristics rendering a combined SPECmark number meaningless. SPEC suite 2 is designed to replace suite 1. SPEC SDM 1.0, published in May 1991, focuses on multitasking software development applications for UNIX-based systems.

SPEC is already working on future benchmark suites and intends to cover other areas such as networking, graphics and input/output. Anybody can write to SPEC for a benchmarks source tape. Both tapes together cost about £1500.

16.5.2 SPEC suite 2

The 20 benchmarks are listed here. See Table 16.3 for a summary.

alvinn   This program is used to train an autonomous land vehicle in a neural network. It is a CPU-intensive program using single-precision C.

Table 16.3. SPEC suite 2 benchmarks

Name	Language	Calculation	Description
compress	C	Integer	File compression utility
eqntott	C	Integer	Boolean equation minimizer
espresso	C	Integer	Programmable array logic generation
gcc	C	Integer	gnu C compiler
li	C	Integer	LISP interpreter solving nine queens problem
sc	C	Integer	A spreadsheet benchmark
alvinn	C	Floating point	Neural network simulation
doduc	Fortran	Floating point	Seven kernel synthetic benchmark
ear	C	Floating point	Human ear simulation
fpppp	Fortran	Floating point	Quantum chemistry
hydro2d	Fortran	Floating point	Astrophysics simulation
mdljdp2	Fortran	Floating point	Quantum chemistry
mdljsp2	Fortran	Floating point	Quantum chemistry
nasa7	Fortran	Floating point	Nasa applications
ora	Fortran	Floating point	Ray tracing
spice2g6	Fortran	Floating point	Analogue circuit simulation
su2cor	Fortran	Floating point	Quantum physics
swm256	Fortran	Floating point	Finite difference arithmetic
tomcatv	Fortran	Floating point	Fluid dynamics
wave5	Fortran	Floating point	Particle in cell simulation

compress   A file compression utility using Lempel-Ziv encoding. This program, written in C, compresses and decompresses a 1 Mb file 20 times.

doduc   A large kernel extracted from a Monte Carlo simulation of the time evolution of a thermo-hydraulic model for a nuclear reactor component. The 5300 lines of Fortran perform little I/O. The code contains many loops and short branches and is not easily vectorizable.

ear   A benchmark supplied by Apple that simulates the human ear. The program's input is a sound file and its output a 1 Mb cochleagram output file. This is a single-precision C benchmark.

eqntott   Translates a logical representation of a boolean equation into a truth table. There are 3400 lines of C; execution is mainly spent in the **qsort()** function.

espresso   One of a collection of tools for the generation and optimization of programmable array logic. Performs heuristic boolean function minimizations. It is completely CPU integer intensive and provides insight into how logic simulation and routeing algorithms can be expected to perform. It has 13 500 lines of C. Almost no paging on most systems.

fpppp   This measures the performance of computations from quantum
               chemistry. The 2700 lines of Fortran do almost no branching.

gcc   The GNU C compiler distributed by the Free Software Foundation.
               It measures the time taken for the compiler to convert 76
               preprocessed source files into optimized Sun-3 assembly language.
               It is representative of work done in a software engineering environ-
               ment. It is a C, integer-intensive program.

hydro2d   This is an astrophysics program that solves the hydrodynamic
               Navier–Stokes equations. It is a vectorizable double-precision
               Fortran program.

li   A lisp interpreter written in C. The benchmark measures the time
               to solve the popular nine queens problem. It comprises over 7000
               lines of LISP. The execution time is dominated by the many
               program short loops and branches and is CPU integer intensive.

mdljsp2   This is a single-precision Fortran benchmark that represents
               quantum chemistry applications. The program solves the equations
               of motion of 500 atoms using the Lennard-Jones interatomic
               potential model method.

mdljdp2   This is a double-precision Fortran version of the previous
               benchmark.

nasa7   A collection of seven floating-point intensive programs. Double
               precision and CPU intensive. There are 2200 lines of Fortran, some
               of which are vectorizable.

ora   Optical Research Associates: traces rays through an optical system
               composed of spherical and plane surfaces. This is a double-precision
               Fortran benchmark.

sc   This is a spreadsheet benchmark that performs standard operations
               such as cursor movement, data entry and calculation. Output is
               directed into a file.

spice2g6   An analogue circuit simulation and analysis widely and heavily
               used in the electronic design automation market. It is a CPU-
               bound floating-point application. There are 18 400 lines of Fortran.
               It stress tests small instruction and data caches. It is unlikely to
               benefit from vectorization or parallelization techniques.

su2cor   This calculates particle masses of elementary particles using the
               statistical Monte Carlo method. It is a vectorizable double-precision
               Fortran program.

swm256   This solves a system of shallow water equations using finite differ-
             ence approximation on a 256 × 256 grid. This is a single-precision
             Fortran benchmark.

tomcatv   This is a 250-line Fortran program performing mesh generation.
             The code is highly vectorizable but creates several very large
             memory arrays.

wave5   This is a single-precision Fortran benchmark. It performs a two-
             dimensional particle in cell simulation used to study plasma
             phenomena.

16.5.3   SPEC system development multitasking

System development multitasking (SDM) consists of two multitasking system
level benchmarks *sdet* and *kenbus1*. Both benchmarks are designed to exercise
CPU, memory, disk I/O and operating system services.

- sdet is a benchmark with AT&T origins. It comprises the execution of a
  number of UNIX commands used in C-based commercial software development including *spell, nroff, diff, make* and *find.*
- kenbus1 is derived from the Monash University Suite for UNIX benchmarking (MUSBUS). The benchmark uses commands and procedures that are
  used in a typical UNIX/C research and development environment such as *cc,
  cat, grep, mkdir* and *rm.*

SDM measures performance by gradually increasing the workload applied to the
system. This is achieved by increasing the number of concurrent copies of the
workload script. The number of scripts is increased until thrashing bottlenecks
occur. The throughput metric is defined as the peak scripts executed per hour.

16.5.4   The Transaction Processing Performance Council

The Transaction Processing Performance Council (TPC) was formed in 1988
with the purpose of developing transaction processing application benchmarks.
Two benchmarks are of particular interest: TPC-A multiuser and TPC-B
multitasking.

The TPC A benchmark dates back to November 1989. It is an interactive
multiuser benchmark representative of an online transaction processing (OLTP)
banking environment. It measures (in transactions per second—tps) the
throughput of a system with the requirement that 90 per cent of all transactions
must have an external user response time of two seconds or less. TPC-A
therefore uses a remote terminal emulator connected to the system under test to
simulate actual users entering transactions.

The TPC B benchmark was created in September 1990. It is a multitasking workload that exercises the database on a system under test. It uses the same banking application as TPC-A but no terminal I/O or network overhead is simulated. TPC-B (like TPC-A) requires that 90 per cent of transactions have a residence time of two seconds or less. IBM results detailed previously were obtained using AIX version 3.2 and Informix–Online 4.00.

16.5.5   Whetstones

This benchmark was created in 1976 by Curnow and Wichman. It is written in Algol and based on a statistical distribution of Algol statements. Fortran, C and Pascal versions are now available. Single- and double-precision versions also exist. It is a CPU-bound benchmark with no I/O or system calls. Hence it may at best be a test of raw system floating-point performance and maturity of the compiler. Results are expressed in MWHETS (millions of whetstones). The higher the number, the better the performance.

16.5.6   Dhrystones

A dhrystone is an old (1984) performance metric. It is composed of approximately 100 C statements. It does not use floating-point, terminal or disk I/O, or any AIX system function. Today the SPEC series of benchmarks are usually used instead of dhrystones. Dhrystone test results are expressed in dhrystones per second.

16.5.7   Linpack

This benchmark was written by Jack J. Dongarra of Argonne National Laboratory. It is coded in Fortran and uses a linear programming problem involving array manipulation to test machine performance. The innermost computational loops of the workload are isolated in one subroutine called the basic linear algebra subroutine (BLAS). Single- and double-precision versions of the benchmark exist. The results are expressed in terms of MFLOPS (millions of floating-point operations per second). The higher the number, the better the performance.

16.6   Competitive summary

We have seen how AIX conforms to industry standards and performs in industry benchmarks. How does it fare against other leading UNIX or personal computer implementations? Table 16.4 is my summary which I feel was accurate at the time of writing.

Table 16.4. AIX competitive summary

Description	AIX 3.2	HP-UX 8.0x	NCR V.4	SCO ODT	SunOS 4.1.2	ULTRIX 4.2a	OS/2 2.0
Scalable kernel	Y		Y				
Efficient I/O	Y		Y		Y		Y
Kernel pre-emption	Y	P	P				
Dynamic linking	Y		Y		Y		Y
Shared libraries	Y	P	Y	P	Y		Y
Streams	Y	Y	Y	Y	Y		
Reliable filesystem	Y		Y				
Disk volume manager	Y	P	Y		Y	P	
Sys. mgt. interface	Y	Y	Y	Y			Y
Good internationalization	Y	Y	P	P	P	Y	Y
Good documentation	Y	Y	P	Y	P	Y	Y
Good connectivity	Y	Y	Y	Y	Y	Y	Y
Good compilers	Y	Y	Y	Y	Y	Y	
Good security	Y	Y	Y	Y	Y	Y	

Y = yes, P = partial

17
A change of attitude

In the fiscal year 1991, IBM sold almost three billion dollars' worth of UNIX products, placing IBM as the world's third largest vendor of UNIX systems. This was a substantial improvement over the previous year and enough to place IBM in the same league as vendors with strong UNIX connections including Sun Microsystems and DEC.

My personal view is that IBM's marketing strategy for the IBM RISC System/ 6000 is not based on straight-line derived revenue or profitability for two reasons. First, IBM is still not perceived by many other vendors or corporates as a significant player in the UNIX marketplace, even though I would argue the above sales figures prove otherwise. Second, and perhaps more significantly, the nineties have meant lean times for most established computer vendors. As the general worldwide recession continues, I believe that computer vendors' aspirations seem now to be sighted on not making a year-on-year loss, rather than on maximizing profits.

In this difficult global computer marketplace I believe that IBM's strategy for the nineties relies heavily on expanding its market share, especially in the open systems marketplace, via IBM's premier open systems computer system the IBM RISC System/6000. How is this being achieved? By meeting the needs of any potential and existing customer by using the full range of information technology facilities such as marketing, technology leadership and manufacturing, supplied by IBM itself or from any IBM business partner. Business partners divide into three categories:

- The value added reseller
- The ex-IBM companies
- Vendor alliances

Let us look at some of marketing strategy changes that I believe have taken place inside IBM, before covering the above three categories.

17.1   Market driven for customer satisfaction

One of the differentiating factors that IBM marketing provided in the seventies was the excellence of the IBM systems engineer. The systems engineer and sales professional were traditionally a team that marketed AIX and other IBM computer systems to existing IBM customers or to new business prospects. Since the beginning of the nineties, IBM has made the change to services marketing, but before we cover that, let us look at the traditional role of the IBM systems engineer.

The established role of the IBM systems engineer was to work with an IBM customer or prospect to determine the best system for that customer's needs. For a large and established IBM customer one or more systems engineers would be dedicated to a particular 'account' and would work solely as technical liaison and account maintenance for the IBM systems used by that customer. At a pre-sales stage the systems engineer worked with the customer to understand the business requirements, determine the most suitable IBM system and plan the installation. After sale and installation, the systems engineer continued to work closely with the customer.

By the mid eighties the emphasis within IBM was on 'getting closer to the customer' and this usually involved spending more time with the customer. It was not uncommon in large IBM customer sites for IBM staff to be located almost full time on the customer premises.

Some of the key phrases that have dominated IBM marketing strategy for 1991 and 1992 include 'market driven' and 'total solutions'. The systems engineering team is now oriented to provide an 'open minded' solution comprising both products and services to help the customer to be more successful; in particular, to provide services to build customer enterprise-wide multivendor information systems based on the principles of 'what you have is what we will support' and 'what you need is what we will help you get'. Here are some examples of services that IBM could provide, taken from real IBM customer situations:

- Performing a technical appraisal of the customer's international and single-vendor corporate computing system and drawing up a plan on how to move this to an open systems UNIX-based platform, incorporating IBM AIX and other UNIX vendors' workstations and minicomputers.
- Project management of a large avionics installation and development project.
- Supplying skilled AIX people to work onsite with the customer to implement a portable streams interface on AIX and non-IBM UNIX systems.

17.2   IBM terms and conditions

IBM now provides many flexible options of purchase and leasing to encourage existing IBM and prospective customers to consider AIX. (Since exact availability, terms and conditions will vary from country to country and from time to time readers should check their IBM electronic customer support or their local IBM marketing representative for exact details.)

17.2.1   The IBM volume purchase agreement

The IBM volume purchase agreement (VPA) offers an enterprise a discount on the price of IBM computer systems based on an agreed yearly purchase quantity. This agreement benefits both the customer and IBM. The customer agrees to purchase a stated minimum quantity of IBM AIX systems over a fixed period, usually one year. This can be a 'worldwide VPA', which is advantageous for international corporations, each of which may make small individual sales, but which when aggregated form a larger commitment. In return IBM discounts the equipment sold to the customer based on total quantity and retail price. This agreement is beneficial to IBM because manufacturing divisions are assured of a guaranteed production quantity in the coming yearly period.

17.2.2   IBM leasing

IBM leasing is often a cost-effective way of utilizing IBM equipment. Depending on the country, there may be good reason why it is more tax efficient to lease rather than to buy. Here is a list of some of the terms that may be possible with an IBM RISC System/6000 hardware and software leasing contract:

- One stop shopping—everything can be included
- Competitive rates vs. the marketplace
- Discounted and fixed IBM maintenance
- Rollover/refinancing
- Interim buyout options
- Fully disclosed IBM contracts

In many countries IBM leasing operates as an independent business unit and offers customers an attractive package in order to secure business.

17.2.3   The IBM trade-in program

Customers who have bought previous IBM UNIX systems, and increasingly customers who have bought another vendor's UNIX system, can trade in that UNIX system for an IBM AIX system. Of course, since these terms are subject to change the reader should contact their IBM marketing representative for full information.

17.2.4   The IBM technology trade-in

In an attempt to become more open to customers, IBM now announces many products well before it is ready to ship them. IBM wants to tell customers what products are coming down the line. However, some customers may be consequently put off from ordering products that may shortly be replaced by newer IBM technology. To prevent this, IBM announced a series of technology trade-in programmes allowing users to buy systems or peripherals today, then to exchange or upgrade them to already announced new systems and components. For example, the current range of high-performance graphics cards (discussed in Sec. 8.7) were announced several months before their 'general availability'. In the interim, IBM customers could purchase existing graphics cards and trade them in when the new cards became readily available. A second example is the model upgrade ability, allowing users of RISC system models 320, 520 and 530 to upgrade their systems to newer higher performing models in the RISC system family.

17.2.5   Discounts to developers and demonstrators

IBM recognized that however good RISC system hardware and AIX software are, they are of little use without good applications support. IBM therefore has a twofold strategy in place to encourage applications developers to support AIX.

First, IBM has a number of internationally placed 'porting centres' whose purpose is specifically to support the conversion of software written for other (typically UNIX) platforms onto AIX. The vendor discusses with IBM the nature and expected effort required for the port and reserves the required time with the porting centre which has a variety of IBM AIX and other systems. But this is not enough—clearly if the applications developer had initially developed for AIX then porting would not be necessary! Therefore to encourage applications developers to use AIX as their UNIX base (and have to port to other UNIX flavours), IBM offers certain financial discounts to bona fide developers of AIX applications. These discounts may also be extended to industrial consult-ants also.

17.2.6   Source code availability

IBM now makes available the complete source code and build guide for AIX to those customers who need to customize and enhance their AIX environment. Since AIX derives in part from USL System V 3.2 +, the Tahoe/Reno BSD 4.3 and OSF/1, source licenses to these are required as contractual prerequisites. IBM is very proud of its version of UNIX. If a customer wants the source to AIX they can have it.

17.3   The IBM value added reseller

The IBM value added reseller (VAR) is an important part of IBM's marketing team, selling the IBM RISC System/6000 to small and medium sized-businesses. The VAR buys IBM RISC System/6000 computers from IBM then resells them together with services and software to the customer. A customer's contact is therefore with the VAR and not with IBM. The customer does, however, normally obtain hardware and software support from IBM unless the VAR elects to provide their own. Traditionally, IBM sold computers to the large corporate customer, but clearly the market for computer systems now extends from the very smallest to the very largest business. VARs are one of the key ways in which IBM can penetrate the open systems marketplace, especially specific segments of industry or customers who have little or no previous computing skills or utilization. Small business customers do not have the time or resources to staff in-house computer departments; they are interested in using a RISC system as a tool in their business. They are typically interested in buying a complete systems solution from a VAR supplier, and usually the VAR has specific knowledge in a customer's business sector and will be able to tailor an existing package for the customer's use. The IBM marketing salesforce works hand in hand with the VAR, usually by understanding a customer's needs, then by identifying the best VAR that satisfies a customer's requirements.

17.4   IBM companies

In the nineties IBM realized that it needs to restructure its business radically into increasingly autonomous companies to increase profitability. This restructuring has taken the form of variable IBM ownership across a range of product businesses, marketing and service companies—from wholly owned, majority owned or minority owned to no ownership at all. These companies can also be categorized into two groups: first, companies like Lexmark who were part of existing IBM worldwide development; second, companies like Metaphor who are the result of recent IBM acquisitions. This new structure is designed to allow each company greater local management control, allowing it to react faster and be more flexible toward changes in the information technology marketplace, and, most importantly, each company is now a genuine profit centre, buying services and products to manufacture its products. In the past, it may have been common for the more profitable sectors of IBM to subsidize the lesser; this will not happen in the future. Further, should a wholly or part-owned IBM subsidiary register year-on-year losses then IBM would be very likely to sell off its shareholding to the highest bidder. This provides greater local management focus on reducing cost, for example, within IBM the increasing trend of hiring contractors to meet varying workload demands instead of taking on permanent staff.

17.4.1 Lexmark International

In March 1991, Lexmark International Inc., an independent company, was formed from IBM's former typewriter and office printer business. The name Lexmark was created by combining 'lex' an abbreviation of lexicon (meaning 'pertaining to words') and 'mark' (referring to 'marks on paper'). IBM holds a 10 per cent equity interest in the company, the balance being owned by Clayton and Dubilier Inc. IBM has entered into several manufacturing, marketing and distribution agreements with the new company. For example, one such agreement enables Lexmark's line of printers and supplies to continue to be sold under the IBM brand name through the established IBM worldwide dealer and distribution network.

17.4.2 Metaphor Computer Systems

Since October 1991, the California-based Metaphor Computer Systems has become a wholly-owned subsidiary of IBM. Metaphor is now focusing on integrating its data interpretation systems (DIS) into the IBM product family. DIS combines a graphical user interface with relational database technology. It allows nontechnical business professionals to access multiple databases and to construct their own applications.

17.5 Vendor alliances

Imitation is surely one of the sincerest forms of flattery. IBM has already learnt to its cost in the PC marketplace what imitation and innovation can lead to if not cultured correctly. In the early eighties IBM legitimized the growing personal computer marketplace, at the time occupied by computers running the CP/M operating system. The IBM personal computer was explosively successful, but today IBM is not a majority manufacturer in this marketplace nor indeed the leading manufacturer by revenue or volume. The standard that IBM created is now dominated by other manufacturers. In 1987 IBM introduced the IBM Personal System/2. This computer and its complementary operating system, IBM Operating System/2, was designed to regain the leadership of the PC marketplace through technical innovation. I believe that this strategy has not so far succeeded as is evidenced by the current volumes and revenues of Personal System/2 computers against regular ISA or EISA bus systems. It has faltered because IBM did not cooperate closely enough with other industry vendors. Thus its revolutionary rather than evolutionary strategy has not yet had the desired effect.

So what is IBM's strategy for gaining market share with the IBM RISC System/6000? I believe it is not only to produce technical leadership but also to work cooperatively with other industry vendors, and, in so doing, encouraging them to use this IBM technology as their standard. IBM now has agreements with Wang, Bull, Motorola and Apple. All these vendors will be working with IBM to promote the IBM POWER architecture standard in the marketplace. What are the details?

17.5.1 IBM and Apple

In July 1991, IBM, Apple and Motorola signed an agreement to work together to produce an advanced family of UNIX-based RISC workstations based on the IBM Performance Optimized With Enhanced RISC (POWER) architecture as already used in the IBM RISC System/6000 family. The parts of the agreement are discussed below.

The PowerPC architecture

'PowerPC' is a term used to describe the shrinking of the current three-chipset POWER architecture into a single physical chip. These new integrated processor chips will be designed in the Somerset design centre in Austin, Texas. PowerPC will also be manufactured by Motorola and will be incorporated into future systems by IBM and Apple as well as any other vendor who wants to buy the architecture.

The PowerOpen platform

PowerOpen is an implementation of a UNIX operating system built upon the PowerPC architecture. PowerOpen has five components:

1 The base layer is the hardware POWER or PowerPC architecture defined previously. The PowerPC architecture does not mandate the use of the MicroChannel bus.
2 The operating system layer will be provided by an OSF/1 kernel-based implementation of AIX.
3 The user interface in PowerOpen will be either OSF/Motif or the Macintosh interface provided with A/UX, Apple's implementation of UNIX.
4 An application binary interface (ABI) will be defined to allow products written to run on mixed IBM or Apple, hardware and software platforms. Current IBM AIX applications will be binary compatible with this ABI.
5 To produce software emulation of the DOS and Macintosh architectures, enabling existing software to run under PowerOpen.

Taligent

Taligent is the name to a joint venture company of IBM and Apple whose task is to design the operating system, compilers and tools that will form the PowerOpen platform. The company is headed by CEO Joseph Guglielmi, a former IBM corporate vice-president.

A key emphasis in the design of all of this software is that it is based on object-oriented software technology. The intent is to design systems that are more reliable and robust using object-oriented programming techniques. In the late 1980s IBM was working on a new object-oriented operating system in a project called 'Patriot Partners', drawing on the expertise of companies such as Nextstep and Metaphor. Apple too was working on a similar project called 'Pink'. This had similar object-oriented deliverables, and in a meeting of minds in December 1991, Apple chairman John Sculley, IBM president Jack Kuehler and IBM general manager Jim Cannavino formed the joint venture Taligent under the leadership of Guglielmi. Taligent is staffed by IBM and Apple employees with new employees hired as necessary. Taligent is located in Cupertino, California. Although the target design points for Taligent are products that will run on POWER and PowerPC platforms, the operating system that will be produced will be available to run on any hardware platform and Taligent will license its software technology and systems to any requesting software vendor.

17.5.2   IBM and Bull

Bull, the French computer systems manufacturer, is another vendor that has signed a manufacturing and marketing agreement with IBM. In a major shift away from Bull's MIPS and Motorola processor-based workstations, Bull will use the IBM POWER and PowerPC architectures and other IBM components in its future systems.

From a marketing standpoint, Bull will market these future RISC systems (in competition with IBM RISC systems) to Bull customers. The POWER architecture may become Bull's strategic RISC architecture for future systems. It is certainly sensible for there to be binary compatibility between future Bull RISC and IBM RISC System/6000 systems and this will be achieved if technically and politically possible.

Bull is also leading the cooperative development efforts with IBM to produce a range of symmetrical multiprocessing RISC systems based on its multiprocessing expertise.

17.5.3   IBM and Motorola

Together, IBM, Motorola and Apple are cooperatively manufacturing the new IBM RISC System/6000 processors. Motorola and IBM have set up a joint design facility in Austin to develop three versions of the PowerPC chip: an entry-level processor for laptops, a mid-range processor for desktop systems and a high-end processor for workstations. Apple and IBM are creating a fourth PowerPC processor for entry-level desktop systems. Motorola will be principally responsible for the manufacture of PowerPC processors. The implementation is initially expected to be in complementary metal oxide semiconductor (CMOS) using 0.5 micron technology. (That is to say, the distance between individual circuit tracks inside the integrated circuit is 0.5 millionths of a metre; the smaller the distance the better.) The first PowerPC microprocessor (the model 601) was produced in October 1992. Motorola hopes to move to a 0.35 micron process and increase the processor chip speed to 100 MHz by 1995.

17.5.4   IBM and Wang

Fiscal years 1989 and 1990 were difficult years for Wang. The company, founded in 1951 by Dr An Wang and later handled by his son Fred Wang, has experienced declining sales and profitability. In the summer of 1991 IBM and Wang Laboratories announced a strategic business alliance, allowing Wang to market IBM products. The alliance is intended to help Wang transform itself from a provider of minicomputer hardware solutions to a provider of software and systems integration solutions. Wang are reselling IBM's RISC System/6000 and Personal System/2 products under the Wang logo. In addition, Wang are marketing the IBM Application System/400 to Wang VS customers who convert their VS applications to run under the AS/400.

17.6   OEM marketing

The overall original equipment manufacturer (OEM) market worldwide for electronics is estimated to be as much as 500 000 million US dollars. Around the world many companies in the information technology industry have established themselves firmly as OEM suppliers. IBM, on the other hand, until recently has not. Although IBM is the world's largest manufacturer of semiconductor chips, it has historically produced these chips only for its own needs, but this is no longer true.

Today, IBM has initiated significant new agreements with customers in the OEM marketplace. IBM is now open to supply OEM customers with hardware technology, services, maintenance and software. From personal systems to enterprise systems, subassemblies or chip sets, IBM is keen to participate. As an example, when IBM announced its industry-leading one gigabyte, 3.5 inch hard disk drive, it made it available in the OEM marketplace before it was even incorporated into RISC system products.

Besides the OEM agreements already described with Apple and Motorola, IBM has already won several non-RISC system deals. These include customers such as Hitachi, Mitsubishi and Thompson-CSF.

The message is clear—through OEM marketing and development IBM can deliver more solutions to more customers. OEM sales provide greater market access, technology expansion, early product feedback and, most importantly, increased profitability.

17.7   Future developments

Future hardware developments that IBM announce will be built soundly on the PowerPC architecture and its alliances with Motorola and IBM. During 1993 OEM manufacturers have had acccess to PowerPC components to produce PowerPC architecture notebooks and laptops of between 50 and 150 SPECmarks during 1994 (comparable to the performance of today's RISC system Model 520H). By 1995 a processor performing at least 500 SPECmarks and executing at a clock speed of 100 MHz would seem to be possible.

The principal new software innovation that IBM is working hard to deliver is the integration of the OSF/1 kernel into the AIX. Already, in an announced statement of direction, IBM believes that OSF/1 compatibility is key to its future, because it hopes that the OSF/1 will be the leading open systems operating system by the end of this century.

17.8   Summary

The IBM RISC System/6000 workstations and servers offer excellent performance and value. In addition, the AIX operating system, IBM's advanced implementation of UNIX, offers an enhanced UNIX environment. It includes a sophisticated systems management tool, hypertext help, real-time programming, adherence to industry standards such as POSIX, ANSI and XPG3 and an affinity to AT&T and Berkeley versions of UNIX. This combination of performance, value, function, ease of use, reliability and standards compliance, in conjunction with IBM service and support, is one that increasing numbers of users are finding it hard to resist.

Just as the IBM PC provided IBM's runaway success for the eighties, I see AIX and the IBM RISC System/6000 as IBM's charmed family for the nineties.

Appendix 1
The history of UNIX and IBM's involvement

Perhaps one of the largest inhibitors to the success of IBM's UNIX computer has been IBM's low-key UNIX marketing strategy. Many important IBM customers have been unaware that IBM has had a long and growing involvement with UNIX computer systems stretching back to a product delivered in 1980, over 10 years ago.

For users new to UNIX this appendix will first examine the origins and history of UNIX, then describe the past and present versions of IBM's UNIX offerings.

A1.1   UNIX history

In 1965, Bell Laboratories (a part of AT&T) joined with General Electric and Project MAC of the Massachusetts Institute of Technology to develop the Multics operating system. Multics did not perform as expected and Bell consequently left the project leaving two people in particular, Ken Thompson and Dennis Ritchie, without a 'convenient interactive computing service'. At that time, Thompson had written a Fortran game called 'Space Travel' which ran on a DEC PDP-7 that was little used at the time. In order to develop new versions of the game, Thompson had to take his Fortran code and cross-compile it on a Honeywell 635 computer which output paper tape that could subsequently be fed into the PDP-7 system. To create a better environment, Thompson took some ideas for a proposed filesystem and demand paging environment on which he had been working and implemented them on the PDP-7. Eventually, the environment was powerful enough for standalone development, and another member of the Bell computing science centre called the system UNIX. UNIX was a pun on the name Multics, since it was designed to do a few things well, whereas Multics was designed to do many things well.

Although this early version was promising it needed more work, and Thompson and Ritchie got their chance to move it to a DEC PDP-11 in 1971 when the patent department at Bell wanted a text processing system. Next Thompson implemented the language called B, an interpreted language based on the language

Basic Combined Programming Language (BCPL). From B, a compiled language called C was developed, and in 1973 the operating system was rewritten in C, an unheard of step at the time but one which was to have great consequences, since this fundamental feature gave UNIX its machine-independent portability.

By 1974 AT&T was selling UNIX to universities who requested it for educational purposes. (Because of a consent decree of 1956, AT&T could not market computer services, nor could they advertise, market or otherwise support the product.)

In 1977, Interactive Systems Corporation became the first value added reseller (VAR) of a UNIX system, and added some enhancements that were to surface in PC/IX. Interactive's first hardware platform was Onyx computers, a company founded by Bob Marsh and Kip Myers.

From 1977 to 1982, Bell combined several AT&T UNIX variants into a single system and named it UNIX System III, the first commercial version of UNIX. Bell Laboratories later added more features calling the new product UNIX System V (there was never a System IV). Meanwhile, people at the University of California at Berkeley had developed a variant of UNIX and called it BSD for Berkeley Software Distribution. One of the 'Berkeley enhancements' that was significant was the use of the Termcap database and the Curses library for driving different ASCII terminals in a device-independent manner. AT&T have added their own implementation called Terminfo.

From the mid-eighties then, there were two fundamental flavours of UNIX, System V and BSD. This was to change in 1990 with the introduction of UNIX System V release 4, which integrated both BSD and UNIX System V versions into a single unified product.

In 1991, AT&T separated its UNIX operations from its computer systems division and set up UNIX System Labs (USL). Since that time the ownership of USL has broadened to include Amdahl, Fujitsu, Novell and Sun, to name but a few. USL's chief function involves the support and licensing of UNIX System V. USL has close connections with UNIX International (UI). UNIX International, like OSF, is a nonprofit-making organization, and exists to promote UNIX System V and to provide input to USL regarding future enhancements to USL products.

Table A1.1 summarizes UNIX development.

A1.2   PC/IX

The first IBM computer system to run an IBM licensed version of UNIX was nothing more than an unmodified IBM Personal Computer XT powered by a 4.77 MHz Intel 8088 processor, 256 kb memory and 10 Mb of hard disk. This version of UNIX was a port of AT&T UNIX System III. The port was performed by Interactive Systems Corporation, now owned by Sun Microsystems. PC/IX was first announced in the spring of 1984. PC/IX was supplied on

Table A1.1. U N I X development milestones

Year	Description
1969	First UNIX on PDP-7 (written in assembler)
1971	PDP-11 version (written in assembler)
1972	UNIX version 2
1973	UNIX versions 3 and 4
1974	UNIX version 5 (written in C)
1975	UNIX version 6 (programmer's workbench)
1979	UNIX version 7
1980	IBM maxi/UNIX (based on UNIX version 7)
1982	UNIX System III (AT&T standard, base for PC/IX)
1983	UNIX System V release 1 (base for IX/370)
	IBM VM/IX
1984	UNIX System V release 2 (base for AIX version 2.1)
	IBM PC/IX
	IBM XENIX for IBM System 9000 and IBM PC AT
1985	IBM Interactive Executive
	IBM AIX version 2.1 for IBM RT PC system (base for AIX version 3.1)
1988	IBM Secure XENIX
	IBM AOS (based on BSD 4.3)
1990	UNIX System V release 4
	IBM AIX version 3.1
1992	IBM FTX (based on UNIX System V release 4)
	IBM AIX/ESA
	IBM AIX version 3.2
1993	USL UNIX system VR4.2

nineteen, 5.25 inch low density floppy disks and installed in only 30 minutes. A very full featured multiuser package, it included a base operating system and seven subsets:

- Programming tools including C and SNOBOL compilers
- Communication tools including a printer spooling subsystem and terminal emulation products
- Program development tools like SCCS and *make*
- Text processing tools like *nroff*
- Standard UNIX games programs
- Accounting record and site-specific billing programs
- Other Interactive specific tools such as the full-screen interactive systems editor (INed), DOS disk read and write utilities

All this for only $900 in 1984, including manuals which were almost reproduced verbatim from the original AT&T memos and manuals—a real bargain.

A1.3   XENIX

In the early eighties Microsoft became interested in UNIX. This was not altogether surprising since Microsoft's DOS operating system had certain similarities to UNIX right from early times. The ability to redirect output, pipes, the internal format of device drivers, and even some of the early DOS technical documentation was UNIX like. Microsoft licensed UNIX System 7 from AT&T, customized it for the personal computers and called it XENIX.

In early 1984 IBM introduced a benchtop microcomputer called System 9000. Initially this system ran the computer system operating system (CSOS), a simple operating system that IBM believed would cater for this machine's destined marketplace, that of the office or laboratory for use by engineers, scientists or technicians. The specification of this machine however, with a Motorola 68000 processor, up to 40 Mb of hard disk and 5 Mb of RAM, also made it an ideal entry-level UNIX system. This, coupled with the already strong use of UNIX by the scientific community at the time, prompted IBM to offer XENIX for this system.

Following this announcement, IBM also announced XENIX for the IBM Personal Computer AT. Whereas PC/IX had run on an Intel 8086 processor in real mode, XENIX required an Intel 80286 processor or better and ran in protected mode. Other requirements were really only a 20 Mb hard disk and a 5.25 inch high-capacity disk drive. Also available were three additional packages: first, a programmer's toolkit including a C compiler and assembler as well as traditional UNIX programming tools such as the lexical analyser *lex* and the compiler compiler *yacc*; second, a text formatting package comprising the *nroff* and *troff* programs; and third, a system extension package including some TCP/IP networking, extra accounting and editing programs, and migration aids for existing PC/IX users.

In late 1988 IBM introduced *Secure XENIX*. This was a little-advertised product that functioned on either IBM PC AT or PS/2 systems. Secure XENIX introduced the concept of *least privilege* and enforced security using *mandatory* and *discretionary security* policies. Secure XENIX had the option of full TCP/IP support.

In 1988, Microsoft handed over development of XENIX to the California-based Santa Cruz Organization (SCO). Under the direction and control of SCO, SCO XENIX is now based on AT&T UNIX System V.3. It is now a very different product in substance and character and competes directly with IBM AIX PS/2. SCO XENIX includes a component called Open Desktop which is a basic UNIX system packaged with a database and the OSF/Motif windowing system. It also now features a complete set of programming tools for users to develop programs in that environment.

A1.4   AIX PS/2

This is IBM's version of UNIX for the PS/2. It is the result of a joint development between the California-based Locus Computing Corp. and IBM. AIX PS/2 was originally based on a highly modified version of UNIX 4.1 BSD.

AIX PS/2 runs on any IBM PS/2 with an Intel 386 SX or better processor. It represents a very complete implementation of UNIX and includes the following components:

- Base operating system
- Operating system extensions, including *vi*, INed editors, administration, mail and basic networking utilities (UUCP plus)
- C, Pascal and Fortran compilers
- Text formatting tools
- DOS-Merge, DOS integration software
- X-Windows, OSF/Motif, X-Desktop
- TCP/IP networking
- Application development and X-Windows development and debugging tools

In order to be price competitive with other UNIX offerings for personal computers, AIX PS/2 is sold in components from the base operating system upwards. For the user who runs just AIX applications, only the base operating system needs to be purchased.

DOS-Merge is a component that allows AIX PS/2 to provide one or more IBM DOS sessions concurrently using the VM86 'Virtual 8086 mode' of the Intel 386 processor. DOS sessions can be full screen or windowed onto an X-Windows system screen. Since the DOS session provides full real mode emulation of DOS, it is possible to run Microsoft Windows in real-mode concurrently with other AIX tasks and commands. Because the VM86 mode of the processor is used to provide DOS, these sessions run without impacting the performance of regular AIX tasks, unlike the IBM RISC System/6000 which needs to emulate the Intel 8086 processor in software. DOS-Merge also provides support for dedicating hardware adapter cards to one or more DOS sessions.

Because this is a full implementation of UNIX, AIX PS/2 can serve as an entry-level multiuser commercial UNIX system with a number of ASCII attached or LAN users, running character-based or X-Windows applications.

The X-Windows component allows the user to run and develop applications under X-Windows at version 11 release 5. Also included in the X-Windows component is the popular X-Desktop software from IXI, an earlier version of that shipped with the IBM RISC System/6000.

Initially, AIX PS/2 included specific support for the IBM transparent computing facility (TCF), a development that provided a heterogeneous computing network for PS/2 AIX and mainframe AIX systems. TCF is a very advanced product developed by Locus Computing Corporation that enables user facilities including:

- Automatic file duplication, replication and recovery. Files may be stored locally and remotely for reliability. Should a remote fileserver fail, a local AIX program can continue to operate on local files which are automatically re-synchronized with network copies when the network becomes available again.

- Process migration. This allows a program to run in the environment best suited for its operation. An AIX application can be compiled and run in either an AIX PS/2 or mainframe AIX environment. Dynamic process migration allows the movement of programs from the PS/2 environment to the mainframe environment as the overall heterogeneous system load changes. This includes the ability to *remote fork* an application, where a program can start another instance of itself on a remote mainframe node.

Though TCF showed much early promise, it is not now seen as the future direction for AIX in heterogeneous environments including AIX on IBM mainframe platforms, therefore it is now not included in the latest releases of AIX PS/2.

As with any personal computer based UNIX system, installation and maintenance require a significant amount of care. Most IBM PS/2 systems are not equipped with a tape drive, which means that loading the operating system and utilities is usually performed selectively from diskette. An end-user AIX PS/2 configuration requires the installation of about 40 diskettes and needs 60 Mb of space, but a fully configured development AIX PS/2 system may require the installation of over 120 diskettes and over 200 Mb of disk space. For these reasons, a serious development system should be fitted with a tape drive.

AIX PS/2 is positioned as an entry level to the IBM AIX family. How well does it live up to this claim? IBM has had only moderate success in marketing AIX PS/2 as the UNIX system of choice for personal computer users. Why? First, AIX PS/2 predominantly runs on IBM PS/2 computers and provides only limited support for IBM compatibles. This is because AIX PS/2 cannot use the IBM Personal Computer BIOS which is written to the requirements of a single-tasking operating system like DOS. Instead, AIX PS/2 addresses the hardware directly, and because other vendors' non-MicroChannel bus-based machines have various hardware differences they will not necessarily work with AIX PS/2. Second, in the personal computer UNIX marketplace there is no *de facto* agreed standard for binary application compatibility.[1] The marketplace for AIX PS/2 systems therefore is typically a small configuration, multiuser commercial system. For example, a customer may develop a simple character-based application on an IBM RISC System/6000 for its worldwide series of offices. Smaller offices may not justify their own IBM RISC System/6000 so the application could be ported to an IBM PS/2 running AIX PS/2 for these smaller branches.

Ironically, since the cost of the IBM RISC System/6000 is now very low, it can outperform a high-end IBM PS/2 in terms of performance per pound spent, thus making the choice of AIX PS/2 more difficult.

---

[1] A potential 'standard' is the Intel iBCS (Intel binary compatibility software) specification for personal computer UNIX. This allows applications written for one vendor's personal computer UNIX to run on another vendor's UNIX without recompilation. AIX PS/2 does not yet conform to this standard.

Table A1.2. The models in the RT PC family

Model	Size	Disk interface	Processor
10	Desktop	ST506	ROMP
15	Desktop	ESDI	ROMP
20	Floorstanding	ST506	ROMP
25	Floorstanding	ESDI	ROMP
115	Desktop	EESDI	APC
125	Floorstanding	EESDI	APC
135	Floorstanding	EESDI	FAPC

The future of AIX PS/2 then is at a crossroads. IBM clearly needs to provide or resell a PS/2-based UNIX product, because the potential market place, that of existing IBM PS/2 users, is large. With the advent of OSF/1 and its porting to IBM PC, PC-compatible and PS/2 platforms, I would expect AIX PS/2 to undergo radical changes.

A1.5   The IBM RT PC system

The IBM RISC Technology Personal Computer (RT PC) was IBM's first hardware platform specific to the UNIX operating system.[2] By understanding the characteristics of the RT PC the IBM RISC System/6000 can be seen as an evolutionary rather than revolutionary development.

The RT PC was a family of desktop and deskside minicomputers running the operating system AIX. AIX had always been a merge of USL UNIX System V release 2 and BSD 4.3. A typical desktop and deskside RT PC is shown in Fig. A1.1. Actually, during the evolution of the family both processor speeds and hard disk interfaces changed leading to the models shown in Table A1.2.

In Europe the RT PC was sold as the IBM 6150 microcomputer system. Within IBM the machine was simply called the RT.

A key feature of the RT was its RISC processor. RISC in this context represents 'reduced instruction set computer' and means the production of a microprocessor whose instruction set is limited to useful instructions heavily used in most programs. A smaller instruction set can be executed more quickly. In fact the RT processor had 118 instructions, more than most traditional RISC processors. The initial processor developed was called ROMP (research OPD micro processor) and reflected the cooperation of the IBM research and office products division in the processor design and manufacture. Later enhancements in technology effectively increased the processor clock speed leading to the advanced

[2] Actually early RT PC systems ran an IBM internal operating system called CPR but this was never sold as a product. Equally, AIX version 3 was developed initially upon the RT PC but never released on this platform.

Figure A1.1.   A desktop and deskside RT PC.

processor computer (APC), and later with the model 135, the fast advanced processor computer.

Memory management was performed using IBM virtual memory management chips which interfaced with the virtual resource manager layer of the AIX operating system.

The physical construction of the RT was as follows. A plastic case (copper sputtered to help shield from stray electromagnetic radiation) contained a single planar card containing two different sets of computer buses and support circuitry. The first bus was the ROMP storage channel which interconnected four special slots: one processor, one floating point and two system memory. The second bus was IBM PC AT compatible and was for connecting peripheral cards such as disk, graphics and terminal I/O.

The modular nature of the design enabled RT systems to be easily upgraded. For example, from the first floorstanding model 20 to the model 125, right up to the model 135, by steadily replacing processor, disk controller, memory cards, etc. The planar card in the RT did not change in its design and included not only the AT and dedicated system bus but also a DMA controller, two serial ports, a keyboard and mouse interface. It also contained an I/O channel converter (IOCC).

Limits on the RT system included a maximum of 16 Mb of system memory (40 bits wide: 32 bits of data and 8 bits of error correction), two 5.25 inch floppy disk drives, three internal 5.25 inch hard disk drives (900 Mb total) and fully populated AT bus slots, six for the desktop models and eight for the floorstanding systems. Early RT systems used the Seagate ST506 disk interface, replaced by the enhanced small device interface (ESDI) in later models, then by the faster enhanced ESDI (EESDI).

Other peripheral support was provided using AT form factor cards. Initially these were IBM Personal Computer AT cards, though later RT systems used RT-specific cards. Examples of cards included: the APA graphics adapter cards for graphics displays running X-Windows; the SCSI adapter to connect external hard disks; the $\frac{1}{4}$ inch tape support card; and a variety of high-performance synchronous and asynchronous communications cards.

The initial release of AIX for the RT was version 1.0 then later version 2, culminating in version 2.2.1. An extremely fortunate design move (predating AT&T UNIX System V release 4), AIX version 2 was always a merge of UNIX System version V and Berkeley BSD. A key feature of the software architecture was that AIX was built on a low-level software component called the virtual resource manager (VRM). VRM controlled the real hardware and provided an idealized and 'virtualized' machine interface to AIX. This was done to optimize AIX's use of the real hardware and also enabled, in principle, the RT to be a platform for other operating systems, for example PICK.

This version of AIX also brought some (helpful) baggage from PC/IX including the printing subsystem and the INed full-screen editor. Aside from the standard UNIX facilities provided by the AT&T and BSD levels previously indicated, a number of AIX features are of note:

1 *HFT support*: an IBM terminal subsystem that allowed an arbitrary number of separate full-screen virtual terminals to be opened on a single physical screen. The user switched through these with a key sequence.
2 *Stanza-based configuration* in many of the traditional UNIX system files giving rise to fewer configuration errors.
3 *DOS affinity*: the ability to run DOS programs via a hardware or software Intel PC emulator, translate DOS commands into UNIX ones with the DOS shell and allow satellite DOS systems to share AIX files or log on to AIX hosts with AIX access for DOS products.
4 *IBM affinity* using the SNA services program that provides SNA support and via other IBM host terminal emulation programs.
5 *X-Windows support* on native RT graphic displays.
6 *Enhanced software maintenance and installation* using layered software product installation, and the ability to back out selective AIX installed products and features.
7 *Enhanced diagnostics* using standalone diagnostics and service disks with low-level errors reported to a planar-controlled LED error display.

A1.6   Academic operating system

While IBM would have preferred customers of its RT PC systems to use AIX, many universities and educational establishments had standardized on the *de facto* UNIX in the educational environment, that is BSD.

In order to satisfy the requirements for regular BSD, the IBM Academic Information Systems (ACIS) group at Palo Alto ported the BSD 4.3 level of UNIX, calling the result the academic operating system (AOS). From an architectural point of view this version of UNIX ran 'native' on top of the raw RT PC hardware and not upon VRM. Only genuine education customers could buy ACIS, since IBM wanted to promote AIX as the standard UNIX operating system for RT machines.

Some of the ACIS features, for example the Andrew programming toolkit, were not available for AIX and so for some educational customers AOS was a must. Some of the highlights of AOS were:

- It was a port of BSD level 4.3.
- It included the X-Windows networked windowing system.
- It included the Andrew toolkit, an extensible object-oriented graphical toolkit for building X-Windows applications.
- It included the Metaware C compiler.

Those who used AOS were always favourably impressed by it. It soon became clear, however, that an AOS equipped RT was not price competitive enough for some universities. In an effort to produce a machine which could be more useful to these environments IBM introduced model 6152. This was a standard IBM PS/2 model 60 with two special MicroChannel cards. One card contained a modified ROMP processor and support circuitry, the second up to 8 Mb of RISC processor memory. The 6152 was able to run AOS, but much more cheaply than the RT system. Additionally, using the Intel 80286 processor it could also run DOS or OS/2 version 1. Internal versions of this system were enabled to allow concurrent running of AOS and one other operating system.

The IBM 6152 therefore has the distinction of being the first machine I know capable of concurrently running UNIX and DOS or OS/2.

A1.7   Fault-tolerant UNIX

FTX is a native port of the UNIX System V release 4 operating system designed to run on the IBM System/88 fault-tolerant computer system. The IBM System/88 is IBM's highly fault-tolerant computer. The architecture of the machine uses hardware redundancy to achieve continuous availability. For example, all hard disks, memory and central processors are duplicated. In the event of a failure of any single component the system continues and automatically telephones the IBM support centre. IBM customer support arrives with the replacement part and can *hot plug* the replacement.

Initially the System/88 was powered by a Motorola 68000 series processor and ran the virtual operating system (VOS). Today the latest members of the System/88 family are powered by Intel i860 RISC processors with between 32 Mb and 256 Mb of main memory. What also surprised many people was IBM's decision to implement the USL UNIX System V release 4 on this platform. The operating system is called FTX (release 2).

Actually, this is not so surprising since the System/88 is based on the Stratus range of computers. FTX meets a number of international standards including System V Interface Definition (SVID) issue 3, POSIX 1003.1 and X/Open's XPG3. FTX includes the standard virtual filesystem (VFS), TCP/IP networking and NFS and RFS file-sharing. FTX also includes the X-Windows graphical interface and the Open Look graphical environment.

IBM positions the System/88 as a high reliability, hardware fault tolerant system. The IBM RISC System/6000, for example, can never become as fault tolerant as the System/88 because a single system does not include hardware duplication, nor does the MicroChannel bus support hot pluggability.

A1.8   Mainframe UNIX

IBM has had a number of IBM mainframe (see Sec. 13.2) system UNIX developments. To date however, they have all had a common disappointing bottom line, that is to say, they have not sold well. It would be wrong to infer, however, that this was a reflection on the technical quality or abilities of the various offerings; the first IBM mainframe UNIX called *maxi/UNIX* was an early excellent UNIX implementation. Low sales figures represent the solid established base of IBM mainframe users using IBM's traditional mainframe operating systems—VSE, VM and MVS. These users have traditionally been interested in moving up the scale of IBM's vendor operating systems, perhaps from VSE to MVS, while being able to maintain object code compatibility of applications written even decades ago. But times are changing. Today many new and existing corporate IBM customers have already made the decision to move to a company-wide open systems strategy based on the UNIX operating system. Therefore I would expect a dramatic increase in the sales of IBM mainframe AIX in the medium term.

A1.8.1   *maxi/UNIX*

maxi/UNIX was a version of UNIX produced as a result of a joint project between Bell Labs and IBM to implement UNIX on the IBM 370 mainframe. The project was started at IBM Yorktown in 1978, and a working version completed in only 18 months. maxi/UNIX ran on top of the IBM time-sharing system (TSS) operating environment. Though very successful at the time, maxi/

UNIX was never made into a formally supported IBM LPP but remained an IBM PRPQ (see the glossary, Appendix 5, for details).

A1.8.2   VM/IX

Though maxi/UNIX was an excellent product it was based on a TSS which was not strategic. IBM began to develop a version of UNIX that ran as a guest under IBM's VM operating system. The product of this labour was VM/IX, developed jointly by Interactive Systems Corp. and IBM and shipped in 1983. IBM's VM operating system is not only an operating system but also a kind of hypervisor (see Sec. 13.2.1). The operating system presents a logical 'virtual machine' to programs that run under it. These programs can be simple applications or, in the case of VM/IX, an entire operating system in itself. That is to say, the VM/IX product required the customer first to install the IBM VM operating system, then to install VM/IX under it. Speaking honestly, the VM/IX product had several limitations that made it less than useful in a business environment. For example, it utilized IBM 3270 screens and would not support ASCII terminals.

A1.8.3   IX/370

One of the major performance problems with VM/IX was that both UNIX and the controlling VM operating system believed that they owned the whole machine. Since both operating systems tried hard to optimize memory and other resources, the result was operating systems conflict and generally poor perform-ance. IBM mainframe architecture supports special instructions known as *assists* that enable child operating systems, such as running under VM, to operate more efficiently. In an effort to improve performance, IX/370 did not use the VM/IX product as a code base but went back to the maxi/UNIX code. It included TSS and packaged it under VM trying to take advantage of hardware assists where possible. IX/370 also allowed the attachment of ASCII terminals in a somewhat painful manner. ASCII terminals had to be connected to a separate IBM Series/ 1 computer which was then connected to the IBM mainframe.

A1.8.4   AIX/370

AIX/370 was announced in March 1987. It provided a tightly integrated distributed mainframe UNIX environment in conjunction with the transparent computing facility (TCF). The TCF cluster was a collection of TCF nodes connected via an Ethernet or Token Ring network. A TCF node is an AIX/370 system or an IBM PS/2 running AIX/PS2 version 1.2.1 or later. In addition, AIX/370 supported ASCII terminals attached to the IBM PS/2 or IBM RT PC system.

Like its predecessors though, AIX/370 was not a native implementation of

AIX, it ran as a 'guest' under the supervision of the VM or VM extended architecture operating systems.

By the late eighties it was clear to IBM management that a radical change of direction was required for future IBM mainframe UNIX products. The current offerings were just not commercially successful. These were some of the drawbacks:

- Not a native implementation of UNIX but running under another operating system. This had a performance penalty.
- Running under VM meant that customers had to be knowledgeable with IBM's VM operating system too. Not particularly likely if the customer just had experience with UNIX, and if they had VM experience then why not implement their new application under VM instead of UNIX?
- Connecting ASCII terminals was via another specialized IBM computer system (for example the IBM Series /1), adding to the cost and skills required for an IBM mainframe UNIX solution.
- The cost of IBM's UNIX route was as competitive as its main rival, that of Amdahl, which provided a native UNIX implementation called UTS.

The product that addressed these points is AIX/ESA.

A1.8.5   AIX/ESA

AIX/ESA is the current implementation of UNIX for the IBM mainframe. It extends IBM's family of current AIX offerings to any IBM mainframe containing the Enterprise Systems Architecture (ESA). In developing AIX/ESA, IBM has sought to overcome the limitations of its previously mainframe UNIX offerings and to produce a serious UNIX implementation that can serve hundreds of interactive users attached via standard ASCII terminals. Answering another customer request, AIX/ESA is the first implementation of IBM mainframe UNIX that can run native. In fact three modes of operation are supported:

- *Native mode*   AIX/ESA runs natively on the ESA processor and has full control of all resources.
- *Logical partition (PR/SM) mode*   PR/SM is a hardware feature of an IBM mainframe that logically partitions the mainframe into several smaller ESA systems, each with its own set of peripherals. AIX/ESA can execute within a logical partition.
- *Virtual machine mode*   AIX/ESA may run underneath the VM/ESA operating system. In this mode VM acts as a hypervisor controlling the real processor and peripherals. VM presents a 'virtualized machine' to AIX/ESA which runs as a guest operating system.

AIX/ESA is particularly noteworthy because it is IBM's first announced implementation of a UNIX operating system based on the Open Software

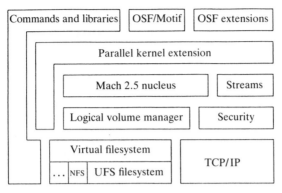

Figure A1.2. AIX/ESA nucleus.

Foundation OSF/1. The principal components of OSF/1 which form the nucleus of AIX/ESA are shown in Fig. A1.2.

The fundamental component of OSF/1 is the Mach kernel from Carnegie-Mellon University with extension from Encore Corporation to permit symmetric multiprocessing. Core OSF/1 technology also incorporated into AIX/ESA includes:

- The portable STREAM communications interface from Mentat
- The AIX logical volume manager
- Security features from SecureWare
- The OSF/1 VFS and UFS filesystems, based on the Berkeley BSD fastfile system
- TCP/IP
- Threads
- OSF/Motif and X-Windows client support
- Commands and libraries from AIX and BSD
- Compliance with X/Open's Portability Guide 3 (XPG3)

Connecting interactive users

One of the greatest technical challenges in implementing any form of UNIX on an IBM mainframe is the support of interactive users. A UNIX system with ASCII terminals operates using a character-based full duplex link. In this scheme, as the user presses a key on the ASCII terminal, that character is sent to the user's application program on the system and then echoed back to the user's terminal screen. IBM mainframe terminals, and indeed the entire IBM mainframe architecture is *block mode* oriented. In this form of communication no characters are sent from an IBM Block mode terminal to the application until the user has pressed the Enter key. Because most UNIX applications need to process input character by character some method of connecting ASCII screens to an AIX/ESA needed to be devised.

The solution was to connect all ASCII terminals via an IBM RISC System/6000. The RISC system is connected to the IBM mainframe using a special MicroChannel 'channel' attachment card. Recall from Sec. 13.2.2 that a channel is the fundamental form of IBM mainframe to peripheral connection highway. Under AIX/ESA a special device driver called the remote TTY driver (RTY) communicates with a remote TTY server via the channel attachment. The RTY device driver presents a standard TTY system call interface to AIX. The RTY server drives serial lines on the RISC system to which user terminals are attached. Within the RTY server, the terminal buffer manager collects the responses for all ASCII terminals being serviced into a single buffer and when it is full, or when a timeout occurs, sends the buffer to the host. In this way, individual keystrokes from ASCII terminals are *not* sent as blocks of size 1 byte to the IBM mainframe. This new strategy overcomes a limitation of many of IBM's previous UNIX offerings which could become overloaded when a significant number of users logged on, because now users share a single block communications data packet.

Appendix 2
IBM hard disk interfaces

Many different types of hard disk interface are used in today's workstations and UNIX computers. It is valuable to look at these interfaces and the terms used to describe them. This provides a reference point from which to assess the latest IBM serial link disk technology.

A2.1   The Seagate ST506 disk interface

One of the first hard disks designed for personal computers and workstations was the Seagate Technologies model ST506 5 Mb hard disk. This had a full-height 5.25 inch form factor.

The interface to this hard disk was a controller usually contained on a separate card plugged into the PC or workstation expansion bus. The hard disk was connected to this adapter with two ribbon cables, one for commands, the other for data. The hard disk had a third four-wire connector supplying 12 and 5 volt DC power. The data were sent at 5 megabits per second from the controller card to the hard disk electronics using the modified frequency modulation (MFM) encoding technique.

The ST506 was the first hard disk from Seagate; subsequent disks had different part numbers but maintained the same electrical interface which was named the *ST506 interface*. The earliest versions of the IBM RT PC system used 40 Mb and 70 Mb ST506 hard disks. Later the data transfer rate was increased to 7.5 megabits per second and data encoded on the hard disk using run length limited (RLL) encoding. This encoding method had been used for some considerable time by IBM on mainframe disks. Of course to use RLL a new hard disk and controller was required.

Many early personal UNIX systems stored the geometry of the hard disk (that is to say the number of cylinders, heads and sectors per track) on the first addressable sector of the hard disk. The first time that the disk was low-level formatted it was common to ask the user a number of questions to determine this low-level information.

On early IBM personal computer systems another strategy was employed, that

311

of drive type numbers. A table in read-only memory mapped a drive type number to known drive characteristics, such as heads, cylinders and sectors per track.

A2.2   The enhanced small device interface

The next step forward was the enhanced small device interface (ESDI), developed by Dal Allan of ENDL Consulting, California. This was usually implemented on a separate card that plugged into the I/O bus of the computer. Later models of the IBM RT PC system used the ESDI disk interface. As with ST506, an EDSI controller card was plugged into the workstation and this connected to the ESDI disk with two ribbon cables (control and data) and a third cable supplied the DC power.

Unlike ST506 however, raw data was sent to the hard disk and encoded at 10 megabits per second, twice as dense as with MFM. ESDI also had intelligent media management, being able to substitute bad disk sectors automatically, thus presenting the device driver with an apparently error-free disk. ESDI also had the ability to inform the controller of its hard disk geometry, and the operating system could use this information regarding the number of tracks and sectors to its advantage by trying to place files in the physical UNIX filesystem in logically adjacent sectors or tracks.

On late models of the IBM RT PC system, IBM introduced the EESDI interface, which comprised a faster ESDI controller; you could, for example, use standard ESDI disks with either controller.

A2.3   Integrated drive electronics

The next logical step was to integrate the controller electronics onto the hard disk itself, eliminating the need for a controller card altogether. This is the approach used for example in the IBM RISC System/6000 model 320H. This is commonly known as the IDE interface, or by the IBM name direct bus attach (DBA). There are many different types of DBA, for example 8 bit, 16 bit, enhanced 16 bit. In the IBM implementation, DBA hard disks have a single edge connector which is powered by a single ribbon cable supplying control, data and power.

A2.4   Small computer systems interface

SCSI represents the current industry standard for interfacing peripherals to UNIX workstations. IBM's implementation of SCSI conforms to the ANSI X3.131-1986 standard. The IBM RISC System/6000 uses SCSI to interface all internal and external hard disks (save the IDE attachments of the 320H system and the serial link disks described in Sec. 8.1).

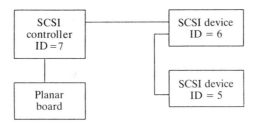

Figure A2.1.   SCSI physical configuration.

SCSI uses a 50 conductor wide bus to transfer control and data information to up to eight addressable SCSI devices. Internal SCSI devices are powered by a four-wire cable; external SCSI devices from the external enclosure power supply. Each SCSI device has assigned a unique ID from 0 (the lowest priority) to 7 (the highest). ID 7 is normally assigned to the controller itself as shown in Fig. A2.1.

Each SCSI device may have up to eight logical units or subdevices for a theoretical total of (8 × 7) 56 devices per adapter card (not recommended for bandwidth reasons). Physically, the RISC System SCSI adapter must be within six metres of the hard disks it controls. This is because the adapter has a *single-ended* SCSI bus which means that its signal pins have voltages in the range 0–5 volts. (Another more costly solution might be to provide a SCSI adapter card with a *differential bus*. In that scheme hard disks can be up to 25 metres away because the adapter outputs are via a differential voltage.)

SCSI hard disks, like IDE (DBA) hard disks, have most of their controller electronics mounted on the hard disk itself. This includes automatic bad sector management.

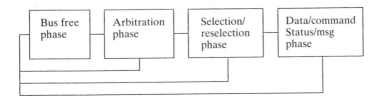

Figure A2.2.   SCSI bus phases.

A2.4.1   *How does the SCSI bus work?*

In order to transfer data between the source (*initiator*) and the destination (*target*) the SCSI bus goes through a set sequence or phases as shown in Fig. A2.2:

1   In the *bus free phase* no initiator or target is using the bus and it is available for use by any connected device. A device needs to wait for a free phase before it can start a request.

2   In the *arbitration phase* an initiator puts in a request for control of the bus.
    Earlier we said that the SCSI bus is a prioritized bus and that ID 0 has the
    lowest priority, with ID 7 the highest. The initiator now sets the data line
    representing its ID. For example, a device whose ID was 4 would wait for a
    bus free phase then set data line 4 high (there are 8 data transfer lines). After
    setting the line the initiator waits an *arbitration delay* period during which
    time any higher priority initiator (IDs 5–7 in this example) may assert its
    data line. If this happens our initiator has to start all over again and wait for
    a bus free phase. If no higher priority device wants control our initiator is
    now able to move to the next stage.

3   In the *selection/reselection phase* the initiator places its own ID on the SCSI
    bus together with the ID of the desired target. The target device recognizes
    this and sends back a confirmation message to the initiator allowing the final
    phase to begin.

4   Thence begins the final *message, command, data* and *status* phase. The
    message phase is optional and may negotiate such things as the required data
    transfer rate or subdevice (logical unit) specific information.

5   Next the command sequence begins by transferring a *command descriptor
    block* from initiator to target. This is usually either a 6 or a 10 byte block.
    The command block indicates to the target to prepare for a data transfer.
    Information may be sent in either direction according to the definition of the
    operation code.

6   After data is transferred the target sends back a status byte to the initiator.

A2.4.2   SCSI performance

Data is transferred from the SCSI device to the SCSI controller synchronously
or asynchronously at the fastest data rate that both items support. As the word
suggests, asynchronous transfer means that each byte of data must be sent then
acknowledged before the next byte can be transmitted. This byte-by-byte
handshaking between initiator and target slows down the theoretical SCSI
transfer rate to about 3 Mb per second. In synchronous mode, multiple bytes of
data can be transferred to a destination. After the transfer is completed a block
acknowledgement is sent. This method increases the maximum data transfer rate
to about 5 Mb per second.

An important performance booster in the design of SCSI is the ability of
multiple commands to be simultaneously in progress on a single SCSI bus, that
is, there is concurrent activity. For example, a SCSI bus may have two connected
SCSI hard disks. While one disk head has had a command issued to seek across
the disk to a distant track, a second SCSI hard disk could be transferring data to
the SCSI controller. In a multiuser or multitasking environment this is an
important advantage.

Overlapped command processing is possible because once a target has received a command descriptor block it can disconnect from the bus. This means another initiator is freed to send commands to another target while the first target is processing.

Early members of the RISC system family provided an SCSI-1 adapter using a single MicroChannel card. Newer members of the family make use of more advanced adapters. At the time of writing the current position was as follows:

- Model 220: integrated SCSI-1 interface using on-planar NCR SCSI controller chips.
- Models 530, 540, 550, 560, 950 use a single MicroChannel card using a 16 MHz Western Digital WD33C93A processor providing an SCSI-1 interface. This achieves a burst data rate of 4 Mb per second or, including command overhead, approximately 3 Mb per second.
- Models 340, 350, 355, 360, 365, 370, 375, 570, 580 and 970 incorporate the SCSI-1 adapter on the planar. This provides the same functionality as for the plug in card except that 'twin tail' (see Sec. 12.4.2) connections are not allowed.
- In late 1992, IBM announced a MicroChannel SCSI-2 adapter. This supports a data transfer rate of up to 10 Mb per second, achieved by using a 20 MHz Western Digital WD33C93B processor and altering firmware to deal with the faster SCSI bus, target mode and command tag queuing.[1] The RISC System model 980B comes equipped with the adapter as standard.
- In June 1993 IBM announced a differential SCSI-2 adapter. It has the facilities of the regular SCSI-2 adapter but it also enables SCSI devices to be connected at distances of up to 19 metres.

Both SCSI-1 and SCSI-2 adapters support the 40 Mb per second BusMaster MicroChannel mode.

The SCSI-1 interface supports a 4 Mb, the SCSI-2 a 10 Mb and the 9333 serial link disk an 8 Mb per second data transfer rate from SCSI to RISC system processor. These data transfer speeds are not the performance determining areas when one considers that hard disks are currently capable of transferring information from their platters at about only 3 Mb per second. One of the interesting characteristics of the 9333 serial link drive is that data transfer rates can rise to up to 8 Mb per second by simply adding more disks into the serial link subsystem. An equivalent SCSI system is limited in throughput when more that one disk is attached to the SCSI adapter simply because only one disk can be sending or receiving data at a time. Still, SCSI is the best general-purpose high-speed peripheral interface available and future developments, for example SCSI-3 (with a 16-bit data bus), will improve performance still further.

---

[1] Target mode enables the adapter to behave as a target device instead of the normal source. Tag queuing allows commands to be accepted from the host and queued prior to execution.

Appendix 3
Bibliography and further information

A3.1   Bibliography and references

For more information in a particular area, readers may wish to contact the standard bodies or vendors, or refer to the following list:

Bach, M. J. (1986). *The Design of the UNIX Operating System*, Prentice-Hall, Englewood Cliffs, N.J.

Bornat, R. (1984). *Understanding and Writing Compilers*, Macmillan Press, London.

Braca, M. (1991). 'X Display Management', *UNIXworld*, McGraw-Hill, New York, Vol. 8, No. 4, April 1991.

Comer, D. (1988). *Internetworking with TCP/IP*, Prentice-Hall, Englewood Cliffs, N.J.

Gibbs, B. (1992). *Demystifying the Object Data Manager 1 and 2*, lecture from IBM Field Television Network (FTN), IBM, USA.

Groves, R. and R. Oehler (1989). *IBM Second Generation RISC*, proceedings from the International Conference on Computer Design, 3 October 1989, IEEE, Boston, M.A.

Harris, C. (1993). *The IBM RISC System/6000*, McGraw-Hill, London.

Heller, D. (1991). *Motif Programming Manual*, Vol. 6, No. 1, September 1991, IBM, USA.

IBM (1982). *The 801 Minicomputer*, proceedings from the Symposium on Architectural Support for Programming Languages, IBM, USA.

IBM (1990). *Power Processor Architecture*, IBM, USA.

IBM (1990). 'IBM RISC System/6000', *IBM Journal of Research and Development*, January 1990, IBM, USA.

IBM (1991). *The IBM UK Annual Report*, IBM, UK.

IBM (1992). *IBM RISC System/6000 Performance Enhancements, Tools and Offerings*, handouts from live television presentation.

IBM (1992). *The IBM Technical Disclosure Bulletin*, IBM, USA.

IBM (1992). *AIX Version 3.2 and RISC System/6000 Announcements Overview*, IBM, UK.

IBM (1993). *IBM RISC System/6000 Facts and Figures*, IBM, UK. G320-9878-10.

The following online publications are from the IBM RISC System/6000 Hypertext Information Base Library. Publication SC23-2163-04:

AIX Technical Reference: Base Operating System and Extensions
AIX Technical Reference: Kernel and Subsystems
AIX Technical Reference: Graphics
AIX Technical Reference: User Interface
Communications Programming Concepts
General Programming Concepts
InfoCrafter/6000 User's Guide
Assembler Programming Guide
7015 POWERserver Hardware Technical Reference.

Keller, T. (1992). 'AIX 3.2 Memory Load Control', *AIXpert Journal*, IBM, USA, February 1992, pp. 17–25.

Kuenning, G. (1987). *UNIX Papers, Article Real Time UNIX*, Macmillan Inc., Indiana.

Oehler, R. and M. Blasgen (1991). *IBM RISC System/6000: Architecture and Performance*, IEEE, Boston, MA.

OSF (1992). *Internationalisation Made Easy*, OSF, Cambridge, MA.

Tannenbaum, H. S. (1987). *Operating Systems Design and Implementation*, Prentice-Hall, Englewood Cliffs, N.J.

Wong, C. (1992). 'The Top 10 UNIX Companies of 1992', *UNIXworld*, McGraw-Hill, New York, Vol. 9, No. 12, December 1992, pp. 46–56.

For a list of IBM publications used in the writing of this publication, see Sec. A3.3.

A3.2   Useful addresses

International telephone numbers are given.

Bristol Technologies Inc.
898 Ethan Allen Highway, Ridgefield, Connecticut, CT 06877.
Tel: 1-203-438-6769

IBM UK
National Enquiry Centre
389 Chiswick High Road, London W4 4AL
Tel: 44-81-747-0747
Technical Publications Centre
PO Box 117, Basing View, Basingstoke, Hampshire RG21 1EJ
Tel: 44-256-343-000

IBM US
>   Armonk
>   New York 10504, USA
>   Tel: 1-800-IBM-6676, ex. 990

IBM Austin Development
>   IBM Corporation
>   Advanced Workstation Division
>   11400 Burnet Road, Austin, Texas TX 78758, USA.

IXI Limited
>   62–74 Burleigh Street, Cambridge, CB1 1OJ
>   Tel: 44-223-462131

Locus Computing Corporation
>   9800 La Cienega Boulevard, Inglewood, CA 90301-4440
>   Tel: 1-310-337-5017

Open Software Foundation
>   11 Cambridge Center, Cambridge, MA 12142
>   Tel: 1-617-621-8895

SPEC
>   c/o NCGA
>   2722 Merrilee Drive, Suite 200, Fairfax, VA 22031-4499
>   Tel: 1-703-698-9600 ex. 318

Visual Edge Software
>   Distributed in the UK by Protek Software, 1 York Road, Maidenhead,
>   Berkshire SL6 1SQ
>   Tel: 44-628-759-59

X/Open
>   X/Open Company Limited
>   Apex Plaza, Forbury Road, Reading, Berkshire RG1 1AX
>   Tel: 44-734-508311

A3.3   IBM publications

IBM publishes a large number of technical AIX publications that provide detailed information in particular areas of AIX. The following orderable publications are recommended to enhance your understanding of AIX. All of the following publications were used as background reading material for this book. For more complete details including abstracts, the reader should use IBM Electronic Customer Support or contact their IBM Technical Publications Centre.

GA19-5576	The IBM RISC System/6000 Handbook
GG22-9487	AIX v3.1 access control lists
GG22-9493	AIX SNA services/6000 profile configuration
GG22-9494	Sun to IBM RISC System/6000 migration guide
GG22-9495	DEC VAX/VMS 5.4 to IBM RISC System/6000 AIX version 3.1 migration guide
GG24-1690	IBM Personal Computer PC/IX
GG24-3376	TCP/IP tutorial and technical overview
GG24-3382	AIXwindows programming guide
GG24-3458	X.25 Guide
GG24-3489	Aix distributed environments: nfs, ncs, rpc, ds migration
GG24-3584	A plain man's view of the IBM MicroChannel
GG24-3570	Printing for fun and profit under AIX V3
GG24-3589	AIX V3 for the IBM RISC System/6000 national language support
GG24-3611	IBM RISC System/6000 NIC tuning guide for Fortran and C
GG24-3629	Writing a device driver for AIX V3
GG24-3633	The IBM RISC System/6000 as real-time system
GG24-3666	Cooking with SNA and 3270 emulators on the IBM RISC System/6000
GG24-3692	AIX/V3 X.25 communications
GG24-3695	Xstation 120/130 (install, config, tune)
GG24-3700	Experiences in using AIX NetView service point
GG24-3711	Predicting execution time on the IBM RISC System/6000
GG24-3735	AIX consumer transaction/6000
GG24-3750	AIX V3.1 additional authorization: an example
GG24-3814	Upgrading to AIX 3.2, the inside story
GG24-3850	AIX 3.2 national language support (NLS)
SA23-2619	IBM RISC System/6000 technology
SC23-2409	High availability cluster multiprocessing, systems administration
SC23-2482	AIX software and data distribution/6000 user's guide
GC67-0210	IBM family applications catalogue
G325-0060	The AIX applications catalogue (US publication)
GU59-8129	The AIX applications directory (UK publication)
GK2T-0237	General information and planning kit

A3.4   Further information

In a publication of this size it has not been possible to include information on all aspects of the IBM RISC System/6000. An outline of the known omissions is given in the following pages.

A3.4.1   Transaction processing

IBM now supplies two products, Enterprise Computing in a New Age (Encina) and Customer Information Control System/6000 (CICS/6000), allowing customers to implement business transaction processing (TP) applications. A detailed review of either of these products warrants publications in themselves, so only an overview is presented here.

Before discussing either product it is useful to clarify just exactly what business transaction processing is. In a transaction processing system, one execution of an application program processes a single transaction. This may not be any different to a regular business application interacting with a database. However TP applications make some of the following additional requirements:

- High availability—many TP systems, for example, banking cashpoint systems, are required to be available 24 hours a day, 7 days a week.
- Swift and consistent response time—businesses typically use TP systems to provide services to their customers. In order to offer high levels of customer service the underlying TP application must provide fast response times. Additionally, for operators to have faith in their system, *consistent* response times are required.
- Atomic access and update of shared resources—TP applications concurrently access and update shared data. Individual transactions must complete sucessfully without interfering with any other transactions, that is, be 'atomic' in nature. Any serious TP system must provide the following individual transaction:
  —Commit: to save changes made successfully in a transaction
  —Rollback: to put the database to the state it was in before the transaction started
- Crash recovery—the computer system may need to be restarted after an unexpected shutdown, for example, a power loss. Upon restart the TP system must be able to *back out* any changes to restore system consistency.
- Forward recovery—the TP system must be able to recover a completely lost database using two components: first, a historical database backup; and second, a record of changes successfully made to that database. This is known as forward recovery.

IBM's TP strategy for the IBM RISC System/6000 uses the CICS/6000 and Encina products on the existing base AIX and AIX distributed computing environment. This is shown in Fig. A3.1.

A3.4.2   Encina

The Encina family is a suite of five modular products that allow customers to start designing and to begin initially implementing distributed transactional applications that run in a heterogeneous, networked computing environment.

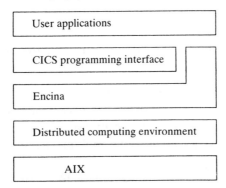

Figure A3.1.   CICS and Encina layering.

The products are based on technology provided by the TransArc Corporation. The components are: executive, server core, monitor, structured file service and peer-to-peer communications service.

Executive

The Encina executive contains core APIs for defining transactional clients and servers. First, transactional-C (Tran-C) is a high-level API that simplifies transaction demarcation, concurrency control and exception handling. Transaction-C is made up of a set of macros and library routines for ANSI C. Figure A3.2 is a simple example of a transaction definition in Tran-C.

The second API, called transactional RPC (TRPC), extends the DCE RPC with transaction semantics. This is important since if a standard RPC fails, the client cannot usually determine whether the message never arrived at the server, whether the server failed during the computation, or whether the return message was lost. When a transactional RPC fails however, the encompassing transaction is aborted.

The executive also contains the distributed transaction service (TRAN) which is the means by which a consensus is reached among transaction participants as to whether to commit or abort. This service provided the logic for the two-phase commit protocol.

```
transaction { ...

debit (salaryExpense, amount);
credit (accountsPayable, amount);
enterAuditData (employeeIdentifier, amount, date);
            }

onCommit
   printf ("Transaction succeeded\n");

onAbort
   printf ("Transaction aborted\n");
```

Figure A3.2.   A sample transactional-C program.

Server core

The server core provides for the management of recoverable data and includes components such as:

- The *lock service* to implement serialization of transactions.
- The *recovery service* to provide the undo/redo logic required to implement rollback after abort and roll-forward after system failure.
- The *volume service* to provide the multiple physical and mirrored disk support.
- The *log service* to provide a write-ahead log for storing transaction outcomes and updates to recoverable data.
- The *TRAN/XA* interface to provide access to XA supporting databases such as the majority of modern database packages. The XA interface is the X/Open standard for initiating and coordinating subordinate database transactions.

Monitor

The executive and server core components form a toolkit that allows an applications developer to write client/server applications supporting transactional remote invocation, distributed two-phase commit processing and the management of recoverable data. The *monitor* extends the toolkit with three environment services, allowing a complete solution of distributed online transaction processing. The three services are the development, execution and administration services.

- The *development environment* allows the applications developer to interconnect with a wide range of front end tools and fourth-generation languages, for example OSF/Motif or the forms editor JAM.
- The *execution environment* augments the toolkit with facilities to provide better availability, performance and security.
- The *administration environment* allows centralized and simplified systems administration. This includes the ability to monitor active clients, server availability and load, or auditing information.

Structured file service

The Encina structured file service (SFS) provides a record-oriented filesystem, offering transaction integrity and supporting ISAM-compliant and VSAM-style programming interfaces. It is provided to overcome the typical UNIX and DCE distributed filesystem limitations which treat files as a single stream of bytes. Multiple file layouts are supported by SFS including entry sequenced, relative and B-tree. SFS uses authentication tools from DCE as its base.

Peer-to-peer communication service

The Encina peer-to-peer communication (PPC) service is composed of two subcomponents: the PPC executive and the PPC SNA gateway.

- The *PPC executive* contains programming interfaces for issuing APPC (that is, IBM SNA, LU6.2 style) communications packaged into a TCP/IP protocol stream. It supports the IBM, CPI-C interface.
- The *PPC gateway* allows an Encina program to communicate directly with a host program via the LU6.2 protocol interface.

I would recommend that an applications developer writing TP applications afresh would be best advised to write Encina applications. It is, however, more likely that they would be migrating and/or modifying existing CICS transaction processing applications to run in the AIX environment. For this CICS/6000 should be used.

A3.4.3 CICS/6000

CICS/6000 was designed to be part of the CICS family which already extends to the OS/400, OS/2, MVS and VSE operating systems. By supporting a substantial subset of the CICS/MVS programming interface an applications developer can easily migrate applications written in COBOL or C.

Many commercial applications require only character screen support. CICS provides this via basic mapping support (BMS). CICS applications using the minimum level of BMS for 3270 are portable unchanged from host mainframe CICS systems. The minimum level of BMS support is sufficient for most 3270 applications. CICS/6000 also includes support for OSF/Motif. An OSF/Motif application can now start a transaction using the external call interface.

Some of the techniques available to a CICS TP developer include:

- Data integrity—using explicit and implicit mechanisms. Explicit mechanisms include commit and rollback. When a single transaction involves updating several databases on different systems, a process known as *two-phase commit* is required to complete the transaction reliably.
- Transaction routeing—a terminal operator may execute a remote transaction in any other CICS in the network. for example, from CICS/6000 to CICS/MVS.
- Function shipping—a program transparently accesses remote data.
- Distributed program link—a local CICS program invokes a remote CICS program.
- Distributed transaction processing—a local CICS program uses the APPC protocol to communicate with another system.

CICS/6000 provides the programmer with traditional CICS application development and system management facilities such as the CICS command interpreter (CECI), the run-time resources definition facility (CEDA) and the screen design aid.

A3.4.4   Callpath

Callpath is a software product linking the RISC system to various vendor telephone systems. Callpath enables the applications developer to automate many aspects of agent activity in customer databases with telephone calls to and from their clients, providing those clients with a faster and more effective service. Typical client areas include universities, government offices, airlines, hospitals and banks.

For example, within IBM Callpath is used to provide a faster and more effective computer helpdesk facility. Users experiencing problems in accessing or using their computer systems typically call a central helpdesk. As the helpdesk answers the telephone, Callpath can determine the identity of the caller (based on the inbound telephone extension), and place an information screen in front of the helpdesk professional. This may include the name of the user, the computer equipment owned by the user and a historical log of previous reported questions and problems. The helpdesk professional therefore gains a headstart in being able to assist the user before that user has even spoken a word. It may be that in conversation with the user their problem is best handled by another Helpdesk professional so Callpath can 'transfer' the information screen thus far displayed to another helpdesk person.

Another way in which Callpath can help increase business productivity is to provide users with a computerized messaging service. For example, a customer could call my office while I was absent. Callpath could play my personalized voice message which could ask the caller to leave a voice message. After the message was left, Callpath could automatically send an electronic message to my IBM Professional Office System indicating that a voicemail message was waiting. I could then call my extension and, using a 'touch-tone' phone, retrieve, play, pause or otherwise manipulate the waiting voicemail.

A3.4.5   Speech server products

The speech server series of products enables an applications developer to produce business applications that respond to, process or output spoken text. At the most fundamental level the products allow a user to talk into a microphone and have their words recognized electronically into text which can then be either stored in a flat file format or passed to an application. Alternatively, information may be presented to the user audibly.

To take advantage of these facilities three components are required:

1 A RISC system with the AIX Speech Client/6000 software installed controlling an M-Audio capture and playback hardware adapter. This needs to be connected to a suitable microphone and loudspeaker. This RISC system is the system with which the user interacts.

2 A RISC system with the AIX Speech Server/6000 software installed controlling one or more IBM speech accelerator type 1 or type 2 cards. The type 1 card supports one client session, the type 2 card two sessions. Cards may be placed into a server machine (subject to slot availability) to cater for up to eight active speech sessions.

3 A LAN connection between the client and server machines hardware.

In a typical scenario, an applications developer will have fully integrated audio into the user's application. Using the dedicated speech application programming interface, audio signals are received by the M-Audio capture card in the client machine and transmitted to the speech accelerator card and software in the server machine. The words are matched against the 20 000 word supplied library and translated into text which is then fed back to the client machine for processing in the application. At other points in the application data is sent outward to the M-Audio capture and thence to the loudspeaker under application control.

In a typical environment one server machine serves up to eight client machines interconnected across a LAN. However, a minimal environment could run both client and server components within a single machine should this be required.

A3.4.6   Hub management

Hub management is a part of the Netview product family and allows the management of LANs that incorporate the IBM 8250 multiprotocol intelligent LAN hub. It aids LAN management by collecting and reporting statistics per hub port and per LAN, and offers LAN-level security by preventing unauthorized users from network access.

For more marketing or technical information on these products please contact your IBM marketing representative.

Appendix 4
Abbreviations

AADU	AIX access for DOS users
ABI	Application binary interface
ACIS	Academic information system
ACL	Access control list
AEP	Application environment profile
AES	Application environment specification
AFS	Andrew filesystem
AIC	AIX interface composer
AIX	Advanced interactive executive
ANDF	Architecture neutral distribution format
ANSI	American National Standards Institute
APAR	Authorized problem analysis report
API	Application program interface
APPC	Advanced program-to-program communication
ARP	Address resolution protocol
ASCII	American standard code for information interchange
ATK	Andrew toolkit
BEAR	Break-even after release
BIOS	Basic input output system
BIST	Built-in self-test
BNU	Basic networking utilities
BOS	Basic operating system
BSC	Binary synchronous communication
BSD	Berkeley software distribution
CAE	Common applications environment
CASE	Computer-aided software engineering
CCS	Common communications support
CCW	Channel control word
CD-ROM	Compact disk read-only memory
CE	Customer engineer (now renamed CS)
CGM	Computer graphics metafile

CICS	Customer information control system
CISC	Complex instruction set computer
CLM	Cluster lock manager
CMOS	Complementary metal oxide semiconductor
CMS	Conversational monitor system
CMVC	Configuration management version control
COBOL	Common business oriented language
COP	Common on-chip processor
COSE	Common open software environment
CPI	Common programming interface
CPM	Control program for microcomputers
CPU	Central processing unit
CR	Carriage return
CRC	Cyclic redundancy check
CS	Customer support, the IBM service organization
CSOS	Computer system operating system
CUA	Common user access
CUT	Control unit terminal
DAC	Discretionary access contro
DAS	Dual attach station
DAT	Digital audio tape
DBA	Direct bus attach
DBCS	Double byte character set
DBMS	Database management system
DCE	Distributed computing environment
DEC	Digital Equipment Corporation
DFS	Distributed file system
DFT	Distributed function terminal
DIS	Data interpretation system
DLC	Data link control
DLL	Dynamic link library
DPS	Display PostScript
DRAM	Dynamic random access memory
DSLO	Distributed systems licence option
DTE	Data terminal equipment
EBCDIC	Extended binary coded data interchange code
ECC	Error correction code
ECMA	European Computer Manufacturers Association
ECS	Electronic customer support
EGA	Enhanced graphics adapter
EISA	Extended industry standard architecture
ENCINA	Enterprise Computing in a New Age
EOF	End of file

ESA	Enterprise Systems Architecture
ESC	Escape
ESCON	Enterprise systems connection
ESDI	Enhanced small device interface
ESP	Engineering support processor
FDDI	Fibre distributed data interface
FIPS	Federal information processing standard
FP	Floating point
FTN	Field television network
FTP	File transfer protocol
FX	Fixed point
GDDM	Graphical data display manager
GID	Group identification
GKS	Graphics kernel system
GL	Graphics library
GML	Generalized markup communication
GPR	General-purpose register
GTO	Graphic terminal option
GUI	Graphical user interface
HAS	High availability system
HAT	Hash anchor table
HCON	Host connection
HFT	High-function terminal
HIPPI	High-performance parallel interface
iBCS	Intel binary compatibility standard
IBM	International Business Machines
IC	Integrated circuit
ICMP	Internet control message protocol
IDE	Integrated drive electronics
IDP	Internet datagram protocol
IDRC	Improved data recording cabability
IEEE	Institute of Electrical and Electronics Engineers
INED	Interactive systems editor
I/O	Input/output
IOCC	Input output channel converter
IP	Internet protocol
IPC	Interprogram communication
IPL	Initial program load
ISA	Industry standard architecture
ISAM	Indexed sequential access method
IT	Information technology
JFS	Journalled filesystem
JIS	Japanese Industry Standard

kb	Kilobyte
LAN	Local area network
LAPI	Layered API
LF	Line feed
LP	Logical partition
LPP	Licensed program products
LV	Logical volume
LVM	Logical volume manager
LU	Logical unit
MAC	Mandatory access control
MAU	Multistation access unit
Mb	Megabyte
MBCS	Multibyte character set
MFM	Modified frequency modulation
MHz	Megahertz
MIB	Management information base
MIF	Maker interchange format
MRI	Machine-readable information
MVS	Multiple virtual storage
NCS	Network computing system
NCSC	National Computer Security Commission
NDIS	Network driver interface support
NETBIOS	Network basic input output system
NFS	Network file system
NIDL	Network interface definition language
NIST	National Institute of Standards and Technology
NLS	National language support
NSP	Netview service point
NT	New technology
NVRAM	Nonvolatile random access memory
NVT	Novell virtual terminal
OCS	On-card sequencer
ODM	Object data manager
OEM	Original equipment manufacturer
OIA	Operator information area
OLTP	Online transaction processing
OPD	Office products division
OSF	Open Software Foundation
OSWC	Open Systems and Workstations Consultancy
PC	Personal computer
PC DOS	Personal computer disk operating system
PCB	Printed circuit board
PCI	PC interface

PCL	Printer control language
PCSIM	PC simulator
PFT	Page from table
PIO	Programmed input/output
PLB	Picture-level benchmark
PMP	Preventative maintenance package
POS-ID	Programmable option select ID
POST	Power-on self-test
POWER	Performance optimization with enhanced RISC
PP	Physical partition
PR/SM	Processor resource/systems manager
PS/2	Personal System/2
PSM	Persistent storage manager
PSS	Persistent storage segment
PTF	Program temporary fix
PU	Physical unit
QLLC	Qualified logical link control
RAM	Random access memory
RARP	Reverse address resolution protocol
RAS	Reliability, availability and serviceability
RETAIN	Remote technical assistance information network
RFT	Request for technology
RGB	Red green blue
RISC	Reduced instruction set cycles
RJE	Remote job entry
RLL	Run length limited
RLM	Resource licence manager
RM	Resource manager
ROM	Read-only memory
ROMP	Research OPD microprocessor
ROS	Read-only storage
RPC	Remote procedure call
RT	RISC technology
RTY	Remote TTY
SAA	Systems application architecture
SAF	Service access facility
SAK	Secure attention key
SBCS	Single-byte character set
SCLM	Software configuration and library manager
SCSI	Small computer systems interface
SDE	Software development environment
SDLG	Synchronous data link control
SDM	System development multitasking

SDS	Software development system
SDT	Static debug trap
SFS	Structured file service
SGID	Set group ID
SGML	Standardized general markup language
SIMM	Single inline memory module
SIPO	System installation productivity option
SLIP	Serial line interface protocol
SMIT	Systems management interface tool
SMTP	Simple mail transfer protocol
SNA	Systems network architecture
SNMP	Simple network management protocol
SOCC	Serial optical channel converter
SPC	Software publications centre
SPEC	Standard Performance Evaluation Corporation
SPOT	Shared product object tree
SPP	Sequenced packet protocol
SQL	Structured query language
SRC	Systems resource controller
SRF	Standard record format
SRN	Service request number
SSC	Systems support centre
SSCP	System services control point
SSDO	Single source dual object
SSSO	Single source single object
SSU	Selective subsystem update
SUID	Set user ID
TCB	Trusted computer base
TCF	Transparent computing facility
TCOS	Technical Committee on Operating Systems
TCP/IP	Transmission control protocol/Internet protocol
TCSEC	Trusted computer system evaluation criteria
TCW	Translation control words
TFTP	Trivial file transfer protocol
TIFF	Tagged image file format
TLB	Translation lookaside buffer
TLI	Transport layer interface
TP	Transaction processing
TP	Transaction programs
TPC	Technical Publications Centre or Transaction Performance Council
TRAN	Distributed transaction service
TRPC	Transactional RPC
TSR	Terminate and stay resident

TSS	Time-sharing system
TTM	Time to market
TTY	Teletype
UDP	User datagram protocol
UI	UNIX International
UID	User identification
UIL	User interface language
USL	UNIX System Laboratories
UTC	Universal time, coordinated
UUCP	UNIX-to-UNIX copy program
UUID	Universal unique identifier
VG	Volume group
VGA	Video graphics array
VGDA	Volume group descriptor area
VM	Virtual machine
VM86	Virtual mode 86
VMM	Virtual memory management or virtual memory manager
VOS	Virtual operating system
VP	Value point
VPA	Volume purchase agreement
VPD	Vital product data
VPN	Virtual page number
VRM	Virtual resource manager
VSE	Virtual storage extended
VTAM	Virtual telecommunications access method
WAN	Wide area network
XA	Extended architecture
XCOFF	Extended common object file format
XDE	X-Windows debugging environment
XDF	Extended data facility
XDMCP	X-Windows display management control protocol
XDR	External data representation
XIO	Extended input/output
XPG	X/Open portability guide

Appendix 5
Glossary

AFS

Networking software originally developed at CMU. Included in OSF DCE.

AIX

Advanced interactive executive. IBM's UNIX system announced for the PS/2 and the IBM RISC System/6000. AIX is POSIX compliant.

A/UX

UNIX for Apple computers.

BSD

Berkeley Software Distribution. UNIX from the University of California at Berkeley. The latest and final version of BSD is 4.4. Many of the major enhancements seen in UNIX were originally developed for BSD UNIX.

C

A general-purpose programming language and the language of choice for the UNIX industry. IBM offers C in AIX and SAA.

Curses

Programming tools for screen management. AIX offers standard and extended curses.

C2

One of the ratings in the US Department of Defense trusted systems evaluation criteria (the 'orange book'). The orange book defines a series of classes or levels such as: D—no security; C1—discretionary access control such as logon; C2—C1 and auditing; B1—C2 plus mandatory access control.

Code point

The numeric value a character is assigned within a code set. For example 'A' is at code position 0x41 in ASCII.

Daemon

Pronounced 'demon'. A background, never-ending process normally started and controlled by AIX performing a service to requestors. For example, the error daemon collects and logs errors, or the printer daemon receives queued file print requests.

DMA

Direct memory access. Transfer of data between the memory and a peripheral (or another memory) without intervention of the processor.

GSL

Graphics subroutine library. The IBM support provided on AIX workstations for the device-independent manipulation of two-dimensional data.

Hard file

The IBM term for a hard disk drive usually used to describe 5.25 inch and smaller hard disks.

Hypertext

Text organized and accessed by a relational database.

IEEE

The Institute of Electrical and Electronics Engineers, based in the USA.

ILS

International language support. Another term to describe NLS.

ISO

The International Organization for Standardization. Produces standards on many topics including fonts for internationalization.

Kerberos

An encryption-based third-party authentication mechanism for network security developed at MIT. Included in OSF DCE.

Mach

A Carnegie-Mellon University developed version of UNIX. Mach was an experimental operating system supporting multiple threads and muliple processors. The Mach kernel is at the heart of the new OSF/1 operating system.

MIPS

Millions of instructions per second, a measure of a processor's horsepower. It is usually compared with a known system such as a DEC PDP11/780 that has a MIPS rating of 1.

NFS

Network File System. A protocol from Sun Microsystems for the network transparent sharing of filesystems among computer systems connected via TCP/IP. IBM offers NFS on AIX and SAA platforms.

NLS

The IBM preferred name of internationalization. Stands for 'national language support'. Outside IBM also means 'network license server' (see RLM).

ODM

The object data manager. A data manager intended for storing system information. Information is stored and maintained as objects with associated characteristics and methods. Can also be used to manage systems data for user programs.

Opcode

Operation code. A component part of a machine instruction telling the processor to do something. The opcode identifies the type of instruction. For example, in the POWER processor architecture, the opcode to add a number to a register is opcode 12, whereas the opcode to add two registers together is opcode 31.

OSF

The Open Software Foundation. A nonprofit-making foundation whose objectives include vendor-neutral, hardware-independent software based on industry standards. Founding members were IBM, DEC, HP, Apollo, Siemens and others.

OSF/1

UNIX-based operating system developed by the OSF. OSF/1 has a Mach kernel and system calls and libraries based in part upon AIX. OSF/1 will be integrated into all IBM UNIX workstations at a later date.

POSIX

Portable operating systems for computer environments. A detailed set of standards for a portable operating system developed by the IEEE. IBM belongs to the POSIX committee. AIX is POSIX compliant.

PRPQ

Program request for price quotation. IBM customers may request a software or hardware function to be implemented upon IBM systems. If there is a good IBM business case for the product or software package to be produced it may be implemented for the requested customer. After this the technology is then normally made available to other IBM customers as a PRPQ.

RISC

Reduced instruction set computing or reduced instruction set cycles. RISC architecture strives to minimize the number of machine instructions, and to optimize the number of machine instructions that require just one cycle of the processor. The results are simplified processor logic and enhanced processor performance.

RLM

Resource licence manager. This is IBM's name for the network licence server component of network computer system (NCS).

ROS

Read-only storage. The IBM name for read-only memory. ROS or ROM is an example read-only memory technology.

RS232

A standard for connecting computer systems with serial interfaces. More formally known as the Electronic Industries Association (EIA) 232D standard. The publication *RS232 Made Easy* by Martin D. Seyer is a good source of information (ISBN 0-13-749870-5).

SDS

Software development solutions. IBM's CASE product for the IBM RISC System/6000. It is composed of an integrated set of basic tools (SDE Workbench), an integrator to allow the incorporation of existing tools. The last component, CMVC, provides configuration management and version control.

SIPO

System installation productivity option. A set of IBM software products packaged on a single set of 'stacked' tapes. The AIX 3.2 SIPO is program number 5750-AET and it allows a customer to order on a single tape base AIX and optional components. The AIX SIPO tape also contains a header to enable the RISC system to boot and install standalone from that tape.

SNMP

Simple network management protocol. The network management protocol of choice for TCP/IP based LANs.

SPEC

System performance evaluation cooperative. A suite of benchmarks, commonly summarized by the term 'SPECmark'. The SPECmark is designed to replace older benchmarks made obsolete by advances in chip design and compiler technology. IBM is a member of SPEC.

SSC

Systems support centre. A single point of contact for IBM hardware and software problems. By purchasing or leasing the software an IBM customer is automatically entitled to service. Hardware service is provided free during the warranty period and for a cost thereafter.

STORAGE

The IBM term for memory.

SVID

System V interface definition. An AT&T document defining the standard interfaces to be used by UNIX System V application programmers.

SVVS

System V verification suite. A set of programs to test compliance to SVID.

TSR.

Terminate and stay resident program. This is a method used under the DOS operating system to expand the operating system dynamically. Typically, the program comprising the TSR is first executed, after which it installs itself. An interactive TSR then often checks for a particular user keyboard sequence that indicates the user wants to talk to the TSR. A communications TSR normally hooks a software interrupt and waits for that interrupt to be called. Under DOS this is a common way for a Microsoft Windows program to call a TSR communications driver.

Two-phase commit

In a two-phase commit procedure, the transaction processing system first asks each resource manager (RM) to prepare to commit, then, when each RM has signalled readiness, asks each to commit, or, if there are any RM signals that it cannot commit, asks each to back out.

VAR

Value added remarketer. An IBM accredited VAR is a software house that buys IBM RISC System/6000 and AIX from IBM, packages this with their own applications software and resells this machine to a customer. Depending on how the VAR chooses to operate, the customer may receive hardware and software support from IBM, or from the VAR and IBM combined.

VPD

Vital product data. This relates to detailed information about an IBM product. For example, the date and plant of manufacture, revision and subrevision levels of a hardware card and any on-card firmware. Many IBM devices and most IBM adapter cards have special command sequences that can retrieve this information which may be used for configuration and diagnostics.

X-Terminal

A dumb terminal which can act as an X-Windows graphics display server. X-terminals usually boot up from a LAN-connected workstation in order to load their X server.

X-Windows

The UNIX industry's graphics windowing standard developed at MIT.

Index

I
R

RE